FAULT LINES

THE CULTURAL LIVES OF LAW

Edited by Austin Sarat

**EDITED BY DAVID M. ENGEL
AND MICHAEL MCCANN**

Fault Lines

Tort Law as Cultural Practice

STANFORD LAW BOOKS

*An imprint of Stanford University Press
Stanford, California*

Stanford University Press
Stanford, California

Printed in the United States of America on acid-free, archival-quality
paper

Library of Congress Cataloging-in-Publication Data

Fault lines : tort law as cultural practice / edited by David M. Engel
and Michael McCann.
        p. cm.—(The cultural lives of law)
    Includes bibliographical references and index.
    ISBN 978-0-8047-5613-6 (cloth : alk. paper)—
    ISBN 978-0-8047-5614-3 (pbk. : alk. paper)
    1. Torts.   2. Culture and law.   3. Torts—United States.
I. Engel, David M.   II. McCann, Michael W., 1952-   III. Series:
Cultural lives of law.
    K923.F37 2009
    346.03—dc22   2008054141

Typeset by Thompson Type in 10/14½ Minion Pro

Contents

List of Tables and Figures   ix
Contributors   xi

Introduction: Tort Law as Cultural Practice   1

DAVID M. ENGEL AND MICHAEL MCCANN

Part I: On Legal Culture and Cultural Analysis of Tort Law

1. Law, Liability, and Culture   21

   DAVID NELKEN

2. Torts and Notions of Community: More Observations
   on Units of Legal Culture   39

   KEEBET VON BENDA-BECKMANN

Part II: Different Approaches to Cultural Analysis of Tort Law

3. India's Tort Deficit: Sketch for a Historical Portrait   47

   MARC GALANTER

4. Liability Insurance at the Tort-Crime Boundary   66

   TOM BAKER

5. Juries as Conduits for Culture?   80

   VALERIE P. HANS

6. Framing Fast-Food Litigation: Tort Claims, Mass Media,
and the Politics of Responsibility in the United States   97
   WILLIAM HALTOM AND MICHAEL MCCANN

Part III: Injury and Identity: Race, Gender, Sexuality, and Tort Law

7. Discrimination and Outrage: Exploring the Gap Between
Civil Rights and Tort Recoveries   119
   MARTHA CHAMALLAS

8. Regulating Middlesex   137
   ANNE BLOOM

9. Whiteness, Equal Treatment, and the Valuation of Injury
in Torts, 1900–1949   156
   JENNIFER B. WRIGGINS

Part IV: Issues of Risk and Responsibility

10. The Role of Tort Lawsuits in Reconstructing the Issue
of Police Abuse in the United Kingdom   175
   CHARLES R. EPP

11. Lawyers and Solicitors Separated by a Common Legal System:
Anti-Tobacco Litigation in the United States and Britain   192
   LYNN MATHER

12. Suing Doctors in Japan: Structure, Culture,
and the Rise of Malpractice Litigation   211
   ERIC A. FELDMAN

13. The Role of the Judiciary in Asbestos Injury Compensation
in Japan   233
   TAKAO TANASE

Part V: Causation, Duty, and Obligation

14. Discourses of Causation in Injury Cases: Exploring Thai
and American Legal Cultures   251
   DAVID M. ENGEL

15. "Nobody Broke It, It Just Broke": Causation as an Instrument
    of Obfuscation and Oppression 269

    ANN SCALES

16. The Cultural Agenda of Tort Litigation: Constructing
    Responsibility in the Rocky Mountain Frontier 287

    JOYCE STERLING AND NANCY REICHMAN

    Acknowledgments 309
    Notes 311
    Bibliography 329
    Cases, Statutes, and Agency Reports 361
    Index 365

List of Tables and Figures

Tables

6.1	Frames Mentioned in Newspapers, 2002–2003	108
6.2	References to Actors in 2002–2003 Articles on Food-Related Litigation	111
12.1	Medical Malpractice Claims in Japan, 1992–2006	214
12.2	Case Filing Fees Paid by Plaintiffs	217
12.3	Number of Licensed Attorneys and Total Population of Japan	218
12.4	Number of Licensed Female Attorneys in Japan	219
12.5	Length of Time Between the Filing and Final Judgment of Malpractice Cases and Civil Cases in District Courts, 1994–2006 (in months)	220
12.6	Tokyo District Court, Specialized Medical Court (*shūchūbu*), 2001–2007	224
16.1	Tort Litigation in Denver Trial Courts, 1862–1917: Disposition of Cases Against Railroads and Tramways	295
16.2	Winners of Judgments and Trials in Cases Against Railroads and Tramways: Denver Trial Courts, 1862–1917	296

Figures

11.1	Smoking and Legal Compensation for Illnesses	201
16.1	Percentage of Tort Cases Involving Transportation Defendants	295

Contributors

TOM BAKER is Professor of Law at the University of Pennsylvania Law School. He is the author of *The Medical Malpractice Myth* (2005) and *Insurance Law and Policy: Cases, Materials and Problems* (2008).

KEEBET VON BENDA-BECKMANN is the head of the Project Group Legal Pluralism at the Max Planck Institute for Social Anthropology in Halle, Germany. Her most recent publications include *Order and Disorder: Anthropological Perspectives* (2007) (ed. with F. Pirie) and *Social Security between Past and Future: Ambonese Networks of Care and Support* (2007) (with F. von Benda-Beckmann).

ANNE BLOOM is Associate Professor of Law at the University of the Pacific McGeorge School of Law. A former public interest attorney, she has published articles on mass torts, the plaintiffs' bar, and the role of tort law in shaping sexual identity.

MARTHA CHAMALLAS holds the Robert J. Lynn Chair in Law at the Moritz College of Law at Ohio State University, where she received the University Distinguished Lecturer Award in 2007. She is the author of *Introduction to Feminist Legal Theory*, 2nd ed. (2003) and a forthcoming book (with Jennifer Wriggins), *The Measure of Injury: Race, Gender, and the Law of Torts*.

DAVID M. ENGEL is SUNY Distinguished Service Professor of Law at the University at Buffalo Law School. A former president of the Law & Society Association, his publications include *Rights of Inclusion: Law and Identity in the Life*

Stories of Americans with Disabilities (2003) (with Frank W. Munger), which received the Myers Outstanding Book Award.

CHARLES R. EPP is Associate Professor of Public Administration at the University of Kansas. His book, *The Rights Revolution* (1998), won the American Political Science Association's C. Herman Pritchett Award.

ERIC A. FELDMAN is Professor of Law at the University of Pennsylvania Law School. He is the author of *Blood Feuds: AIDS, Blood, and the Politics of Medical Disaster* (ed. with Ronald Bayer) (1999), *The Ritual of Rights in Japan: Law, Society, and Health Policy* (2000), and *Unfiltered: Conflicts over Tobacco Policy and Public Health* (with Ronald Bayer) (2004).

MARC GALANTER is the John & Rylla Bosshard Professor Emeritus of Law and South Asian Studies, University of Wisconsin–Madison and Centennial Professor, Department of Law, London School of Economics and Political Science. A former president of the Law & Society Association, his books include *Competing Equalities: Law and the Backward Classes in India* (1984 and 1991), *Law and Society in Modern India* (1989), and *Lowering the Bar: Lawyer Jokes and Legal Culture* (2005).

WILLIAM HALTOM is Professor in the Department of Government and Politics at the University of Puget Sound. He is the author of *Reporting on the Courts* and (with Michael McCann) the multi-award winning *Distorting the Law: Politics, Media, and the Litigation Crisis* (2004).

VALERIE P. HANS is Professor of Law at Cornell Law School. Her books include *American Juries: The Verdict* (2007), *The Jury System: Contemporary Scholarship* (2006), *Business on Trial: The Civil Jury and Corporate Responsibility* (2000), and *Judging the Jury* (1986).

LYNN MATHER is Director of the Baldy Center for Law & Social Policy and Professor of Law and Political Science at the University at Buffalo, State University of New York. Her co-authored book, *Divorce Lawyers at Work: Varieties of Professionalism in Practice* (2001) won the C. Herman Pritchett award from APSA. She has served as president of the Law & Society Association and chair of the Law and Courts Section of APSA.

MICHAEL MCCANN is Gordon Hirabayashi Professor for the Advancement of Citizenship at the University of Washington. He is director of the Law, Societies, and Justice program and the Comparative Law and Society Studies Center. McCann's books include *Rights at Work: Pay Equity and the Politics of Legal Mobilization* (1994) and *Distorting the Law: Politics, Media, and the Litigation Crisis* (2004), each of which has won multiple awards.

DAVID NELKEN is Distinguished Professor of Legal Institutions and Social Change at the University of Macerata in Italy. He is also Distinguished Research Professor of Law at the University of Wales, Cardiff, and Honorary Professor of Law at the LSE, United Kingdom, and "Wiarda" Chair in the Faculty of Law, Utrecht, The Netherlands. Recent publications include *Comparative Law: A Handbook* (2007), *European Ways of Law* (2007), and *Exploring Legal Cultures* (2007).

NANCY REICHMAN is Professor and Chair of the Sociology and Criminology Department at the University of Denver. She is the co-author of *Ozone Connections: Expert Networks in Global Environmental Governance* (2002).

ANN SCALES is a Professor of Law at the University of Denver College of Law. She is the author of *Legal Feminism: Activism, Lawyering, and Legal Theory* (2006).

JOYCE STERLING is Professor of Law at University of Denver Sturm College of Law. Her publications include *After the JD: First Results of a National Study of Legal Careers* (2004).

TAKAO TANASE is Professor at Chuo Law School. He has published numerous books and articles in Japanese and English, including *Contract and its Related Practices* (1999) and *Civil Society and Responsibility* (2007). In 2005, his work was honored with a series of papers at the Sho Sato Conference, Boalt Hall School of Law, University of California, Berkeley.

JENNIFER B. WRIGGINS is the Sumner T. Bernstein Professor at the University of Maine School of Law. She is currently working on a book with Martha Chamallas *The Measure of Injury: Race, Gender, and the Law of Torts*.

FAULT LINES

Introduction

Tort Law as Cultural Practice

DAVID M. ENGEL AND MICHAEL MCCANN

The chapters in this book examine tort law's norms, institutions, and procedures as cultural practices. Few observers, regardless of their academic background, their role in relation to tort law, or their political leanings, would challenge the assertion that tort law is a cultural phenomenon. Nor are they likely to reject our working proposition that tort law plays a role in constituting the very cultural fabric in which it is embedded. Yet, despite this consensus, it is surprising to discover that a rigorous exploration of tort law's cultural dimensions has rarely been attempted and that there is virtually no agreement across disciplines as to how such a study should be conducted. Tort law as a form of cultural practice has remained terra incognita. Even the pathways into this unexplored territory are but dimly perceived.

In this volume, a group of leading legal scholars and social scientists has embarked on a voyage of exploration. Drawing on the pioneering work of important precursors, these authors have begun to map the uncharted land. Their work not only identifies useful roadways for those who might follow, but it also demonstrates a variety of techniques by which the journey might be attempted. This collection makes no claim of completeness nor does it claim to have identified a single superior methodology or discipline. Rather, it identifies a large, potentially important area of inquiry and offers some illustrative attempts by a talented group of scholars to reveal the riches that future explorers might discover there.

This initial foray has two important features. First, it is multidisciplinary. The contributors come from different academic fields and departments, including law, political science, sociology, anthropology, policy studies, and psychology. Through an ongoing conversation about their work, this diverse group of scholars generated mutual understandings and exchanges of insights, making this a truly *inter*disciplinary effort. Second, the collection is explicitly committed to comparative cross-cultural and historical study. Although some of the essays focus on tort law in the United States, others examine practices in quite different social and cultural settings, especially in Asia and Europe. Some draw comparisons across two or more societies or time periods. For reasons we will explain shortly, we think that such a comparative, multi-sited cultural approach to the study of tort law by interdisciplinary scholars is a relatively novel and, we hope, important contribution.

Cultural Dimensions of Tort Law Doctrine

Select any opinion from a first year U.S. torts casebook and you will find references to culture—both explicit and implicit—on nearly every page. As appellate court judges construct the common law of torts case by case, they use building materials that they quarry from their social and cultural environment. The resulting legal edifice reflects its surroundings even as it attempts to reshape them. Cultural elements are everywhere apparent in the practices and products of tort law. For example, the jury, drawn from an imagined but largely fictitious "community" in which cultural values and social norms are said to be shared, makes crucial pronouncements in tort cases about proper and improper conduct. In making these decisions, jurors are expected to deploy an avatar, the ubiquitous "reasonable person," who embodies typical cultural and social practices found in the community. Judges, too, rely on their presumed knowledge of the cultural environment when they dismiss some cases on the grounds that no "reasonable" jury could view them as meritorious, when they characterize certain behaviors as outrageous or acceptable, or when they express concern that tort law might suppress some activities to which they assume society assigns a particularly high value. All of these typical tort law practices rest on an assumption that judges, lawyers, and jurors are able to "read" their own culture to determine what is considered reasonable, outrageous, or valuable and that they can—and should—rely on such readings to inject cultural norms, values, and behaviors into the tort law system.

Some researchers have sought to highlight and analyze the cultural expressions they discover in tort law texts, but the cultural dimensions of tort law are apparent not only in case law doctrine. It is not enough to sift through the opinions of appellate court judges like an archaeologist in search of cultural shards. Culture is not some "thing" outside of tort law that may or may not influence legal behavior and deposit artifacts in the case law reporters. Rather, tort law and culture are inseparable dimensions of a single domain in which risk, injury, liability, compensation, deterrence, and normative pronouncements about acceptable behavior are crucial features.

Conceptual Limitations Resulting from the Tort Reform Debate

Because tort law expresses and constitutes cultural meanings on so many different levels, one might expect to find an extensive interdisciplinary literature exploring their interrelationships. It is somewhat surprising, then, to discover that scholars have generally neglected systematic analysis of this topic. Legal scholars have by and large confined their attention to culture as they see it reflected as an extralegal influence in appellate court opinions (see, e.g., Shapo 2003) or to nonempirical allusions to presumed cultural norms such as individualism, adversarialism, rights consciousness, and litigiousness. Social scientists have tended to focus on quantitative demonstrations that judges, jurors, and litigants have not, in fact, run amok or brought industries and medical professionals to their knees, as the media typically suggest. Tort law as an element or domain of culture has, however, gone largely unexamined.

This book is intended to address what we consider an important gap in the literature about tort law. The subject of culture is the purloined letter of tort law scholarship, almost too obvious to consider in a rigorous and systematic way. Yet we think there is another reason for this curious neglect of what should be a central topic for tort law scholars. Interdisciplinary researchers have allowed politics to set their research agenda. The debate over "tort reform" has, for more than two decades, defined the terrain that is considered legitimate and important for sociolegal research to explore.

Contemporary sociolegal scholarship on tort law has a surprisingly short history. As recently as twenty-five years ago, it would have been accurate to say that empirical research on the criminal justice system was broader, deeper, and far more sophisticated than research on tort law, although crimes and torts are closely related phenomena. Over the past quarter century, however, social scientific research on tort law has flourished. We can no longer complain that we know little about the actual workings of tort law in the United States or the flow of cases from relatively informal or unofficial contexts through lawyers' offices and into the courts.

Even as our knowledge of the tort system has expanded, however, our insights into "tort law and society" have been limited by the predominant theoretical and policy frameworks. Of these, the most influential by far is the debate about the so-called "litigation explosion" conducted in the halls of Congress, the pages of popular magazines and newspapers, and the multiple forums of academia. The contours of this debate are now familiar. Tort "reformers" assert that tort litigation in the United States has vastly increased, that greedy plaintiffs sue at the drop of a hat, and that unscrupulous lawyers encourage thousands of frivolous lawsuits in order to collect their contingent fees (e.g., Boot 1998; Howard 1994; Huber 1988; Olson 1991). These assertions are widely accepted as factually accurate by much of the public, and they are repeated by news reporters, media commentators, politicians, and talk show hosts (see generally Haltom and McCann 2004), often accompanied by distorted or unverifiable urban legends about supposedly ridiculous lawsuits that clog our courts (Baker 2005; Daniels and Martin 1995, 1998; Galanter 1998; Haltom and McCann 2004; Hayden 1991).

Not surprisingly, much of the current sociolegal research on U.S. tort law has been undertaken in response to the litigation explosion critique and the "tort reform" movement it has spawned, with its call for caps on noneconomic and/or punitive damage awards, the elimination of joint and several liability, the establishment of screening panels for medical malpractice cases, and other restrictions on claiming and recovery by tort plaintiffs. Empirical research has been largely positivistic, behavioral, and quantitative, designed to measure whether tort litigation has actually increased over time or is "excessive" in comparison to other types of litigation (e.g., Galanter 1983; Saks 1992). It has examined not only the supposed excesses of clients and lawyers but also the actual behavior of jurors, who have also been the targets of critics because of their supposed credulity, irrationality, and largesse in bestowing enormous damage awards on undeserving plaintiffs (examples of important empirical research on juries include Hans 2000; Lempert 1993; MacCoun 1993; Vidmar 1995, 1999; Vidmar, Gross, and Rose 1998). Further, a growing body of research examines patterns in damage awards themselves, with particular attention to punitive damages, since empirical evidence appears to contradict the critics' assertion that such awards are excessive and out of control (see, e.g., Daniels and Martin 1998; Finley 1997; Galanter and Luban 1993; Saks 1992).

Studies such as these have provided a far more extensive picture of the entire tort law "pyramid," beginning with injurious incidents in the pyramid's base and tracing the cases that injured persons perceive as wrongful as they travel through various levels of the tort law system—lawyer interviews, negotiations, filing of complaints, trials, verdicts, postadjudication processing, and appeals—or are abandoned. One of us (McCann) has dubbed this the "realist" school of empirical research on tort law. We view most empirical scholarship on tort law as a direct response to the tort reformers and the litigation explosion debate. Empirical research has therefore been shaped largely by immediate policy concerns of a very particular kind and has been aimed at debunking unsupported, anecdotal assertions about tort law with sophisticated, scientifically valid evidence.

We applaud and endorse much of the realist research on tort law, and we acknowledge that it has shed valuable light on a subject of great importance to American society. Yet this book arises out of a concern that the demands of this policy debate have been overly influential in determining our research agenda and have limited the theoretical significance of sociolegal scholarship on tort law. We wish to reclaim a broader, more culturally informed view of tort law that is not entirely shaped by immediate policy debates. We suggest that the scholarly foundations of such a view already exist, both in research on American society and in comparative studies of injuries and tort law in other societies around the world.

Toward a Cultural Approach to the Study of Tort Law

Scholars use the term *culture* in many different ways, and we do not attempt to advance any singular concept or approach in the book (see Friedman 1997; Nelken 2004). Nevertheless, the cultural analysis that the authors in this volume offer exhibits some clear and consistent themes. In general, they view cultural analysis as attending to the experiential frames of meaning through which social life is understood and transacted. As such, culture is not a separate variable to be isolated and studied for its independent causal significance, but rather it refers to the discourses, logics, and norms that structure and render meaningful the practices of humans in various social contexts. Culture is not distinct from either the institutional processes that organize social life or the instrumental pursuits of interest by citizens, but rather it is constitutive of both. Our approach focuses on cultural understandings and norms as they are *enacted* in social practices. Culture, we might say, is practical meaning-making activity at work. To study tort law from a cultural perspective thus is to inquire about the specific categories of meaning construction that inform tort law practice, to locate these within densely mapped contexts of social interaction, and to examine their interrelationships with other forms of knowledge—especially other domains of legal discourse and extralegal moral, religious, technical, and familial discourses—that constitute social life. In other words, we ask how tort law is nested within and matters for the larger web of relationships and for the widely shared ways of thinking, talking, and acting that organize social life in particular times and places.[1]

In this sense, law, and tort law in particular, is a rich subject for cultural analysis. On the one hand, legal texts, ideas, and conventions are an important *source* of cultural values and understandings in most social contexts, and legal institutions are dynamic sites for making sense of the interplay among people negotiating social relationships through the use of legal resources (see Swidler 1986). On the other hand, legal practice in most societies offers a large, often transparent *window* through which one can view cultural norms, values, and practices in action, including those that are not necessarily "legal" in pedigree. After all, we know that judges, juries, attorneys, and litigants often draw on a wide array of cultural values, many of which are not uniquely or directly derived from formal law, in practical interactions within institutionalized legal settings such as courtroom trials (Conley and O'Barr 1990; Merry 1990; Rosen 2006; Yngvesson 1993). When we recognize further that the language, concepts, and images associated with law saturate mass-generated popular culture in television, movies, novels, cartoons, and the like, the cultural dimensions of law become at once more salient, more complex, and more challenging (Haltom and McCann 2004). Legal norms are distinguishable from, yet often intricately related to, extralegal norms such as religious, moral, technocratic, professional, and other group-based norms or values. Although law and culture can be understood as analytically distinct categories, therefore, in practice they are inseparable and mutually constitutive. A *cultural approach* to the study of tort law thus emphasizes the ways that legal practice is embedded within the larger framework of cultural norms, routines, and institutional relations (Greenhouse et al. 1994; Rosen 2006). It revels in identifying the complexities of those relationships, which often are ripe with paradox, contradictions, and puzzles for the sociolegal analyst.

Specifically, the authors in this book view tort law as one set of cultural responses to the broader challenges of addressing risk and assignments of responsibility, compensation, valuation, and obligation related to injury that may be shared with or addressed by a range of other social institutions. Most scholarship by professional legal scholars addresses the black-letter constructions of these concepts and values by scrutinizing official reasoning by judges. But even that scholarship underlines the indeterminacy, contested character, contingency, and changing meanings of official tort law constructions. Indeed, it has become commonplace among empirically oriented scholars to view tort law as one of the most discretionary, dynamic, and indeterminate areas of legal activity in the United States. Its open-textured qualities allow great latitude for meaning making by all the actors in the tort law system and make tort law a particularly important site for the articulation and dissemination of cultural norms and images.

Moreover, there is much reason to think that the actual black-letter rules of tort law do not tightly constrain decision making by judges, juries, litigants, attorneys, and ordinary disputants. Key concepts, such as proximate cause and assumption of the risk, are notoriously slippery and easy for result-oriented advocates and judges to manipulate. The doctrine of strict products liability, considered revolutionary when it was widely adopted in the 1960s, soon became riddled with elements appellate court judges drew from the negligence regime it had supposedly replaced. By the time the American Law Institute promulgated the so-called Products Liability Restatement in 1998,[2] "strict liability" was all but banished from the text. Moreover, even when judges endorse relatively "strict" versions of strict liability and instruct juries to apply them, empirical studies have often demonstrated that the issue of fault remains central to the jury's—and the public's—assumptions about blame and liability in American society. Hence our chosen title for this volume, *Fault Lines,* which underlines the broader discursive themes that permeate tort disputes in many contexts regardless of doctrinal categories.

Broadly speaking, empirical studies have further demonstrated how cultural understandings of risk and responsibility have shaped legal discourse and decision making from the everyday experience of "naming" an injury to decisions to "claim" a right, to advance a dispute, to contact an attorney, and to formalize claims in official legal forums (Engel 1984; Haltom and McCann 2004). "The identifying elements of legal culture," posits David Nelken in Chapter One of this volume, "range from facts about institutions such as the number and role of lawyers or the ways judges are appointed and controlled, to various forms of behavior such as litigation or prison rates, and, at the other extreme, more nebulous aspects of ideas, values, aspirations, and mentalities" (see p. 22) As such, cultural studies of tort law expand our understanding about the intersections of official legal doctrine and the broader normative or disciplinary discourses and institutional practices that constitute social life.

Advantages of the Comparative Perspective

Our emphasis on comparative study of cultural legal practices follows from these basic assumptions. We stress the comparative dimension, because we believe it is difficult to discern, much less to theorize about, the cultural aspects of tort law without comparisons to other social contexts where the perceptions of injury and risk, adjudication and compensation, are quite different (Nelken 1997). Comparison of variability across space and time can, for one thing, help to identify elements of contemporary U.S. tort law that may go unnoticed, be taken for granted as common sense, and thus be accorded little analytical attention. The focus on differences across space and over time enhances understanding of practices that we may overlook in our own culturally grounded experience. Moreover, the comparative enterprise can aid in analytical efforts to connect tort principles and practices to broader discourses, norms, and institutionalized relations in which the former play a constitutive role. It can aid in identifying the complex interdependencies as well as tensions among tort law and insurance institutions, health care providers, government regulators, and the like in different cultural settings. At the same time, comparative analysis can aid in normative assessment regarding the merits or failures of both tort law and broader constellations of practice in various times and places. This is essential to informed judgments about how well tort processes perform as well as to debates about institutional reform, even though that is not a primary goal of our inquiry. For American readers, comparisons to other societies can highlight the unique—some would say peculiar—features of our common law approach to tort law, tied as it is to the contingent fee, extensive pretrial discovery, and an expansive role for civil trial juries (Chase 2005). Finally, knowing more about cultural practices related to torts is arguably valuable for the larger enterprise of theorizing in sophisticated ways about law generally. If legal systems are as pluralistic, loosely coordinated, and "messy" as much contemporary scholarship insists, more knowledge about particular understudied domains of legal practice should enhance understanding about the larger phenomena of legality.

Our approach in assembling this collection has been comparative in several specific senses. First, many essays compare familiar American practices and institutions to those in other societies, including but not limited to India, Thailand, Japan, the United Kingdom, Canada, and Italy. This explicit cross-national comparative dimension alone renders our volume a unique contribution to the sociolegal study of torts. Second, a number of studies in the following pages emphasize comparisons across moments of history within particular societies, often providing a developmental perspective on how changes in tort practices have been interrelated with other social changes. Both types of comparative analysis will advance our contention that "culture" should not be viewed as static, singular, or essentialized but, rather, should be examined in terms of its multiplicity and variability across time as well as space. The inclusion of some studies of tort law over time should illuminate the conditions in which social responses to injuries change and deliberate efforts at reform are attempted and with what results. Attention to the contemporary forces of globalization in particular may help us to explore changing practices of and debate about tort law in particular research sites. Such attention to challenges of exploring differential practices in various spatially and temporally bounded contexts highlights yet another meaning of our volume's title, *Fault Lines*.

Third, the essays provide comparative perspectives on how tort law constitutes differences among citizens within particular contexts. A number of the essays will interrogate the implications of different tort systems for race, class, gender, ethnic, religious, and other forms of social differentiation. Feminist analysis of the gendered dimensions of tort law and broader cultural norms in particular receives extensive attention in several of the chapters in the volume. Our focus on tort law in relation to all of these forms of social differentiation underscores our commitment to analyzing culture in terms of power relationships and inequalities. We ask how tort law contributes to or challenges the larger patterns of who gets what, when, and how, and of institutionalized privilege and marginalization. To ask how constructions of norms matter in and for tort law is to ask fundamental questions about the organization of social power, hierarchy, and inequality. These are core questions at the heart of our analytical project. And this emphasis on differential distributions of power dividing citizens and social groups in various contexts defines yet a third nuanced connotation of our book title, *Fault Lines*.

Organization and Content

The essays in this book are grouped into five sections. We begin in Part One with two quite different but complementary essays regarding puzzles and challenges faced by cultural analysts of law generally. Both of these essays were written by scholars whom we invited to comment on the separate substantive essays as a group and to provide an overview perspective on tort law as cultural practice. We were drawn to these scholars in part because they are from outside the United States and specialize in the comparative cultural study of legal practices.

David Nelken's essay (Chapter One) adapts his classic, genre-defining work on comparative cultural study of law to tort practices. His organizing idea is "legal culture," a concept directly related to our focus on a cultural approach to analyzing law, thus making it an appropriate essay to start the collection. Nelken structures the essay around two large theoretical issues concerning cultural analysis. First, he raises a series of complex questions about how we choose the appropriate units of comparative cultural study. He argues that a focus on comparisons across nation-states should give way to more nuanced studies of differential microcontexts within nations as well as macrolevel processes such as colonialism and globalism that transcend state boundaries. Second, Nelken addresses the fitting question of what cultural analysis offers or "does" for our understandings of law. The essay weaves explicit references to other studies that follow in the book together with Nelken's own comments about tort practice in the legal culture of contemporary Italy.

Keebet von Benda-Beckmann (Chapter Two) adds a further comment on the concept of legal culture in relation to comparative tort law analysis. Her primary goal is to interrogate the concept of "community," which is frequently invoked in discussions of tort law. For example, analysts often assert that juries are uniquely qualified—as representatives of *the community*—to apply shared norms in performing such tasks as the determination of negligence or the assessment of punitive damages. From an anthropologist's point of view, however, the concept of community that underlies such assertions is incoherent. As von Benda-

Beckmann observes, communities are actually heterogeneous, dynamic, and divided along lines of differential (class, race, gender, ethnic) social power, thus complicating all questions about who can speak on their behalf. Moreover, communities can be defined in many different ways, not only by geography but by common norms and interests, by shared knowledge, or by shared experiences. Even if it were clear which meaning of *community* is intended, there would be no reason to think that juries are more representative than judges. In the end, the concept of community and the representative role of the jury in relation to it should be understood as legal-cultural artifacts that demand interpretation rather than as statements of obvious social facts.

Part Two shifts from general discussion about the puzzles and challenges at stake in cultural analysis of law to four quite different scholarly examples of cultural analysis applied to tort practices. The aim of this section is to underline the very different types of projects through which scholars can explore the cultural dimensions of torts as practical legal activity. While each study focuses on one particular national context, the general analytical approaches and methodologies offer rich models for study and comparative analysis in general.

Marc Galanter (Chapter Three) starts the section with an intriguing macrohistorical study of tort law practice in India since the late nineteenth century. His essay explores why torts play such a minor role in India's robust and flourishing legal system, one in which scarce and congested courts, immense backlogs, reputed litigiousness, and highly visible judicial intervention in public life coexist with low rates of court use by citizens and infrequent resort to tort claims. The essay shows how popular cultural stories of widespread litigiousness mask actual low rates of tort claiming, high rates of delay that discourage tort action, and heavy reliance on criminal penalties to do much of the legal work that torts might otherwise do. Despite some similarities to the United States in this regard, Galanter identifies a growing appetite for tort recoveries specifically in the area of intentional torts involving personal dignity and demands for increased compliance with caregiving duties rather than monetary compensation.

Tom Baker's essay (Chapter Four) explores and problematizes the boundaries between torts and criminalization through the lens of insurance law and practice in the United States. Just as the insurance industry has struggled to define insurance as fundamentally different from, and therefore not about, gambling, so too has the insurance industry struggled to define liability insurance as disconnected from crime. As with the more fully explored relationship between insurance and gambling, the relationship between insurance and crime depends more on culturally and historically specific images and ideas than on logical distinctions that can withstand critical analysis. Therefore, careful study of how the insurance industry ensures that it protects policyholders from tort liability, but not criminal liability, can help us better understand the culturally salient images and ideas that define the boundaries of the civil (as opposed to criminal) justice system.

Valerie Hans (Chapter Five) follows by addressing an equally fascinating question. In short, how and why do core concepts of tort law—judgments of injury, liability, the reasonable person standard, and the appropriateness of compensation—become defined by the jury's infusion of extralegal social norms and cultural understandings into its decision making? Hans draws on existing empirical research to interrogate the various institutional and psychological factors that facilitate the discretionary cultural construction of injury cases by American jurors, enabling her to offer a variety of insights about how and when this mix of generically legal and extralegal cultural norms matters most. Hans thus continues the project of examining the construction of tort law boundaries undertaken by Baker. At the same time, she raises an issue that is addressed in the chapter that follows: what are the sources of knowledge and norms in society that shape tort law?

William Haltom and Michael McCann (Chapter Six) inquire into the sources and content of popular understandings about personal injury from which jurors, judges, attorneys, and litigants enact tort law in practice. Haltom and McCann begin from the premise that much "public interest" tort litigation seeks explicitly to shape public perceptions, debates, and policy preferences on matters of personal injury, including especially harms created by mass-produced corporate products. Using tort litigation against fast-food vendors as a case study, the authors explore how the news media both construct dominant frames regarding legal "responsibility" and highlight key characteristics of participants in litigation over fast food. The study shows that news coverage has privileged cultural norms of "individual responsibility" while ridiculing plaintiffs and, especially, their attorneys, thus skewing moral and political debate in favor of corporate producers and to the detriment of consumers. Media coverage tends to eviscerate the transformative public goals of public interest litigation to discredit its advocates, and to ignore expressed demands for enlarged government responsibility almost entirely. The findings expose the challenges faced by legal advocates of reform as well as document the institutionalized (re)production of legal knowledge and values that shape the cultural context of tort disputes in the United States.

In Part Three, the authors ask how tort law doctrine grapples with fundamental cultural categories such as personhood, mind and body, gender, race, and injury. They carefully examine how tort law attempts to define the injuries humans might suffer and the remedies that tort law provides or denies. In so doing, these authors illuminate the interconnections between tort law and culturally based assumptions about the "essential" qualities of individuals and the perceived status of different kinds of individuals in society. These essays on harms to the body and the mind are therefore deeply concerned with the ways in which tort law responds to issues of inequality, stigma, and discrimination arising in particular from gender, race, and sexual identity.

Martha Chamallas (Chapter Seven) examines the intentional infliction of injury to emotions or reputation through outrageous conduct that evinces racial or gender-based discrimination, harassment, and other forms of oppressive behavior. Tort law has tended to respond ambivalently at best to such claims and to reinscribe cultural patterns of racism or sexism when attempting to define the "outrageous" conduct that would give rise to liability. Chamallas argues that confining these cases to civil rights law has permitted unsympathetic judges to impose rigid limits on antidiscrimination claims, particularly in the workplace, and may reinforce the perception that they are specialized matters somehow separate from the cultural mainstream. To the extent that tort law permits antidiscrimination claims to "migrate" from civil rights law, it can acknowledge their broader cultural acceptance and also reaffirm the role of tort law as an enforcer of core cultural norms.

Anne Bloom (Chapter Eight) focuses on a type of body that is considered culturally anomalous—that of the intersexed person who has biological features of both males and females. Bloom demonstrates how courts may deny tort claims brought by transsexual plaintiffs because the judges impose an "either-or" categorization of the plaintiff's gender. Neither federal nor state law defines how a person's sex is to be determined and, as a result, the courts have been left to devise their own criteria for sexual categorization. To illustrate this, the essay draws upon a variety of tort cases, some involving transsexuals and transvestites but also many ostensibly "run of the mill" tort cases, involving product liability, medical malpractice, and other types of claims, where sexual identity is not directly at issue. An analysis of these cases reveals both the continuing reliance on an understanding of sex as a pre-political biological given in American tort law and the fragility of the assumptions upon which this understanding rests. By continuing to base legal rulings on these assumptions, Bloom argues, courts effectively enforce prevailing binary understandings of gender and, indeed, produce their own legal/cultural norms about what it means to be a man or a woman. Finally, the essay connects the question of tort law's role in the regulation of sexual identity to a broader set of issues about the role of the body as a site of political and legal contestation.

Jennifer Wriggins (Chapter Nine) concludes this section of the book with a survey of race in tort law cases during the first half of the twentieth century. Although race has been extensively researched in the criminal justice system, its role in tort law has attracted very little scholarly attention. In part, as Wriggins observes, this is because tort law was presumed (by white observers) to be white and therefore not racial. Whiteness was understood as the "default" identity of litigants and witnesses, and the tort law decision makers—judges and jurors—were also generally white. Wriggins problematizes these assumptions and shows that whiteness was actually associated with a presumed set of attributes drawn from the culture in which tort law operated. In her comparison of damage awards for black and white decedents in wrongful death and survival cases in Louisiana from 1900 to 1949, Wriggins finds that the use of racist imagery and language was in tension with the general principle of equal treatment. In order to avoid an explicit disregard for equal treatment in tort cases, judges resorted to complicated and essentially segregated analytic frameworks to justify the much smaller damage awards for black versus white decedents. Accordingly, damage awards were sharply skewed by race, and patterns of inequality in the broader society were reproduced in the outcomes of tort litigation.

Part Four shifts attention to the themes of risk and responsibility in tort disputing, focusing on the types of macropolitical issues of legal culture that Haltom and McCann's essay raised. This section offers the most explicit examples of comparative cross-national study in the book, with the four studies variously addressing practices in the United Kingdom, Japan, and the United States.

Charles Epp's essay (Chapter Ten) examines the sudden emergence of tort lawsuits challenging police misconduct in the United Kingdom in the 1980s. He compares the legal culture of the United Kingdom, which traditionally has relied on top-down managerial approaches to accountability issues, to that of the United States, where populist approaches, including tort litigation, have been prominent. The analysis shows that, despite these different national traditions, there has been some degree of convergence. In the United Kingdom, the interaction among activist strategies, jury decisions, and newspaper coverage reconstructed the issue of police brutality and racial bias, generating trends that paralleled familiar U.S. models. The study thus balances attention to differences between legal cultures with interesting insights into the processes by which some degree of convergence can develop in a globalizing world. Even with convergence in institutional strategies on some levels, however, Epp shows how the meanings of similar legal practices can continue to differ in important ways.

Lynn Mather (Chapter Eleven) presents a study that is very similar to Epp's, although she focuses her comparison on the different trajectories of litigation against tobacco companies in the United Kingdom and the United States. Like Epp, Mather places great emphasis on differences between legal institutions and culture in the two countries to make sense of the fact that litigation in Britain was far less consequential than in the United States. Particular attention is extended to expectations and incentives for lawyers, judges, and juries in the two countries, and, following the earlier essay by McCann and Haltom, to media coverage of the litigation campaigns as well as to surveys of public attitudes toward lawsuits seeking recovery for injuries. Mather concludes her study of differences by, like Epp, examining changes in British law that are altering traditional tort practices in the United Kingdom to make them more like those in the United States.

Eric Feldman's study (Chapter Twelve) of medical malpractice litigation highlights what he views as a profound shift in Japanese legal culture. After World War II, the tort law system tended to create incentives to divert litigants and potential litigants from the courts to nonadversarial settings where disputes could be resolved without publicity and without the articulation of new social norms. At the most, tort law functioned as an early warning system to alert the ruling elites that they must create new institutional responses to important social issues. In contemporary Japan, however, things have changed. Tort law now attracts larger numbers of claimants who appear galvanized by an emergent sense that formal legal activity is socially acceptable and efficacious. Structural and procedural reforms have both legitimated tort litigation and made it more feasible than in the past. Medical malpractice litigation thus provides a striking illustration of a significant transformation of Japanese legal culture in the direction of adversarial legalism and away from a presumed avoidance of tort law.

Takao Tanase (Chapter Thirteen) raises similar questions about the evolution and current characteristics of tort law in Japanese legal culture, but he suggests that in the Japanese context adversarial legalism is by no means an end in itself. Tanase's study focuses on tort claims related to asbestos exposure, a problem discovered relatively recently in Japan. He observes that tort victims and their lawyers do indeed appear quite willing to press their claims, not only before workers' compensation tribunals but in court when necessary. Nevertheless, Tanase contends, the claimants support the collective goal of "equal justice" over the individual goal of "full compensation" in these cases. Viewing the Japanese government as the party primarily responsible for these calamities, litigants seek solutions that provide some compensation to every victim rather than ensuring that a few victims receive the full payment they may deserve. Moreover, the ultimate goal of litigation is to forge an administrative-compensation system that will remove asbestos cases from judicial control. As one of the litigants observed, "Litigation is necessary to make compensation available without litigation."

Part Five explores three key tort law concepts—causation, duty, and obligation—across time and space. All three concepts are highly contested sites in which varying meanings are asserted by different groups of social actors. Here we see with some clarity how legal and cultural interpretive frameworks can sometimes clash and at other times reinforce one another in times of social change and struggles for power.

David Engel (Chapter Fourteen) examines one of tort law's core concepts—causation—in comparative perspective, drawing on materials from the United States and Thailand. Citing Wex Malone's classic article on causation in American tort law, Engel suggests that the causation requirement in tort litigation is a crucial site of tension between legal doctrine and societal norms and beliefs. By analyzing this tension, researchers can better understand why tort law is embraced or rejected—and by whom. In Thailand, it is relatively obvious that the highly simplified concepts of causation in litigated tort cases bear little relationship to the rich, multicausal narratives offered by injury victims in personal interviews. Popular understandings of causation, associated with recent transformations in Thai culture and society, ultimately lead Thai injury victims away from law. In American society, popular discourses of causation are highly variable and contested, but victims tend to construct interpretive frameworks that are distinguishable from tort law and stand in opposition to it. This chapter demonstrates how such discourses shape and are shaped by tort law and how they help to explain the use, avoidance, and variable role of tort law in the handling of injury cases.

Ann Scales (Chapter Fifteen) continues the discussion of causation in her chapter. She notes that prevailing discussions of causation in American tort law are linear, "scientistic," monocausal and constructed in ways that are consistent with an emphasis on individual responsibility and self-determination. Yet such conceptions of causation, she contends, fail to acknowledge long-standing philosophical demonstrations that monocausal explanations are no more than convenient inferences. They are, in the terminology of this volume, cultural constructs and not facts of nature. If the rigid and purportedly scientific concepts of causation applied in modern tort cases are indeed no more than "convenient inferences," then who is it that finds them convenient—and inconvenient? Scales presents a powerful argument that the causation requirements of American tort law systematically disadvantage and cause harm to women. They are the primary consumers of a plethora of pharmaceuticals that are inadequately tested and improperly marketed, while the drug companies rely on stringent causation requirements to shield themselves from tort liability. Scales concludes by suggesting how current causation requirements could be transformed in ways that would recognize the realities of pharmaceutical testing and marketing procedures and the harms they disproportionately inflict on women.

Nancy Reichman and Joyce Sterling (Chapter Sixteen) explore in the final chapter how changes in the social construction of legal "duty" can help to make sense of curious trends in litigation. Duty is usually defined in terms of social relationships; injury is a form of social disruption. Tort law manages definitions of both injury and responsibility. Obligations that appear in legal thought are products of specific contextual factors that have to be understood and explained. Using trial court cases and Colorado Supreme Court cases filed in Denver from 1862 through 1917, they probe the types of factors that affect the development of the concept of duty. How does the type of injury, the status of the parties involved, the relationship of parties, or the location of the accident influence the court's definition of cases eligible for tort recovery? The authors' analysis of cultural meanings at stake in tort disputes with tramways and railroads provides a host of provocative insights, many of which problematize and deepen familiar arguments about how tort law subsidized corporate development in American history.

PART I

On Legal Culture and Cultural Analysis of Tort Law

CHAPTER ONE

Law, Liability, and Culture

DAVID NELKEN

Few legal domains are as obviously promising for "cultural" analysis as torts, revolving as they do around questions of risk, fault, blame, responsibility, and the limits of the duty to care. Cause and effect can be defined and connected in a wide variety of ways, and attributions of such linkages are shaped (collectively and individually) by where one wants blame to end up. The contributions to this volume show that inquiries into tort law and culture can cover a wide range of topics concerned with culture *in* tort law, tort law *in* culture, and tort law *as* culture. Cultural approaches can provide insight into the role of this kind of law, and studies of different ways of dealing with liability in different societies can highlight their cultural differences.

Notoriously, however, the term *culture* can be used in many ways, ranging from referring to what is most taken for granted to that which is most manipulated. When we are faced with such protean terms as law and culture, the variety of meanings and possible interconnections is almost too large to be mapped. My interest here is only to consider how far the term *legal culture* can be used to add conceptual clarity to this effort to map some of the relationships between law and culture. Some of the contributors actually say that this is their aim: Lynn Mather, for example, tells us that "Tobacco litigation provides an excellent lens for comparative research on legal cultures." But other contributions may also provide us with useful illustrations for this purpose even where the concept is not referred to explicitly. Legal culture can be relevant to their attempts to disclose the different and partially competing cultures that are reflected in any given system of attributions, to trace how the willingness to attach blame for tortlike behavior changes over time, as well as, most obviously, to compare the way liability for harm is attached in different places. Using a framework I have set out elsewhere,[1] I shall first say something about what is meant by the term *legal culture,* and then discuss, in turn, the units of legal culture and the role it plays in explanations.

What Is Legal Culture?

Legal culture, in its most general sense, is one way of describing relatively stable patterns of legally oriented social behavior and attitudes. The identifying elements of legal culture range from facts about institutions such as the number and role of lawyers or the ways judges are appointed and controlled, to various forms of behavior such as litigation or prison rates, and, at the other extreme, more nebulous aspects of ideas, values, aspirations, and mentalities. Like culture itself, legal culture is about who we are and not just what we do.

Inquiries into legal culture try to understand puzzling features of the role and the rule of law within given societies. Why do the United Kingdom and Denmark complain most about the imposition of European Union law but then turn out to be the countries that have the best records of obedience? Conversely, why does Italy, whose public opinion is most in favor of Europe, have such a high rate of noncompliance? Why does Holland, otherwise so similar, have such a low litigation rate compared to neighboring Germany? Why in the United States and the United Kingdom does it often take a sex scandal to create official interest in doing something about corruption, whereas in Latin countries it takes a major corruption scandal to excite interest in marital unfaithfulness? Such contrasts can lead us to reconsider broader theoretical issues in the study of law and society. How does the importance of "enforcement" as an aspect of law vary in different societies? What can be learned, and what is likely to be obscured, by defining "law" in terms of litigation rates? How do shame and guilt cultures condition the boundaries of law and in what ways does law help shape those self-same boundaries?

These few examples are enough to suggest that findings about legal culture can have both theoretical and policy implications. But there may even be more straightforward practical advantages. Knowing more about differences in legal culture can actually save your life. One well-traveled colleague who teaches legal theory likes to tells a story of the way crossing the road when abroad requires good knowledge of the local customs. In England, he claims, you are relatively safe on pedestrian crossings, but rather less secure if you try to cross elsewhere. In Italy, he argues, you need to show about the same caution in both places; but at least motorists will do their best to avoid actually hitting you. In Germany, on the other hand, or so he alleges, you are totally safe on the pedestrian crossing. You don't even need to look out for traffic. But, if you dare to cross elsewhere, you risk simply not being "seen."

The sort of investigations in which the idea of legal culture finds its place are those that set out to explore empirical variation in the way law is conceived and lived rather than to establish universal truths about the nature of law, to map the existence of different *concepts* of law rather than establish *the* concept of law (Tamanaha 2001). In employing the idea of legal culture, in comparative exercises geared to exploring the similarities and differences among legal practices and legal worlds, the aim is to go beyond the tired categories so often relied on in comparative law such as "families of law" and incorporate that attention to the "law in action" and "living law" that is usually missing from comparative lawyers' classifications and descriptions (Nelken, 1995).

The Unit of Legal Culture

There are still many interesting books (e.g., Bell 2001; Blankenburg and Bruinsma 1994; Johnson 2002) and articles (e.g., Feldman 1997, 2001) that identify legal culture with the nation-state. Collections of studies of legal culture often likewise use this as their organizing theme (Gessner, Hoeland, and Varga 1996). Rather than limit ourselves to the state level, however, patterns of legal culture can and must also be sought both at a more micro- as well as at a more macro-level. At the subnational level the appropriate unit of legal culture may be the local court, the prosecutor's office, or the lawyer's consulting room. Differences between places in the same society may often be considerable. Legal culture is not necessarily uniform (organizationally and meaningfully) across different branches of law (Bell 2001). Lawyers specializing in some subjects may have less in common with other lawyers outside their field than they have with those abroad. At the macrolevel, historical membership of the continental or common law world transcends the frontiers of the nation-state. And, increasingly, the implications of these memberships are being challenged and reworked by globalizing networks of trading and other interchanges. We also need to explore

what have been described as the "third cultures" of international trade, communication networks, and other transnational processes (Dezalay and Garth 1996;
Snyder 1999; Teubner 1997, 1998).

Given the extent of past and present transfer of legal institutions and ideas,
it is often misleading to try to relate legal culture only to its current national
context (Nelken, 2003a). For example, some American authors have mistakenly
tried to explain as examples of "Japanese" legal culture standard features of Continental European systems that date back in Japan only to their borrowing of
these legal institutions in the last century. Many aspects of law are the result
of colonialism, immigration, and conquest. Non-European countries frequently
have mixed or pluralistic legal systems that testify to waves of colonial invasions
or imitations of other systems (Harding 2001). Deliberate attempts at the sociolegal engineering of so called "legal transplants" can range from single laws and
legal institutions to entire codes or borrowed systems of law (Nelken 2001). Law
may be remade by wider national culture; but it can also itself help mold that culture. Many current legal transfers can be seen as attempts to bring about imagined and different *futures,* rather than to conserve the present (as the transplant
metaphor might suggest). Hence ex-communist countries try to become more
like selected examples of the more successful market societies, or South Africa
models its new constitution on the best that Western regimes have to offer rather
than on constitutional arrangements found in its nearer neighbors in Africa. The
hope is that law may be a means of resolving current problems by transforming
their society into one more like the source of such borrowed law; legal transfer
becomes part of the effort to become more democratic, more economically successful, more secular—or more religious. In what is almost a species of sympathetic magic, borrowed law is deemed capable of bringing about the same conditions of a flourishing economy or a healthy civil society that are found in the
social context from which the borrowed law has been taken.

The adoption of dissimilar legal models is perhaps most likely where the legal
transfer is imposed by third parties as part of a colonial project and/or insisted
on as a condition of trade, aid, alliance, or diplomatic recognition. But it has also
often been sought by elites wanting to "modernize" their society or otherwise
bring it into the wider family of "civilized" nations. Japan and Turkey are the
most obvious examples (Harding and Orucu 2002; Likosky 2002). Even in Europe some of the laws and legal institutions that people think of as most typically
their own are the result of imitation, imposition, or borrowing. Much domestic
law in the nineteenth century, such as the law of copyright, was mainly invented

as a response to its existence elsewhere (Sherman 1997). There are Dutch disputing mechanisms that are in fact a result of German imposition during the occupation, and which have been abandoned in Germany itself (Jettinghoff 2001). Hence, in advance of empirical investigation, it would be wrong to assume any particular "fit" between law and its environing national society or culture. In addition, the nation-state now has to come to terms with the impact of globalization (Garapon 1995). For some writers, we inhabit a "deterritorialized world"; we can participate via the media in other communities of people with whom we have no geographical proximity or common history (Coombe 2000). Hence, "all totalizing accounts of society, tradition and culture are exclusionary and enact a social violence by suppressing contingent and continually emergent differences." Instead, Coombe says, we must face the "challenges of transnationalism and the politics of global capitalism or multiple overlapping and conflicting juridiscapes."

Claims about the decline of the nation-state can no doubt be taken too far. Given the boundaries of jurisdiction, politics, and language, the nation-state can offer a convenient starting point for comparing legal culture. It is an empirical question how far legal culture at the national level is modified by what happens at other levels. Common influences, cultural interchange, and increasing economic interdependence (or in many cases just dependence) can all produce similarities. But, simultaneously, "increasing homogenization of social and cultural forms seems to be accompanied by a proliferation of claims to specific authenticities and identities" (Strathern 1995, 3).

We also need to take care that our comparisons do not fall into the vices of Occidentalism or Orientalism, of making other cultures seem either necessarily similar or intrinsically "other" (Cain 2000). Given that culture is, to a large extent, a matter of struggle and disagreement, the purported uniformity, coherence, or stability of given national cultures will often be no more than a rhetorical claim projected by outside observers or manipulated by elements within the culture concerned. Much that goes under the name of culture is no more— but also no less—than "imagined communities" or "invented traditions" (though these may of course be real in their effects). There is therefore some danger of reifying national stereotypes (as in the earlier examples of driving practices and pedestrians in different societies) and failing to recognize that legal culture, like all culture, is a product of the contingencies of history and is always undergoing change (Nelken 1995). It is enough to think of the transformations in attitudes toward "law and order" from Weimar to Hitlerian Germany.

One of the most pressing tasks of the comparative sociologist of law is to capture how far in actual practice what is described as globalization in fact represents the attempted imposition of one *particular* legal culture on other societies. Some leading authors argue that we are now seeing convergence toward a modern type of legal culture (Friedman 1994; Garland 2000), and, in particular, the recent growth of prestige of the Anglo American model that is spread by trade and the media. The Anglo American model is seen to be characterized by its emphasis on the care taken to link law and economics (rather than law and the state), procedures which rely on orality, party initiative, and negotiation inside law, as well as more broad cultural features such as individualism and the search for security through legal remedies (Heyderbrand 2001). Others insist that nation-states remain recognizably distinctive, with the extreme of "adversarial legalism" located only in the United States (Kagan 2001, 2007). It has been noted that "ideal" models for export often do not accurately describe how the law operates at home, as, for example, the American legal and regulatory system in practice often relies on inquisitorial methods. National versions of the continental European type of legal system embodied in ready-packaged codes are also being exported, especially to the ex-communist world. In addition, the ideals represented by the "rule of law" itself, as a way of providing certainty and keeping the state within bounds, seem increasingly outdated for the regulation of international commercial exchange by computer between multinational coporations that are more powerful than many of the governments of the countries in which they trade (Scheuerman 1999).

What does seem undeniable is the extent to which legal culture is becoming more of what we could call "relational." With increasing contact between societies there are more opportunities to define one's own legal culture in terms of relationships of attraction to or repulsion from what goes on in other societies. For example, when comparative European prison rates first began to be published in the 1980s, Finland, which was high in the list, decided to cut back on prison building, whereas Holland felt entitled to build more. What mattered was to stay within the norm. Likewise, for many European countries the continued use of the death penalty in the United States serves as a significant marker of the superiority of the former's own legal culture.

Cultural Units and Tort Law

What are the units of tort law that are being analyzed in this book? Any cultural analysis of tort law needs to ask whether this is a useful cross-cultural category.[2] Are the various torts—uniting intentional torts such as racial offence or police misbehavior, with procedures for dealing with road accidents, products liability, or medical malpractice—coherent from a legal point of view? (Or from any other point of view?) What are the boundaries of tort law? As against the search across jurisdictions for "functional equivalents," legal doctrines, and instruments that resolve similar "problems" (an approach that has been a mainstay of comparative law), cultural analysis should make us more sensitive to the power of culture to define what counts as a problem to be solved. If we are interested in legal culture, another way of getting at these questions is to ask about the unit or units we are examining. The culture of tort law looks different when we consider the part played by legislatures, judges, lawyers, juries, or textbook writers. As the contributions to this volume show, there are political and professional struggles between various units—legislatures versus courts, judges versus juries, and so on. And, as part of such struggles, the media play an important role in constructing our perceptions about when tort law is and should be used (Haltom and McCann 2004). It would be more correct to speak of the cultures rather than the culture of tort law (even though we should also not forget that actors arguing about issues of liability may also share many assumptions).

Scholars in the United States (e.g., Shapo 2003) have treated judicial decisions as reflections of and commentaries on such larger cultural battles in society and offered persuasive analyses of the values and interests vying for hegemony. Elaborated through doctrinal discussions and borrowings, tort law also responds to and shapes social developments, and sparks and is subject to political reactions and cycles. Many jurisdictions in the developed world in the twentieth century have seen, for example, consolidation of moves from fault- to risk-based liability, debates over the lottery of using the law of negligence to deal with road accidents, and arguments over the expansion of rules for products liability. The rise of what has been called the "risk society" has led to growing recognition of the unpredictable consequences of modern technological advances. While some say that this makes the case for extending more legal protection, others stress the need to reduce expectations (whether to contrast the alleged "culture of complaint" or to preserve competitive global advantage). Such debates are not disinterested. Many of the contributors to this volume claim that talk of the "litigation explosion" in the United States has a flimsy empirical basis and seek to expose not only the interests of corporations but also the role of gender and racial stereotypes in shaping arguments in and about tort law.

Any definition of tort law's boundaries also depends on how far it circumscribes the range of institutions and discourses it treats as relevant. As various contributions demonstrate, accounts seeking to reveal the culture(s) of tort law cannot afford to limit themselves to examining the work of the courts. The number and type of cases that are litigated depends on recognition of the possibility of claiming ("naming, blaming and shaming"), the choice to employ tort remedies, the possibility of benefiting from alternative remedies or using competing modes of dispute processing, and the strategic choices of lawyers. The agencies and institutions that shape the everyday processing of tort claims—in particular the calculations of insurers and loss adjustors—introduce economic and bureaucratic rationalities that typically have little to do with the cultural messages that judges supposedly wish to convey (Ross 1980; Baker, in this volume). On the other hand, it is simplistic to see tort law as merely a technical instrument for channeling compensation to those who suffer harms. The expressive role of tort law is suggested by the fact that (especially in the United States) a large part of the compensation obtained is needed to fuel the system itself.

In many of the chapters, cultural differences are highlighted by contrasting the way different jurisdictions organize the possibilities of attaching blame and obtaining compensation. In such cross-cultural comparisons of similarities and differences much depends on our cultural starting point. Whereas those comparing the United States with Japan may see the expansion of tort law as evidence of assertive *individualism,* the U.S. authors represented here tend to see it more as showing the extension of *social* responsibility to those who cause damage. The historical research by Joyce Sterling and Nancy Reichman (this volume) reminds us how difficult it was not so long ago even in the United States to obtain relief for negligence. But if difficulties recovering accident damages in the United States can be seen as largely related to capitalist development, the key to the current lower level of relief in Japan or India seems to have at least as much to do with the existence of alternative ways of dealing with or thinking about these problems.

The danger of taking tort law as it currently operates in the United States as our yardstick for comparative research is that it may be too distinctive to serve as a basis for understanding other systems, leading only to the repetitive question of why other places are not like the United States or, less obviously, why other places do not make more use of (tort) law. Are we justified in assuming that being obliged to turn to the police or "a big man" to solve these kind of disputes (Galanter, in this volume) is always an inferior solution? Yes, if we think that the type of modern society India is, or is on the way to becoming, "requires" certain forms of redress. But a cultural approach needs to be aware that the individualistic type of remedies that tort law makes possible can also threaten the bonds of a more group-based type of social order. In Japan, not having to call on your rights is still considered by many the best guarantee of having them (Tanase, in this volume) even if those from more individualistic societies would worry that this leaves you at the mercy of others. Can there be a culturally neutral answer to this dilemma? On the other hand, it is also possible to question whether it now makes sense (if it ever did) to assume that the places we are comparing are really independent. In their case studies Epp and Mather, for example, both argue that recent campaigns to seek tort remedies in the United Kingdom were influenced by developments in the United States and are part of a "global movement." Feldman, in describing the rise of medical malpractice suits in Japan also argues that these are "inspired by the US." At the same time all these authors are cautious about seeing this as evidence of convergence toward the U.S. model.

The Italian Context of Tort Law

Insofar as jurisdictions are in contact with others, it may sometimes be plausible to point to the same variables as shaping developments in tort law. But what about factors that are not a result of such mutual influences? Marc Galanter at one point makes a daring comparison between the situation of the courts in India and Italy. He rightly suggests that procedural difficulties produce long delays in both societies and that the ability to postpone the day of reckoning means that there is often little incentive to settle. But, of course, there are also other factors that distinguish the way tort law operates in each context. Delay in Italy results from a variety of factors that are not replicated in India; for example, politicians are fearful to have a well-functioning justice system because even with the current one only fifteen years ago judges succeeded in driving from office all the existing parties of government. It can be risky to compare different societies without engaging in direct observations. In the absence of careful empirical studies, Galanter finds himself relying on procedural scholars to describe the Italian situation (whereas those writing about the United Kingdom find it easier to quote data produced by empirical sociologists).

It would be wrong to make too much of what is for Galanter not much more than an aside, were it not for the fact, as the chapters in this collection confirm, it is so hard to find English language[3] discussions of the role of tort law in civil law European societies. Scholars in the United States have written more about Japan and Asia (though they sometimes fail to note the extent to which what they see as the legal peculiarities of these places may have descended from civil law imports). Comparing the situation in the United States to that in the United Kingdom, valuable as it is, does not allow us to address these other differences with most of the countries that make up the European Union. Kagan (2001) considers the United Kingdom to be similar to other European societies in not being afflicted with the drawbacks of a system of adversarial justice. But in many (other) respects the two countries do have many similarities that they do not share with continental Europe (Field and Nelken 2007; Nelken 2003b). It may therefore be useful to add something more here about tort law in Italy in the hope that this may encourage more empirical research on the use of tort law in Europe, even if I can only indicate some of the possible aspects that should be taken into account.[4]

In the first place, it is important not to assume that the cultural object "tort law" exists as it does in the United States—even if there is a large overlap with what Italians call "civil responsibility." There are almost no media or popular debates about tort law as a problem as such, and virtually no discussion (outside some restricted judicial circles) of a litigation explosion centered on this area of law. There is, though, a continuing and growing scandal about the level of deaths and injuries at work (alleging that Italy has the highest level in Europe of what Italians call "white death"). Although cases involving large factories make the news, most accidents result from the working practices of the small businesses that are the backbone of Italian industry and increasingly employ immigrant workers for dangerous jobs. Employers are said to often try to buy off criminal proceedings (which provide the evidence for tort claims) and threaten or bribe fellow workers not to give evidence. The response to this problem, however, is usually to call for better regulation by the state[5] rather than stronger remedies in tort.

As an aspect of legal education, tort law is seen as relatively unexciting compared to subjects such as criminal or labor law. Lawyers who do such work tend to be generalists or to combine it as part of their general practice in those fields. Although court judgments provide some material for cultural exegesis (Italian "motivations" are longer than most found in continental Europe), the best place to search for culturally relevant debates are the surrounding doctrinal commentary, which has an altogether higher status than in the common law world. Such discussions include extraordinarily rich analyses of legal approaches to causation, much of which centers on developments in Germany (itself an interesting and recurrent example of the way " internal" legal culture does not necessarily develop in tandem with other features of general culture). Much ink is spilled in drawing lines between "material," "moral," and "existential" heads of damages (the last being the most controversial and misunderstood).

When it comes to the "law in action"—to an extent that is difficult for common lawyers to appreciate—in practicing their trade, tort lawyers typically choose to rely on prosecutors and court experts to establish the facts of cases where both criminal and civil charges arise. This applies both to cases of dangerous driving and the mass torts claims that follow industrial or environmental disasters. Often such lawyers are linked to trade unions or other organizations that feed them their cases. Lawyers are principally oriented to litigation rather than to settlement, and plaintiff lawyers face the problem of delay as a crucial factor exploited by insurance companies offering low settlements. Especially in northern Italy, a new profession of accident brokers has sprung up who act as intermediaries offering a complete service (car replacement service, attached medical expert, and lawyers), and these have made some inroads on the clients who would otherwise turn to ordinary lawyers.

As in the case studies of Japan and the United Kingdom discussed in this book, there are various aspects of institutional factors in Italy that reduce the advantages of litigation as compared to the United States. There are no class actions, no contingent fees (though de facto, there may be "under the table" agreements), and no punitive damages. But it is also a changing scene, and both lawyers and judges have emphasized to me the emergence of new heads of damages and a rise in the number of claims of medical negligence. Although groups or lobbies of victims have scored some victories,[6] consumers have much less clout than in many other developed societies. What is more significant is the changing role of unions. Whereas the extension of job security and pension and other benefits reduced class conflict, job security is now increasingly unavailable or being threatened, and tort remedies may increasingly play a role that used to be left to political bargaining. Such institutional and structural changes play themselves out in a culture that still has no easy equivalent term for *accountability* and where the highly influential catholic and ex-communist ideologies place relatively less stress on individual responsibility to improve society as opposed to loyalty to the group and collective action.

Explaining Legal Culture

Let us assume that we can identify which unit—or, better, units—of legal culture we want to study. The second set of questions concerns how we should employ the concept in the context of our investigations. What is the point in calling a particular pattern of behavior or ideas *legal culture*, and what follows from this? We could use this term, like others such as *legal system* or *legal process,* as no more than scholarly shorthand for pointing to a set of activities or problems. But if we want to utilize legal culture in explanatory enquiries, we shall have to go further than this. The question is: "How much further?" *Culture* is one of those words that is particularly difficult to define and easy to abuse (Kuper 1999). Within anthropology, the process of producing accounts of other cultures is increasingly contested (Clifford and Marcus 1986). How can we avoid the ever-present danger of circular argument? (They do it that way because that is how they do it in Japan, in Holland, or wherever.) Is it best to use the term *legal culture* only as a residual explanation when other explanations run out (Prosser 1995)?

Roger Cotterrell has argued that the term *legal culture* is too vague and impressionistic a concept to be useful in constructing explanations (Cotterrell 1997). Lawrence Friedman, the acknowledged father of the concept, replies that it is no worse than other overarching social science concepts. Even if the concept as such is not measurable, it covers a wide range of phenomena that can be measured (Friedman 1997). In its role in explanations, legal culture can serve to capture an essential intervening variable in influencing the type of legal changes that follow on large social transformations such as those following technological breakthroughs. More generally, "legal culture determines when, why, and where people turn for help to law, or to other institutions, or just decide to 'lump it.'" An inquiry into legal culture would try to explain, for example, why French or Italian women would be more or less likely to turn to the police for help in the case of sexual assault.

Lawrence Friedman is also the author of the classic distinction between "internal" and "external" legal culture. On the one hand, "internal legal culture" refers to the ideas and practices of legal professionals; "external legal culture," on the other hand, is the name given to the understandings, norms, values, and attitudes brought to bear on law by wider social groups. Friedman has increasingly argued that the importance of internal legal culture as a factor in explaining sociolegal change tends to be exaggerated, usually by legal scholars who have an investment in doing so. He has preferred to concentrate on the importance of external legal culture and has given especial attention to how the increasing public demand for legal remedies—what he calls the drive to "Total Justice" (Friedman 1985, 1990)—produces legal and social change. Some of the most stimulating if controversial work in this field, however, has been designed to show, *pace* Friedman, that patterns of legally related behavior are less the result of the way "folk culture" shapes the demand for legal relief and more the consequence of the institutional possibilities provided. There has been considerable debate, for example, about how far the comparatively low use of courts in Japan should be explained in terms of a specifically widely felt Japanese (and, more generally, Asian) religiously based, cultural reluctance to going to law, or whether it is more a result of a deliberate set of government-created disincentives to litigation (Hamilton and Sanders 1992). An important study of litigation rates in Europe by Erhard Blankenburg seeks to explain why the Netherlands has one of the lowest, and Germany one of the highest, litigation rates, despite being so similar culturally and even interdependent economically (Blankenburg 1997). The answer given is that these rates depend less on what people want from law than on the availability of other institutional possibilities for dealing with their disputes and claims. The Netherlands, it is argued, as compared to Germany, possesses a much wider range of "infrastructural" avenues for disposing of cases in ways that do not require court litigation. But as an illustration of the lack of conceptual clarification in this field, we may note that the infrastructural alternatives that Blankenburg calls "legal culture" others would describe as "structural factors," precisely in contrast to cultural ones.

The positivist social science explanatory approach to legal culture typically seeks to assign causal priority between competing hypothetical variables. The interpretative approach, on the other hand, is more concerned with understanding how aspects of legal culture resonate and fit together. It sees its task as faithfully translating another system's ideas of fairness and justice and making proper sense of its web of meanings. In the search for holistic meaning, the insistence on distinguishing internal from external legal culture, or the "demand" for law from the "supply" of law, can obscure as much as it reveals (Nelken 1997). Whereas the first approach uses various aspects of legal culture to explain variation in levels and types of legally related behavior such as litigation or crime control, the second approach seeks to use evidence of legally relevant meaning-making activity and attitudes as an "index" of legal culture. It aims at providing "thick descriptions" (Geertz 1973) of law as "local knowledge" (Geertz 1983). In testing its hypotheses, the positivist approach seeks a sort of sociolegal Esperanto that abstracts from the language used by members of different cultures, preferring for example to talk of "decision-making" rather than "discretion." The rival strategy, concerned precisely with grasping linguistic nuance and cultural packaging, would ask whether and when the term *discretion* is used and what different nuances it carries.

Scholars who adopt the interpretative approach contrast the different meanings of the "Rule of law," the "Rechtsstaat," or the "Stato di diritto," the Italian "garantismo" versus "due process," or "law and order" as compared to the German "innere sicherheit"; they unpack the meaning of "lokale justiz" as compared to "community crime control" (Zedner, 1995). They try to grasp the secrets of culture by focusing on key local terms, which are almost, but not quite, untranslatable. Blankenburg himself explores the meaning of the term *beleid* in Holland that refers to the more or less explicit policy guidelines followed by trusted government, criminal justice personnel, and public organizations in general (Blankenburg and Bruinsma 1994). They examine the idea of the state in common law and continental European countries so as to understand, for example, why civil litigation is seen as essentially democratic in the United States but as antidemocratic in France. For this approach, concepts both reflect and constitute culture, as in the changes undergone by the meaning of "contract" in a society where the individual is seen as necessarily embodied in wider relationships (Winn 1994), or the way that the Japanese ideogram for the new concept of "rights" came to settle on a sign associated with "self interest" rather than morality (Feldman 1997).

An interpretative stance is more ready than the positivist explanatory approach to treat culture as part of a flow of meaning, "the enormous interplay of interpretations in and about a culture" (Friedman 1994, 73) to which the scholar herself also contributes. It is also less interested in drawing a definitional line between legal culture and the rest of social life because it sees this less as a problem for the observer to solve than an aspect of the way legal culture actually works as it reflexively constructs the boundaries of law in society. Institutions thus are not isolated as variables separable from culture, but rather what we identify as institutions are understood as sites of routinized enactment of cultural understandings and practices. Common law systems, for example, tend to focus more on the link among law, economics, and society, while civil law systems focus principally on that among law, politics, and society. In some civil law legal regimes, as compared to the Anglo American pragmatic-instrumental view of law, law may be deliberately treated as more of an ideal aspiration than as a blueprint for guiding behavior, either because of deference to the state project of representing the collective will or under the influence of religious traditions and philosophical idealism. The fact that the latter has a poorer "fit" to globalizing business may partly explain the successful spread of Anglo American lawyering.

What explanations using legal culture are offered by the contributors to this volume? Institutions, structures, and culture, taken singly or together, all figure in arguments about how tort law works or changes. Sometimes—especially in cross-cultural comparisons—these elements are put together, as where Tanase tells us both about the Japanese "mind set" and the way governments there seek to manage disputes centrally. Or the focus may be more on single elements. We learn, for example, of the role played by the statute of limitations in the United Kingdom in blocking tobacco litigation, of the deterrent of having to pay lawyers' fees in advance in Japan, and of the relevance of the specialized bar in the United States as compared to the centralized court system in Japan. For some writers it is important to try to distinguish the specific role of culture, whether this is treated as group mentality, popular legal consciousness, or media projection. But it proves difficult to hold a hard and fast line. Institutions themselves are an expression of culture. Feldman tells us that the introduction of contingent fees in Japan would not of itself alter much, without a change in the wider way of thinking.

Some of the contributors offer instructive contrasts when concentrating on the same jurisdiction. Sterling and Reichman ask why it was so much easier to get compensation for similar kinds of accidents caused by tramways as compared to railways at the same period and place (and make the provocative argument that this is a rare case where "insiders" are treated more harshly). Whatever cross-cultural truths emerge (the importance of public health systems, procedural delays, lawyers' level of organization) putting different chapters together also reveals that similar variables can sometimes have different effects in different places. Thus Epp tells us that in the United Kingdom, media exposure helped focus attention on the structural factors—the institutionalized racism—that lay behind police misconduct; in the United States, by contrast, media stories serve mainly to distract attention from corporate responsibility. Having more than one study of the same place gives us a richer picture. We see how in the United Kingdom tort remedies played a more successful role in campaigns against the police than against tobacco companies. If Tanase emphasizes the distinctiveness of the Japanese system, Feldman shows us how things are changing, at least where it comes to matters of medical malpractice.[7]

It may be appropriate, finally, to ask how these explanations relate to Lawrence Friedman's original proposals for the study of legal culture. Friedman has maintained a strong interest in tort law throughout his long and amazingly productive career. Early on, with Jack Ladinsky, he offered a trail-breaking account of the many factors that helped produce the emergence of remedies for railway and other industrial accidents (Friedman and Ladinsky 1967). And he continued to chart the historical transformations in the relationship between people and the legal system in the United States, as illustrated through the move from a high degree of fatalism to the demand for "total justice" (Friedman 1985). So we could even say that his interest in tort law helped produce the idea of legal culture. As we have noted, Friedman's original framework made space for both internal and external legal culture, but he and later writers have concentrated on exploring the legal consciousness of those not directly involved in administering the legal system. In any case, the discussions in this book about how, why, and when people in India, the United Kingdom, Japan, or Thailand turn to the law fall squarely within the paradigm he created.

While it is a mistake to exaggerate the extent to which people in the United States seek legal remedies to their troubles, there is certainly evidence from these chapters of a much wider gulf between internal and external legal culture in some other places. David Engel, in particular, shows the enormous gulf between internal and external legal culture in Thailand. But even nearer to home, those trained in common law cultures can easily underestimate the importance in continental European countries of the idea that internal and external *should* be kept apart. Examining the legal consciousness of those who use the law suggests that whatever moral messages tort law seeks to communicate frequently has little to do with shaping when people resort to the law. In Sicily, for example, I would suggest that, as in Thailand, personal relationships are all important. But the issue after a road accident occurs is not how to seek merit but how to avoid being outwitted ("fregato").

Interviews conducted by my Sicilian research assistant[8] suggest that in that part of Italy the key question after an accident (even after forms detailing the incident have been exchanged) is not who is to blame but with whom you have to deal. It is important to find out as much as possible about the personal and social background of the person you have been in an accident with, getting information about the reputation of his or her insurance company, the lawyer, garage mechanic, medical expert available to him or her, and in general the person's larger network. Irrespective of what can be gained or lost by reporting the accident to the insurance company, common sense dictates that it is always better to try to reach personal agreement rather than take the case to court or go down any road involving impersonal bureaucracy. Likewise, in choosing an insurance company in the first place it is wise to choose one in which your family or friends work, best of all if they are the top people. In this case they can help you in the search for information as and when it becomes necessary. It is normally possible to get some sense straight after the accident of whether the other person intends to take advantage of you. If this is likely, then you (too) may have to set up false witnesses, compliant mechanics, and experts as well as put pressure on lawyers and insurance employees working on your side.

On the other hand, Friedman's framework can also give rise to problems. It is hardly satisfactory to use the term *legal culture* as a mode of explanation (e.g., of changes in tort law or differences in tort systems) and also use the term to describe the result of what we have explained. There is a real danger this way of falling into tautological arguments (Cotterrell 1997; Nelken 2007). Many aspects of internal and external legal culture are relevant to characterizing Japan as different—but saying that this is what adds up to their legal culture means we can't use it as *explanation* of why Japan has the legal culture it does. This difficulty is compounded when we use the term to explain change. Friedman suggests that legal culture is the name that we can give to the factors that mediate between technological change and the legal response. Over time, he suggests, tort law tends to follow social change. (His example is of the motor car;[9] now with the Internet we are seeing an extension of tort law to threats of invasion of privacy and defamation). But, because tort law can be an index, result, or cause of change, then, as Feldman points out (in this volume), it is often impossible to disentangle which is cause and which is effect.

More generally, Friedman's framework would be considered too positivist by at least some of this volume's authors. Culture is rarely uniform, as Epp points out in talking about the "footholes" in British culture that were exploited by those challenging the police service. Where culture is a "toolkit," it is hard to see it as determining any given outcome. Placing more emphasis on personal responsibility, for example, can cut both ways. It can justify the state imposing more obligations or removing them. When we move to interpretative approaches (e.g., in thinking about Karma), culture is not so much an explanatory factor as the context in which behavior emerges.

Any study of tort law and culture ultimately brings us back to larger issues about the place of law and legality in social life more generally. What do we hope to achieve by our writing, asks Ann Scales (this volume), referring to the futility, as she sees it, of demonstrating repeatedly the inequality and discrimination intrinsic to the way tort law decides on liability? It is certainly a scholarly illusion to think that power differentials disappear simply by unmasking them, but exposing injustice is at least part of such a task. Beyond this, comparative studies of legal culture can provoke us to rethink what we mean by justice and make an important contribution by showing the restrictions on the alternatives we consider as open to us in connecting law to society. We thus come to appreciate that "we," and not only "them," have "culture." As Engel and Hans each reminds us, religious and moral beliefs of ordinary people in the United States as well as in other places have large effects on explaining differences in their attitudes in deciding about liability. And, for better or worse, cultural assumptions also help shape the range of options thought acceptable by political elites.

CHAPTER TWO

Torts and Notions of Community

More Observations on Units of Legal Culture

KEEBET VON BENDA-BECKMANN

David Nelken's discussion of legal culture raises important questions about the criteria for selecting appropriate units of analysis for comparative study. To that astute discussion I add some observations about the concept of community, which appears to be one of the most prevalent units of analysis in discussions of legal culture and American tort law. In fact, many of the American participants in the discussions and presentations that gave rise to this volume referred to the concept of community, yet it was rarely problematized. I suspect that there is a shared but implicit understanding among American scholars that communities are at the foundation of (tort) law and that it is clear what a community is, or rather, what the relevant community is when discussing tort law issues. If examined more closely, their concept of community is sociologically incoherent. "Community" can actually mean quite different things rather than having the unitary (and normatively driven) meaning that is assumed in these discussions about American tort law and legal culture.

In order to understand why the normative concept of community has trumped a more anthropological concept, Roger Cotterrell's (1995) discussion of the legal philosophical foundations of English and American law is helpful, since it suggests the importance of the ideology of community for American legal scholars and practitioners. Cotterrell argues that the English system is characterized by the governing force of law, which he calls "imperium," while the American system is based on the assumption that it is communities with shared values and interest that are at the basis of law. He discusses the implications of the deep communitarian undercurrents in American law for the American legal profession. While the judge is seen as representing authority in the English legal system, judges in the American understanding are regarded as the most important representatives of communities to determine and interpret what the shared values are.

The central role of "community" in discussions of American tort law seem to support Cotterrell's thesis, though the representative role he assigns to the judges might have to be reconsidered in the tort law context, because it is usually said that the American trial jury rather than the judge performs this function. For example, commentators, including participants in the discussions leading to this volume, sometimes debate the roles of judges and juries in awarding punitive damages. An argument offered in favor of the jury's determining punitive damages is that jurors are part of the community and are therefore better positioned to understand and evaluate the conduct of the parties. Those arguing that the judge should determine punitive damages may contend that judges not only have relevant legal expertise but also a more distanced perspective on the dispute, which is more likely to produce the best decision. Thus, in this implicit justification that seems characteristic of American legal culture, the judge appears as a distanced actor, while members of the jury are seen as more directly representing the community and having privileged knowledge of the community's norms and interests as well as of the parties' experiences. Although observers may differ about the respective merits of a decision by a more distanced (judge) or a more immediate (jury) actor, they seem to concur in the underlying assumptions about community in American tort law.

In debates of this kind, the term *community* may be used with many different connotations that would lead to quite different outcomes if they were taken seriously, yet the participants tend to proceed as if they are all using the same term. It may be useful, therefore, to discuss some of the contradictions and problems involved in the concept of community as an appropriate unit to analyze torts. In this brief discussion, I will raise some questions about who in the community is presumed to be represented, who represents the community, and what is represented. Furthermore, I will address the question of what the relevant community might be.

What Is Represented: Cultural Norms and Interests, Shared Knowledge, or Shared Experiences?

Some of the problems of who and what is represented are well known from criminal law: Juries do not represent a community as a whole, but are skewed in terms of class and race. In particular, the poor are underrepresented, which accounts at least to some extent for racial imbalances in criminal justice. This is especially problematic in criminal cases because those who might be expected to hold cultural values most similar to those of the accused are not likely to sit on the jury. That is, the cultural values and interests of criminal defendants are not adequately represented by juries. Although perhaps less urgent in tort cases, where the parties are not so drastically skewed in terms of race or social class, the question to what extent juries represent their community is nevertheless relevant. This is, moreover, linked to the question of what it is that juries are thought to represent. Are they presumed to represent the *cultural* norms of a community or the experiences and perceptions of the parties? Is there reason to think that juries are more representative of communities in either sense than are judges?

Heterogeneity and Mobility

In a small, close-knit, face-to-face community, for example, a small village or a small and homogeneous neighborhood, the members by virtue of belonging to that community might indeed have more or less intimate and firsthand information about the experiences and perceptions of the parties in a tort case. Let us assume, for the sake of argument, that the members of the community do have such information because of their proximity to the parties. Such a jury could not possibly fulfill the requirements of independence. What would that mean for due process? And would that disqualify the whole jury or even the idea of a jury generally?

However, such small, homogeneous communities are not the rule; generally juries represent quite heterogeneous communities. For these communities, the claim that local residents know the experiences of the parties in a tort case and the justice norms of the residents firsthand cannot in its generality be sustained. Most residents would not deny this. Others might think they do, because they derive their information from the local press or television, through the Internet, or through their network within and among the community. But this knowledge will be secondhand at best for most members of the community and thus of the jury. This is a problematic basis for decisions that are meant to reflect local norms and knowledge of the parties' experiences.

Communities are not only heterogeneous; they also fluctuate in composition. According to the U.S. Census Bureau, March 2004, annual moving rates in the United States have slowly gone down from 16.7 percent in 1993–94 to

14.2 percent in 2002–2003, slightly under two-thirds of which is mobility within the same county, and more than one-third within or between different states. This must have implications for the communities and the level of shared knowledge. Though movement, even frequent movement, does not necessarily affect the class, race, and age structures, it does affect the degree of familiarity among the members of a community. How does community formation work with a population that moves on average once every seven to eight years and that has a considerable population that moves more frequently? How do these movers tap into shared knowledge, and how are shared cultural norms negotiated or imposed? Through what institutions and networks do immigrants become members of the community, and how is information of the type we are interested in here disseminated? What is the role of local media and of the new communication media? And to what extent and how do such movers represent their community when they act on juries? Are these mobile people immediately fully represented in juries or is mobility in itself a source of skewed representation?

The argument that members of the community, and by extension members of the jury, know the local norms and the perceptions and experiences of the parties in a tort action is problematic in two regards. First, the argument is based on a concept of community that not only shares cultural norms and interests but also shares common knowledge. This implies a notion of a community as a set of social relationships, a social group with a higher degree of density than a community that shares cultural values only. We shall see that this has implications for what the relevant community might be. Second, the claim of shared experience implies an even denser concept of community. Class, race, gender, and age differences and differences in the concomitant cultural expressions and evaluations are put in parentheses. Thus, even if the members of the community might share knowledge of what happened in the tort case, this does not mean that they understand or have shared the experiences and perceptions of the parties. People with different backgrounds may interpret what happened completely differently. This would be a problematic basis for any jury decision, including a decision to award punitive damages, if the claim is that it is based on shared experience. It also raises important questions about the role of the media and the ways they mediate cultural and social evaluations and interpretations of the events.

Furthermore, the community of the parties, that is, the community that lives closely together in day-to-day life and shares the primary knowledge and experiences of the parties, is in many instances, a different community from the one that is represented by a jury. The community from which the jury is drawn is defined by the administrative boundaries of the jurisdiction.[1] Though theoretically the two could coincide, in practice the scope of these two types of communities is in all likelihood different. And, as we have seen, a community that shares cultural norms and interests is different from a community that shares common knowledge or even common experience. To what extent a jury really represents the relevant community is therefore highly questionable.

Moreover, many tort cases do not arise and are not tried in the communities where the parties reside but in other locations such as the workplace, public spaces, or thoroughfares. If tort litigation takes place far from the neighborhood of the parties, the jury cannot possibly represent any community that is relevant to them. The community the jury represents may be quite different in social composition, might have different cultural norms, and its members would have no direct knowledge of what happened, and no direct knowledge of the justice norms, experiences, or perceptions of the parties.

Conclusion

The communitarian underpinnings of the American judicial system thus seem to have some curious implications for tort law. The claim that jurors have privileged knowledge over judges by virtue of being members of the community is problematic because the former may not represent a community that is relevant for the parties, and because the community, due to mobility and social stratification, is typically so heterogeneous that there cannot be shared firsthand knowledge of the tort, let alone shared normative values, experiences, and perceptions. And if, on the other hand, the community of the victim and jury is so small and close knit that the jury actually shares knowledge if not experience of the parties, then the issue of independence becomes highly problematic.

The confusion in the argumentation arises out of the different connotations of community implied in the claim for shared experience. It seems that the term is no more than a general idea without a referent in actual social life. It is, in short, an ideological tool. As such, it substantiates Cotterrell's central thesis that the American legal system is based on communitarian premises, be it that it is not the judge but the jury that is accorded a privileged status as representing the community. This ideology is not without problems. Such an idea can be freely manipulated by lawyers and media, precisely because it has no clear referent in actual social life. How does that affect issues such as the awarding of punitive damage? One also wonders how much this contributes to public perceptions of the legitimacy or illegitimacy of tort litigation. And finally, one wonders why the judge is not considered to be a representative of the community of his jurisdiction. In many instances, he or she is, after all, elected by that very community. Does being elected mean a lower level or a more distant form of representativeness than being selected for jury service? Why would that be the case? Even if it were clearer what is meant by the term *community,* therefore, it would still be problematic to claim that the jury is more representative than the judge. Reliance on community as a unit of analysis in tort law thus carries with it a number of conceptual problems that tend to be ignored, suggesting that the concept is essentially ideological rather than sociological. If so, we must proceed with caution when we bring the notion of community into our analysis of tort law and legal culture.

PART II

Different Approaches to Cultural Analysis of Tort Law

India's Tort Deficit

Sketch for a Historical Portrait

MARC GALANTER

The Not-Quite Arrival of Tort Law

Doctrinally, India appears to have a tort law modeled on that of England, with some local modifications and statutory supplements. But this is deceptive. The history of tort in India is quite distinctive. The British brought the common law to India in the eighteenth century; in the quarter century following the 1857 revolt, the legal system was rationalized and systematized. A unified hierarchy of courts was established in each region. A series of codes, based on English law and applicable throughout British India, was adopted (Acharyya 1914; Galanter 1968; Stokes 1887). By 1882 there was virtually complete codification of all fields of criminal, commercial, and procedural law; tort was the only major field of law left uncodified.

The need for a tort code was urged by Sir Henry Maine, Sir James Stephen, and the Fourth Law Commission which reported in 1879. An Indian Civil Wrongs Bill, drafted by Sir Frederick Pollock in 1886, at the instance of the Government of India, was never taken up for legislative action (Jain 1966, 658). Looking back from 1914 in a magisterial account of codification, a distinguished advocate found the failure to enact a code "inexplicable" (Acharyya 1914, 306). But a decade later the Civil Justice Committee 1924–25, noting that the matter "had been under consideration for some years," observed that "there is no branch of law which is more free from blame of contributing to the law's delays" (Government of India 1925, 535–36). In 1872, Stephen had asserted that "a good law of torts would be a great blessing to [India because] it would enable the legislature to curtail very greatly many of the provisions of the Penal Code, which are at present called into play on the most trifling occasions to gratify malice" (Acharyya 1914, 217). But half a century later, the diversion to the criminal courts struck the Civil Justice Committee as providential: "A large part of this work [that might be done by tort] is done in India, and is better done, by the criminal courts" (Government of India 1925, 536).

Patterns of Use/Nonuse

Official satisfaction with discouragement of tort litigation reflects a view, prevalent from the early days of British rule, that Indians were excessively litigious and inclined to misuse opportunities for legal remedy to pursue status and carry on feuds. Henry St. George Tucker, a director of the East India Company, complained in 1832 that "the natives of these provinces, to whom the duel is little known, repair to our courts as to the listed field, where they may give vent to all their malignant passions" (Tucker 1853, 21). Others took a more benign view of Indian litigaton. Sir William Hunter thought British courts offered a vent for "the pent up litigation of several centuries" and thought it "only a healthy and most encouraging result of . . . conscientious government . . . [that for the first time Indians] are learning to enforce their rights" (Hunter 1897, 342–43).

To restrain litigiousness and not incidentally raise considerable revenue, India's rulers imposed fees for using the civil courts. A series of enactments, culminating in the Indian Court Fees Act of 1870 (Act VII of 1870), imposed an ad valorem fee, on a regressive scale, on suits for money damages. For a suit to proceed, the claim had to be accompanied by payment of a fee of from 5 to 12 percent of the amount claimed (court fees might be waived for poor parties, and specific statutes might permit actions without payment of court fees).

Although court statistics unfortunately do not separate tort claims, it seems that tort was not a prominent part of the court caseload. A researcher at the Indian Law Institute searched the *All-India Reporter* for tort cases for the period from 1914 to 1965 (Ramamoorthy 1970).[1] In this fifty-two-year period, there were 613 reported tort cases. Strikingly, more than half of these concerned intentional torts. There were 184 malicious prosecution cases and 73 defamation cases, but only 132 negligence cases. That is, for these fifty-two years there were an average of 11.8 torts cases reported each year, including 2.5 negligence cases.

This was a period during which India underwent considerable industrial development and in which motor vehicles and numerous other technical innovations were introduced. It is clear that tort doctrine was not keeping abreast of these developments. Although there is obviously no exact correlation between the types of cases filed in the lower courts and the types that reach the appellate courts, the sparse appellate presence of tort fits with the general view that few tort cases were filed.

In 1970, the professor of law writing on torts in the Indian Law Institute's authoritative *Annual Survey of Indian Law* complained that: "While the surveyors of other branches of the law have to pick and choose from the cases reported during the year, the surveyor on the law of torts has no such option. Hardly a few cases are reported. This year the number is less than a dozen" (Balsara 1970). The infrequency of tort cases reflects a general absence of tort consciousness, manifested in the invisability of torts in standard works on the Indian legal system. In Alan Gledhill's authoritative post-Independence survey of Indian law, there is not a single mention of tort (Gledhill 1951). M. P. Jain's widely used *Outlines of Indian Legal History* devotes only two paragraphs in its 746-page second edition (1966) to tort law, that is, to the absence of codified tort law. The first edition (1952) contained no mention at all.

The Collapse of Civil Litigation

From the consolidation and rationalization of the legal system through the first three decades of the twentieth century, the courts of British India attracted an increasing level of use. Niketa Kulkarni and I have analyzed the available judicial statistics from 1881 forward. We found that the per capita rate of court filings gently and unevenly rose for the half century from 7,198 per million in 1881 to a high of 9,931 in 1933. Then they plunged precipitously. By the time of Independence in 1947 there were only 3,810 suits per million. Twenty years later the rate in the Republic of India was 1,487 suits per million—just a bit more than one-fifth the rate in 1881 and one-seventh the rate in 1933.[2]

The totals are broken down into land cases (rent suits and title suits) and suits for money damages or movable property (which I shall refer to as money damage suits). It is in the latter category that the great collapse of litigation occurs. Money damage suits fall from 6,948 per million in 1933 to 1,482 in 1947 to 905 in 1967. It was not only the rate that fell, but the absolute number of suits. Overall total cases instituted fell from 2.7 million in 1933 to 1 million in 1947; money damage suits fell from 1.9 million to .4 million. This must have been a catastrophe for India's lawyers, especially since they did little nonlitigation work. Although contemporary accounts by lawyers (Galanter 2007) and recent observations by scholars (Mendelsohn 1981; Moog 1997; Pistor and Wellons 1999) confirm the reality of the litigation implosion, there has been no convincing account of the collapse.

Unfortunately, the money damage suits are not broken down, so we cannot separate torts from the more numerous contract and debt cases. But, in light of the consistent reports of low levels of tort claiming, there is reason to think that there was no noticeable increase in filing of tort cases in the middle third of the twentieth century and very possibly a significant decrease.

A Comparative Note on Contracting Civil Court Use

People tend to think of civil court use as expanding with growing consciousness of rights and resources to pursue them. This may be because more attention is paid to litigation in its expansive phases. But there are accounts from other jurisdictions of severe contraction of court use. The United States experienced a contraction of court use during the beginning of the Great Depression years (Galanter 2001, 581–582). In contemporary Britain, a sharp reduction in court use in recent years seems connected with procedural changes that force extensive case development before filing, together with heavy court fees (Dingwall and Cloatre 2006). But the situation that seems most akin to the India story is the deterioration of civil justice in Italy, as described in David Nelken's chapter in this volume. Sergio Chiarloni confirms the point:

> In Italy . . . civil justice contrasts sharply with other state services. Its quality has increasingly deteriorated since Italian unification in the 1860s. Judicial statistics show that the total number of proceedings has vastly decreased since the 1860s, while the proportion of abandoned proceedings has progressively increased. The Italian civil process is largely useless to citizens who ask for justice . . . The party in the wrong may hide behind the extremely long duration of the process. (Chiarloni 1999)

Varano and De Luca (2007, 1) confirm "the deep crisis of the administration of justice in Italy, which is centered on delay." The delay, they conclude, is attributable neither "to a dramatic litigation explosion . . . (n)or to a shortage of judicial resources" (2007, 3). They point to other causes, including "the piecemeal character of the ordinary proceeding" (2007: 16) and "the tendency of most lawyers to increase their incomes by multiplying briefs and hearings" (citing Taruffo 2003, 223–324).

Continuing Low Rates of Court Use and Tort Claiming

Court statistics after Indian Independence are scarcer. But what we have suggests that rates of court use never returned to their pre–Great Depression levels and have remained near the lows they reached after Independence.[3] As court use has declined, there is no indication that tort has flourished. I surveyed all the tort cases reported in the *All-India Reporter* for the ten-year period 1975–84. There were some fifty-six cases (just half as many per year as in the 1914–65 period surveyed by Professor Ramamoorthy, in the section Patterns of Use/Nonuse above). Although these cases did not involve matters of great complexity, either logistical or technological, they took an average of twelve years and nine months from filing to decision. In the twenty-two negligence cases, the most common fact situation was a railroad crossing accident (seven); next was a downed electrical line (three). There is not a single product liability case among the fifty-six, nor any case involving any industrial process or chemical mishap. Nor is there any indication of the presence of massive amounts of evidence, large numbers of experts, or large numbers of parties. To follow up, my student Neil Bjorkman examined all the tort cases reported in the *All-India Reporter* for the years 1989, 1994, 1999, and 2004. The average number of reports annually for those years rose to nine, higher than in the 1974–85 decade and closer to the rate in the Ramamoorthy study. A larger portion (25/36) were negligence cases, including six medical malpractice cases. Apart from this, there was no indication of the presence of any complex technology or logistical intricacy. The modal fact situation (10/36) was the ever-popular downed electrical line. The five private intentional torts (one libel, four malicious prosecution) were outnumbered by six cases involving police or other government wrongdoing. The changes are in directions that might be expected, but of course we cannot eliminate the possibility that they reflect small sample size or changes in the selection practices at the *All-India Reporter*.

Perceptions and Realities of Litigation in India

As in education, health care, and other spheres of activity, India has a dual legal system. India is rightly acclaimed for achieving a flourishing constitutional order, presided over by an inventive and activist judiciary, aided by a proficient bar, supported by the state, and cherished by the public. This is a fitting portrait of what we might call the constitutional tier of the system, comprising the High Courts and Supreme Court, site of the work of a few hundred judges and a few thousand lawyers, where the writ petition procedure provides direct access for constitutional issues of fundamental rights. But there is another and vastly larger tier of courts and tribunals, staffed by hundreds of thousands of judges, officials, and lawyers, where ordinary Indians might go for remedy and protection with everyday problems. These forums are beset with massive problems of delay, cost, and ineffectiveness. Formally, tort is located in the lower tier and is connected to the higher tier only by occasional appeals. As we shall see, the connections, in fact, are thicker.

The old colonial view that the Indian population is extremely litigious is widely believed in India today (e.g., M. Jagannadha Rao [1997] notes that "[l]ike the Americans and others, we [Indians] too are a litigious society"). Even sophisticated observers speak of an "explosion of litigation" in India (Chodesh et al. 1997–98, 27). Actually, this bit of received wisdom is far from the mark. There is considerable evidence that the rate of utilization or invocation of the civil courts by the citizens of India is rather low. Indeed, the per capita rate of civil court utilization in India seems in the range of such famously nonlitigious societies as Japan and South Korea (Galanter and Krishnan 2003, 97–98).

How can it be that so few Indians invoke the courts while there is a widespread perception that the courts are inundated with cases, that frivolous litigation is rife, and that there is an abundance of hungry lawyers? What is the connection between the relative scarcity of litigation and the impression that there is so much of it?

First, the Indian media are saturated with news of court proceedings. But these are almost all cases in the Supreme Court and High Courts, which play an important political role and whose services are very much in demand. But few everyday matters come before these courts—they are appellate courts but have an extensive original jurisdiction to hear matters involving violations of Fundamental Rights, that is, mostly against the state. Ordinary matters such as contracts, divorces, and torts are in the district courts. Certainly the Indian courts are desperately congested, even though the number of cases filed is small on a per capita basis (Debroy 2002). The courts appear to be heavily used because there are relatively few courts. India has only one-tenth to one-sixth the number of judges per capita that are found in the developed parts of the common law world. Indian courts tend to be poorly equipped and inefficient. Apart from the physical and technical deficiencies of these courts, outmoded procedural laws provide abundant scope for delaying tactics, especially interlocutory appeals and stay orders (Chodesh et al. 1997–98, 71; Rajiv Gandhi Institute 1999). Judges, fearful of the bar, lack leverage to discipline lawyers or use the available tools to expedite proceedings (Chodesh et al. 1997–98, 39–40; Moog 1997). Delay is endemic: in 1997, almost one-third of the cases on the dockets of the district courts were waiting anywhere from one to ten years, while a quarter of cases waited for this same period of time in subordinate courts (Rajiv Gandhi Institute 1999, 35).

Cases linger interminably and arrears mount (Bearak 2000). Lawyers, fiercely loyal to existing practices, resist reforms by collective action and by wielding their "street power" (Hegde 1987). Bibek Debroy describes how in 1999 Parliament passed amendments to the Civil Procedure Code intended to reduce delay, but agitations by lawyers (including public demonstrations and strikes) forced the government to back away from the proposed reforms (Bearak 2000; Debroy 2002; Mitra 2000, 32).

One sign of the courts' infirmity is public disdain for these lower courts (Mitra 2000, 32). The public has low (and generally realistic) expectations of law, lawyers, and courts (Rao 1990). Potential users forego the lower courts or avoid them wherever possible, many from ignorance but most from calculation. The source of the low use of courts and lawyers is neither that the courts are congested nor the absence of "legal literacy" among the masses of Indians; it is that lawyers and courts are able to deliver so little in the way of remedy, protection, and vindication (Desai 1981). The courts provide a useful facility for those who wish to postpone payment of taxes or debts and those who wish to forestall eviction or other legal action. Generally, they serve those who benefit from delay and nonimplementation of legal norms—that is, parties who are satisfied with the status quo (as it existed ex ante or after obtaining an interim order) (Jagannadha Rao 1997, 105). "[B]acklog and delay provide a profound disincentive to settlement. Defendants who have achieved preliminary injunctive relief, benefit from the time value of money by refusing to settle, even in cases that they realize they are likely to lose" (Chodesh et al. 1997–98, 31). Observers conclude that in this setting "the honest litigant is impeded in the asserting of his legal rights, while paradoxically enough, the dishonest litigant is encouraged to assert unfounded or exaggerated claims" (Rajiv Gandhi Institute 1999, 18). As a local banker confided to a journalist, "we tell our clients to settle if they have a strong case and to go court if it's weak" (Gardner 2000, 21).

A very high percentage of cases involve government bodies as parties. One analyst estimates that the government is a litigating party in more than 60 percent of court cases and an even higher percentage of cases before tribunals (Richard Messick, personal communication, January 2002). When the government is a litigant it tends to pursue cases simply for delay and engages in relentless appeals even where the chance of winning is remote (Richard Messick, personal communication, January 2002). For example, in the state of Uttar Pradesh, the government has lost virtually every case in which it has participated in the Public Services Tribunal, but it nevertheless still appeals a large percentage of cases to the state's High Court (Messick 2002). Again, Uttar Pradesh's state-owned bus company is involved in thousands of pending motor accident cases, but refuses to make reasonable settlement offers and forces the victims in each case to take the case to trial—which the state loses on most occasions (Richard Messick, personal communication, January 2002). This pattern of scorched earth litigation fills the courts (and tribunals) with meritless claims (and defenses) and discourages meritorious claims by increasing the expense and delay of using these forums.

For those who require vindication and prompt implementation of remedies and protections against dominant parties—women from husbands or relatives, laborers from landowners, citizens from government—the system works only haltingly, partially, and occasionally. Since so many of the potential meritorious claims are absent from the courts, it is not surprising that the claims that are present include a significant portion that are "frivolous" in the sense of being brought or maintained for purposes of harassment and delay.

These patterns are consistent with the low rate of tort litigation, for the potential tort claimant faces a daunting series of obstacles: ad valorum court fees; continuing lawyer fees (no contingency arrangement, lawyers paid by the appearance); successive delays, interlocutory appeals, low awards (judges very worried about windfalls). The claimant who persists until he has judgment in hand then faces a similar gauntlet in pursuing execution.

Given the long delays (and high interest rates at which future value must be discounted), mounting expenses, meager damage awards, and difficulties of execution, the present value of most potential tort claims (and other suits for money damages) is probably close to zero if it is not negative. Indeed, much litigation in India can be described as a "sunk cost auction" in which the competitors invest ever-higher amounts in the hope of staving off larger losses.[4] Widespread popular intuition of this produces avoidance of the civil courts. Many potential seekers of money damages instead pursue criminal complaints or seek injunctive relief, seek another forum (e.g., a tribunal or mediation by police or local *dadas* [big shots]), or simply lump it. Those cases that are brought often involve some additional motivation such as spite, harassment, or tactical maneuver in a wider dispute.

Bhopal and Mass Disasters

If tort law did not connect with the ordinary run of individual injuries, it had even less connection with mass disasters, a not infrequent occurrence in India. Such a negative is hard to document. I can only say that I have never heard of an instance of any industrial explosion, mine cave-in, building collapse, food adulteration, or other mass injury leading to tort claims. Surveys of all the tort cases reported by India's leading series of law reports from 1975 to 1985 did not reveal a single case that arose from such an incident.

What typically happens in disasters is that the government announces that it is making ex gratia payments of a specified amount to the victims. Attributions of responsibility, if pursued at all, would be done by a governmental investigation or perhaps a criminal prosecution or a commission of inquiry. In each case, the inquiry into responsibility is dissociated from the administration of compensation.

Not surprisingly, the virtual absence of tort litigation is associated with an absence of institutional features for facilitating such litigation. Neither contingency fees nor legal aid are present to overcome claimants' financial barriers to access. Although India has a numerous and well-established legal profession, lawyers' role does not include investigation and fact development; specialization is rudimentary; and, barring some recent exceptions, there are few firms or other forms of enduring professional collaboration that would support a division of labor and pooling of resources to support the development of expertise in tort law. The setting in which these lawyers work is devoid of institutional support for specialized knowledge: in this area there are no specialist organizations, no specialized technical publishing, and no continuing legal education; nor is there a vigorous scholarly community.

Indian civil procedure does not include provisions for wide-ranging discovery that would permit factual investigation in complex problems of technology or corporate management. There are no special procedures for handling complex litigation involving massive amounts of evidence or large numbers of parties. Bar and bench, though they contain many brilliant and talented individuals, have a very limited fund of experience, skills, and organizational capacity to address massive tort cases.

In December 1984 India's well-established low-use, low-remedy, low-accountability system received a rude shock when a gas leak at the Union Carbide Corporation's plant in Bhopal killed thousands and injured many thousands more. The shock to the system was not the vast scale of the disaster but its transnational character. Imagine that this had been a purely American event: suppose the gas had leaked at Union Carbide's comparable methyl isocynate operation at Institute, West Virginia, instead of at its undernourished twin in Bhopal. We can readily envision the immense mass tort case, the judicial improvisation of devices to handle it, very likely a settlement for a substantial amount, and possibly even the resulting reorganization of Union Carbide through bankruptcy. It would have been big and unwieldy and would possibly have strained the capacities of the courts, but it would have delivered significant compensation and broadcast powerful preventive signals to many audiences. In spite of the many imponderables, including problems of causation and uncertainty about the final toll of injury, the limited single-event format would have presented a good candidate for more or less satisfactory resolution by the United States' high-cost, high-accountability, high-remedy system of private law.

Imagine, now, that it was an entirely Indian event, with a domestic Indian company in the role of Union Carbide. On the basis of all previous experience, notwithstanding the vastly greater scale of this disaster, it is very unlikely that tort law would have been invoked at all. There would have been an ex gratia payment of compensation (quite meager by Western standards) by the company or the government or both; surely a commission of inquiry, and very likely a criminal prosecution. Buildings collapse, mines cave in, hundreds are killed by poisonous liquor—there is a constant stream of these little Bhopals in India. For example, in December 1995, more than five hundred persons, mostly children, were killed in a fire that swept through a temporary structure housing a school ceremony. Accounts stressed the inadequacy of safety measures and emergency services. The state government announced that it would provide ex gratia payments of Rs. (rupees) 100,000 to the families of the dead and half that to those seriously injured (Bora 1996; Burns 1995). Typically, the law, courts, and lawyers are not involved in establishing accountability or securing compensation.[5] There is no reason to think that an all-Indian Bhopal disaster would have departed from this pattern. (Or, that it would have escaped more than momentarily from the obscurity that surrounded the explosion of a liquefied natural gas storage facility in Mexico City just two weeks earlier in which three hundred people were killed) (http://www.emergency.com/mxcoblst.htm).

In the case of Bhopal, it was the American identity of the malefactor that coupled the disaster and the legal system as they would not have been connected otherwise. The perception of invasive violation and pollution by a foreign intruder generated a sense of shared injury and outrage. At the same time the American connection brought with it the image of an American tort system laden with both sting and largesse. The image was quickly given dramatic embodiment by the arrival in India of American plaintiffs' lawyers, just days after the explosion. But even before the American lawyers arrived, Indian officials were discussing the possibility of recovery in the United States—and at American levels of compensation (Galanter 2002, 175). The reach for an American remedy was the reverse side of a deep pessimism about a remedy in India, coupled with an untroubled confidence in the United States' legal system and anticipation of enormous recoveries. A few weeks after the gas leak, the Chief Justice of India observed "These cases must be pursued in the United States. It is the only hope these unfortunate people have" (Stewart 1985). The export of the legal action to the United States provoked hardly a murmur of dissent at the time.

The Government of India, having equipped itself with statutory authorization as the exclusive representative of the victims, pursued the case in the United States, but its suit was dismissed on grounds of *forum non conveniens* and sent to India. After several years of inconclusive grappling, the Bhopal District Court ordered interim relief, which led to an interlocutory appeal to the High Court of Madhya Pradesh and eventually put the matter before the Supreme Court of India. At that moment, the Government of India concluded a settlement with Union Carbide, which was immediately endorsed by the Supreme Court.

The Government of India and many observers, including some in the judiciary, justified the February 1989 settlement of the Bhopal case as beneficial to the victims by comparing it with the results of further litigation that would have lasted "anywhere from 15 to 25 more years" (*Hindustan Times* 1989). This was not a claim that the settlement represented the victims' true entitlements; rather, it was an assertion that, whatever the magnitude of those entitlements, the unalterable character of the Indian legal system made it inevitable that they could not be obtained before passage of so long a period that the discounted present value of these claims was less than the amount to be delivered under the settlement. The features of the system that insured protracted delay were treated as given and unchangeable.

Far from resolving matters, the 1989 settlement fragmented the controversy and diverted the fragments into several channels. Activists won a retraction of the Supreme Court's initial acceptance of the quashing of the related criminal cases (*Union Carbide Corp. v. Union of India* 1991), which have continued unresolved and have engaged an unappeased following to this day. Campaigns to force Union Carbide's purchaser, Dow Chemical, to engage in clean-ups of the site continue. Sporadic litigation attempting to find an American forum has been rebuffed by the U.S. courts (Galanter 2002, 173). Meanwhile, the distribution of the settlement funds was niggardly and inefficient. An authoritative report observed that "No claim was settled earlier than a waiting period of 7 years. The adjudicatory process involved over 5 visits of two hours each for the claimant. Ultimately the Judge was able to spend no more than 10 minutes on a case" (Fact Finding Mission 2004). After twenty years, the Government of India retained an amount roughly equivalent to the amount it had distributed to the victims. In 2004, the Supreme Court ordered the government to distribute the remaining funds pro rata to the prior recipients (*Union Carbide Corporation v. Union of India* 2004; Muralidhar 2004).

Reform by Bypass

Like some other observers, I expected big changes in the wake of Bhopal that would usher in a new era for tort in India. But no such changes have occurred. The few doctrinal innovations that were stimulated did not inspire reforms that dislodged the low-use, low-accountability, low-remedy system that occupies the courts. Unsurprisingly, few are inspired to take on the Sisyphean task of an overall revamping of the civil justice system. Advocates and activists are more likely to seek a bypass around the gridlock by removing a particular type of claims from the district courts into a special tribunal, or channeling them into the higher courts under the writ jurisdiction, or developing nonadjudicative schemes of compensation. In the twenty years since Bhopal, there have been a number of such developments bypassing the regular lower courts.

Motor Accident Claims Tribunal

The oldest and quantitatively most important of the bypasses are the Motor Accident Claims Tribunals (MACTs), originally authorized by the Motor Vehicles Act, 1939, which conferred on these tribunals exclusive jurisdiction over claims involving death, bodily injury, and property damage arising out of the use of motor vehicles. Typically the tribunal is in fact a judge of the district court sitting as the MACT. Appeal is directly to the High Court of the state. Cases run the full gamut of appeals somewhat faster than do other tort cases. Claimants are not subject to the court fees applicable in civil court filings. Since 1982 there is "no fault compensation" (presently Rs. 50,000 [approximately US$1,200] for deaths, and Rs. 25,000 [approximately US$600] for permanent disability), but claimants may seek more on a "fault" basis.

There are many times more motor accident cases than all other tort cases combined. The tribunals are quite congested and cases are backlogged. For example, some 40,000 to 50,000 cases are pending before Mumbai's eight MACTs. Motor vehicle cases have been the favorite candidates for diversion into the "informal" Lok Adalats (discussed below in the section Lok Adalats and the Thrust to Informalism). In May 2007, five insurance companies petitioned the Supreme Court alleging that the system was in crisis, with as many as 1.5 million cases pending in the claims tribunals and the High Courts. The court ordered the state to indicate the number of cases forwarded to the MACTs (Muralidhar 2004).

Consumer Tribunals

In 1986, Parliament passed a Consumer Protection Act that established a nationwide system of Consumer Tribunals to provide remedies for deficiencies in purchases of "goods and services." Claims were brought for negligent medical treatment, and in 1995 the Supreme Court held that medical services were included under the Act (*Indian Medical Assn. v. V. P. Shantha, A.I.R.,* 1995). A few years later, the Indian Medical Association estimated that more than 10,000 cases of medical negligence had been filed so far in the Consumer Tribunals, of which more than 90 percent were dismissed (Mudur 1998). Although some medical claimants pursue tort remedies in the courts, sometimes via the writ petition route (see section The Ex-Gratia System below), and others file criminal charges against doctors, it appears that the Consumer Tribunals are the principle forum for such claims. It would seem possible for these tribunals to be pressed into service to take up a wide range of product liability claims, but I have seen no reports that they have.

"Constitutional Torts" in the Higher Courts

After the 1975–77 Emergency, the higher courts embarked on an activist expansion of rights, which included "public law remedies" for constitutional torts: illegal detention, custodial violence, police atrocities, and even culpable inaction in failing to protect citizens (Ramanathan 2002). Under the writ petition procedure, courts, typically proceeding on the basis of a report of judicial inquiry or other official report, allowed compensation against the state and sometimes against offending officials, preserving rights to pursue "private law remedies."

Uphaar: Privileged Plaintiffs Use the Writ Bypass

The outstanding instance of tort recovery from private parties grew out of the response to the June 1997 fire at the Uphaar Cinema in New Delhi in which 57 persons, many from affluent families, were killed (Halarnkar and Chakravarty 1997, 30). A group of families launched a coordinated campaign of litigation against the cinema owners, the Electricity Board that housed a defective generator in the basement of the theater, indifferent regulators, and ill-equipped responders. In November 1997, the association filed suit in the Delhi High Court (using the writ petition procedure), asking Rs. 22.1 crores (about US$4.9 million) compensation and Rs. 100 crore (about US$22 million) punitive damages (to be used to set up a trauma center). In April 2003, the court ordered compensation of Rs. 21 crores to the families of the deceased, and Rs. 1.04 crores to the 104 injured theatergoers. Fifty-five percent of these damages were assessed against the theater owners and 45 percent shared by three government units (the Electricity Board, the Municipal Corporation, and the Police Licensing Bureau). In addition, Rs. 2.5 crore (the earnings of the owners from the theater's unauthorized seats) was awarded to establish an accident trauma service (Chakravarty 2003, 44).

While the Uphaar case opened a path to tort relief in disasters, it is very much the exception that proves the rule. The event was big news, the plaintiffs were affluent and well organized, and they were represented by a dedicated lawyer who did not charge for his services (Kaur 2003); also, the defendants included governmental as well as private parties, the wrongdoing included violations of statutory duties, and the civil proceedings were entwined with criminal prosecutions. The writ petition procedure was pressed into service; it could suffice without a trial because "the judges felt that a conclusion could be reached on the basis of official reports without going into disputed questions of fact requiring massive volumes of evidence" (Dhavan 2003). The writ petition path seems to be followed in a fair portion of the small number of reported tort cases. Of the thirty-six cases in our four-year sample, almost half (seventeen) arrived in the High Court via a writ petition, rather than on appeal. Of course, we do not know how many writs of this type—presumably a large number—were denied admission. In spite of the inability of courts to hold trials in writ cases, only one of the seventeen was dismissed on the ground that the writ procedure was not appropriate where there were disputed matters of fact. The other sixteen managed to finesse this problem by a variety of devices: by resorting to an existing report, ordering an inquiry, deriving admissions from the pleadings or oral arguments, or finding that the dispute was about a question of law.

The discretionary attention of the higher courts is a scarce resource. Public outrage, astute lawyering, or judicial sympathy can capture such attention for an occasional tort case, but, as the late Professor S. P. Sathe (2002, 144) concluded, "[a]wards of compensation under the writ jurisdiction can be nothing more than tokenism." Even claimants blessed by such attention do not escape the common fate when the path of remedy runs through the ordinary courts. The criminal proceedings that accompanied the Uphaar civil case have been stuck in the trial court for a decade. In April 2002, the Delhi High Court directed the Sessions Court to conduct the trial "day-to-day" without break and to wrap up by December 15, 2002 (*Hindu* 2002). After another five years of legal maneuver (*Hindustan Times* 2007), the defendants were convicted and sentenced in November 2007, initiating a series of petitions and rulings leading to the Supreme Court's September 2008 cancellation of the Delhi High Court's allowance of bail in a satellite case involving defendants' destruction of documentary evidence (Indo-Asian News Service 2008).

Lok Adalats and the Thrust to Informalism

The dominant themes of court reform since the mid-1980s have been informality, conciliation, and alternative institutions rather than vindication of rights through adversary processes in mainstream adjudicative institutions. The most prominent and widespread expression of the new informalism is the proliferation of judicially sponsored Lok Adalats, a form of mandatory mediation. Cases on the docket of a local court (or tribunal) are transferred to a Lok Adalat list and then taken up before a mediator or panel of mediators, who are typically retired (but sometimes sitting) judges, senior advocates, or local notables (The Legal Services Authorities Act 1987 [amended 1994], Sec. 20 [1]; Moog 1997, 135–138; Ramaswamy 1997, 98). Legal rules are not binding on the judge. If there is a settlement, there is no appeal; if there is no settlement, the case is returned to the court docket (Galanter and Krishnan 2004).

Although the term initially was used to refer to a transitory forum, staffed by volunteers and convened from time to time, rather than to a continuing institution with fixed location and personnel, it has been extended to cover:

> permanent Lok Adalats [that] have . . . been introduced in the various Government departments that provide services . . . [including] the telephone companies, the electricity board, the municipal corporations, the city development authorities and the insurance companies . . . Today Lok Adalat-type mechanism is being invoked by Government Departments and public sector agencies to settle pension and provident fund claims, bank debts, consumer grievances and similar small claims of a civil or revenue nature. (Menon 2000, 56–57)

Generally, the largest cases in Lok Adalats are claims by motor accident victims transferred from the MACTs. This is the only type of case counted separately, and statistics are compiled of the compensation awarded in these cases. Lok Adalats resolved over 10,000 motor accident cases per month during the four years (475,545 in forty-seven months) from January 1998 to the end of November 2001) (data provided to the author by the National Legal Services Authority). Since the claimants in motor accident claims are typically passengers or pedestrians on the one hand and the defendants are typically companies or government agencies on the other, these cases "tend to be contests between the relatively rich and the relatively poor, the powerful and the weak" (Kassebaum 1989, 7).

The name Lok Adalat (literally, people's court) reveals that its sponsors seek to stress their indigenous character and "rich tradition," even though they have little resemblance to earlier institutions (Mehta 2000) and there is little drawing on indigenous practices. Lok Adalats display no evident community input, nor is there any participative character to the proceedings. These forums are dominated by judges both as organizers and presiders, and the role of lawyers is notably diminished. With little lawyer input and no recourse to appeal, judges enjoy more extensive discretion than in regular courts. Judges are frequently paternalistic, overbearing, or perfunctory in dealing with individual parties, but the judiciary and government are enthused about the virtues of Lok Adalats and have been enlarging their scope and powers.

The Ex Gratia System

The MCATs, the Consumer Tribunals, and the Lok Adalats handle large numbers of tort claims on a routine basis, while tort suits in the regular courts remain rare. But possibly all tortlike claims are outnumbered by ex gratia payments— that is, where the injurer or a government body makes a payment to a victim or survivors or dependents without acknowledging any obligation or entitlement, or making any claim that the amount is proportional to fault or injury. What typically happens in disasters is that the government announces that it is making ex gratia payments of a specified amount to the victims. For example, when four people were trampled to death in a March 1989 stampede at the New Delhi railway station, the railway announced an ex gratia payment of Rs. 5,000 [approximately US$320 at then current exchange rates] to the kin of the deceased and of Rs. 1,000 to the injured. A departmental inquiry was ordered, and a criminal case was registered on the basis of the negligent announcement that was thought to have triggered the stampede (*Hindu* 1989).

Ex gratia payments are made to victims of natural disasters, terrorist attacks, and communal riots (Sharma 2004). At the end of 2005, the Union Cabinet topped up the ex gratia payments to over 20,000 victims of the 1984 anti-Sikh riots that followed the assassination of Indira Gandhi. Expectations of ex gratia payment have been institutionalized in provisions like those cataloged on the Web site of the Government of Delhi, which gives information on payments for the following categories of persons: victims of the 1984 riots; Jammu and Kashmir migrants; victims of "hit and run" cases; persons affected by communal riots, bomb blasts, fire, floods, and "major disasters" (http:/dcnorth.delhigovt .nic.in/relief&rehabilitation.htm). For example, in cases of "Fire and other accidents" there is payment of Rs. 100,000 in case of death (Rs. 50,000 for minors); Rs. 50,000 for permanent incapacitation; Rs. 20,000 for serious injury; and Rs. 1,000 for minor injury.

The givers insist that ex gratia payment is not compensation but is merely humanitarian assistance designed to help the victim deal with the immediate situation. The idiom of ex gratia payments is of unilateral action, absence of obligation, ability to pay rather than fault, and need rather than entitlement. But contests about fault and entitlement may be conducted in ex gratia language. In 1997, an accident at the National Thermal Power Corporation's power station in Ramagundam led to a work stoppage and a demand by the union for suspension of three superintendents for being negligent and payment of Rs. 500,000 to the next of kin of the three deceased employees. "The management pointed out that it had released Rs. 1 lakh as ex gratia to the next of kin . . . and offered employment to a member of each of their families" (*Hindu* 1997, 6).

The line between ex gratia payment and tort recovery is often blurry. For example, in 2005, the Delhi High Court took up the case of a teenage girl who had suffered a botched spinal operation at a government hospital (*Hindu* 2005). After the Government indicated its willingness to bear the cost of reparative treatment:

> As regards payment of ex gratia to the victim, Mr. Malhotra [government's counsel] said that the Government was not ready to pay more than Rs. 20,000 to her.
>
> Reacting to the proposal, Mr. Justice Sen said that it was a too small amount and that he was thinking of paying a much larger amount to her.
>
> When Mr. Malhotra submitted that the Government would abide by whatever amount the Court ordered, Mr. Justice Sen raised it to Rs. 1,00000.

The judge "made it clear" that the ex gratia payment would not preclude the victim's right to sue for additional compensation.

The Future: A Second Coming of Tort Law?

I noted earlier that there is no foundation (as least as measured by per capita court use) for the widespread belief that India is a highly litigious place. Curiously, that belief coexists with a view widespread at least among educated urban Indians that decent people have as little as possible to do with the courts. We are told, as in Japan, that avoidance of courts reflects a cultural distaste for suing. This antilitigation story, too, seems a misreading of the Indian scene. There is an evident demand/appetite for tort recovery, although it does not manifest itself in what appears to Americans the heartland of tort—that is, personal injury claims against private parties for negligent behavior. We see that whenever there is access to a useable procedure (as in the MACTs, in the Consumer Tribunals for medical malpractice, and in the High Courts' writ jurisdiction for constitutional torts), there is willingness to make claims about injuries; and in at least some instances where there is persistent demand for remedies, courts are responsive and inventive in providing them. Because the district courts are not a viable forum, the action is in tribunals, in the writ jurisdiction, and in the realm of ex gratia payments, with some spillover into the criminal process.

The pattern that emerges is reminiscent in some ways of the pre-Independence flourishing of intentional torts and in the readiness to invoke criminal law to settle scores. One theme that seems constant is a great appetite for action to punish intentional incursions on one's dignity or well-being. The desire to punish is prominent, as is the connection to criminal law. Another theme that is emergent is seeking compensation in case of injury, but such compensation need not be in the form of mulcting the wrongdoer/injurer. Responsibility is frequently based on ability to pay and duty to care for one's dependents rather than entitlement growing out of wrongdoing. The connection between accidental wrongdoing and compensation is not very firm, and there seems to be little interest in facilitating recovery on a routine basis.

So tort in India resembles a river whose main channel is dammed up by forbidding obstacles, but the force of the stream finds other channels, forming a vast and intricate delta. Tort recovery in ordinary negligence cases in the regular courts is obstructed by delay and expense, but the demand for recovery and punishment seeks out new forums and new procedures. In a setting of booming economic activity and rising expectations, the question is whether the main channel can be dredged, which of the new channels will become stabilized and able to handle heavy traffic, and how they will connect with one another.

CHAPTER FOUR

Liability Insurance at the Tort-Crime Boundary

TOM BAKER

Liability insurance defines the boundaries of tort law-in-action in a variety of ways. As a formal matter, tort law generally ignores whether defendants have liability insurance, as well as the prevailing verbal and dollar limits on that insurance (Stapleton 1995).[1] Yet, liability insurance is close to a de facto element of tort liability whenever the potential defendants are individuals, and liability insurance even shapes claims against large, well-funded organizations (Baker 2006; Black, Cheffins, and Klausner 2006; Zeiler et al. 2007; cf. Baker and Griffith 2008). Tort liability certainly exists out from under the liability insurance umbrella, but tort lawyers do not go out there very often, because there is less return in it. While there are exceptions, lawyers prefer to ask a liability insurer to pay—because paying claims is the business of liability insurance (Baker 2001). For this reason, liability insurance must be counted among the sites in which to investigate the relationship between tort law and culture. Whatever legal culture is, it surely affects liability insurance institutions, and these, in turn, affect—and are affected by—the development of tort law.

This chapter explores how liability insurance mediates the boundary between torts and crime. Liability insurance sometimes separates these two legal fields, for example, through the application of standard insurance contract provisions that exclude insurance coverage for some crimes that are also torts. These exclusions largely remove these crimes from the reach of civil law, as demonstrated, for example, by the dearth of tort claims involving domestic violence, molestation, and other assaults, notwithstanding the prevalence of these crimes in the

United States (Wriggins 2001). With respect to these crime-torts, liability insurance operates to create a greater de facto separation between tort and criminal liabilities where, de jure, the two liabilities would appear to overlap.

Perhaps less obviously, liability insurance also can draw parts of the tort and criminal fields together. For example, professional liability insurance civilizes the criminal law experience for some crimes that are also torts by providing defendants with an insurance-paid criminal defense that provides more than ordinary means to contest the state's accusations. Notable examples include the recent spate of high-profile, white-collar prosecutions involving former executives from Enron, HealthSouth, and WorldCom, in which directors' and officers' liability insurers helped fund the criminal defense (Brickey 2006). The availability of liability insurance for criminal defense both reflects and signals that these crimes are more like torts than other crimes and, perhaps, that the defendants are not real criminals (cf., Mann 1991; Singer and Husack 1999).

On the books and in theory, criminal and civil liability are governed largely by independent norms and institutions (Steiker 1997; but see Becker 1968). In effect, tort and criminal liability occupy different legal dimensions and thus the idea of a boundary between them might seem to make little sense. An act can be both a crime and a tort, and whether it falls into one of those categories typically has little to do with whether it falls into the other. The most obvious exception to the independence of tort and criminal law occurs when criminal law supplies a legal standard to tort law, for example, through the doctrine of negligence per se (Dobbs 2000, 215). Here, the dominant spatial metaphor is overlap, not boundary.

In practice, however, torts and crime do constitute different fields in the "good fences make good neighbors" sense, and, continuing that metaphor, liability insurance forms part of the fence between them. Liability insurance distinguishes between people and acts that are governed by the "hard treatment" of criminal justice institutions (Hart 1968) and people and acts that are governed by civil justice. Only the state has the power to "govern through crime" (Simon 2007), but liability insurance markets help determine the extent to which civil justice retreats in response.

As Kenneth Abraham has described, liability insurance grew up together with tort law over the course of the twentieth century (Abraham 2008). Liability insurance did not exist until the 1880s, and in the nineteenth century tort claims were rare events (Abraham 2008; Rabin 1999). In a symbiotic relationship, the new tort liabilities associated with industrialization, the automobile, and other new forms of activity created a demand for liability insurance, liability insurance stimulated the growth of tort claiming, the growth of tort claiming increased the demand for liability insurance, and so on. (See also Pandya 2007, Syverud 1994, and Yeazell 2001.)

Like the underlying tort liabilities to which they apply, liability insurance policies might at first seem to be unrelated to the criminal dimension of the legal universe. Indeed, one can search the early liability insurance literature in vain for any reference either to crime or criminal liability. This silence is consistent with the traditional view of liability insurance offered by philosophers of tort law. In that view, tort liability comes first, creating rights and obligations, and liability insurance comes second, merely shifting the financial burdens of these tort obligations to the insurance pool (e.g., Stapleton 1995; Waldron 1995). Wherever tort law goes, liability insurance follows, and there is no need in the liability insurance arena for consideration of the nature or limits of the underlying liability, except perhaps when there are economic or technical issues that affect the operation of liability insurance itself.

Yet, as Mary Coate McNeely first described in the *Columbia Law Review* in 1941, liability insurers have from the beginning struggled to separate liability insurance from crime for reasons that are not purely economic or technical (McNeely 1941).[2] Moreover, as I shall argue, this struggle affects the underlying tort liabilities themselves, challenging tort theorists' hierarchical understanding of the relationship between tort and liability insurance.

McNeely (1940) locates the struggle over liability insurance coverage for crime-torts within a larger story about "Illegality as a Factor in Liability Insurance," and the story she tells is a familiar one in the insurance law genre. Denials of insurance coverage based on broad principles and exhortations to public policy gradually but surely fail, leading insurance underwriters to sharpen their pencils and write exclusionary provisions in their insurance contracts that courts largely enforce (e.g., Rossmiller 2007). The preoccupation with crime is also familiar within the insurance genre. Life and fire insurers struggled for much of the ninetenth century to avoid association with crime (Baker 1996; Zelizer 1979), and the insurance adjuster as detective remains a staple of crime fiction today.[3]

Allowing for differences in style and ambition, much of McNeely's article could have been written today. Insurance institutions continue to refine the standard form contract provisions they use to exclude coverage for tort claims aris-

ing out of crimes, and they continue to justify this effort using the forms of reasoning that she identifies: consequentialist reasoning that distinguishes among
illegal acts according to ideas about incentives that today we call moral hazard
(see e.g., Heimer 1985) and moral reasoning that distinguishes among illegal acts
according to degrees of blameworthiness.

Few commentators today would agree with McNeely's ultimate conclusion,
however. She predicted that the emerging concept of liability insurance as a victim compensation fund would replace the old-fashioned concept of liability insurance as protection for the defendant and, as a result, liability insurers would
gradually abandon the effort to exclude coverage for torts arising out of crimes.
Today this prediction seems as quaintly utopian as the related but more familiar
prediction that the concept of social insurance would take over tort law (cf. Sebok 2003). To be sure, liability insurance *is* a victim compensation fund, but it
is not only that—and not even primarily that, except in workers compensation
(which hardly is considered to be liability insurance anymore) and, perhaps, in
auto insurance. Indeed, the move to extend the compensation idea beyond workers compensation has made very little progress in the nearly seventy years since
McNeely's article (Abraham 2008). The one possible exception may have been
products liability, but whatever force there was in the social insurance concept of
product liability law is, at the very least, dissipating (Schwartz 1981, 1992; also,
cf. Stapleton 1995).

In the sections that follow, I expand on four points suggested by a contemporary rereading of McNeely's mid-twentieth-century treatment of liability insurance and crime. First, I confirm that liability insurers continue to use contract
provisions that exclude claims arising out of criminal acts. Second, I demonstrate that the crime-tort separation in liability insurance cannot be explained by
economic incentives alone. Morality matters, too. Third, I argue that this separation both reflects and reinforces a concept of liability insurance as protection
for defendants, rather than as a fund for victims. Fourth, I argue that this concept of insurance, in turn, both reflects and reinforces an understanding of tort
claims as encounters between particular plaintiffs and defendants, rather than as
a price-setting or loss-spreading insurance mechanism.

In a concluding section, I describe situations in which liability insurance
provides coverage for criminal defense costs. I argue that this extension of liability insurance into the criminal field suggests that liability insurance institutions could cover a broader swath of crime torts than they do, providing further

support for the claim that consequentialist reasoning, alone, cannot explain the observed relationship between liability insurance, torts, and crime.

Excluding Crime-Torts from Liability Insurance Contracts

Liability insurance contracts today limit liability insurers' responsibility for crime-tort losses in four ways.

First, although liability insurance contracts provide broad defense and indemnity coverage for tort proceedings and tort damages, they typically do not provide defense coverage for criminal proceedings, and, to my knowledge, they never provide any coverage for criminal fines or penalties.[4] This means, for example, that a driver charged with driving under the influence (DUI) after running over a pedestrian, will get a tort defense lawyer from his insurance company, but not a criminal defense lawyer. Moreover, if the driver is assessed a fine as part of his punishment for a DUI conviction, the insurance company will not pay or reimburse him for that fine, even though the insurer will readily pay much larger amounts of money to settle the associated tort action or to satisfy a tort judgment.

The fact that some liability insurance policies today do provide criminal defense coverage (as I will discuss in the concluding section of this chapter) brings this aspect of the separation into greater relief. Indeed, the fact that no liability insurance policies appear to have provided criminal defense coverage in the 1940s may explain why McNeely did not mention it. This aspect of the crime-tort separation in liability insurance may have been so obvious and accepted that she did not even notice it.

Second, liability insurance contracts generally contain clauses that exclude coverage for claims arising out of intentional injuries by the insured. These clauses do not explicitly withdraw liability insurance from crime torts. But, in addition to the obvious economic explanation (moral hazard), they reflect concerns about the propriety of insulating people from the consequences of criminal actions. Indeed, when enforcing intentional harm exclusions, courts commonly stress the criminal nature of the conduct in question and refer in moralistic terms to the public policy concerns that would be raised by providing insurance for crime.[5] This justification is an echo of the earlier, general principle McNeely described. Although courts today would be unlikely to uphold the denial of coverage based on this broad principle in the absence of an explicit contract provision,[6] the principle nevertheless retains some value as an explanation for these contract provisions.

Third, some liability insurance contracts contain clauses that exclude coverage for punitive damages, and some courts allow insurance companies to refuse to pay for punitive damages even in the absence of such exclusionary language (Sharkey 2005). Like exclusions for intentional harm, these explicit and implicit exclusions for punitive damages do not directly withdraw liability insurance from crime, but they do withdraw liability insurance from punishment, a defining aspect of criminal remedies (Hart 1968). Moreover, courts that allow insurance companies to refuse to pay punitive damages commonly stress the criminal nature of the conduct in question and the similarity between punitive damages and criminal fines (Sharkey 2005). Instead of withdrawing liability insurance entirely from the tort claim in question, a punitive damages exclusion withdraws coverage from the quasi-criminal aspect of the tort law remedy. Like the public policy-based prohibition of insurance for intentional harm, the prohibition on insurance for punitive damages appears to be on the wane.[7] Nevertheless, the reasoning behind both prohibitions suggests that explicit exclusions for intentional harm and punitive damages in liability insurance contracts can be understood as part of the crime-tort separation.

Fourth, many liability insurance contracts contain additional clauses that specifically state that the insurer will not pay for tort claims arising out of criminal acts, whether the resulting injuries were intentional or not. These clauses are the most explicit manifestation of the crime-tort separation, and they include broadly worded exclusions that eliminate coverage for foreseeable injuries from any "criminal act" as well as more narrowly worded exclusions that eliminate coverage for injuries related to specific crimes, such as molestation. These criminal act exclusions appear in some professional liability insurance policies that include coverage for some criminal defense costs, so the tort-crime separation in those parts of the tort and liability insurance field is far from complete. But these criminal act exclusions have also begun to appear in homeowners' insurance policies, which never provide coverage for criminal defense costs (Eidsmore and Edwards 1998/99). The homeowners' insurance company may still have to pay for some or all of the tort defense costs of the alleged criminal, and that tort defense obligation gives these crime-tort cases a settlement value for insurance companies (Pryor 1997). Nevertheless, the insurers putting these clauses in their contracts clearly aim to reduce the extent to which they have to pay for any costs related to criminal activity, and the courts on the whole support that effort (Baker 2008, 449).

The Limits of the Moral Hazard Explanation

For people accustomed to thinking about law in economic terms, moral hazard might at first seem to provide an obvious and important part of the explanation for the insurance contract provisions just described. Moral hazard—the tendency for insurance to reduce the incentive to prevent loss—is a longstanding concern in all kinds of insurance, and liability insurance is no exception (Baker 1996). Almost all tort liabilities involve harm that potential defendants can avoid to at least some degree, if only by reducing the extent to which they or people they control engage in activity that may cause harm. Indeed, in economic analysis, loss prevention is the primary justification for tort liability (Shavell 1987). Thus, to the extent that liability provides an incentive to take care, all liability insurance creates at least the potential for moral hazard (Shavell 1979).

In that regard at least, insurance for crime-torts is hardly alone. The issue is whether the incentive problem becomes significantly more serious when a tort is also a crime. If so, then moral hazard provides a satisfying explanation for the crime-tort separation. If not, we need to look elsewhere.

As a moment's reflection should be sufficient to make clear, criminal liability does not exacerbate the moral hazard created by liability insurance. Rather, criminal liability reduces moral hazard. Adding criminal liability on top of tort liability helps offset the moral hazard of providing insurance for the related tort liability, at least as long as the criminal penalty is not insured, and, to my knowledge, it never is.

When the criminal penalties include going to jail, the presence or absence of liability insurance seems likely to have little or no effect on incentives. Even a short stay in a jail cell surely would loom larger in the imagination than an uninsured tort liability. Moreover, if the person in question knows a lot about the real-life operation of the tort system, she knows that the odds are strongly against a tort lawsuit if there is not any insurance (Gilles 2006). Given almost any prospect of criminal law enforcement involving imprisonment, the presence or absence of liability insurance seems likely to affect only slightly the expected cost of crime, ex ante.

It is of course possible to imagine a crime-tort for which the only criminal liability is a small fine, and for which there is no significant shame or other nonmonetary sanctions attached to a criminal conviction. In that event, the criminal liability would not do much to offset any moral hazard created by the insurance that covers the associated tort. But I predict that insurance companies would be willing to offer tort liability insurance in all such cases (subject to ordinary moral hazard control measures), because the small size of the fine relative to the potential injury would indicate that society does not strongly condemn the activity and therefore that the moral objections to the insurance would not be substantial.

Traffic laws provide a good example. Speeding, crossing a solid yellow line, going the wrong way on a one-way street, and other traffic law violations are, as McNeely (1941) described, criminal offenses in many jurisdictions, and these traffic violations are subject to fines that are small relative to the potential harm. Yet, insurance against tort liabilities for traffic crime-torts is universally available. True, insurance will not pay for the speeding ticket or any other traffic-related fine. But the cost of those fines pales in comparison to the potential damages that a liability insurer would readily pay in the event a serious accident results from the traffic law violation.

I do not mean to suggest that liability insurance for crime-torts never poses a moral hazard problem. Instead, I simply suggest that the criminal status or label does not create or exacerbate the moral hazard and, all other things being equal, the potential for criminal liability actually reduces that problem.[8] Of course, all other things often are not equal. In particular, crime-torts do seem more likely to involve intentional harm than other torts. But the higher degree of moral hazard that might be created by providing liability insurance for such crime-torts results from the intentional nature of the harm, not from the criminal status of the offense.

A further demonstration of the limits of the moral hazard explanation comes from the fact that there is an easily implemented and arguably more effective approach to managing the moral hazard of liability insurance for intentional harm than simply excluding coverage under the liability insurance contract. Under this alternative approach, the liability insurance contract would provide coverage for the tort, and the liability insurance company would manage the moral hazard by subrogation—that is, by going after the insured to recoup the money paid to the victim.[9]

If anything, this pay-and-then-subrogate approach would provide greater deterrence than the current approach of excluding insurance coverage for intentional harm. Because of the liability insurance exclusions, almost no one bothers to bring a tort claim for many crime-torts, unless there is a third party who was merely negligent or who can be held vicariously liable (Rabin 1999), with the result that the civil law in action often provides no real sanction for the criminal tortfeasor (Baker 1998a; Pryor 1997).[10] For crimes involving family and friends, the absence of civil sanction can mean there is no legal sanction at all, because family and friends are reluctant to call in the criminal law, as the domestic violence and acquaintance rape situations suggest (Wriggins 2001).

Providing liability insurance for intentional harm could change that situation. With liability insurance money at stake, the civil law process would at the very least announce the wrong and, possibly, shame the defendant (Hampton 1992). In addition, the public nature of the tort suit and subsequent subrogation action might even increase the chance that criminal prosecutors would get involved.

Moreover, plaintiffs might well refuse to settle without some payment of "blood money" on the part of the defendant, as occurs in drunk driving tort claims (Baker 2001). Even a small blood money payment is more than the zero payment that would be assessed when a plaintiff cannot bring a tort action because there is no liability insurance policy that makes the claim worthwhile for a contingent fee lawyer. As a repeat player, the liability insurer would enjoy some advantage over the individual plaintiff in actually collecting money from the wrongdoer, so the defendants may well be required to pay even more money in subrogation (cf., Gilles 2006 on the difficulties involved). In combination, the blood money and subrogation possibilities may have the superficially surprising consequence that intentional tortfeasors whose liability insurance policies include coverage for intentional injuries would be more likely to pay some of their own money to plaintiffs than intentional tortfeasors whose liability insurance policies exclude that coverage.

If the real problem with insuring domestic violence, rape, and other assaults were moral hazard, then something like this pay-and-then-subrogate approach would at least be on the public policy agenda for discussion. Yet it is not. The leading appellate decision supporting this approach, the New Jersey Supreme Court's decision in *Ambassador Insurance v. Montes*,[11] has been confined to its facts.[12] Jennifer Wriggins's (2001) proposal to require personal liability insurance policies to cover domestic violence has gone nowhere. And I can barely even persuade my law students to consider the benefits of liability insurance for intentional harm.

Why? Because their main concern about insurance for crime-torts is not, in fact, the effect of liability insurance on incentives. Instead, as my students strenuously argue, it is simply not fair for law-abiding liability insurance policyholders to have to pay, through their insurance premiums, for the costs of rapists' or arsonists' crimes. They object, in other words, that *liability insurance protects defendants,* and that some defendants—rapists and arsonists for example—do not deserve the protection.

Of course, as I always respond, potential victims also share the costs of any liability insurance compensation, either through their own liability insurance premiums or through the prices that they pay for goods and services that they buy from businesses with liability insurance, just as consumers share the costs of products liability and workers share the costs of workers compensation (cf. Stapleton 1995). I respond, in other words, that *liability insurance protects victims.* If any victims deserve that protection, victims of serious crime-torts like arson and rape surely do.

McNeely surely would have agreed with this argument, as would Justice Traynor and other supporters of the social insurance approach to tort liability, but not my students. "Nice move," is the typical response, "but I'm not persuaded." Almost universally, my students remain firmly of the view that liability insurance protects the defendant, and that it is wrong for liability insurance to provide that protection in a case involving a "real" crime.

Although this classroom experience hardly constitutes conclusive proof, repetition over many years has persuaded me. Liability insurance separates crimes from torts, not primarily because of concerns about the increased cost due to moral hazard, but rather because of moral objections to including some criminals in the liability insurance pool.[13]

The Crime-Tort Separation and Liability Insurance as Defense Protection

The crime-tort separation not only reflects a concept of liability insurance as protection for defendants, it also reinforces that concept. Intentional harm and criminal act exclusions produce a claims-handling structure that regularly *performs* the understanding of liability insurance as defendant protection. In that structure, insurance adjusters regularly investigate whether tort claims arise out of crime and, if so, they initiate the legal process that permits them to withhold or withdraw insurance protection.

The following (long) quotation from an article by two insurance defense lawyers illustrates this point:

> The axiom that bad facts make bad law could not have been any truer than in the case of Robert A. Berdella. In 1984, Berdella, a Kansas City, Missouri area resident went on a four-year torture and killing spree. Over that period of time Berdella killed at least six men, all in gruesome fashion . . . When police investigated Berdella's home, they found human skulls, photographs of men being sodomized and tortured, and journal notes describing the torture . . . The criminal record indicated that Berdella injected the victims with drugs and kept them alive for his "perverted desires.
>
> Civil suits were filed against Berdella's estate by the victim's families for wrongful death. Although Berdella had only $63,000 in personal assets, he did have a homeowners insurance policy with $100,000 per occurrence limits (arguably each murder could have been a separate occurrence). Berdella was insured by Economy Fire and Casualty Company (Economy). In the wrongful death actions, the plaintiffs attempted to trigger coverage by alleging that Berdella's actions amounted to negligence. In response, Economy filed a separate declaratory judgment action, citing its common policy language found in all home liability policies (in one form or another) that excludes liability coverage for bodily injury or property damage "expected or intended" from the standpoint of the insured.
>
> The Court of Appeals ruled that the mere fact that Berdella pled guilty to three counts of second degree murder did not establish that he intended to kill the three men for purposes of the civil or the declaratory actions . . . By finding that Berdella intended to torture his victims but did not expect or intend to kill them, the court handed the case back to the jury. This decision also placed the case back into the realm of potential coverage under Economy's homeowner's policy.
>
> The rest is history. The resulting jury verdict in the civil case, one year after the Court of Appeals ruling on the declaratory judgment action still stands today as the highest compensatory award in United States legal history. The livid jurors awarded the Stoops family $5 billion ($2.5 billion for wrongful death and $2.5 billion for "aggravating circumstances"). Although Economy had planned to appeal the verdict, its policy of insurance also covered pre-and post-judgment interest on the entire judgment. The interest on $5 billion amounted to $600,000 a day! Economy was forced to settle the claim rather than appeal and risk insolvency on the outcome of one appeal. Economy paid the Stoops family $2.5 million. The death claims presented by the Howell and Ferris families were settled out of court for undisclosed sums. (Eidsmore and Edwards 1998/99)

The Berdella case is just one particularly graphic example from an entire genre of moral monster stories that have emerged in the insurance case law out of the effort to enforce the crime-tort separation. These stories feature drunken brawlers, wife batterers, child molesters, doctors and dentists who rape sedated patients, and other moral monsters who commit a second crime by asking the insurance company to pay for their first one. Among published opinions, the Berdella case is unusual principally in the fact that the insurance company lost. For that reason, it played an important, "never again" role in the subsequent effort to include a criminal acts exclusion in some homeowners' insurance policies.[14]

It is easy to see these moral monster stories as a *result* of the crime-tort separation, but they also *reproduce* that separation. They allow insurance companies to occupy the moral high ground while refusing to pay victims who indisputably deserve compensation. The stories place the spotlight of attention on the moral monster, not the deserving victim, and they appropriate the victim's wrong for the insurance company. In the process, they legitimate a crime-tort separation that makes the outrage in the Berdella insurance case the fact that Berdella's insurance company had to pay, rather than the fact that the company for years refused to pay the victims' families (cf. Baker 1995, describing the claims story of the immoral insured; Ericson et al. 2003, describing insureds as suspects).

At least in part as a result of the crime-tort separation in liability insurance, the more clearly intentional or criminal the harm, the less likely the perpetrator will be called to account in a civil forum, and the less likely the victim will receive real compensation, given the well-recognized inadequacy of the public compensation funds for criminal victims[15] (e.g., Levmore and Logue 2003) In my view, this result is morally objectionable, but that opinion is only tangential to my main point here: Ideas about the nature of liability insurance affect tort law on the ground (cf. Ewald 1991 on the power of "insurance imaginaries").

There are, it should be acknowledged, two mitigating developments in U.S. tort practice. First, the growth of what Robert Rabin has aptly named "enabling torts" means that victims sometimes are able to recover from noncriminal third parties whose conduct can be causally linked to the crime, although this growth has been subject to counterattack in the form of legislative restrictions on joint and several liability (Rabin 1999). For example, a building owner may be sued for inadequate security in the event of a rape or other assault in the building. Second, common law rules relating to insurers' duty to defend and settle claims have facilitated a practice of "underlitigation"—for example, pleading an intentional tort as a negligent tort—that may help victims in cases in which the evidence on intent is less than clear (Baker 1998a; Pryor 1997). Notwithstanding these developments, however, domestic violence, acquaintance rape, and most other assaults remain largely outside the reach of tort law—not because of technical limits on what can and cannot be the subject of liability insurance, but rather because of an understanding of, and commitment to, liability insurance as defendant protection.

At a more general level, the crime-tort separation in liability insurance and the accompanying moral monster stories also reflect and reproduce an understanding of a tort claim as an encounter between a specific plaintiff and a specific defendant, rather than as the price-setting or loss-spreading mechanism that a social engineer might describe. There are, of course, other institutions that promote this individualized, corrective justice understanding of tort law, but the crime-tort separation in liability insurance is special because it operates within an institution—insurance—that, in so many other ways, promotes the price-setting and loss-spreading approaches.

Thanks in part to the crime-tort separation, a liability insurance claims file is not just an administrative record classifying the nature and economic value of bodily injury or other harm. Instead, the claims file is also an inquiry into the state of mind of the defendant. Like every other aspect of the claims-handling process, this inquiry undoubtedly becomes routinized and subject to rules of thumb that reduce the individualized nature of the inquiry (Ross 1970). Nevertheless, the crime-tort separation provides an additional fault line, beyond those provided by tort law, along which the bureaucratic claims-handling process can break down, releasing the individualized drama of litigation.

Conclusion

This chapter has explored how liability insurance separates the tort and criminal fields by withdrawing insurance protection for crime-torts. Before concluding, I will complicate this picture by briefly describing how liability insurance makes the criminal law experience more like the tort law experience for some defendants in some cases.

Despite the exclusion of coverage for criminal fines and penalties, some liability insurance contracts do provide coverage for criminal defense costs. I have found this criminal defense coverage in two kinds of liability insurance policies:

(1) in professional liability policies sold to high-status professionals, such as directors' and officers' liability insurance[16] and medical liability insurance,[17] and (2) in an excess liability insurance policy available to members of the National Rifle Association.[18]

This coverage civilizes, to at least some degree, the criminal defense experience by providing the means for the criminal defendant to contest the state's allegations. In-depth exploration of this insurance coverage awaits future work. Topics to be addressed include the history of the coverage, the reasons offered by liability insurers for its introduction, and whether there was any resistance on the part of insurance regulators or courts; whether there are features of the criminal liabilities likely to be covered that suggests they are somehow less "criminal" than paradigmatic crimes; and what, if anything, liability insurers do to address potential adverse selection concerns (i.e., that policies with this coverage might be systematically more appealing to higher risk applicants).

For present purposes, the existence of these limited forms of criminal defense coverage simply highlights the absence of this protection in other forms of liability insurance and also provides additional evidence that liability insurers could, as a technical matter, expand the range of services they provide to defendants accused of crime-torts, without running into insurmountable moral hazard or adverse selection problems. This strengthens the claim that economic incentives do not adequately explain the crime-tort separation in liability insurance.

CHAPTER FIVE

Juries as Conduits for Culture?

VALERIE P. HANS

Conventional wisdom holds that juries are the purest method for incorporating social norms and cultural understandings into the civil justice system. This is held to be particularly true in tort cases. In *Tort Law and the Public Interest,* Yale Law School Professor Peter Schuck argues that "The institution of the jury, as much as legal doctrine, infuses tort law with new life and meaning in the light of new configurations of social facts and values" (Schuck 1991, 18). That is so, he maintains, because of the inherent flexibility of tort doctrine: "Tort liability, more than most areas of law, mirrors the economic, technological, ideological, and moral conditions that prevail in society at any given time ... The master ideas that drive tort doctrine—reasonableness, duty of care, and proximate cause—are as loose-jointed, context-sensitive, and openly relativistic as any principles to be found in law" (Schuck 1991, 18).

This chapter examines the conventional wisdom that the American civil jury is a key element in incorporating social, economic, and cultural elements into the tort system. Of course, law itself is so thoroughly intertwined with cultural understandings that one cannot divide "law" and "culture" without doing disservice to both phenomena (Rosen 2006, xii–xiii). Instead, the claim is that the use of core legal concepts of tort law—judgments of injury, liability, the reasonable person standard, and the appropriateness of compensation—depend centrally on the jury's infusion of social norms and popular cultural understandings into its decision making. The jury's normative understandings may be loosely tethered to official law (Ewick and Silbey 1998) or may reflect extralegal norms and values that circulate in mass culture (Haltom and McCann 2004; this volume). Legal rules, commonsense understandings of the law, and extralegal norms all constitute the broader legal culture, of which juries are a part. Without the tort jury's reliance on culturally sensitive interpretations of core legal concepts, the tort system arguably risks becoming static and unresponsive.

After first reviewing the legal landscape, I turn to an interrelated set of questions about juries and their cultural norms, understandings, and expectations. If these cultural phenomena affect jury tort verdicts, what psychological and social processes are involved? Are they distinct to juries or just as apt to be found in decision making by judges?

Finding that jurors have a set of preexisting ideas, understandings, and values about important tort elements, I identify basic themes in the jury's commonsense justice about tort claims. I also take up the issue of civil jury nullification, in which juries reject the application of a legal rule that is at odds with community notions of justice. These cases present an excellent opportunity to observe the influence of cultural factors on jury decision making. This chapter draws on existing research that pertains to some of these questions, while suggesting other issues worthy of empirical examination.

The Legal Landscape: Expansion of the Jury's Ability to Inject Cultural Norms, Sentiments, and Understandings into Tort Cases

I begin by examining more closely, and qualifying a bit, Schuck's thesis that tort law and tort doctrine openly invite the jury's infusion of community norms and values. Tort law and civil procedure have developed in some ways that facilitate and in other ways that restrict the infusion of the civil jury's commonsense understandings and cultural values into the resolution of tort cases. One set of doctrinal and procedural developments addresses the scope of the jury trial right, while another set bears on the contemporary civil jury's structure and composition.

A variety of legal rules and reforms have ensured the jury's continuing presence in civil adjudication, and therefore the jurors' ability to inject cultural understandings into their decisions. Most significant are the constitutional guarantees. The constitutional right to a federal civil jury trial in the United States is provided through the Seventh Amendment of the U.S. Constitution, which preserves the right to a jury "in suits at common law, where the value in controversy shall exceed twenty dollars" (U.S. Constitution, 7th Amendment). The civil jury today is preserved as the fact finder of those types of issues that the civil jury historically decided in common law courts as opposed to equity and admiralty courts. But in part because courts of equity and common law merged, the Supreme Court has eschewed a strict historical test in favor of a multifaceted analysis that recognizes the value of civil jury adjudication (Field, Kaplan, and Clermont, 2007, 1461–1463; Gertner and Mizner 1997, I9).

Congress has further reflected its support for community judgment in civil matters by including a jury trial right in certain new statutory causes of action (Marder 2005, 45). As a consequence of these developments, the civil procedure casebook authors Richard Field, Benjamin Kaplan, and Kevin Clermont conclude that "the federal jury right will likely remain expansive, now extended beyond the clearly common-law realm to reach many new causes of action that give legal relief and reach the merged procedure's various gray areas on the frontier between law and equity, but go no further" (Field et al. 2007, 1508).

In state civil trials, the U.S. Supreme Court has never held that a jury is required, but constitutional provisions and statutes safeguard the right to a civil jury in most state courts (Gertner and Mizner 1997, I14–15; Sward, 2001). The significance of the constitutional provisions is evident when we compare the continuing presence of the civil jury in the United States with its fate in other countries such as England, the birthplace of the jury, which has all but abolished the civil jury (Lloyd-Bostock and Thomas 2000).

Other legal rules preserve the jury's domains of influence. Distinctions between law and fact, for instance, reserve factual questions for the jury, leaving judges to decide matters of law, although clearly judges also make factual determinations in a variety of ways in, for example, judging evidence admissibility and ruling on motions to dismiss (Allen and Pardo 2003). The U.S. Supreme Court preserved jury fact finding in patent cases (*Markman v. Westview Instruments, Inc.* 1996), while allocating claims construction to the judge. And it has up to this point avoided a broad complexity exception to the civil jury trial right. Appellate courts seemed to be headed down this path in the 1980s, when the Third Circuit found a complexity exception based on due process grounds, but other circuits have reached the opposite conclusion or have remained silent on the matter (Lempert 1981–1982).

There have been continuing efforts to remove punitive damages fact-finding from the jury. In *State Farm Mutual Automobile Insurance Company v. Campbell,* business corporations submitted an amicus brief arguing that research demonstrated that juries could not rationally decide punitive damages (Brief of Certain Leading Business Corporations as Amici Curiae in Support of Petitioner 2003, 2–5). The Supreme Court decided the case in favor of the petitioner State Farm. Although it concluded that the particular award was unreasonable and excessive, it remanded the case back to the lower courts. It did not accept the amici's conclusion that juries were unable to adequately perform punitive damages assessments. Instead, the Court further enunciated the importance of guidelines for judicial evaluation of juries' punitive damage awards (*State Farm Mut. Automobile Ins. Co. v. Campbell* 2003), and has reiterated the need for jury guidance in punitive damages more recently as well (*Philip Morris USA v. Williams* 2007).

In addition to these legal rules and decisions that preserve a place for the jury in civil justice, other laws facilitate the ability of the jury to inject community values and sentiments into the verdict. The cases outlining the constitutional requirements for jury selection, including the law's insistence on drawing juries from representative cross-sections of the population, enable the jury to reflect normative values (Vidmar and Hans 2007). Representativeness is critically important because it is assumed that juries will bring the broad community's common sense of justice to bear on legal cases. To the extent that juries are diverse, they should incorporate a range of different experiences and cultural perspectives. These distinct views can be debated and discussed in the jury deliberation.

Jury deliberation's exchange and debate provide an opportunity for both informational and normative influence, that is, for information available to community members to be shared, and for normative pressures to operate. Representative juries debating the evidence can identify and correct individual misunderstandings and inform the group about limitations in particular perspectives about the evidence. The representative jury thus possesses the capability to inject diverse cultural understandings into the decision-making process (Kahan, Hoffman, and Braman in press).

Some scholars point out that the jury deliberation functions to reduce error and individual biases (Ellsworth 1989, 206). Certain community sentiments, such as racial prejudice, might be counteracted or lessened by the presence of people of different races. But the potential benefits of diversity go beyond that. Compared to homogeneous groups, diverse groups representing multiple perspectives tend to engage in better quality decision processes. In an important mock jury experiment, Samuel Sommers (2006) combined participants into six-person mock juries of either all whites or of four white and two black members of the jury pool. Diverse juries deliberated longer, discussed a wider range of topics, and were more accurate in their statements about the case. The presence of diversity on the jury affected the white jurors. Whites in diverse juries made fewer factual errors and raised more issues, compared to the members of all-white juries.

However, other scholars note that at times group decisions are more rather than less susceptible to the influence of bias than individual decisions (Kerr, MacCoun, and Kramer 1996). Majorities tend to rule in juries. Whatever cultural norms and understandings are incorporated into decision making are likely to favor the norms and understandings of the majority. And group decisions are in some instances more polarized than might be expected from knowing the initial judgments of the individual group members. Polarization processes may produce decisions that reflect more extreme versions of prevailing community and group norms. Representative juries are more likely to include dissenting perspectives, which should reduce polarization.

Tort doctrine also contributes to the jury's expression of community norms and culture, as the quote from Peter Schuck suggested. Perhaps most significant is the fact that the concept of "reasonableness" is so central to tort law. And who better than a representative group from the community to say what is reasonable?

Many of the core elements in negligence law require the fact finder to apply a reasonable person standard. The Restatement (Second) of Torts (American Law Institute, 1965), for example, allows an actor to use "reasonable force" in defending against another when the actor "reasonably believes" that the other is about to inflict harmful or offensive contact (§63). The definition of offensive contact is one "that offends a reasonable sense of personal dignity." The general standard that applies in negligence cases is reasonable care under the circumstances (§283). Juries stand in for the community in answering each of these questions of what a reasonably prudent person would do in the particular circumstances of a case. Arguably, because they include a range of individuals, juries are likely to be better than judges at this task.

The reasonableness standard is objective rather than subjective. That is, it doesn't depend on what a particular individual might have believed, but rather what reasonable people would believe under the circumstances. The concept is open-ended and flexible, allowing the jury to incorporate changing standards of behavior and community expectations into their decision making. Juries apply their understandings of community judgments of reasonable behavior, whether it is the reasonableness of the defendant's behavior or that of the plaintiff's. Thus, cultural understandings in multiple manifestations are integrated into legal decisions via the reasonableness concept.

In addition to flexibility in intentional tort and negligence determinations, the jury also is given relatively free rein in deciding damage awards. There are very few constraints placed on juries. Some jurisdictions do not permit attorneys to suggest a specific dollar amount because of concerns about undue influence on jury damage awards. Jurors complain about the lack of guidance in arriving at damage awards (Greene and Bornstein 2003; Mott et al. 2000).

A final feature of tort cases that gives the jury latitude is that judicial instructions in the law are presented in a way that makes them difficult to understand and hence apply. The current approach that many judges take to instructing the jury in the law operates to minimize the impact of law and to maximize cultural sentiments and normative understandings. Jury instructions are often written with heavy doses of legalese, making them difficult for lay people to understand (Tiersma 1999). Judges read the instructions orally, in court. Often just one set of instructions, all given at one time at the end of the evidence presentation, is provided to the jury. All of these factors decrease the jurors' capacity to understand the law.

In sum, constitutional principles, tort doctrines, and court procedures carve out specific issues for the tort jury and allow the jury in torts trials latitude to incorporate cultural norms, understandings, and expectations into their decisions.

Contraction of the Jury's Ability to Inject Cultural Norms, Sentiments, and Understandings into Tort Cases

Yet there are competing currents in legal doctrine and procedure that restrict the jury's role and scope. A number of legal rules and changes have functioned to reduce the jury's role, or have restricted the jury's ability to incorporate lay sentiments and values into tort dispute resolution, counteracting the expansive trends noted earlier.

The first point to note is that over the last several decades there has been a general decline in trials and a specific drop in jury trials as a means of resolving disputes (Galanter 2004b). Some federal judges, notably Patrick Higginbotham

(2002), have confessed that in recent years they have felt pressure to do what they can to settle the civil lawsuits that come before them. A trial is seen as a failure, and more specifically the judge's failure, to avoid the expenditure of government resources spent on public trials. Numerous factors encourage party settlements over trials. Scholars have documented the dramatically declining use of trials, and more specifically jury trials, to resolve cases including torts disputes (Galanter 2004b, 460–476; Resnik 1993). For instance, in 1962, one in six federal torts claims went to trial; by 2002 that figure was one in forty-six (Galanter 2004b, 466).

In addition to settlement pressures, several legal and procedural devices limit jury determinations. Summary judgment now ends many cases at an early stage, cases which otherwise might have been litigated and determined by juries. Similarly, the *Daubert* trilogy of scientific evidence cases increased the judge's gatekeeping role in expert testimony (*Daubert v. Merrell Dow Pharmaceuticals* 1993). Judges today often keep from the jury evidence that in previous decades juries would have heard and evaluated (Berger 2005, S64–S65). Even the law/fact distinction that I identified previously as a means of reserving issues for jury determination can contrarily be employed to prevent the jury from reaching other issues by describing them as questions of law for the judge. Allen and Pardo (2003) take issue with the law-fact distinction, arguing that the seemingly simple categorization of law and fact is plagued with line drawing problems. So some matters that could properly be jury issues may be decided by the judge.

During a civil trial, judges may employ other devices to limit the evidence that juries can hear or to narrow the decisions that they make. All of these methods seem to constitute efforts to constrain jury decision making and limit the infusion of community sentiments and biases. They appear to be based on the assumption that the jury is a powerful vehicle for the injection of community norms into the law, and the policy judgment that this tendency must be controlled. For example, bifurcation of trial issues (such as asking the jury to arrive at a determination of liability before permitting the jurors to consider any evidence pertaining to damages) limits what the jury can know at any one time, preventing juries from considering the whole context of a case as they make multiple decisions. Similarly, special verdicts force the jury to consider single aspects of a case in answering particular questions rather than delivering a general verdict. It is another attempt to reduce the contextual effects that might be present in a trial with only a general verdict. As early as the 1950s, law professor Leon

Green observed that the use of special interrogatories "provides the appellate courts with every opportunity to examine the evidence and to substitute their own conclusions for those of the jury" (Green 1956–1957, 358).

Because of worries about the possible injection of jury sentiments, juries are not permitted to learn many interesting facts that would be relevant to their judgments outside the courtroom, like whether an injured driver was wearing a seat belt or not, or whether a particular party has insurance or not (Diamond and Vidmar 2001). Nonetheless, research has found that juries rely on their own experiences and assumptions about the likelihood of insurance or seat belt usage.

Finally, civil jury verdicts, particularly damage awards, are often adjusted after trial by the judge, replacing the jury's decision with the judge's. And legislative decisions to place caps or upper limits on damage awards, a tort reform supported by powerful defendant lobbies that has been adopted by a number of states, also replace the jury's individualized judgment with the general determination of the legislature about appropriate limits on awards.

All of these developments have constricted the jury's role and ability to inject cultural sentiments into the legal determination of specific cases. Either the jury is not allowed to participate in the decision, or it is restricted or limited in another way. Of course, the exclusion of the jury as decision maker is also a cultural act. It's a value-laden choice to prefer the blackletter and bright line rules, substituting judicial or legislative determinations for those of the jury. Both the expansion and the constriction of the jury in tort cases should be understood as value-driven actions.

The Psychological Process of Cultural Infusion: A Closer Look at Juror Decision Making

Looking at research on jury decision making, we can observe that all of the scientific models of juror and jury decision making either implicitly or explicitly acknowledge the central role of cultural understandings. Whether it is the story model, described below, or alternative approaches that feature Bayesian analysis or highlight the integration of information (Albertson, Farley, and Hans 2004), in all models there is a presumption that a juror's legal decisions are affected by the juror's attitudes, views, preconceptions, and values.

The most popular theory of how jurors arrive at verdicts is the story model (Pennington and Hastie 1992; Vidmar and Hans 2007, 132–137). As jurors listen to testimony, they begin to organize the evidence in the form of a narrative or story that is based on familiar story structures. The story typically includes motives, character assessments, important events, and states of mind. Relying on prior knowledge of the world, jurors fill in gaps in the testimony to complete the narrative. Jurors may ignore information that contradicts their emerging narrative. The consistency, plausibility, and completeness of the developing story determine whether it will be accepted.

Jurors then learn about the law applicable to the case, review the available verdict options, and select the verdict that best matches this narrative they have developed. So, for example, if jurors draw on commonly circulating stories about money-hungry plaintiffs to downgrade a particular plaintiff's claimed injuries, a verdict in favor of the defendant provides the best match for the money-hungry plaintiff story. Psychological research on juror decision making has confirmed the link between narratives and verdict choices (Pennington and Hastie 1992). Haltom and McCann (2004, 297–299; this volume) describe how public reaction to the jury decision in the McDonald's coffee spill case reinforced beliefs in outrageous plaintiff behavior and may have led to a drop in awards.

Many elements of the story model offer opportunities for, indeed require, the transmission of popular cultural understandings. World knowledge and experiences with typical story structures (beginning, middle, end, good guy/bad guy) are culturally dependent. Jurors draw on them to judge the parties' character, their credibility, their motivations, and how much weight to give their evidence. These decisions are driven by social norms, popular understandings, and what common stories come to mind. Of course, communities are heterogeneous bodies, stratified along such dimensions as gender, race, ethnicity, religion, and income (Benda-Beckmann this volume; Engel this volume). Norms and narratives may diverge across or bridge these differences.

In thinking about the verdict-matching phase, it bears repeating that shared cultural understandings are already reflected in statutory and common law principles (Rosen 2006). That is, legal rules themselves, in the criminal or civil context, are highly likely to reflect as well as shape community norms of improper behavior (Robinson and Darley 1995). However, in important stages of the story model in which the jury learns the law and applies the law to the facts, there remains what might be described as an extralegal dimension. The closer a factual situation is to a prototype of improper behavior that is widely shared by community members, the more likely it is for the jury to conclude that the defendant is negligent.

The significance of lay prototypes of law was explored by Vicky Smith in the criminal justice context (Smith 1991; Smith and Studebaker 1996). She discovered that how jurors applied the law to the facts of a case depended on prototypes that jurors had about specific crimes. The closer a set of facts came to the prototype, the more likely a guilty verdict. There is a clear civil justice analogy. The closer an accident or potentially negligent act is to the prototype, the more likely there will be a finding of negligence.

A study of mock jurors responding to sexual harassment cases showed the importance of common stories about sexual discrimination in the workplace to the verdicts that these jurors reached (Huntley and Costanzo 2003, 42). Mock jurors who favored the defense explained the evidence in a way that diverged from jurors who favored the plaintiff. Defense jurors were more apt, for example, to see the employee as overly sensitive, and to critique her behavior and character, while plaintiff jurors evaluated the employee positively and perceived the problem of sexual harassment as systemic in the company (Huntley and Costanzo 2003, 40–42). These perceptions of the evidence and related story themes of plaintiff and defense irresponsibility translated into defense and plaintiff verdicts. In applying the law to the facts, jurors depend on culturally-shared understandings in multiple ways—in the determination of facts, in the understanding of law, and in the way in which the law is seen to fit the facts.

The Commonsense Justice of the Civil Jury

The story model suggests that community notions of justice play an important role in shaping the narratives that jurors develop about the evidence, in comprehending the law, and in the verdict-matching process. I turn now to identifying and describing several community notions implicated in the tort context. Here I draw on the important work by Norman Finkel in his book, *Commonsense Justice* (Finkel 1995), as well as Neal Feigenson's book, *Legal Blame* (Feigenson 2000), which extends common sense justice ideas to the civil justice system. Finkel, focusing on the criminal law, contrasts the law on the books with commonsense justice, which is what citizens think is fair:

> These commonsense notions are at once legal, moral, and psychological. They provide the citizen on the street and the juror in the jury box with a theory of why people

think, feel, and behave as they do, and why the law should find some defendants guilty and punishable and others not. Black-letter law also has its theories of human nature, culpability, and punishment. But there is mounting and persuasive evidence that the "law on the books" may be at odds with commonsense justice in many areas. (Finkel 1995, 2)

In Finkel's view, commonsense justice is not simply folksy sayings and clichés, or quick public opinion poll readings, but rather deliberative, conscious judgments that are exquisitely sensitive to the specific factual contexts and "foundational" issues of justice (Finkel 1995, 5). Finkel identifies different areas in which commonsense justice is at odds with the legal rules. For example, in self-defense and right-to-die cases, commonsense justice is more expansive and more generous than the blackletter law, whereas in insanity defense cases, it is more constricted.

In *Legal Blame,* Feigenson describes the interplay between commonsense justice and the law in the civil law context. He argues that juries attempt to achieve "total justice," by which he means that juries are more focused on the big-picture justice of the outcome than the strict following of legal rules (Feigenson 2000, 16). He identifies several ways in which juries strive for total justice (Feigenson 2000, 16–18).

First, juries aim to achieve balance between the parties. The behavior and responsibility of both plaintiff and defendant are taken into consideration. Feigenson asserts here that jurors desire one party to prevail or win, arguing that jurors prefer a single theory of the case with a winner and a loser (Feigenson, 2000, 16–17). However, in my work I have seen juries make an effort to compare the parties' relative responsibilities; they often display a cheerful willingness to split the outcome to achieve measured justice (Hans 2000).

Second, they take into account all the information they believe is relevant to the inquiry. Insurance, for example, although legally excluded as a formal matter, is relevant to the juror's evaluation of the whole picture. Insurance information may slip out at trial; or jurors may draw on personal experiences or assumptions about how insurance operates as they consider the full context of the case (Diamond and Vidmar 2001).

A third aspect of the commonsense justice of the civil jury is that the decision is reached holistically, rather than in separate, sequential stages. Evidence from different sources may be commingled. Causation elements may blur into compensation elements. The use of bifurcation and special verdicts, mentioned earlier, likely disrupts this element of commonsense justice.

To these insights I would add the following observations about the common-sense justice of the tort jury. Juror judgments reflect strong attention to the personal responsibility of the parties (Engel 1984; this volume). Jurors draw on their culturally shaped expectations of reasonable and responsible behavior to judge the plaintiff as well as the defendant. These expectations are context specific and appear also to be identity specific. As with the reasonable woman test that makes intuitive sense to apply in sexual harassment cases, jurors in tort cases involving business corporations appear to use "reasonable corporation" expectations—and even "reasonable large corporation" expectations—to assess the behavior of the corporate defendant in the case (Hans 2000; MacCoun 1996). Sterling and Reichman's (this volume) historical analysis of railroad and tramway torts in the Rocky Mountain frontier reveals how higher expectations about business responsibility may change over time, influenced by patterns of personal injury and by emerging ideas about risk, safety, and individual versus corporate liability. Tort jurors today expect a higher standard of care from corporate defendants compared to individual defendants. These higher expectations translate into a greater willingness to hold corporate actors liable for their harm-causing actions (Hans 2000; MacCoun 1996).

Another element of commonsense justice is the civil jury's treatment of the plaintiff. Despite widespread beliefs to the contrary, the tort jury is not reliably proplaintiff. Some years ago, David Engel (1984) interviewed members of a local community and discovered a strong tendency to criticize the people who brought lawsuits. Tort jurors likewise take a critical stance. Although severely injured plaintiffs can arouse sympathy, jurors also subject the plaintiffs' claims to searing scrutiny (Haltom and McCann 2004, 297–299; Hans 2000, 28–31). Is the injury real? What did the plaintiff do to make it worse? Did the plaintiff see the doctor at the first opportunity? Jurors are alert to ways in which the story could be one of plaintiff blame rather than defendant irresponsibility—or something in between.

In sum, tort jurors approach their decision making so as to reach an outcome that most closely resembles their perception of total justice in a given set of circumstances. Total justice does not necessarily equate with full compensation for plaintiffs, but rather is influenced by jurors' sense of fairness and their perceptions of the comparative responsibilities of the parties under particular circumstances.

Judge Versus Jury:
Whose Culture or Commonsense Justice Is It Anyway?

If social norms and extralegal cultural understandings are part and parcel of juror decision making, their influence is not necessarily unique to the jury as fact finder. Judges as elite members of the community may be just as likely to reflect and inject social norms and cultural sentiments into their legal decisions. More than a century ago Oliver Wendell Holmes made the following observation about judges: "The felt necessities of the time, the prevalent moral and political theories, intuitions of public policy, avowed or unconscious, even the prejudices which judges share with their fellow-men, have had a good deal more to do than the syllogism in determining the rules by which men should be governed" (Holmes 1887, 1).

An interesting angle on the role of cultural understandings in judges and juries comes from judge-jury agreement studies (Robbennolt 2005). In surveys of judges who preside over jury trials, the judges have provided researchers with their own hypothetical verdicts. The researchers then compare the judge's hypothetical verdict to the jury's actual decision to arrive at a measure of judge-jury agreement. In a substantial majority of the cases, both judge and jury would reach the same verdict (Diamond and Vidmar 2003; Eisenberg et al. 2005; Hannaford, Hans, and Munsterman 2000; Heuer and Penrod 1994; Kalven 1964; Kalven and Zeisel 1996). Likewise, studies examining the factors that predict jury verdicts repeatedly show that the strength of the evidence presented at trial—whether evidence strength is measured by the judge's rating or the jury's collective assessment—is the major determinant of jury verdicts (Eisenberg et al. 2005, 186–189; Visher 1991). When the evidence is strong for one side, both the jury and the judge are likely to decide in favor of that side.

This judge-jury convergence appears to be just as characteristic of civil verdicts as it is of criminal verdicts. The earliest study of civil juries, done as part of the Chicago Jury Project but never fully analyzed, found that in civil cases judge and jury agreed 78 percent of the time on the verdict, and when they disagreed juries were about as likely to find for the plaintiff as for the defendant. Juries were somewhat more generous than judges would have been in damage awards (Kalven 1964, 1065; Kalven and Zeisel 1966, 63). More recently, in a study of 172

Arizona civil jury trials by Hannaford et al. (2000, 371), judicial ratings of evidence favorability were consistent with jury verdicts 84 percent of the time. Likewise, the smaller Diamond et al. study with 50 Arizona civil jury trials found a substantial judge-jury agreement rate (Diamond et al. 2003, 35). But another result from the Diamond et al. study flipped the judge-jury generosity finding of the Kalven and Zeisel project. Arizona judges would have recommended damage awards that were about 10 percent more generous than the jury's actual awards.

Another analysis of the data collected in the Hannaford et al. (2000) study reinforces my claim that there is much overlap between judge and jury in civil cases, and indeed some of the supposed cultural biases of the jury are not much in evidence. I analyzed judge-jury agreement in the Arizona civil jury project to test the widely held view that juries are biased against business corporations (Hans 1998, 341). Included in the larger study of Arizona jury reform was information about civil jury verdicts and judicial ratings of the overall probative value of the trial evidence—favoring the plaintiff, favoring the defense, or evenly balanced. I divided the sample into cases in which individuals were defendants and those in which businesses or corporations were defendants. If juries were strongly proplaintiff when plaintiffs sued businesses, then one would expect to see high proportions of plaintiff verdicts even in instances in which the judge saw the evidence as favorable to the defendant. That did not happen. Instead, jury verdicts tracked the judge's rating of evidence. When judges rated the evidence as favorable to the plaintiff, juries usually arrived at plaintiff verdicts, but not more so in business defendant cases (81 percent in business defendant cases and 88 percent in individual defendant cases). Likewise, when judges saw the evidence as favoring the defense, juries usually found for the defense (69 percent in business defendant cases and 60 percent in individual defendant cases). Thus, employing the judge's evaluation of the trial evidence as a control, I found no support for the view that juries are more proplaintiff or antibusiness than judges. If antibusiness sentiments are part of cultural understandings that affect civil verdicts, the sentiments seem to be shared by juries and judges alike. If juries hold higher expectations of corporate defendants, as described earlier, then judges are likely to as well, although this possibility has not yet been systematically examined.

Even though judges bring with them an aura of rationality, a long line of research in political science points to the continuing importance of a judge's attitudes and political leanings in explaining their judicial decisions. Furthermore, the various cognitive biases that are so readily attributed to juries also are found in judges. A growing body of research by my colleague Jeffrey Rachlinski and his collaborators shows that judges are subject to many of the same cognitive biases as laypersons (Guthrie, Rachlinski, and Wistrich 2001). In their powerful book, *Minding the Law,* lawyer Anthony Amsterdam and psychologist Jerome Bruner make a compelling case for the importance of storytelling and narrative for judges as well as jurors (Amsterdam and Bruner 2000).

The point of this section is that, contrary to the conventional wisdom that juries are distinctive in incorporating cultural understandings into legal decisions, judicial decision making reflects culturally created views as well. The relative importance of cultural understandings to judge and jury decision making has not been thoroughly studied. But one could safely speculate that judges and juries have somewhat different sets of cultural understandings derived from the judge's relatively privileged position as well as legal training and financial security. Because they are markedly less representative of the community than juries, judges are apt to reflect a more elite, narrow slice of community views, and especially to differ on their sense of total justice (Hans 2000, 226–227).

Civil Jury Nullification

One useful way to study the role of cultural norms and understandings on tort jury decisions is to examine instances in which a formal legal rule is at odds with popular views. That is related to the idea that civil juries might nullify the law by injecting community sentiments and values into tort decisions in such circumstances. When scholars discuss jury nullification, they usually focus on criminal law. Since civil jury verdicts that are inconsistent with the law and evidence may be overturned by a judge no matter whether they are for the plaintiff or the defendant, strictly speaking a civil jury on its own cannot nullify the law as irrefutably as an American criminal jury can with its unreviewable acquittal. Nonetheless, judges may be reluctant to overturn civil jury decisions, suggesting that civil juries have opportunities to nullify the law in practice (Noah 2001).

Perhaps the best example of civil jury nullification can be shown through the competing comparative and contributory negligence regimes. For years, in many American jurisdictions, a contributory negligence regime prevailed in which any contributory fault on the part of the plaintiff automatically barred all recovery.

If a plaintiff was found to be slightly at fault, even a clearly negligent defendant could escape responsibility. This all-or-nothing approach diverges from the commonsense justice of the tort jury, whereby civil jurors are keen to evaluate the responsibility and reasonableness of both parties and balance the equities. Many jurisdictions moved to comparative negligence, in which the fact finder assesses the proportion of liability due to each party, including the plaintiff, and the damage award is apportioned accordingly (Field et al. 2007).

Kristin Sommer, Irwin Horowitz, and Martin Bourgeois (2001) examined whether the perceived unfairness of various negligence rules could affect mock juror decision strategies in negligence cases. They crafted a product design defect case that included evidence of defective design but also evidence that could lead to an inference that the plaintiff was partially at fault. A third of the participants were told to follow "strict liability" instructions, in which they were to find the defendant liable if the design was defective. Another third of the participants received comparative negligence instructions, in which they were to assess the relative proportions of liability of the parties, including the plaintiff. A final third were to decide the case using contributory negligence instructions; if the plaintiff was at fault, there could be no recovery.

The researchers found that the different instructions shaped the way that the mock jurors reportedly perceived the fault of the parties. The mock jurors who decided the case under contributory negligence were more likely to say that the plaintiff was not at all liable (24 percent) than the mock jurors who got the comparative negligence instructions (8 percent). Because finding any plaintiff fault under a contributory negligence regime required a defense verdict, mock jurors adjusted their ratings of plaintiff fault accordingly (Sommer, Horowitz, and Bourgeois 2001, 313). They seemed to work backward from what they perceived to be a just result in the case.

A second study of the phenomenon used mock juries deliberating in groups as opposed to individuals. The researchers found that contributory negligence juries were more likely to absolve the plaintiff of fault completely, compared to the comparative negligence mock juries (Sommer et al. 2001, 315). Because the contributory negligence approach was at odds with the total justice dimension of lay justice, the mock jurors and juries were motivated to perceive plaintiff fault in such a way as to be fair and consistent with norms of distributive justice, even when they departed from black letter law.

Conclusion

In this chapter, I've explored the conventional wisdom that the civil jury is a prime instrument in ensuring that popular cultural norms and expectations are reflected in tort case decisions. The legal rules governing tort cases already produce and reflect societal views of responsible and irresponsible behavior. Yet as juries find the facts and apply the law to the facts, there is ample room for additional incorporation of community notions of justice.

Much is made of the open-ended flexible concepts of tort law. Yet consider the chapter's discussion of competing currents surrounding the civil jury's role. Some developments have reinforced and expanded the jury's ability to reflect commonsense justice in tort decisions, while others have restrained and restricted the jury. The open-endedness of tort law has become a politically charged battleground.

Carol Rose wrote a journal article some years ago tracing doctrinal developments in property law (Rose 1988). She observed a cyclical pattern, finding that decisions that asserted bright-line rules—what she called "crystals"—in property law were followed by others that introduced greater flexibility—or "mud" (her term again)—into property law concepts. Then the cycle began again. Attempts to develop and apply bright line rules would appear to succeed for awhile, but then their inapplicability or inability to do justice in a sufficient number of cases would require a more open-ended approach. However, the lack of specificity would likewise be found wanting, driving the desire for more crystalline rules.

The same might be said of tort law developments. The growth of tort liability in the 1960s and 1970s was followed by retrenchment and restriction in the 1990s and beyond (Henderson 2005). Henderson concludes that by the 1990s negligence law in the United States had either halted or reversed the expansions of the earlier years, arriving at what he calls a "stable equilibrium" (Henderson 2005, 192, 227). Developments that have alternately expanded and contracted the jury's opportunity to speak with the community's voice also appear to follow a cyclical pattern. The cycling between judge and jury does not remove popular culture from tort law decisions but is likely to change its substance. This reinforces the critical importance of studying popular understandings of law and legal culture, with the goal of understanding how the production and circulation of norms and understandings at once reflect and shape official law and law in action.

CHAPTER SIX

Framing Fast-Food Litigation

Tort Claims, Mass Media, and the Politics of Responsibility in the United States

WILLIAM HALTOM AND MICHAEL MCCANN

Cultural studies generally focus on discursive practices and the contesting constructions of knowledge or meaning in particular times and places. Empirical study of legal culture varies widely in the specific manifestations of practice mobilized as primary data. As the essays in this volume illustrate, familiar modes of data generation include written historical texts, personal interviews, court records, written legal opinions, and ethnographies. One particularly useful data resource for cultural study of law in modern societies, we think, is the various products of mass media. These might include news editorials, popular movies or television shows, novels and poetry, music, or news reporting. This chapter focuses on these last cultural texts, news articles, to study efforts of public interest lawyers to use tort lawsuits for the purpose of reforming and regulating corporate production, sales, and marketing of fast food. This specific study is part of a large multi-issue project interrogating how public interest tort litigation at once reflects and shapes political discourse about the "politics of responsibility" in the United States. We are particularly interested in the ways that the culturally prominent stigmatization of personal injury lawyers, tort plaintiffs, and personal injury litigation generally might affect efforts of public interest advocates using tort litigation to challenge corporate power and advance consumer welfare. Our essay anticipates essays regarding tort litigation in the areas of tobacco and asbestos by Epp, Mather, and Tanase in this volume.

Food Wars: Populist Litigators, Fat Warriors, and the Politics of Responsibility

Fast food has become a lightning rod for contests among many different interests and values in modern American society. It thus is important at the outset to locate the recent litigation campaigns regarding fast food within the larger organizational terrain of activists and interests regarding high-calorie, high-fat fast food as well as within the general ideological terrain of debate regarding differential responsibility for consumer health and welfare. Some sophisticated academic studies have been written recently about contemporary debates regarding obesity, casting a wary eye on the moralistic, quasi-prohibitionist campaigns for personal discipline (Kersh and Morone 2002; Saguy and Riley 2005). These studies are quite insightful, but legal activists and litigation campaigns are often overlooked or included among the moralists in simplistic and misleading ways. We thus offer a very brief classification of actors involved in the food wars, emphasizing in particular their interests and orientations to the ideological politics of assigning responsibility. These categories are ideal types, and many individuals or groups cross the boundaries of several categories. But this brief discussion at least enables us to identify the larger political debates at stake and the unique position occupied by the litigators.

We find it useful to identify five general groups of advocates in the food wars. First are the *corporate producers and vendors of fast food.* These organizations generate huge revenues and profits from fast food, which provides them considerable material interest in the defense of fast-food consumption and resistance to tort lawsuits (see Schlosser 2001). Such corporations also invest tremendous sums in advertising and market the expeditious victuals, much of the advertising aimed at young people, minority citizens, and low-income groups generally. Ideologically, they tend to urge that consumers must take responsibility for the choices of which foods and how much food they consume. In short, individual consumers must accept responsibility for their diets, and neither corporations nor the government nor the public should bear the burden or costs of unhealthy choices, although government may rightly assume some responsibility for promoting research and care for individuals whose health problems result from inherited genetic predispositions. In public forums, most corporate spokespeople support education and voice admonitions about healthy eating, although a few brazenly responded to legal challenges by parading new ultrafat products like Hardee's Monster Thickburger, Culver's Jumbo Bacon Butterburger Deluxe, and Burger King's Double Whopper with Cheese. "We've been pretty up front about what we are doing . . . People would be hard-pressed to assume it was anything other than what it was," a Hardee's spokesperson told the *Wall Street Journal* (Gray 2005). In short, the consuming public must regulate itself.

A second group involved in obesity discourse consists of *various diet peddlers and exercise gurus* who promote fitness, health, and low-fat bodies through disciplined personal effort. Like fast-food marketers, such entrepreneurs profit from their appeals to responsible individuals and market mechanisms, although their message of personal discipline typically urges abandoning or diminishing intake of fast food and spending more time in the gym than in inexpensive eateries. This message permeates contemporary mass media, thus leading some scholars to allege that the purveyors are charlatans generating a national "moral panic" about fat and health. At the same time, however, these players tend to be the least directly involved in public debates over responsibility for obesity, and they almost never participate in policy forums or address issues related to possible government responsibilities. They thus rarely show up on news coverage of the issue, so we accord them little further attention in this study.

A third group features *scientific health experts, medical specialists, and research organizations* who are concerned about obesity and lead or sponsor research into the problems of obesity and its potential remedies. This group includes many prominent advocates who appear frequently in press coverage of the obesity issue (Brownell and Horgen 2003; Nestle 2003). Although quite diverse, most players in this category agree that, as the American Obesity Association (AOA) puts it, "obesity is a leading cause of mortality, morbidity, disability, and discrimination in health care, education, and employment . . . (T)he health consequences of obesity are as significant or greater than smoking, problem alcohol consumption and poverty." Moreover, this group of advocates generally takes the most complex view of the health issue and distributes responsibility for remedies well beyond individual self-regulation. Because obesity results from a "combination of genetic, environmental, and behavioral factors," the AOA focuses its attention primarily on government responsibility and secondarily on corporate responsibility for what the association views as the "biggest health problem" facing the nation. Indeed, the AOA appeals to government for dramatically increased research support, nutrition education, consumer protection, antidiscrimination enforcement toward obese persons, increased corporate regulation by the Food and Drug Administration (FDA) and the Federal Trade Commission (FTC), insurance reform, and radically revised government investment patterns in food production subsidies and tax policies. In short, while scientific experts rarely directly bite the corporate hand that often funds them, their policy orientation to responsibility tends to differ greatly from private corporations and entrepreneurs. Some critics find these folks as misguided as the profit-driven diet gurus, but their motives are generally more benign. Because they do participate directly in public debates over responsibility for consumer health, we include their impact within our study.

The fourth group is our primary interest in this paper: the *liberal public interest litigators* who challenge fast-food vendors and producers through tort lawsuits and related forms of litigation. This too is a somewhat diverse group, although the core activists build on a history of consumer-oriented public interest litigation, were active in tobacco or other types of products litigation, and adopt a public posture clearly identified with the Naderite consumer litigation legacy of "public interest liberalism" (McCann 1986). They labor the hardest to shift the focus away from individual responsibility for unhealthy diets and to the shared responsibility of corporate vendors and government regulators who are supposed to serve the public interest. Indeed, the primary concern of these activists is to use tort law to increase corporate accountability and government action to ensure responsible corporate action in food production and marketing. At best, consumer health is just one of many benefits from the campaign for corporate responsibility, transparency, and responsiveness to concerns about social justice. This point is illustrated by one of the most celebrated legal actions by fast-food litigators, the successful case exposing McDonald's famous french fries as less than fully vegetarian. While health issues were at stake, the case was won by arguing how corporate deception caused a Hindu consumer to transgress his religious code, and its primary gain was in advancing corporate honesty and transparency in marketing. In short, most fast-food litigation has aimed primarily to highlight a mix of corporate and government responsibility for issues of consumer welfare and justice.

Finally, a fifth advocacy group has battled to challenge social practices, especially by corporations, that discriminate against obese persons (see Kirkland 2008). These *antidiscrimination activists* for "fat rights" shift attention away from obesity as a health problem and toward its manifestation as a social justice issue. Like the consumer accountability activists, antidiscrimination activists focus on corporate irresponsibility—both by employers and peddlers of antifat services or products—as the problem and increased government responsibility as the solution. However, these activists do not generally target fast-food production or marketing, so their efforts are outside the scope of this study.

Relationships Among Key Actors

Fast-food litigators most often find themselves in direct opposition to corporate interests and their political supporters. Where the latter trumpet individual responsibility and market solutions, the former identify corporations and their control over markets as the problem and responsive government—whether courts, legislators, or administrative bodies—as the solution. Fast-food litigators thus typically find themselves as uneasy allies with health experts, who also look to increase government action for promoting consumer welfare but are less openly hostile to corporations, less committed to democratic accountability as an end or means, and generally far less politically adversarial or partisan. It seems fair to say that litigators depend on the scientific experts to advance their cause far more than do health experts depend on, and actively ally with, the experts. Our study will investigate some continuities and some divergences in media coverage of actions and agendas initiated by these two groups.

Food Wars: Legal Framing Strategies Derived from the Tobacco Wars

A few years old, the legal campaign against the allegedly deceptive marketing and consumption of fattening foods pursues long- and short-term strategies shaped in part by successful legal campaigns against tobacco corporations in the 1990s. After decades of failed efforts to use judicial proceedings to call Big Tobacco to account for its deceptive marketing of its addictive, deadly products, both private and public trial attorneys scored impressive victories and fees in the courtroom, then in backroom bargaining, during the second half of the 1990s. Several of the attorneys who landed blows for both the public good and their private bank accounts in fighting tobacco quickly saw new possibilities for health reforms in challenging fast-food producers on similar grounds. The earlier campaign provided a corps of experienced reform leaders, a potentially winning legal strategy, and substantial financial resources for the crusade against fatty foods.

Tobacco Wars produced only minimal regulatory control and no victories in the courtroom from the 1950s through the late 1980s (Haltom and McCann 2004; Mather 1998). The tobacco industry, which generated many billions of dollars in revenue each year, simply had too much political and social power for conventional tort litigation. In specific engagements, armies of tobacco lawyers used what one observer called "Scorched Earth, Walls of Flesh" (Zegart 2000, 85) tactics to destroy challengers. Beyond courtrooms, Big Tobacco expended considerable resources for campaign financing and congressional lobbying schemes; reminded Americans how many jobs in production and especially retail sales enriched the citizenry and the nation; and relied on state and federal governments to recognize their enormous revenues from taxing tobacco sales. The tobacco industry also developed a powerful ideological defense. It effectively mobilized the traditional American ideals of "individual responsibility" to insulate its production and profiteering from public control. After all, tobacco spokespersons repeated, consumers must bear the burden for the products that they buy and ingest. This is why in the 1960s, when it could no longer deny the well-demonstrated health dangers from tobacco consumption, the industry agreed to federal requirements about publicizing such dangers in the marketing and packaging of their products, thus somewhat ironically further reducing corporate liability for consumer choices because consumers could no longer plead ignorance about health risks (Haltom and McCann 2004, ch. 7).

Health advocates, public interest groups, and lonely legal crusaders are as materially disadvantaged against Big Mac as were the diminutive political Davids challenging the Goliath of Big Tobacco. Like tobacco, the vending and marketing of fast food generate billions of dollars yearly for corporations capable of wielding considerable clout in Congress and throughout the regulatory establishment despite the FDA or other officials. Like tobacco, fast food provides a steady diet of jobs, sales revenues, and taxes on which government leaders depend. Traditional lobbying efforts to put the issue on the legislative agenda have been an important part of the new consumer movement against the fast-food industry, but, as on many other issues, reformers recognize the low chances for success by this route alone.

Moreover, the traditional American ethic of "individual responsibility" has presented an even more formidable cultural stumbling block for reformers using tort litigation against the fast-food industry because fast food differs from tobacco in at least three fundamental ways. First, fast food has not been demonstrated to be physically addictive in the ways that eventually were proved for tobacco, so consumers' choices of different foods are arguably less fettered than the actions of dependent, needy nicotine users. Second, whereas the health risks of tobacco can be isolated and vary little with exogenous factors, the dangers of fast food are inseparable from the effects of other life choices about exercise, overall diet, and the like as well as genetic predispositions. Demonstrating how fast food contributes to heart attacks thus is more difficult than making the causal linkage between a lifetime of smoking and lung cancer. A third related difference is that small uses of tobacco have been proven to be dangerous, both in contributing to long-term health risks and raising the risk of addiction. This is not true for fatty fast foods, which seem to pose little risk when eaten in moderation. Both institutionally and ideologically, then, the challenges facing fast-food warriors in courts of law and mass-mediated society parallel but exceed those for anti-tobacco reformers.

Nevertheless, the new advocates of consumer health have resorted to institutional strategies developed by previous generations of liberal public interest advocates—targeted personal injury litigation coordinated with multidimensional publicity campaigns exposing the irresponsible actions of corporate producers and the dangers of their products. Strategic litigators aimed to bypass some of the formidable institutional capacities of corporations to block congressional and bureaucratic initiatives while focusing attention directly on specific wrongdoers. Moreover, many activists believe that litigation is a very effective way to draw press attention, increase public consciousness, and leverage elite support for expanded state policy initiatives involving public health risks. Individual cases of litigation have generated modest attention from the press, while the overall legal campaign has generated considerable attention in a short time.

Less strategically and more tactically, litigation-minded food fighters followed the antitobacco strategists' three most effective substantive claims to advance their respective cases before the courts of judges, juries, and public opinion alike. First, the antitobacco campaign accelerated in the late 1980s and 1990s when litigation revealed conclusively a long history of deception and duplicity by industry officials. These exposures significantly undermined the credibility of corporate producers and marketers as well as their claims about the informed, free choices of consumers. Critics of the fast-food industry have similarly leveled the claim about inadequate disclosure and even deception. Virtually every lawsuit has contended that fast-food marketers fail to produce adequate or accurate information about fat, sugar, and chemical contents of the expeditious victuals they peddle. Such was at the heart of the claim by Hindus and other vegetarians against McDonald's about misrepresentation of french fries, a claim that produced a formal apology and a $12 million settlement. It also was the core point of the argument by Caesar Barber, who filed legal claims challenging McDonald's, Burger King, Wendy's, and KFC for his excessive, dangerous weight. Judges in a number of cases have explicitly opened the door for further litigation on this claim about misrepresentation of information to consumers.[1]

Second, just as antismoking activists spotlighted marketing to and addiction of children, both scientific and legal challengers to the fast-food industry have targeted corporate marketing aimed at impressionable children. "Everybody is looking at children as the vulnerable point in this," notes Marion Nestle, a professor of nutrition at New York University (Stern 2004; see also Nestle 2003). One notable campaign in Seattle pressured the school board to reject the exclusive contracts with Coca Cola for school vending machines that came with corporate payouts to the underfunded districts. As in tobacco cases, corporate profiteering from junk food sales at the expense of the most vulnerable consumers proved to be a promising target in the courts and mass media alike.

Third, the biggest transformation in the antitobacco campaign came when state attorneys general shifted the debate over the relative responsibility of consumer choices about whether to smoke to the involuntarily assumed public costs of health care caused by tobacco sales (Mather 1998, 2008). Attorneys showed that smoking imposed billions of dollars in tax and insurance costs paid by ordinary people who never lit up the noxious product. These claims became the basis for massive lawsuits and state-negotiated payouts by the tobacco industry in the late 1990s, in many ways fundamentally redefining the terms of the battle (Haltom and McCann 2004). A similar logic seems to be the next step in the food fights as well. Fast-food critics like to cite a controversial Surgeon General's report that obesity can be linked to 300,000 deaths and $117 billion in health costs each year, almost as much as smoking, and dozens of times the costs of the Enron scandal, thus raising the question whether those who are obese or contribute to obesity should absorb their fair share of costs. Indeed, reformers cite another study showing that each obese person incurs an average of $1,500 more in annual health costs than does a healthy person (Banzhaf 2004). "Some argue that there is a right to voluntarily engage in unhealthy behaviors, but there certainly is no right to require others to subsidize the huge costs" (Banzhaf 2002, 2). Identification of collectively shared costs thus has provided a critical component of reformer appeals for an increased government role in requiring full disclosure about, in limiting production of, and in encouraging healthy alternatives to the fast food that is bloating the body politic.

As consumer activists see it, corporate deceptions, vulnerable publics, and drains on public coffers may mitigate or moderate "Individual Responsibility" perspectives, but lobbyists and campaign contributors stymie reforms in legislatures. "(I)f legislators don't legislate, then litigators will litigate" (Banzhaf 2004). Tort litigation offers a twofold promise. Successful litigation might directly force corporations to internalize some costs of marketing or production and, hence, alter their practices (Banzhaf 2002). This would require huge punitive damages awards, which may be unlikely in the near term. A second, short-run promise of litigation is to get the general issue onto the public agenda and to mobilize support for legislative or other forms of governmental regulatory action.

Publicization and mobilization through lawsuits, however, depend on the efficacy of litigation strategies to overcome powerful, persisting perspectives through "frame-breakers" such as the three strategic gambits adapted from the Tobacco Wars. Of course, if such strategies are to succeed, the agents who execute the stratagems cannot interfere with or contradict the reframing activities. If food fights are to emulate successes in the Tobacco Wars, food fighters must strike poses and craft tactics that complement strategic themes such as those rehearsed above.

Food Fighters' Legal Tactics Against Fat and Fast Food

Among other litigation-oriented food fighters, John Banzhaf III, an energetic professor at the George Washington School of Law and a public interest lawyer, has formulated the reframing strategies reviewed earlier. Deemed a "Trial Lawyer's Trial Lawyer" and one of the 100 most influential people in Washington DC, Banzhaf developed his reputation as founder of the Action on Smoking and Health (ASH) campaign fighting Big Tobacco, winning him designation as the "Ralph Nader of the Tobacco Industry." He loves to generate publicity for his legal campaigns and is successful at litigating and publicizing, as his Web site attests (http://banzhaf.net/). Perhaps no one has contributed more to making the

Big Mac "rival Big Tobacco as public health enemy No. 1 in the nation's courts" (Stern 2002). Banzhaf and his students have sponsored or consulted in much of the most important litigation efforts against the fast-food industry to date.

Banzhaf's crusades against Big Tobacco and various other corporate practices have earned him a variety of unflattering designations, including "radical," "legal flamethrower," and even "legal terrorist" (see Banzhaf 2004). This is one reason why Banzhaf always makes it clear that "not only does he not make a cent from the suits that he inspires, he would, in fact, much rather not bring them in the first place. He would love it if the government would overhaul the food industry to make people healthier, just as he would have preferred the government to take action on smoking unprompted" (Stern 2002). In short, Banzhaf assiduously anticipates and rebuffs charges by critics that he is greedy, litigious, and irresponsible. Instead, he proudly displays the mantle of the responsible public citizen and legal leader seeking sensible legislative and administrative policy reform.

Banzhaf's attention to creating both an image as a ferocious adversary of irresponsible corporate power and an image as a public-interested idealist exemplify the self-conscious efforts of the new health litigators to portray themselves as pure, noble, publicly spirited, and credible advocates for change. No doubt these reform lawyers are very aware of the pervasive negative images of trial lawyers and civil plaintiffs as inherently greedy, opportunistic, and manipulative (Galanter 2005).[2]

News Coverage of Food Fights

The strategies and tactics of campaigns against obesity, fat, and fast food tend to generate coverage in major U.S. newspapers, but findings suggest that the *quantity* of attention may be less than crusaders anticipate and that the *quality* of such coverage may cut against crusaders' designs. We have analyzed how articles, features, and editorials characterized strategic *frames* regarding responsibility and tactical *participants* in fights over fast foods. Whether the context involves litigation or not, reformers tend to confront a marked tilt toward "individual responsibility" frames relative to frames that publicize "corporate responsibility" or "governmental responsibility." In newspapers' spot coverage of specific cases or of general litigation, the predominance of individual responsibility frames is exacerbated. Even spot reports tend to characterize participants in "food fights" differentially. Plaintiffs and plaintiffs' attorneys are described in net-negative terms, while civil defendants and their attorneys often are not described at all.

Methodology

Our methodology for the study was simple and relatively orthodox. We first ran two searches in LexisNexis Academic for 2002 and 2003, when the most prominent lawsuits made the news.[3] Nondomestic newspapers,[4] irrelevant articles, and duplicated stories discarded, the search netted 166[5] articles in which obesity litigation had been prominently featured in major domestic newspapers over this period and 264 articles that did not involve litigative efforts but concerned crusades against obesity, fat, or fast food. Articles were coded by trained research assistants according to schemes grounded in earlier studies and revised after experimentation in pilot studies. The coding aimed to discern conceptual themes (frames) used to make sense of the disputes or issues at stake as well as characterizations of actors and their motives. The 166 articles in the Litigation Sample yielded 1,548 coded frames and 3,731 coded actors. In the 264 articles in the Non-Litigation Sample, coders found 2,098 frames and 6,407 characterized actors.

Responsibilizing Framing

Table 6.1 reveals interesting consistencies and fascinating variations across thematic frames. We restrict ourselves here to advantages and disadvantages that appear in the sampled coverage from leading U.S. newspapers. From these data, articles about litigation appear to emphasize the responsibility and duplicity of corporate entities substantially more than do articles that raised no specific cases or litigation campaigns. However, articles that mentioned no specific lawsuits tended to sound themes of governmental and of parental responsibility much more often than articles that featured specific lawsuits or litigation. At best, Table 6.1 makes food litigation to date seem to produce mixed results in publicizing its preferred frames in newspapers and, by transitivity, in other mass media informed to a significant degree by newspapers' coverage. Let us review Table 6.1 in some detail.

Whatever else they may do, articles consistently discuss differential responsibilities for consumer welfare. In our combined sample of 430 articles, we found

TABLE 6.1

Frames Mentioned in Newspapers, 2002–2003

Each cell features the column percentage in its upper left corner and the number of cases in its lower *right corner*.	Litigation Sample		Non-Litigation Sample		Totals across Samples	
Individual Responsibility	38%		37%		37%	
		588		767		1355
Corporate Responsibility	30%		23%		26%	
		463		475		938
Governmental Responsibility	4%		14%		10%	
		62		288		350
Parental Responsibility	4%		13%		9%	
		59		275		334
Corporate Duplicity	13%		4%		8%	
		193		93		286
Plaintiffs & Corporations Share Responsibility	4%		6%		5%	
		63		130		193
Attorneys' Fees or Motives	6%		0%		3%	
		98		1		99
Public Costs	1%		3%		2%	
		17		69		86
Column Totals	100%		100%		100%	
		1543		2098		3641

SOURCE: Original data are with the authors.

3,456 references to one of our various responsibility frames. This underlines that "the politics of responsibility" is very much at the heart of fast-food fights in and out of courts, as it is in most areas of American politics.[6] The two frames most commonly coded—"Individual Responsibility" and "Corporate Responsibility"— accounted for nearly two-thirds of all themes detected (and nearly three-fourths of responsibility themes). Governmental and parental responsibility each added about one-tenth of frames coded. Explicit references to the perspective that consumers and corporations might or should share responsibility appeared in only about one coding in twenty.

When we contrast litigation and nonlitigation samples, different patterns of responsibilities emerge. The columnar percentages for "Individual Responsibility" and "Plaintiffs and Corporations Share Responsibility" are quite similar whether articles mention litigation or not. Of course, "Individual Responsibility" is the far more common frame by a factor of six or more. Articles that mentioned civil actions yielded "Corporate Responsibility" considerably more often (by columnar percentages) than did articles that did not raise litigation, so litigation strategies and tactics may increase the net likelihood that the populist anti-corporate frame will reach readers and journalists who build on newspapers' coverage.[7] In this regard, the legal activists had some success in preaching their message and identifying their foes. By contrast, the "Non-Litigation Sample" features more than three times more uses (by columnar percentages) of "Governmental Responsibility" than does the "Litigation Sample"; by absolute numbers the ratios approach five to one.[8] In sum, coverage of litigation in general or of specific lawsuits tends to promote relative emphasis on the responsibility (and the duplicity) of food producers and marketers but also tends to retard relatively the discussion of governmental responsibility.

Adding other frames to attributions of responsibility, we note as we scan the "Litigation" column that the two most common prodefendant frames ("Individual Responsibility" and "Attorneys' Fees or Motives") slightly outnumbered pro-plaintiff frames ("Corporate Responsibility" and "Corporate Duplicity"), while in "Non-Litigation" articles "Individual Responsibility" alone offset attributions of corporate and governmental responsibility combined. If "Parental Responsibility" is understood as a variant on individual responsibility and hence favored by civil defendants, then the two most common prodefendant themes account for nearly half of all detected themes in "Non-Litigation" articles.

Frame analysis results in a complex set of patterns, but one conclusion seems unambiguous in Table 6.1: "Individual Responsibility" is nearly a constant by columnar percentage. Thus, the cultural frame most advantageous to defendants in food fights (whether inside or outside courtrooms) is not dislodged or attenuated by coverage of litigation in general or of specific cases. The relative gains in attributions of corporate duplicity and corporate responsibility in reports of cases might justify uses of tort litigation to publicize food fighting, but such gains might be offset by declining attention to the responsibility borne by governments, not to mention that articles that do not mention lawsuits are almost devoid of attacks on the motives and billing of attorneys. In short, litigation has produced coverage targeting its corporate foes, but this frame falls well short of attention to personal discipline, and the effort to elevate government duties has failed miserably. Lawsuits are presented as contests between private parties, consumer plaintiffs, and corporate foes, with the latter receiving less "blame" (attribution of responsibility) than the former, while government is largely out of the picture except perhaps as a disinterested adjudicator of the dispute.

Portraying the Players

Coding characterizations of prominent agents and actors produced more dramatic, less ambiguous results. Coders were asked to mark each time a positive or negative descriptive term was used regarding the personal character or motivation of one or more participants in disputes about fast food. Such descriptive terms are especially important in stories that focus on locating subject responsibility, for they mark subjects as either deserving or undeserving of respect, credibility, support, or sympathy. At lawslore.info/ we explain how coders enumerated characterizations of eleven actors or agents.[9] Table 6.2 summarizes characterizations.

The totals of references (rightmost column) differ greatly between samples.[10] Articles in the Litigation Sample characterized corporate defendants, consumer plaintiffs, or plaintiffs' attorneys four out of five references (79 percent). In the Non-Litigation Sample, corporate defendants and consumer plaintiffs accounted for 68 percent of characterizations, although lawyers for consumers or victims plummeted almost to zero. Moreover, the two most referenced sets of actors reversed their positions: Corporations or Defendants plunged from 39 percent of all references among Litigation articles to 25 percent of all references among Non-Litigation articles; Consumers or Victims climbed from 30 percent to 43 percent of all references. References to government or to experts were twice as common by percentage among Non-Litigation articles as among Litigation articles. Other actors were addressed seldom.

Most profiles of positive, negative, and neutral references also differed markedly across the samples.

- Corporations and defendants did not vary much; negative characterizations of civil defendants outnumbered positive depictions by two to one in each sample.
- The ratio of positive to negative references for consumer-plaintiffs plunged from almost 8:1 in the Litigation Sample to "merely" about 3:1 in the Non-Litigation Sample even as the overall proportion of references to civil plaintiffs increased by about 43 percent in the latter sample.
- Descriptors of plaintiffs' attorneys, more than 5:1 negative in the Litigation Sample, were almost absent in other articles.
- "Government" and "Experts" alike were almost twice as prominent by percentage among Non-Litigation articles as among Litigation articles

TABLE 6.2

References to Actors in 2002–2003 Articles on Food-Related Litigation

Litigation Sample

Actors/Agents	Positive		Neutral		Negative		Total		
	n	row %	n	row %	n	row %	n	row %	col %
Corporations/Defendant(s)	286	20	596	41	570	39	1452	100	39
Consumers/Plaintiff(s)	83	7	416	37	631	56	1130	100	30
Victims' Attorney(s)	25	7	224	59	131	35	380	100	10
Government(s)	17	9	153	78	27	14	197	100	5
Expert(s)	3	2	157	94	8	5	168	100	5
Judge(s)	7	6	103	94	0	0	110	100	3
Corporate Interests/Group(s)	1	1	104	98	1	1	106	100	3
Public Interest Group(s)	2	2	55	62	32	36	89	100	2
Medical Doctor(s)	0	0	53	86	9	15	62	100	2
Corporate/Defense Attorney(s)	2	7	26	87	2	7	30	100	1
Diet Peddler(s)	0	0	2	29	5	71	7	100	0
Litigation Totals	426	11	1889	51	1416	38	3731	100	100

Nonlitigation Sample

Actors/Agents	Positive		Neutral		Negative		Total		
	n	row %	n	row %	n	row %	n	row %	col %
Corporations/Defendant(s)	338	21	630	39	633	40	1601	100	25
Consumers/Victim(s)	326	12	1442	53	953	35	2721	100	43
Victims' Attorney(s)	0	0	3	75	1	25	4	100	0
Government(s)	107	18	360	62	115	20	582	100	9
Expert(s)	20	3	604	96	8	1	632	100	10
Judge(s)	0	0	3	100	0	0	3	100	0
Corporate Interests/Group(s)	6	5	101	87	9	8	116	100	2
Public Interest Group(s)	27	11	188	79	23	10	238	100	4
Medical Doctor(s)	19	6	269	88	18	6	306	100	5
Corporate/Defense Attorney(s)	0	0	0	0	0	0	0	100	0
Diet Peddler(s)	60	32	108	58	17	9	185	100	3
Nonlitigation Totals	903	14	3708	58	1777	28	6388	100	100

SOURCE: Original data are with the authors.

and approached a rough balance of valence in part due to the preponderance of neutral references.

- Assessments of corporate interest and public interest groups were not common and tended to be neutral, the ratio of negatives to positives for public interest groups notwithstanding.
- Defense attorneys had almost no profile in either sample.

Table 6.2 suggests that Litigation articles paint a far more negative picture of tort litigation as a forum for the food fights than do other articles. Corporations and other civil defendants come off about as well in one sample as the other, but plaintiffs and consumers fare far worse in articles that generally or specifically raise lawsuits. Disadvantage food fighters! Legal representatives for self-styled victims, almost invisible when litigations are not invoked, become a substantially negative feature of litigation coverage. Meanwhile, counsel for corporations are virtually uncovered.

In sum, newspapers dramatically reproduced and amplified assaults by corporations and their front groups on advocates of consumers' rights and mobilizers of legal crusades seeking to expand public policy. One need not agree with the ends or means of junk-food fighters to recognize their failure in shaping how newspapers portray, and hence influence, the struggle to reassign responsibility. These dominant narratives that circulate in our mass culture not only discredit legal mobilization campaigns but defame the causes themselves by debasing the victims and their representatives.

Beyond the Numbers: A Brief Look at Sample Text

Readers at this point may be weary and wary of our numbers. Hence we provide a brief glimpse of actual characterizations of lawsuits, examining the case of Caesar Barber's legal claim against five fast-food restaurants. The interplay of caricatures of the plaintiff and ridicule of his attempted reframing exposes the considerable costs of publicization through litigation.

Barber's lawsuit was covered gleefully in scores of print and electronic news venues. The articles that we surveyed were cast in the mold of standard legal lore about frivolous litigation—focusing on the outrageous claim and obese, seemingly undisciplined character of the plaintiff, accented by assessments that the lawsuit was "ridiculous," "senseless," baseless," "irresponsible," "frivolous," and the like. Headlines underlined the message with parody: "Whopper of a Lawsuit" (*ABC NEWS.com*), "Want a class-action with that burger? (*FOXNEWS*), "Lawsuit: Hold the Fat" (*Newsday*); "Fast Food Junkies Sue Eateries Over Fatty Food" (*Boston Herald*); "Would you like fries with that lawsuit?" (*CNN*). Opinion essays quickly followed, with titles such as: "Fat Police Are Here," "Sue Your Way to Fame and Fortune," "In war on fat, it's the food's fault," and "Burger fans view lawsuit as bum steer," which ends with the line "We sue too much in this country" (Michael Stetz, *San Diego Union-Tribune*). In the *Time Online* commentary, "A lawsuit to choke on," the editorialist concluded that "Americans are going to have to decide if they want to be treated like adults." "It's not your fault. And there's money to be made," noted columnist Kathleen Parker. An *Online News* alternative website stated what most journalists hinted at more subtly: "Big Fat Man Sues Self for Being Such a Dumbass."

Even the careful, astute reader might miss, amid such jocular condescension, that this lawsuit, like others, was a classic act of legal mobilization to draw public attention to the issue of fast-food vendors' pervasive deceptions, the huge profits that they provide, the collective costs they impose, and the need for government regulatory action (see Mather 1998; McCann 1994). Only a few stories noted as well the fact that doctors, nutrition experts, consumer groups, and even FDA officials and the Surgeon General praised the lawsuit for raising an important public issue. Meanwhile, corporate-funded opponents displayed their art by quickly making the story another memorable, if quite distorted, icon. One group ran a prominent full-page ad in major magazines, showing a huge naked belly falling over belted pants, bearing the title "Did you hear the one about the fat guy suing the restaurants? It's no joke. He claims the food was too cheap so he ate too much! Learn more about the erosion of personal responsibility and common sense. Go to: ConsumerFreedom.com." A second ad dressed up the picture with $100 bills tucked into the tight jeans, and the headline "Trial lawyers' next cash cow." That may not be the last word, but it surely seems to capture the reigning conventional wisdom reproduced by news media at this moment in history.

Implications

We develop two different levels of generalizable implications from the findings presented previously.

The Limits of Tort Litigation in Shaping Public Agendas

Tables 6.1 and 6.2 make us question any presumption that publicity is an unalloyed resource for fast-food fighters. Our framing analysis of news constructions of the junk-food fights confirms the cultural challenge that confronts corporate reformers (see Hans 2000; Saad 2003). The individual responsibility ethic and "blame game" logics in news narratives about tort litigation inform our legal system and broader culture. This benefits private diet gurus and exercise peddlers as well as corporate producers but disadvantages those who seek a larger role for government in counterbalancing each. Moreover, the uneven, often subtle, but undeniable tendency to stigmatize plaintiffs as irresponsible, undisciplined, and greedy and to debase the normative designs and political message of their litigation campaign likewise burdens litigation. Hindu vegetarians suing McDonald's over latent beef products in french fries got reasonably balanced coverage—perhaps due to the principled, religious lifestyles and the explicitly deceptive corporate practices they documented—but an overweight working-class African American male received quite negative treatment, perhaps reflecting ways in which his obesity was filtered through a lens of racial and class stereotypes. Finally, trial lawyers representing consumer plaintiffs in tort suits, despite self-conscious efforts to act in a self-sacrificing and publicly spirited manner, have garnered unflattering treatment in news coverage.

If coverage of food fights parallels and reinforces findings about antitobacco litigation, that need not mean that litigation wastes reformers' time and resources. After all, tobacco litigation forced massive buyouts by corporate producers of tobacco and some modest changes in marketing practices. Likewise, a few fast-food restaurant chains, most notably McDonald's, moderated "supersizing" practices and added ostensibly healthy, low-calorie items (adult Happy Meals, salads)—for health-conscious adults—to their menus in the aftermath of several lawsuits. But other restaurants defiantly added larger, higher calorie, and more fatty products as well (Gray 2005). More important, litigators aiming to pin responsibility on corporate foes do not automatically foment discussions of expanded government regulation, insurance reform, increased medical benefit subsidies, or other statist policies at odds with individualistic, "blame game" frames privileged by tort law. Indeed, litigators who seek to reassign responsibility for widespread harms may impede and divert the very agendas they would set. It is almost astounding, for example, that the debate over fast food has barely acknowledged the class-based factors at stake in consumption of food that is, above all, cheap and accessible and heavily marketed as well as fast (see Associated Press 2004; Torrant 2003).[11] All in all, these data incline us to doubt that tort litigation to increase consumer health against corporate profit-making capacities will be able to surmount obstacles from mass-communication processes and practices.

The Mass Production of Legal Culture

Most generally, we want to suggest through our study that the mass media play a fundamental role in the production and reproduction of law itself. After all, we live in a cultural environment where images of law saturate the news we read, the television shows and movies we watch, the novels we indulge, the cartoons that make us laugh, the jokes we exchange with each other, the entire range of mass-mediated knowledge. To the extent that law is understood as a body of knowledge, a complex tradition of discourses, symbols, logics, and modes of reasoning, so must we confront the means by which that knowledge is generated, circulated, consumed, and incorporated into practical action. It is not enough to recognize, with realists, the gap between popular narratives and official practice, between legal fantasy and legal reality. Nor is it enough to follow some cultural scholars in simply interrogating isolated cultural texts. Rather, the narratives about law that we absorb from corporate-produced entertainment and infotainment become essential parts of our legal imagination, vivid referents that constitute our actions as legal subjects in everyday life—as jurors, lawyers, and officials, but also as workers, students, consumers, neighbors, family members, and the like. To put it most plainly, newspapers, magazines, television shows, and other organs of the mass media are every bit as much institutions of legal construction (including torts) as are judicial trials, administrative rule-making processes, and police decisions in the street. Indeed, citizens act on mass-produced images, understandings, and expectations identified with law as they assume roles as legal actors, infusing official legal processes with constructions of the "outside" mass culture, verifying a continuous circulation of knowledge that we identify as law, as legal "reality," across the many domains of modern life. Regardless of the institutional site where legal practice is studied, we miss a great deal if we ignore the degree to which mass-produced knowledge of and about tort law is present and powerful, contributing to the ongoing constitution of legality.[12]

PART III

Injury and Identity

Race, Gender, Sexuality, and Tort Law

Discrimination and Outrage

Exploring the Gap Between Civil Rights and Tort Recoveries

MARTHA CHAMALLAS

The connection between tort law—the premier system designed to protect against civil wrongs—and civil rights is an undertheorized topic that only sporadically attracts the attention of scholars. It is not always appreciated that proven discrimination on the basis of race or sex may not amount to a tort and that even persistent racial or sexual harassment may not be enough to qualify for tort recovery. In the law school curriculum, for example, discussions of social equality tend to be confined to public law courses, such as constitutional law or employment discrimination.

For quite some time, the best candidate for situating a tort claim for discriminatory behavior has been the tort of "outrage," or "intentional infliction of emotional distress," as it is commonly referred to, with its key threshold requirement of proof of "extreme and outrageous" conduct on the part of the defendant. At first blush, the intentional infliction tort seems particularly well suited to capture harassment and other discriminatory harms that create hostile environments for targeted groups of workers: unlike many other tort claims, it dispenses with the need to prove physical harm and responds to an abusive course of conduct over a period of time, rather than simply to discrete harmful acts. So far, however, the use of the intentional infliction tort for this purpose has been limited and erratic. A variety of legal and cultural forces have served to keep civil rights in its place and preserve tort law for more traditionally framed dignitary harms divorced from considerations of equality.

The particular focus of this chapter is on the intersection of torts and civil rights law, the place where outrage and discrimination meet. It is part of a larger inquiry into the degree to which the concepts and values of civil rights law have migrated or can be expected to migrate into tort law (Chamallas and Wriggins 2009). Through interrogating the development of the intentional infliction tort, this chapter highlights some important ways in which tort law has reflected and been constrained by prevailing cultural views about the nature of serious injury and the boundaries of decent behavior. In particular, the topic provides an opportunity to see how gender ideology has both facilitated and closed off recovery for so-called "dignitary" harms that produce emotional distress. The evolution of the infliction tort also offers a case study into the relationship between law and cultural change, exploring how initial doctrinal conceptions and the original framing of a cause of action can affect later judicial interpretations and block new cultural norms from finding their way into the law.

This chapter begins with a brief description of the current legal terrain. I then present a history of the intentional infliction tort, with particular emphasis on how early courts and commentators treated issues of gender, race, and sexuality. The chapter then chronicles feminist criticism of and attraction to the tort after civil rights, reflecting a continuing struggle to find the right "location" for claims of sexual exploitation and demands for recognition of sexual autonomy. I conclude by explaining why some progressive scholars have recently taken a turn toward tort law with its universal principles, in recognition of the limitations of the identity-based approach of civil rights.

The Current Legal Terrain

At present, the laws regulating cases of discriminatory workplace harassment are technically complex and vary greatly from state to state. Victims of sexual, racial, or other kinds of discriminatory harassment typically may assert at least three potential claims: a federal and a state statutory civil rights claim for discrimination and a tort claim for intentional infliction of emotional distress. From a practical perspective, the advantage of bringing a tort claim for plaintiffs is that it offers the prospect of greater amounts of damages, in contrast to recoveries under civil rights statutes which typically impose a low cap on damages. Indeed, a recent empirical study of sexual harassment cases conducted by Professor Catherine Sharkey found that including a tort claim in such cases increased an award on average by $137,176 after controlling for independent variables that might affect the level of damages (Sharkey 2006, 39).

Beyond this immediate practical impact, however, the degree of migration from civil rights to torts is also a significant index of cultural transformation, a marker of whether new understandings of categories such as "sexual harassment" and "hostile environment" have become mainstream and have altered traditional thinking about the proper domain of tort law. As one leading commentator on the subject has stated, when a court declares that a recurring type of conduct is "outrageous," it is making "an official determination of the moral seriousness of the conduct" (Givelber 1982, 52).

That civil rights would migrate from its "home" in constitutional and antidiscrimination law into other areas is not surprising, given that the antidiscrimination principle is now a widely shared cultural norm (Koppleman 1996, 1). The harms of discrimination have been extensively catalogued and theorized, both in the debate over "hate" crimes and through the development of various theories of discrimination under the U.S. Constitution, federal civil rights law, and related state statutes (Franke 1997, 691; Lenhardt 2004, 803; Wang 1997, 47). What has emerged is a multifaceted injury—with both a personal and a social dimension—that can now be transported and absorbed into preexisting bodies of law.

Predictably, however, given the strong countervailing social forces, the migration from civil rights to torts has also been vigorously resisted. The contemporary legal picture of the intentional infliction tort reflects this struggle. Currently, there is considerable variation in treatment among the states, ranging from hefty migration in some states to a complete cut off of torts claims in others. Through the complex welter of cases, one can see two basic approaches: The majority of courts treat the claim of intentional infliction as a mere "gap filler" that comes into play only when no other remedy is available. A minority of states, however, treat the claim as an independent cause of action that provides mutual reinforcement for civil rights as an important public policy of the state.

Some "gap filler" states set the bar of proof of "outrageousness" so high that they allow recovery only in extremely aggravated cases—some might say bizarre cases—that do not resemble the typical hostile working environment case which, by definition, already entails proof of severe or pervasive harassment (*Hoffman-LaRoche, Inc. v. Zeltwanger* 2004, 447). The mutual reinforcement states, on the other hand, are more likely to find the defendant's conduct outrageous if it also violates civil rights provisions (*Coates v. Wal-Mart Stores, Inc.* 1999, 1001–1008). These courts find it fitting that the state's public policy is expressed in both domains. Lower courts in California, for example, have even adopted a per se approach in harassment cases in which a violation of state civil rights law automatically results in a finding of outrageousness (*Fisher v. San Pedro Peninsula Hospital* 1989, 858).

The Tort of Intentional Infliction Before Civil Rights

The current reluctance to use the intentional infliction tort as a vehicle for civil rights is partly rooted in legal tradition. The traditional framing of the tort has had a long shelf life, outlasting the social norms and ideologies that first surrounded it. Originally, the infliction tort was part of a reform aimed at liberalizing recovery for emotional distress more generally. Unlike the statutory civil rights claims, the tort was not directed toward fostering the goal of social equality and did not arise in response to a social movement to expand civil rights. Indeed, before the mid-twentieth century, the tort was repeatedly used to reinscribe traditional gender ideologies and to reinforce race segregation and white racial privilege.

By legal standards, the intentional infliction tort is a "new" tort, established only in the late 1940s, largely through the writings and efforts of two academics, William Prosser in his role as Reporter for the Restatement (Second) of Torts, and Harvard law professor, William Magruder. In this formative period, the claim was viewed as filling an important gap or deficiency *within* tort law to provide a remedy for serious, nonphysical injury caused by behavior that seemed unquestionably immoral to judges. At the time, there was a felt need to create a new tort because the older torts—such as assault, battery, and slander—were so engrafted with technical limitations that they often did not capture some of the worst forms of intentionally harmful behavior.

Since its inception, the intentional infliction tort has been knee-deep in issues relating to gender, sexuality, and personal morality. As the tort designed to redress dignitary harms, it originally reflected dominant cultural conceptions of "male honor" and "female chastity." Thus, the early cases were primarily interested in protecting "respectable" women against conduct that threatened their reputation for sexual propriety (Pruitt 2004, 419–445). Women sometimes recovered for emotional distress when they were falsely accused of immoral sexual conduct, in cases that did not meet the technical requirements for an actionable libel.

Prosser noticed this gendered aspect of the tort early on, remarking that "nearly all the plaintiffs have been women" (Prosser 1939, 887–888). Prosser's remark about the predominance of female plaintiffs is interesting because he used it to support a broader claim that courts in intentional infliction cases had permitted recovery only in cases of "extreme" mental disturbance in which there was "convincing objective testimony to attest to its genuineness." Trading on familiar gender imagery of the fragile, female plaintiff easily hurt by callous or brutal behavior, Prosser's rhetoric was meant to allay fears that courts would be misused by plaintiffs seeking money for fictitious injuries. He had confidence that in their case-by-case adjudication, judges would be sensitive to context and could tell the "difference between violent and vile profanity addressed to a lady and the same language addressed to a Butte miner." It was self-evident to Prosser that ladies and other vulnerable persons suffered disproportionately from mental distress and should have their claims acknowledged as "real wrong[s] entitled to redress." For Prosser, the female gender of the plaintiffs served to legitimate their injuries and to justify recognition of the new tort.

This solicitude for the fragile, female plaintiff also surfaced in Magruder's seminal article on emotional disturbance (Magruder 1936, 1047–1055). Magruder was troubled by a line of slander cases in which female plaintiffs falsely accused of unchastity failed to recover because they could not prove special damages, that is, pecuniary damages stemming from injury to their reputation. One old case, for example, involved a false statement by a defendant who claimed to have had sexual intercourse with the plaintiff, a married woman (*Allsop v. Allsop* 1860, 534). When the plaintiff heard about the false rumor, she suffered humiliation and physical illness, but lost her case because she could not show pecuniary loss. Magruder considered the result unjust and declared that she should be able to recover for intentional infliction of emotional distress. In tune with prevailing attitudes among legal elites, Magruder apparently believed that accusing a married woman of adultery was clearly intolerable conduct that could be expected to result in severe emotional distress and illness. For Magruder, when it came to matters of sexual propriety, the relational and social harm of defamation converged with the more individualistic harm of emotional distress.

The sympathetic attitude of legal commentators shifted markedly, however, when the claim of injury asserted by a female plaintiff grew out of a solicitation to have sex, rather than an accusation of unchastity. Magruder is remembered for his oft-quoted assertion that "there is no harm in asking." The famous quote was actually imbedded in the following text indicating there was no clear judicial position on the issue: "Women have occasionally sought damages for mental distress and humiliation on account of being addressed by a proposal of illicit intercourse. This is peculiarly a situation where circumstances alter cases. If there has been no incidental assault or battery, or perhaps trespass to land, recovery is generally denied, the view being, apparently, that there is no harm in asking" (Magruder 1936, 1055).

Magruder's statement was somewhat cryptic because he did not directly endorse the view that sexual solicitations were intrinsically harmless, but merely speculated as to why courts might deny recovery in such cases. For a formal law review article, however, the use of the phrase was a bit flippant, and perhaps memorable for that reason. It certainly left the impression that Magruder believed that the courts were correct in their apparent belief that sexual solicitation was harmless conduct and distinguishable from more condemnable conduct, such as a false imputation of unchastity.

In later articles, Prosser reiterated the "no harm in asking" phrase and left no doubt that he also agreed with its substance (Prosser 1939, 888–889). He classified a solicitation to have sex as a mere insult or indignity which "amount[ed] to nothing more than annoyance" and contrasted it to "extreme outrage" which justified legal recovery. Prosser's demarcation line between "extreme and outrageous" conduct, on the one hand, and "mere insults, indignities, threats, annoyances, petty oppressions or other trivialities," on the other, would subsequently play a major role in the development of the intentional infliction tort, once it was included in the Restatement commentary and cited by a number of courts (Restatement of Torts 2d 1965, 73).

In addition to minimizing defendants' conduct in sexual solicitation cases, Prosser also faulted the responses of plaintiffs in such cases. He argued that if a plaintiff genuinely suffered as a result of such behavior, her suffering should be regarded as "exaggerated, unreasonable, and beneath the notice of the law." By 1956, Prosser's tone grew sarcastic. In his notable article, *Insult and Outrage*, he discussed how courts in different jurisdictions had treated the "dire affront" of "inviting an unwilling woman to illicit intercourse" (Prosser 1956, 46–47), clearly signaling that he did not regard such situations as "dire" at all. He was particularly worried that the "chivalry of the southern courts" would lead them to grant recovery in solicitation cases.

When they wrote in the mid-1930s to the mid-1950s, Prosser and Magruder were in an unusual position to shape the law, precisely because there was no settled doctrine or clear trend. The case law the professors analyzed was sparse, inconclusive, and itself reflected conflicting cultural and regional attitudes toward sexual conduct and the limits of tort law. Some courts displayed open hostility toward plaintiffs who sued for damages related to a solicitation of sex. For example, in one early New York case, a trial court brusquely dismissed a plaintiff's complaint, stating that there could be no recovery for "words of persuasion" that were meant "to induce plaintiff to grant [the defendant] the favor of sexual intercourse with him" (*Prince v. Ridge* 1900, 454–455). As Prosser's "southern chivalry" remark indicated, however, the issue was not so easy for other courts. A 1903 Kentucky appellate court, for example, gave more serious and thorough examination of a plaintiff's claim that she had been injured by a solicitation to have sex, although also ultimately denying recovery (*Reed v. Maley* 1903, 1081–1084). These courts worried that the solicitation itself could be offensive and harmful because it implied that the plaintiff was the kind of woman who might accept the offer and thereby impugn her reputation for sexual propriety.

Not surprisingly, when Prosser analyzed this body of cases, he lacked a feminist sensibility to plumb the facts to see whether there was any coercion, threat, or pressure behind a solicitation to have sex. Rather, his analysis categorized sexual solicitations uncritically as mere "offers" or "invitations" that plaintiffs were free to accept or reject. Moreover, when race entered the picture, Prosser's stance against recovery in solicitation cases intensified. Prosser singled out one case as "worthy of note" because, according to Prosser, "the lady [in the case had] accepted the invitation and then sued for the insult" (Prosser 1956, 46nn33). That case, however, involved an allegation of rape by an African American woman, Cora Scruggs, who was the lone passenger in the colored compartment of a midnight train leaving Memphis (*Dickinson v. Scruggs* 1917, 901–902). Scruggs claimed that the porter made "indecent proposals to her, offer[ed] her money and attempt[ed] familiarity with her person." She testified that she refused his advances, but that just before the train reached its destination, the porter confronted her coming out of the lavatory, pushed her back into the room and, despite her active resistance, forcibly raped her, badly injuring her back in the process.

In 1917, Scruggs won a jury trial for "assault" and was awarded $1,800 in damages. The trial court directed a verdict in her favor because it regarded Scruggs's testimony as essentially uncontradicted. Tellingly, the porter who had allegedly raped the plaintiff did not testify. In its defense, however, the railroad tried to prove that the plaintiff had "yielded for a consideration," based solely on testimony of a different porter who had allegedly spoken with the plaintiff on the return trip back to Memphis. Over the plaintiff's denials, he testified that Scruggs told him that she had given in to the porter because she was afraid of him. She purportedly also stated that because the porter never paid her the $10 and breakfast he had promised, she would make the company pay for it. By this testimony, the railroad hoped to show plaintiff was a loose woman who had agreed to have sex for money.

On appeal, the court reversed Scruggs's award and ordered a new trial. Because it viewed the testimony of the porter on the return trip as contradicting the plaintiff's testimony, it ruled that the issue of liability should have been submitted to the jury. Most importantly, the appellate court rejected the trial court's view that, standing alone, "improper advances" made to a passenger in the defendant's car would be enough to sustain the verdict. It disagreed with the trial court's view that the solicitations by the porter were actionable, even if the plaintiff eventually submitted to him and even if she were offered money for her submission.

For the appellate court, the plaintiff could not recover if it turned out that she submitted to intercourse, not out of fear alone, but for money as well. It held that "lascivious proposals, if later voluntarily accepted, would not create liability upon defendant's part." Its holding implicitly endorsed the view that in this case there was no harm in asking, the plaintiff's fear notwithstanding.

In *Insult and Outrage,* Prosser referenced *Scruggs* in his discussion of the "no harm in asking" doctrine and in support of the majority view that a solicitation for sex does not lead to liability. However, Prosser apparently misread the appellate court's opinion as containing a finding that Cora Scruggs had voluntarily agreed to have sex, rather than as a contested case in which the issue should have gone to the jury. It was in the footnote to *Scruggs* that Prosser stated that "it was worthy of note that there is at least one case in which the lady accepted the invitation and then sued for the insult" (Prosser 1956, 46nn33). He never mentioned the race of the plaintiff.

Prosser's casual and perhaps intentionally humorous mention of *Scruggs* is disturbing to the contemporary eye because it plays into pernicious stereotypes of black women as promiscuous by nature and thereby "unrapable" (Painter 1992, 209–210; Wriggins 1983, 103). His cursory classification of the case as one in which an "invitation" was "accepted" gave no hint that the plaintiff had alleged that she had been raped, that her account had been believed by the trial court, and that the alleged rapist never appeared to give testimony for the defense. Prosser's classification of the case effectively erased the plaintiff's uncontradicted allegations of fear and coercion and greatly minimized her injury.

Like most legal commentators in the pre-civil rights era, Prosser did not offer a critique of how race affected judicial treatment of claims for emotional distress. Instead, he merely noticed race as one of several cultural factors that might enter into the decision-making processes of courts and juries—most often in Southern states—when they assessed the quality of a defendant's conduct. In the 1950s, Prosser treated racial segregation as a fact of life and noted that a defendant could not be liable for "doing no more than he has a legal privilege to do, even though he may do it with very bad manners, and in doing it cause acute mental distress" (Prosser 1956, 49–62). He reported that, in the absence of some applicable state civil rights statute, there could be no liability for refusing to admit a black person to a school, restaurant, or shop. Recovery for the humiliation and wounded pride of excluded minorities was not cognizable under existing law and customs that authorized such discriminatory treatment. However, Prosser was aware that many courts did recognize and place a value on white racial privilege. He noted that, pursuant to the common carrier rule, white plaintiffs had recovered for their distress at being put in a Jim Crow car, characterizing such conduct as a "gross insult" and "of a kind highly offensive to a reasonable man."

As described in Jennifer Wriggins's chapter (this volume) *Whiteness, Equal Treatment and the Valuation of Injury in Torts, 1900–1949*, a racial double standard permeated judicial decisions in the pre-civil rights era. Compare *Scruggs* to a 1905 decision from a Texas appellate court involving a claim for insult by a white female plaintiff (*Gulf C. & S.F.Ry. Co. v. Luther* 1905, 523). The case arose from an incident in the "ladies waiting room" of a railway station, reserved at that time for white women, their children, and their white male escorts. The incident occurred when one of Mrs. Luther's children spilled water from a cup onto the floor. Luther, a white married woman, claimed that the black female attendant insulted her by insinuating that her child had purposefully spilled the water and that she had looked at the plaintiff in a "vicious and angry" manner. Luther alleged that she was afraid of the attendant and suffered great mental distress as a result of the disturbing encounter. The appellate court upheld a $2,500 jury verdict, stating that the plaintiff was entitled to be "treated with respect and kindness." In striking contrast to *Scruggs,* Mrs. Luther's allegations of fear and distress were not erased or diminished. In this case, white racial privilege served to validate her claim of injury and justify an award, despite the fact that she suffered no physical assault or direct physical harm (Wriggins 2005b, 143–148).

Seen through a lens of gender and race, the history of the tort of intentional infliction of emotional distress presents a picture of limited protection against intentionally cruel and offensive behavior, largely reflective of dominant cultural attitudes toward women and racial minorities. Before the era of civil rights, courts were willing to use the new tort to protect some "respectable" white women against conduct that threatened their reputation for sexual propriety and moral rectitude. Courts used the emerging tort to reinforce prevailing standards of moral purity and redress "wounded female honor" in cases in which women claimed that they were inaccurately treated as fallen women or whores. Seen in this way, tort law helped to police what historian Judith Walkowitz describes as the boundary between "the fallen and the virtuous" and to assure that women in the latter category did not suffer in cases of "mistaken identity" (Walkowitz 1998, 7–9). Additionally, the traditionalist gender ideology served to clear the way for more expansive recovery for emotional distress within tort law (Welke 2001, 203–234). The new tort grew in part because it proved effective at reinscribing dominant cultural beliefs about white femininity.

The limited protection afforded female chastity and honor, however, did not extend to women who claimed that male solicitation of sex caused them harm. The Catch-22 logic of the traditionalist sexual ideology seem to play out in the following way: If a woman accepted the solicitation, she proved she was not respectable and did not deserve legal protection; if she rejected the solicitation, she established herself as respectable, but could not be heard to complain that she suffered cognizable harm by being required to do so. In effect, when courts refused to regard offensive solicitations, without more, as potentially actionable behavior, they placed a higher value on male sexual initiative than on female injury in cases of "mistaken identity" and required even respectable women to prove their virtue in everyday encounters.

Not surprisingly, the early cases did not use the intentional infliction tort as a means to protect an individual woman's sexual autonomy or right to self-determination. The courts were not inclined to inquire whether a woman "welcomed" the particular sexual advance or whether particular attentions were "unwanted," to borrow from the vocabulary of contemporary sexual harassment law. For the most part, tort law reflected what Professor Orit Kamir describes as an "honor culture," a cultural system highly dependent on one's relative standing in society in which "reputation is all" (Kamir 2006, 6–7). In such cultures, Kamir explains, a person's honor "can be easily lost through the slightest social error, or stolen by another" and requires "specific, daily (sometimes ritualistic) behavior" (Kamir 2006, 9) to police the boundary between the honorable and the disreputable. In the early days of the infliction tort, the assumption seemed to be that although virtuous women would, by definition, be offended by sexual overtures, men should nevertheless be given leeway to test the virtue of women, at least to some degree. This simple equation did not allow much room to investigate the meaning to be ascribed to the "solicitation" in question—whether it was a display of power, a sign of disrespect, or a show of affection—or whether the defendant's conduct could fairly even be described as a solicitation of sex. Nor did it lead courts to question the validity of the madonna/whore dichotomy that attempted to lock women's identities into stagnant sexual categories.

By the early 1960s, moreover, the leeway given to defendants in solicitation cases expanded considerably, as the notion that respectable women were offended by sexual solicitations came to seem quaint. The earlier view that had linked solicitations to have sex to a libel-like claim for impugning a woman's virtue disappeared, without yet being replaced by a new understanding of the harms that could be caused by aggressive sexual conduct. At this point in the pre-civil rights era, tort law provided a "safe haven" for male sexual initiative.

Additionally, in its early days, the abuses of power addressed by the infliction tort did not encompass abuses of white racial privilege. The infliction tort provided little protection against severe emotional distress inflicted by racist behavior, nor was it used to recognize the extreme vulnerability of racial minorities to suffering at the hands of whites. During this period, the protection against racial insult or race-based humiliation was more likely to be afforded to white than to minority plaintiffs. The mantle of respectability that allowed some white women to claim protection against emotional distress was typically denied to women of color, in line with prevailing racial stereotypes of black women as promiscuous by nature and impervious to sexualized injury. On issues of race, tort law tended to reinforce white supremacy by providing white claimants damages for the "outrage" of being treated with insufficient deference by black attendants or for mistakenly being assigned to a "colored" facility. Until the injustice of racial hi-erarchy was challenged by the civil rights movement, there was little recognition that discriminatory treatment of racial minorities might qualify as intolerable and outrageous conduct and form the basis of a tort claim for emotional distress. Before civil rights, tort law was more engaged in vindicating wounded feelings of white racial pride than in compensating for harms of racial subordination.

The Tort of Intentional Infliction After Civil Rights

Given the historical limitations of the infliction tort, it is not surprising that when Catharine MacKinnon and other feminist activists first agitated for a legal remedy for sexual harassment in the mid-1970s, they steered clear of tort law (MacKinnon 1979, 164–174). MacKinnon's case for a civil rights remedy for sex-ual harassment was predicated on what she regarded as the fundamental inad-equacy of tort law to redress systemic harms of sexual coercion. She saw a need for legal protection specifically linked to sex discrimination, arguing that tort law inevitably failed to capture the "group-defined" nature of the injury and to connect sex-linked torts to other forms of discrimination faced by women.

By locating sexual harassment claims under civil rights law, MacKinnon hoped to redirect the law away from the "disabling (and cloying) moralism" of tort law to a more equality-centered jurisprudence that comprehended sexual harassment's role in maintaining women's inferior status in the workplace. When MacKinnon's *Sexual Harassment of Working Women* was published in 1979, the time was ripe for law reform centered around identity-based concepts of discrimination, in line with the newly acquired cultural consciousness of the pervasiveness of sex discrimination forged by the second wave women's move-ment. Rather than try to remake tort doctrines to accommodate sexual harass-ment claims, MacKinnon thought it best to free sexual harassment from tort law, to give it its own name, and a home in civil rights law.

At the time, there was little awareness or discussion of same-sex harassment or other forms of abusive conduct beyond the paradigmatic male/female model of harassment by which female employees were victimized by male supervisors and co-workers. Proving that harassment was "based on sex" was then seen as giving litigants an opportunity to focus the law's attention in the right place, that is, on how women's sexuality was used to force women out of jobs, and deny them promotions and other benefits of employment. For the most part, feminist energies in the 1980s and early 1990s were poured into establishing sexual harassment as a violation of federal civil rights law. As Ann Bloom indicates in her essay, *Regulating Middlesex,* concern for addressing other forms of bias surfaced only later, after courts and scholars had struggled with the meaning of "sex" discrimination under the statute (Hebert 2001, 439; Schwartz 2002, 1697).

An early argument for revising tort law to address harassment on a more universal basis, however, came from black feminist critic, Professor Regina Austin (Austin 1988, 4–18). Her 1988 article was prescient in identifying multidimensional harassment as a major problem that tort law should address. Austin was mainly concerned with abuse suffered by low-income workers. She described how the law imposed few penalties on supervisors who routinely intimidated and ridiculed workers, provided only that they refrained from doing so in transparently racial or sexual terms. She maintained that because class oppression was not prohibited under federal civil rights law, supervisory "mistreatment that would never be tolerated if it were undertaken openly in the name of white supremacy or male patriarchy is readily justified by the privilege of status, class or color of collar" (Austin 1988, 4).

Austin was not hopeful about the prospects for meaningful tort reform, given her view that tort relief had so far been limited to "the extraordinary, the excessive and the nearly bizarre in the way of supervisor intimidation" (Austin, 1988, 18). She was not willing to give up on tort law completely, however, because of its distinctive capacity to create a norm of respectful treatment by supervisors premised on the dignity of all workers. Her article was one of the first to show how multidimensional harassment could fall through the cracks of civil rights statutes and how "racism and sexism obscure and are obscured by the perniciousness of class oppression" (Austin 1988, 4).

The arguments first presented by MacKinnon and Austin set the stage for contemporary debates about the virtues of status-based versus universal approaches to protection against harassment. Reflecting MacKinnon's legacy, there is still skepticism that tort law is so inherently individualistic and tied to outmoded gender and racial ideologies that attempts to reshape it along civil rights lines are bound to be futile (Scales 2004, 307). However, as the limitations of status-based civil rights protection have been realized in recent years, there has been a renewed interest in universalism among legal commentators (Bernstein 1997, 445; Coleman 2004, 239; Ehrenreich 1999, 1; Fisk 2001, 73; Parkes 2004, 423). Now that it looks like the federal civil rights claim is firmly established, the debate has shifted to what supplemental protection torts might provide and how the norms of tort law might be influenced by civil rights. The recent calls for reform are tempered, however, by a realization of the limits of law to effect cultural change, especially in the minefield of gender and racial politics.

In large part due to the development of the hostile environment claim under the civil rights statutes, there is now something for tort law to borrow to give meaning to outrageous conduct in intentional infliction cases. In some respects, the development of sexual harassment law in the last thirty years has been remarkable, contributing to a cultural transformation in the way sexualized conduct in the workplace is understood and evaluated, at least in some quarters (MacKinnon 2004, 672).

Simply put, the emergence of sexual harassment law has challenged the belief that there is no harm in asking. The entire body of sexual harassment law is premised on the view that solicitations for sex and other sexualized conduct in the workplace can produce harm, most notably in instances when they are backed by economic coercion or pressure or serve to reinforce the subordinate status of a group of workers. In marked contrast to the attitude of early torts cases which presumed that women were always free to accept or refuse sexual solicitations, sexual harassment law now recognizes how disparities in power and status can produce offers that cannot be refused and can construct unequal working conditions for targeted workers. This deprivatization of the injury of sexual harassment and separation of sexual harassment from the category of consensual sex was the pivotal move toward legal recognition of the claim under civil rights law. The change in vocabulary from "solicitation" to "harassment" effectively conveys the distance traveled, from harmless offer to form of abuse.

These innovations from civil rights could be transported to tort law to help make a transition from an honor-based to a dignity-based conception of outrageous conduct. Under such a dignity-based system informed by civil rights, the inquiry would center on whether defendant's conduct, as a whole, had the effect of seriously harming the plaintiff by targeting her as a second-class citizen who did not deserve to be treated with equal respect and consideration. Under this approach, the discriminatory aspect of the harassment is part of what qualifies it as outrageous conduct and sets it apart from less virulent forms of incivility, rudeness, or disrespect.

This transition from honor to dignity characterizes Canadian law, which has successfully woven equality principles into its fundamental notion of human dignity. Canadian courts see equal treatment as an essential component of human dignity, in contrast to U.S. courts which tend to separate the two concepts. Thus, the Canadian Supreme Court has defined human dignity along civil rights lines declaring that:

> Human dignity means that an individual or group feels self-respect and self-worth. It is concerned with physical and psychological integrity and empowerment. Human dignity is harmed by unfair treatment premised upon personal traits or circumstances that do not relate to individual needs, capacities, or merits. It is enhanced by laws which are sensitive to the needs, capacities, and merits of different individuals, taking into account the context underlying their differences. Human dignity is harmed when individuals and groups are marginalized, ignored or devalued. (*Law v. Canada [Minister of Employment & Immigration]* 1999: 530)

Under the Canadian vision of human dignity, it is far easier to characterize group-based forms of harassment as serious harms that warrant protection under both statutory and tort law.

Revising the tort of outrage along civil rights lines could provide redress in some cases that currently fall outside the categories of civil rights. As federal civil rights law has matured, it has become complex and rigid. Compared to the universal principles of tort law, statutory civil rights protection turns on proof of discrimination based on certain specified grounds. Thus, there are perennial struggles over what constitutes "sex-based" discrimination or what qualifies as discrimination based on race or national origin. Equally harmful and related forms of discrimination, such as discrimination based on sexual orientation or language, are not covered by federal civil rights law. Many contemporary forms of bias are hard to fit under the traditional categories. There is little space, for example, for same-sex harassment, multidimensional discrimination, or discrimination against subgroups (Chamallas 1992, 132; Crenshaw 1992, 1467; Schwartz 2002, 1697). This focus on the group status of the victim also makes it difficult to reach bias directed at persons because of how they perform their identity (e.g., the effeminate man or transgender woman) or against persons who refuse to cover their identity and resist assimilation (e.g., the African American woman who wears corn rows) (Caldwell 1991, 769; Carbado and Gulati 2000, 1259; Case 1995, 31; Yoshino 2002, 769). Although scholars have called for expanding the meaning of race and sex discrimination to reach such complex claims and complex claimants, for the most part, the federal courts have not bought these arguments (Abrams 1994, 2479).

Given the limitations of civil rights law, it is not surprising that there has been a turn to tort law, where plaintiffs are not required to pinpoint the motivation behind their harassment or mistreatment. The availability of tort law could prove particularly important, for example, in a case of same-sex harassment in which the abuse consisted of forbidding the plaintiff from speaking Spanish in the presence of the harasser (*Lucerno-Nelson v. Wash. Metro. Area Transit Auth.* 1998, 1). Because tort law would permit plaintiffs to cumulate incidents of different types of harassment, it could also relieve women of color and other multiply-burdened claimants from having to split their identity and separate conduct directed at them "as women" from behavior taken against them on the basis of their race or ethnicity (Austin 1989, 540). In a postmodern age, it is useful to have tort protection available to avoid such contests about identity.

These potential benefits of tort law to harassment victims, of course, are only speculative and depend largely on whether judges and juries would regard defendants' conduct in such "complex" harassment cases as outrageous. MacKinnon's early reservation that, in the hands of judges interpreting tort law, protection against harassment might be stunted by traditional moralism and honor-based ideologies remains a live issue, especially in same-sex harassment cases or cases brought by plaintiffs who do not conform to contemporary models of respectability.

Concerns about the possible "domestication" of harassment law, however, extend beyond fears of judicial interpretation of tort doctrines. After more than three decades of enforcement of civil rights laws, it has become clear that conservative cultural forces can and will influence the meanings placed on the law, regardless of whether the claim carries the label of torts or civil rights. Thus, one compelling complaint of feminist scholars is that enforcement of sexual harassment law in everyday life can serve to reinscribe old ideologies, rather than to empower women to resist discrimination. For example, in her ethnography of an industrial electronics plant in Southern California, sociologist Beth Quinn explained how male employees interpreted sexual harassment law mainly as a requirement to use "appropriate language" when they were in the presence of "ladies," while retaining the traditional belief that any woman who "put up with" crude behavior was, by inference, not a lady (Quinn 2000, 1166–1179). Quinn saw little sign that the existence of sexual harassment law operated as an incentive for women to resist sexist behavior in this male-dominated workplace. Instead, most female employees took a skeptical view of the benefits of sexual harassment law, believing that filing a complaint was a risky and ineffectual tactic, likely to reinforce their "outsider" status, without appreciably reducing the incidence of sex-based insults, demeaning "jokes," or physical aggression. When harassment law is seen in this sobering light, it is easy to understand why most contemporary feminists doubt that reform of harassment law will likely produce immediate changes "on the ground." Instead, the focus tends to be on the more modest goal of providing sufficient protection to those few victims who decide to buck the conventional wisdom by resorting to law.

Since MacKinnon first argued against using tort law to remedy sexual harassment, the legal and cultural landscape has changed considerably. There is less concern that association with tort law will contaminate sexual harassment law, especially given the danger that the claim might well be stripped of its radical elements even if it stays within civil rights. Instead, there is a growing sense that locating harassment claims solely within civil rights law may now serve to further marginalize the claim. Confined within civil rights, it can look like a claim that has no place in the core curriculum, describes only a particularized harm, and imposes only a special statutory duty that does not reflect a widely shared cultural norm. In the century following the civil rights and women's movements, there is more pressure to mainstream civil rights values and to connect the core concepts of equality and dignity in U.S. law.

In its relatively short life span, the intentional infliction tort has illuminated the complicated relationship between law and culture that often characterizes legal reforms. In its early days, the tort served as a repository for dominant cultural views on gender, race, and morality, mainly operating to reinscribe the line between the respectable and the dishonored. Before the civil rights era, the dignitary harm addressed by the infliction tort tended to protect women's chastity, but not their autonomy or self-determination. For some white female plaintiffs, however, the tort did provide a measure of relief for suffering caused by unusually cruel behavior. And in this way, it could be said that gender opened up the tort and tort law more generally to an assessment of sex-linked behavior beyond physical violence.

Once the intentional infliction tort was established, moreover, it became a potential vehicle for protecting a new equality-centered conception of dignitary harm influenced by the black civil rights and women's movements. In the post-civil rights era, the notion that gender or racial harassment amounts to "outrageous" behavior resonates with employees and others who have been exposed to the norms and effects of statutory civil rights laws. Notably, however, the infliction tort has yet to be transformed into a claim for injuries to dignity stemming from sexual, racial, or other group-based bias or devaluation. In most states, the tort is a mere gap filler reserved for claims that stand apart from "ordinary" harassment and workplace discrimination. The legacy of the "no harm in asking" doctrine and the trivialization of women's harm stemming from sexual overtures that characterized the early days of the tort continues to affect contemporary legal judgments, making it seem that harassment claims do not belong in torts. The current struggle over the meaning of "outrageous" conduct and the slow migration of civil rights values into tort law reveals the interplay of law and cultural change and the degree to which courts will authorize "new moral values to be woven into the fabric of law" (Gergen 1996, 1709–1710). We will know that civil rights has finally "arrived" when it makes it into tort law.

CHAPTER EIGHT

Regulating Middlesex

ANNE BLOOM

I was born twice: first, as a baby girl, on a remarkably smogless Detroit day in 1960; and, then again, as a teenage boy, in an emergency room near Petroskey, Michigan, in 1974.

From *Middlesex* (Eugenides 2002, 3)

The Concern of the magistrates was less with corporeal reality—with what we could call sex—than with maintaining clear social boundaries, maintaining the categories of gender.

(Laquer 1990, 135)

Middlesex is the title of a best-selling book in the United States. Authored by Jeffrey Eugenides, it is a fictional account of the life of an intersexual, who is raised as a girl until puberty, when she makes the decision to live life, more or less, as a male. Like many intersexuals, the protagonist of *Middlesex* struggles with feelings of monstrosity. Although fictional, the themes of *Middlesex* echo those of the real-life saga of David Reimer, whose story was publicized widely a few years ago, in another best-selling book titled *As Nature Made Him: The Boy Who Was Raised as a Girl* (Colapinto 2000). David was not born intersexed but, rather, as a biological male, named Bruce. At about six months of age, however, Bruce's penis was destroyed during a botched circumcision. On the advice of medical experts, David's parents decided that the appropriate course of action was to reconstruct Bruce as a girl, who they renamed Brenda.

Over the next several years, Bruce/Brenda underwent several surgeries, in which his penis and testes were removed. Somewhat later, he took estrogen and grew breasts. Although his doctors reported otherwise, Bruce/Brenda suffered severe psychological problems stemming from the sex change operations and related treatments. At the age of fourteen, following several threats of suicide,

Bruce/Brenda made the independent decision to become a male again. This, of course, required more surgery to, among other things, remove his breasts and reconstruct his penis.

Inspired by the biblical tale of David and Goliath, Bruce/Brenda also decided to re-christen himself as David. About ten years later, David went on to marry a woman and to father several children through adoption. In 2000, he agreed to make his story public, with the hope that greater knowledge about his experience might help to prevent other infants and small children from being forced to undergo sex change operations before they are old enough to give meaningful consent. A few years later, for reasons that are not entirely clear, David Reimer took his own life.

David Reimer and his family did not attempt to sue the doctors who recommended the sex change in his instance. Had they attempted to sue, they most likely would have been precluded by legal doctrines in tort law that protect doctors from liability when the medical procedures are consistent with the custom of the profession and where they have obtained the patient's consent. In the case of intersexed children and children with severe genital injuries, it was, and remains, standard practice for doctors to perform sex change operations on boys with damaged penises and on children with ambiguous genitalia. Doctors readily obtain the consent of the children's parents, who are eager to do whatever they must to help their children conform to cultural expectations about what their children should look like. For both reasons, it would be difficult to establish tort liability in U.S. courts through a breach of the standard of care.

It is not inconceivable, however, that a court would rule otherwise. In 1995, the Constitutional Court of Colombia heard the claims of a young Colombian man who underwent a very similar experience to David Reimer. Like David Reimer, the plaintiff in the Colombian case had undergone a surgical sex reassignment, following a traumatic injury to his penis. In a precedent-setting ruling that is being watched by specialists in sex-change surgery around the world, the Colombian Court held that parents cannot give consent on a child's behalf to surgeries to determine sexual identity. Instead, the court held the surgery must, in most instances, be delayed until the child has an opportunity to comprehend the nature of the surgery and give meaningful consent (Sentencia T-477/95 1995).

What is perhaps most remarkable about the Colombian Court's ruling is its recognition of the role that cultural expectations played in the decision to subject the Colombian child to surgery in the first place and in its own rulings about what actions were appropriate. Specifically, the ruling noted the surgery might have been motivated by societal intolerance of bodies that do not live up to cultural expectations about sexual difference. If that were the case, the Court reasoned, it would constitute discrimination for the Court to place its imprimatur on this intolerance by allowing the practices to go unchallenged.

At stake in the Colombian case, and in other cases involving individuals with bodies that do not clearly conform to cultural expectations, is the legitimacy of one our most deeply held cultural understandings. Conventional wisdom holds that sexual identity occurs "naturally" as a binary category, which consists of two "opposite" sexes: male and female. But, as the two stories recounted above suggest, the question of sexual identity is often much more complex than this. As it turns out, many bodies, even in nature, simply do not fit very well into the rigid boundaries of a male/female classification. Others do not comport with cultural expectations about the characteristics that are typically associated with the two categories.

Instead, doctors observe physical characteristics which defy a binary categorization of sex on a regular basis: men with breasts, women with facial hair, and, of course, intersexed individuals whose genitalia cannot be distinguished clearly as either male or female. Doctors respond to this dilemma with medical treatment aimed at helping the body to comply with the cultural demand. In David Reimer's case, and in the case of many other infants who suffer from a traumatic penis injury, the recommended treatment is often to surgically reassign the infant into a girl (Ben-Asher 2006). Other nonconforming bodies may be provided with prostheses (e.g., breast implants and penile implants), hormone therapy, or other treatments, such as electrolysis, to help them better fit the norm.

However, some individuals, like David Reimer and the protagonist in *Middlesex*, refuse to conform. More commonly, there are problems in transition. Sex reassignment surgery fails, implants rupture, or someone is incarcerated before their sex change is complete. Quite frequently, the law is called upon to mediate the resulting conflicts. When that happens, U.S. courts face their own dilemma. Should they, like doctors, follow the lead of cultural expectations and insist that bodies fit into a male/female classification? Or should they, like the Constitutional Court of Colombia, recognize that the categories themselves may be grounded in intolerance of sexual difference and refuse to enforce them?

This chapter explores the role of U.S. tort law in negotiating this dilemma. I argue that, in contrast to the Constitutional Court of Colombia, U.S. courts routinely embrace and, indeed, enforce an understanding of sexual identity that is deeply rooted in cultural assumptions about what is "natural" and "normal." The most fundamental of these cultural understandings is the assumption that sexual identity occurs "naturally" as a binary category, with distinct physiological features associated with each sex. U.S. courts enforce this understanding of sexual identity not only in cases involving intersexuals and transsexuals, I argue, but in other contexts as well, when individuals have acted to reconstruct and/or amplify their sexual identity in ways that "mess with nature."

The remainder of the essay is divided into four sections. The first section provides an introduction to some of the scientific and medical issues surrounding sexual identity. The next section addresses the theoretical issues that guide my analysis of the cases that follow. The third section provides some historical background on how U.S. courts have responded to questions about the biological "nature" of binary sexual identity. The fourth section looks at several tort cases to show how tort law operates to enforce cultural understandings about sexual identity as naturally binary.

The "Science" of Sexual Identity

When a child is born, we ask: "Is it a boy or girl"? When we ask this question, we assume that sexual identity is binary. You are born either male or female, with identifying characteristics that allow the doctor to assign you to your appropriate category. Even at birth, however, many bodies do not fit neatly within the rigid boundaries of a male/female classification. Perhaps because of this, sex classification experts struggle to identify reliable criteria for assigning sexual identity.

By one conservative estimate, 1 in 2,000 children are born intersexed (Hermer 2002) and approximately 1 in 100 people have bodies which differ from the standard traits of a male or female (Blackless et al. 2000). Some intersexed children display ambiguous genitalia, such as children born with the external genitalia of a male but with ovaries instead of testes. Others have genital features that seem under- or overdeveloped as compared to other children. An apparent "girl," for example, might be born with an enlarged clitoris that looks like a penis. Alternatively, an apparent "boy" might be born with an extremely small penis, which doctors refer to as "micropenis."

In some instances, however, the external genitalia are not ambiguous, and the intersex condition is not discovered until puberty, when the child begins to exhibit developmental patterns that are at odds with the initial sex designation. This was the case with the protagonist of *Middlesex*. At birth, the child's external genitalia appeared to be that of a girl. During adolescence, however, she began to develop traits that were more classically "male," such as a deepening voice and a failure to menstruate. Upon closer examination, doctors discovered undescended testes and the presence of male (XY) chromosomes.

Under a chromosome-based classification system, the protagonist in *Middlesex* and many real people with this condition are categorized as male because of the presence of both an X and a Y chromosome. Individuals with two X chromosomes, on the other hand, are typically designated as "female." Many individuals, however, have a chromosomal makeup that places them somewhat outside a simple XX versus XY classification.

Some babies, for example, are born XXY or XYY; others are born with only one X or extra Xs. In other words, chromosomal structure is considerably more variable than a simple XX = female and XY = male classification. In general, the existence of a Y chromosome results in a male classification, and the absence of a Y chromosome results in classification as a female. Such classifications can be confusing, however, particularly when the individual develops physical traits that do not fit clearly within their designated categories. Even in seemingly unambiguous cases (i.e., a clear XX or XY), chromosomal analysis can result in confusing classifications. Some XX individuals, for example, have both ovaries and external genitalia that appear male (Ben-Asher 2006, 51–52, n2). Others have undescended testes and female-appearing genitalia.

For medical experts, the appearance of external genitalia tends to be considered more important than chromosomes in determining sexual identity. Current medical protocols, for example, indicate that newborn boys should have a penis that is at least 2.5 centimeters long and newborn girls should have a clitoris that is no larger than 1 centimeter (Ben-Asher 2006, 61). Children who do not conform to these norms are designated for medical treatment, including hormone therapy and surgery, to help them more closely approximate the traits of either a male or female classification.

Although ambiguous genitalia pose no physical health risk, the birth of a child with ambiguous genitalia is deemed by medical experts to be a "social emergency" requiring immediate medical attention (American Association of Pediatrics [AAP] Policy 2000, 138). As a practical matter, it is much easier to construct an artificial vagina than an artificial penis. Because of this, it remains

standard practice within the medical profession to perform a sex change operation on children with unusually small penises or other "under-masculinized"
traits, even if their chromosomes fit the XY classification as male. XX babies with
enlarged clitorises, on the other hand, are not converted into boys but undergo
surgery to either remove or alter the clitoris to conform to medical expectations
for girls.

The theory underlying these practices embodies two fundamental principles.
The first principle is that it is essential to designate all babies as either male or
female as quickly as possible. The second is that children cannot develop "proper
gender identity" unless their bodies exhibit consistent male or female traits (Levit 1998, 240). Under these protocols, "proper gender identity" means identifying
as either a male or female, with the appropriate, matching genitalia. Individuals without appropriate genitalia are slated for surgery and counseling and individuals who fail to develop an appropriate gender identity are diagnosed with
"gender identity disorder."

Medical protocols on the appropriateness of transsexual surgery for adults follow essentially the same principles. With adults, however, candidates for surgery
must have already developed a proper gender identity. Because of this, sexual
reassignment surgery is recommended for adults only when the individual has a
demonstrated history of identifying clearly as either a male or female. Individuals who espouse a more ambiguous sexual identity do not qualify (Spade 2003).

Much of the science to support these principles was developed in the 1950s
and 1960s. Although the principles adhere strictly to a conceptualization of sexual identity as "naturally" binary (male/female), they also reflect the consensus
of the medical community at the time that the development of sexual identity in
any given individual was primarily a product of "nurture" rather than "nature"
(Ben-Asher 2006). As a result, experts believed (and many still believe) that sexual identity can be altered with surgery and appropriate social conditioning.

As it turns out, the poster child for the nurture over nature perspective was
David Reimer, whose initial conversion from a biological male to a biological
female was widely reported as an unequivocal "success" in critically acclaimed
articles published in peer reviewed journals and highly publicized media accounts which concealed his name. Although this perspective has been widely
questioned since David Reimer went public with his subsequent change back to
being a male, doctors in the United States continue to perform sex change opera-

tions on infants and children. This is largely because, regardless of whether the doctor adopts a view of sexual identity that is grounded primarily in nurture or nature, there is still a perceived need to identify the child as either male or female, and surgery is one means of perfecting the categorization.

In sum, despite evidence to the contrary, medical protocols continue to operate on the assumption that sexual identity is, or perhaps *should be,* binary. Moreover, binary sexual classification is assumed to be natural and the categories of male and female are presumed to have certain natural characteristics, such as penises and clitorises of a particular size and shape. Put differently, the American medical community treats sexual identity and the classification of individuals into males and females as if the categories were a precultural, biological given.

This is so despite the fact that, for many years, scientists spoke of sexual identity in terms of *one* sex, rather than two (Laquer 1990). And, even today, the existence of a "middlesex" is acknowledged in other cultures. Many Native Americans, for example, recognize intersexuals as a separate sex, which they refer to as "two spirit." And, in India, Pakistan, and Bangladesh intersexuals are identified as "hijras" who are neither male nor female. All this suggests that sexual identity might be better understood as a *cultural* category that is mediated, at least in part, by normative expectations (Laquer 1990). I explore this possibility, and the role that law plays in this process, in the sections that follow.

Constructing Sexual Identity

If doctors observe bodies that defy a binary classification, why not abandon the classification scheme for one that seems more workable? Laquer (1990) argues that the conceptualization of sex as binary is a relatively recent cultural phenomenon that took place in the late seventeenth and eighteenth centuries. This reinterpretation of bodies took place in tandem with other political and cultural developments, including the rise of evangelical religion, Lockean ideas of marriage as a contract, and postrevolutionary feminism, all of which led to greater emphasis on binary sexual differentiation.

Others present a somewhat more complex historical view of the development of contemporary understandings of sexual difference while still acknowledging the important role of culture in shaping these understandings (Cadden 1993). The studies agree, however, that our understanding of sexual difference is not based entirely on biological observation but is "explicable only within the context of battles over gender and power" (Laquer 1990, 11). Moreover, because these battles play out in the form of competing narratives, cultural texts play a role in generating sexual difference.

Medieval scientists conceptualized sexual identity in terms of one sex instead of two primarily because "[l]anguage constrained the seeing of opposites and sustained the male body as the canonical human form" (Laquer 1990, 96). The conceptualization of sexual identity in terms of two sexes, on the other hand, grew out of a cultural climate that emphasized the importance of physical, and especially sexual, difference. Although the cultural settings were quite different, in both instances, scientific understanding of sexual identity was shaped by "the rhetorical exigencies of the moment" (Laqueur 1990, 243)

Judith Butler makes a similar argument in *Bodies that Matter* (1993). Butler analyzes gender (including sexual identity) in terms of how language and performance construct gender/sex in particular discursive contexts. Language does not simply create cultural categories (such as males and females), however, but extends to the *production* of material subjects, including human bodies, which correspond with the regulatory demands of a particular discourse (Butler 1993).

This conceptualization of sexual identity questions both the categorical distinctions between nature and culture, and the parallel distinction between sex and gender (Butler 1993, 223–226). These distinctions assert that culture and gender accrue to ontologically preexisting or "biological" matter, such as biological sex. Butler argues, however, that this binary opposition between bodies (matter) and cultural constructions leads to a misconception of sexuality as either biological and natural ("sex") or culturally constructed ("gender"). In fact, Butler suggests, both gender and sex are more likely the product of processes of *both* biological and cultural construction.

In making this move, Butler effectively asks us to transform our thinking about the stability of biological matter. In her analysis, the category of "matter" becomes a "process of materialization," in which matter is materialized as an effect of cultural practices. In *Bodies That Matter,* Butler illustrates the materialization of sex and gender through a practice she calls "girling" (Butler 1993, 232–233). Girling is a process that is compelled by the naming of a girl as a girl. The symbolic power of this naming, in turn, effectively "governs the formation of a corporeally enacted femininity" (Butler 1993, 232). In other words, gender and sex are produced and maintained through the repetition and citation of authoritative speech and actions. Seen in this way, gender and sex are not the products of nature, or even a particular choice, but are instead the effect of particular discursive practices.

Butler's argument seems quite radical because it suggests that sexual identity is constituted by something other than naturally occurring biological differences. But, in many ways, Butler's theory provides a powerful explanation of contemporary medical protocols concerning sexual identity. The fact that medical texts describe the birth of a child with ambiguous genitalia as a "social emergency," for example, is indicative of the extent to which medical experts are themselves cognizant of the fact that the situation poses more of a cultural, rather than medical, dilemma.

The situation is said to constitute a social emergency, Butler's theory suggests, because it reveals a gap between the cultural demand that sexual identity be binary and the reality of human experience. How doctors respond to this gap between the normative demands of sexual identity and what Butler would call the performance of sexual identity is also revealing. Although ambiguous genitalia pose no threat to the physical health of the child, surgical reconstruction and other physical treatments are typically employed almost immediately to literally *construct* binary sexual difference onto bodies that do not comply on their own. With this move, doctors expose their own role in the construction of sexual identity by, among other things, delineating and reconstructing bodies to fit within normative expectations (see Laquer 1990 17).

Although the medical community is aware that these activities are problematic from a health perspective (among other things, the surgeries pose risks of sexual dysfunction), the treatments are defended on psychological grounds (Weil 2006). David Reimer's story and other anecdotal evidence, however, suggest that the psychological benefits of surgery are far from clear (Weil 2006). Because of this, the Intersex Society of America opposes cosmetic genital surgery on children (Weil 2006). At the same time, the Society supports assigning children a gender at birth, primarily because its members believe that it is unfair to expect intersex children to combat normative expectations of binary sexual identification on their own.

As Butler notes, this process of classifying individuals into binary categories is clearly an artificial and "forcible" act, with its own consequences, including reification of the hegemonic, binary regime (Butler 1993, 232). Scientific and cultural narratives that insist on a view of sexual identity that privileges binary sexual identification play an important role in this process. So does the law.

Legal Narratives

Most of us associate the study of law with formal rules and regulations and with the legal institutions that play a role in enforcing societal norms and obligations. But "the formal institutions of law" are "but a small part" of the legal universe "that ought to claim our attention" (Cover 1983, 4). Legal narratives are of equal, if not greater importance. Like other cultural narratives, legal narratives send a "message" about how the world is constituted (Merry 1990, 9). Because of this, legal narratives can become hegemonic and, as a result, operate as a mechanism of social control.

Legal narratives about sexual difference have taken two somewhat divergent paths in the United States. On the one hand, courts have moved in the direction of avoiding sex-based distinctions that are founded on stereotypes and mistaken assumptions. In *Craig v. Boren* (1976), for example, the Supreme Court proclaimed that there is a "weak congruence between gender and the characteristic or trait that gender purport[s] to represent" (*Craig v. Boren* 1976, 199). Because of this, the court held, gender-based distinctions should be scrutinized closely to ensure that sex-based generalizations comport with factual realities.

In other rulings, however, courts have adhered strictly to sex-based generalizations that embody popular assumptions about biological differences between males and females. One important example of this in the area of women's rights is in the court's use of a lower standard in assessing discrimination in sex discrimination cases than is employed in race discrimination cases. In cases alleging race discrimination, courts employ a "strict scrutiny standard," in which the government must demonstrate a compelling state interest in treating people differently. Sex discrimination cases employ a less stringent standard, known as "intermediate scrutiny," which requires only that the challenged differences in treatment be substantially related to an important governmental objective (Tribe 2000; see also Chamallas, this volume).

The use of a lower standard for sex than is employed for race is justified by the proposition that there are meaningful, biological differences between men and women that apply to every individual (Levit 1998, 66). In *Michael M. v. Superior*

Court of Sonoma County (1981), for example, the Supreme Court ruled that biological differences between boys and girls provided an adequate justification for sex-based differences in California's statutory rape law (*Michael M. v. Superior Court of Sonomoa County* 1981, 464). And, in *Nguyen v. INS* (2001), the Court upheld different rules for attainment of citizenship by children born abroad out of wedlock, depending on whether the mother or the father was the American, on the ground that "basic biological differences" between men and women affect parent-child relationships in meaningful ways (*Nguyen v. INS* 2001, 57).

Other court rulings reflect cultural expectations about what sexual difference should look like. For example, courts have upheld employers' decisions to fire women who wear pants (see, e.g., *Tamimim v. Howard Johnson Co.* 1987) or refuse to wear makeup (Bartlett 1994). And employer policies that terminate men for having long hair or wearing jewelry have also withstood legal challenge (Levitt, 99–100). The rationale in these cases is nearly always the same and involves the reasoning that the dress codes do not discriminate on the basis of sex but, rather, require both men and women "to dress in conformity with the accepted standards of the community" (see, e.g., *Harper v. Edgewood Board of Education* 1987).

Courts enforce similar expectations in cases involving transsexuals. In a 1993 case decided by the Washington Supreme Court, for example, a corporate dress policy that required a preoperative transsexual to dress in a unisex fashion against the advice of her doctor was upheld as an acceptable policy for the employer to enforce (*Doe v. Boeing* 1993). Central to the court's reasoning was the fact that the transsexual plaintiff was still a "biological male."

Rulings like these suggest the extent to which American law continues to enforce sex- and gender-based distinctions believed to be grounded in nature or a pre-cultural, biological reality. In each of these cases, courts rely on an understanding of sex as "naturally" binary and associated with particular physical characteristics. In doing so, they employ a form of biological essentialism in determining the rights and remedies to be afforded to the complaining parties.

Cases involving transsexuals, of course, often pose serious challenges to these assumptions. In one recent case, a Kansas court suggested that, in cases involving transsexuals, courts might consider abandoning an approach that relies on a binary conception of sexual identity. The case involved a male to female transsexual who, after sex reassignment surgery, married a biological male. After her husband died, her husband's son from another marriage sought to disinherit her from her husband's estate on the ground that the marriage was invalid because both parties had been born male (*In the Matter of the Estate of Marshall G. Gardiner* 2001).

In attempting to adjudicate the case, the Kansas intermediate court of appeal noted the difficulty in determining what constitutes a male or female. After considering an array of factors employed by medical experts, including appearance of the genitalia and chromosomes, the court concluded that it could not rely on only one factor because the question of sexual identity was "far more complex" than could be captured with a single factor (*In the Matter of the Estate of Marshall G. Gardiner* 2001, 127). Ultimately, the court suggested "it is only the [individuals] themselves who can and must identify who and what they are" (ibid.).

On appeal to the Kansas Supreme Court, the higher court reversed the intermediate court of appeals and instructed the trial court to rely solely on dictionary definitions of what constitutes males and females. According to the definitions employed by the court, a "'male' is defined as designation or of the sex that fertilizes the ovum and begets offspring" and a "'female' is defined as designation or of the sex that produces ova and bears offspring" (*In the Matter of the Estate of Marshall G. Gardiner* 2002, 213). A male to female postoperative transsexual cannot qualify as a female, according to this definition, the court concluded, because the "ability 'to produce ova and bear offspring' does not and never did exist" (ibid.).

What is especially fascinating about this opinion is the large number of people that it excludes. If we take the court seriously, individuals who cannot fertilize an ovum or ovulate do not qualify as either male or female and are thereby precluded from enjoying any of the benefits of the binary sex regime. In other words, sex is not only natural and binary in this legal narrative but also linked closely with reproductive capacity.

Torts and Sexual Identity

Legal narratives about sexual identity and difference have also played an important role in the development of American tort law. As Chamallas (this volume) notes, recovery for mental distress in American tort law was made possible, in part, because it proved effective at reinforcing cultural beliefs about the emotional sensitivity of white women. And, in a similar way, cultural conceptions of "male honor" and "female chastity" inflected the development of the tort of solicitation (ibid.).

This section looks at more contemporary cases to show how tort law continues to operate to enforce cultural expectations about sexual difference. Drawing on cases in three different areas of tort law—wrongful death/survival claims, products liability, and medical malpractice—I argue that cultural and legal narratives both enforce and reproduce a binary conception of sexual identity that links sexual classification to bodies that look and operate in particular ways.

Wrongful Death/Survival Claims

Christie Littleton was born Lee Cavazos Jr. and designated a male at birth (*Littleton v. Prange* 1999). At the age of twenty-seven, however, Christie underwent sex assignment surgery and became an anatomical female. A few years later, she married Jonathan Littleton and lived with him until his death. After he died, Christie filed a medical malpractice claim against her husband's doctor in her capacity as the surviving spouse. The doctor argued, however, that the case should be dismissed because Christie was not a "real" woman and therefore could not be the surviving spouse of Jonathon Littleton. The trial court agreed and entered summary judgment for the doctor (*Littleton v. Prange* 1999, 224).

On appeal, the court noted that since Texas did not recognize marriages between persons of the same sex, the key question before the court was whether "Christie [is] a man or a woman?" In attempting to answer this question, the court acknowledged that Christie currently had the "anatomical and genital features" of a female and that she had "the capacity to function sexually as a female" (*Littleton v. Prange* 1999, 225). The court also acknowledged that many physicians would consider her a female. For the court, however, the most important question was not what Christie looked like now but whether Christie was "created and born a male" (*Littleton v. Prange* 1999, 231). Because Christie's female anatomy was "all man-made," the court reasoned she was not a "real" woman (*Littleton v. Prange* 1999, 230). As a result, her marriage to Jonathan Littleton was illegal and she could not recover as his surviving spouse.

As the *Littleton* case illustrates, many tort claims, including wrongful death, alienation of affection, loss of consortium, and negligent infliction of emotional distress, rely upon the existence of a marital relationship for the plaintiff to establish a claim. When that relationship comes into question as a result of questions about the validity of the marriage, then the claim itself may be in jeopardy. In the case of transsexuals, for those courts (and there are many) that refuse to recognize a marriage between a transsexual and an individual of the same birth sex, tort litigation of this kind is not an option for the recovery of damages stemming from negligent or intentional conduct that had an impact on the marriage (see also *Bume v. Dr. Roy J. Catanne* 1971 [rejecting similar claims brought by male to female transsexual wife]).

Littleton is also indicative of the extent to which the courts' confusion over how to determine sexual identity can lead to somewhat unexpected results. *Littleton* relied upon the designated sex at birth to determine sexual identity. As two lesbians discovered recently, however, this means that, under *Littleton,* a male to female transsexual may legally marry another female in Texas. Interestingly enough, the marriage received the blessings of the president of the Texas Conservative Coalition, which ordinarily opposes same sex marriage, because, anatomy aside, "[t]hey are *legally* a man and a woman" (Kurtz 2000).

The ruling also raises questions about the legal status of those millions of Americans who do not clearly qualify as a man or a woman, in terms of their chromosomes or external genitalia at birth, and of those individuals whose external genitalia and/or sexual identification change significantly during puberty. Under the court's ruling, these individuals are also precluded from bringing tort claims that rely upon the existence of a marriage between two individuals whose sexual identity classifies them as members of the "opposite" sex (cf. Chamallas, this volume, noting how, in a similar way, gender ideology historically closed off recovery for certain types of "dignitary" harms).

Products Liability

In cases involving transsexuals, the law's role in regulating sexual identity is often directly at issue. As in the *Littleton* case, the court must face the question of what constitutes a man or a woman directly. In other tort cases, however, tort law may act more subtly to enforce and reproduce sex and gender norms in litigation that does not ostensibly address such questions. An example of this can be found in the regulation and litigation surrounding breast implants.

Like genitalia, breasts have tremendous symbolic import in the differentiation of sexes. Medical literature describes breasts of an appropriate size and shape as "essential" for a female's mental health and well-being (Spanbauer 1997, 183). Individuals with breasts that are deemed too small are diagnosed with a condition called "micromastia" (flat-chestedness) and, along with those who have lost breasts due to mastectomy, are recommended for reconstructive surgery. Others choose to undergo implantation surgery without a medical diagnosis, so as to "emphasize something specifically *female* about themselves" (Allen 1994, 83–84). Silicone implants were, and remain, extremely popular because they look and feel more "natural" than other options, such as saline implants or prostheses (Coniff 1997).

Tort law became involved in regulating breast implantation practices when some individuals began to claim that silicone implants ruptured and leaked, causing serious injuries. The first products liability lawsuits were filed against the manufacturers in the early 1970s. Nearly all of these cases settled under conditions of secrecy. In the fall of 1991, however, the Food and Drug Administration (FDA) obtained access to some of the court documents and, after reviewing the documents, the FDA called for an immediate moratorium on some uses of silicone implants.

Because of concerns about safety, the FDA urged plastic surgeons to immediately stop using silicone implants in patients undergoing implantation for "purely cosmetic" purposes (Gladwell 1992). Exempted from the moratorium, however, were silicone implants used for purposes of reconstructing breasts lost to mastectomy or the correction of "micromastia." The agency explained its decision to allow for this exemption by citing the unique physical and psychological "need" of individuals in these categories for access to the much more natural looking silicone implants (Gladwell 1992).

An explosion in breast implant-related lawsuits followed. Many of these cases were consolidated into a class action, which ultimately settled (*Lindsey v. Dow Corning Corp.* 1994). Some implant recipients, however, chose to proceed with individual litigation, outside the class settlements. Despite the early litigation successes, public opinion began to turn against these individual implant recipients, and manufacturers began to win a very large percentage of the individual cases.

Although sexual identity was not directly at issue in the breast implant litigation, the law operated in these cases to enforce and reproduce cultural understandings about sexual identity as naturally binary and associated with certain bodily characteristics. What is interesting about breast implantation practices, however, is that, much like sex reassignment surgery, the practices effectively re-produce a natural conception of sexual identity, while simultaneously exposing its artificiality. This is because, to the extent that implantation surgery is successful and the artificial breasts seem "real" to all observers, breast implantation practices help to regulate and produce a conception of sexual identity, in which females appear to naturally have breasts of a certain size and shape. At the same time, surgical implantation practices reveal a gap between the cultural message that binary sexual categorization is natural and the physical experience of being male and female, which sometimes requires artificial help to "fully approximate the norm" (Butler 1993, 232).

The FDA's regulatory decisions played a role in reenforcing the cultural message that binary sexual categorization is natural and, specifically, that breasts of a particular size and shape are necessary to qualify as a woman. This is most clearly seen in the FDA's conclusion that, despite concerns about the safety of silicone implants, it would continue to allow restricted use of silicone gel implants for those women seeking reconstruction of breasts lost to mastectomy or seeking treatment for micromastia.

Like genital surgery on intersex infants, from a safety perspective, the FDA's decision is difficult to understand. If there was a problem with the safety of silicone implants, then the agency should have pulled silicone implants from the market for all purposes, especially since alternatives to silicone implants, such as saline implants and prostheses, were readily available (Yang 2001). The FDA's decision begins to make more sense, however, when we consider, as the FDA apparently did, that the absence of natural-looking breasts in adult women constitutes a "social emergency" (cf. AAP Policy 2000, 138 [protocol for ambiguous genitalia]). Under these circumstances, the risks associated with silicone implants were, in the FDA's view, outweighed by the fact that the alternatives did not provide women with breasts that appeared sufficiently natural (Kessler 1992).

Like the FDA's regulatory actions, the valuation of claims in the breast implant litigation also enforced a conception of natural binary sexual identity by valuing the claims of individuals who underwent surgery to replace a breast more highly than those who underwent surgery for enlargement purposes. The implicit message of this differential valuing is that it is wrong to "mess with nature," for purposes other than reconstructing a "natural" state of affairs (e.g., reconstruction after mastectomy). There is ample evidence, for example, that "juries tend to be more sympathetic" to individuals who undergo breast implant surgery for what is perceived as "purely reconstructive" rather than cosmetic purposes (Collins 1997; see also Chamallas, this volume, noting that "traditional moralism . . . remains a live issue especially in cases brought by plaintiffs who do not conform to contemporary models of respectability").

A similar issue came up in a breast implants case that raised the issue of whether a claim for strict liability based on design defects should be available as a potential cause of action for implant recipients who did not undergo implant surgery to replace a breast lost to mastectomy (*Artiglio v. Superior Court of San Diego County* 1994). Ultimately, implant recipients were allowed to proceed with strict liability-based claims, without regard to the implant recipients' motivations for obtaining the implants. The court noted, however, that there were important differences between using the implants for purposes of "restoring the body to natural form" and using them to "enhance esteem and add to life's enjoyment" (*Artiglio v. Superior Court of San Diego County* 1994, 1395). In this way, the court signaled, once again, that sexual identity is natural.

Medical Malpractice

One of the issues raised by the experience of David Reimer and other individuals who undergo sex reassignment surgery as an infant or small child is whether the individuals might later bring tort litigation against the doctors for malpractice and/or battery. There are no reported cases to date of such litigation in the United States. Several cases have been brought in Australia and Colombia, however, and these cases suggest that such litigation is also on the horizon of the U.S. legal landscape.

In Australia, one of the more publicized cases was brought by Tony Briffa, an intersex activist, who is attempting to sue his doctors for medical malpractice in reassigning him as female, including castration at age seven and hormone treatments beginning at age eleven (see Bragge 2005). Like David Reimer, however, Briffa never identified as a female and, at age thirty, reassigned himself as a male.

Other cases in Australia indicate that a court order may now be necessary before a physician may perform sexual reassignment surgery. In *In Re A (A Child)* (1993), an Australian court determined that, in a case involving genital injury after birth, a court order was required before a physician could reassign the child to a different sex. Physician and parental decisions to operate on children born intersexed, however, still require no outside authorization or approval. Instead, it is considered standard medical practice for the doctors to recommend, and the parents to authorize, surgery to make the child conform to a male or female sex at a very early age.

It is in Colombia, however, where courts have confronted the question most extensively. The Constitutional Court of Colombia has now heard three cases involving the question of surgery on intersexed infants. In two of those cases, the court issued rulings restricting the ability of parents and doctors to consent and perform the surgery (Sentencia Su-337/99 1999; Sentencia T-551/99 1999). The third case ruled in favor of a young man who had already undergone such surgery and determined that the consent given by his parents was insufficient (Sentencia T-477/95 1995).

These rulings have significantly altered the practice of surgery on intersexed infants in Colombia. Today, most physicians in Colombia will no longer perform the surgery without a court order. Encouraged by these rulings, intersex activists in the United States are also pursuing the possibility of suing physicians who perform the surgery at a very early age. Cases which result in a loss of sexual function and/or in which the adult gender identity conflicts with the surgically created sex are considered the most promising. As in Colombia and Australia, parental consent to the surgery poses a key challenge to the success of such litigation, as does the tort doctrine that bars medical malpractice claims when the doctor's actions are consistent with prevailing professional customs.

Conclusion

The foregoing cases reveal both the reliance on an understanding of sex as "naturally binary" in American tort law and the fragility of the assumptions upon which this understanding rests. By continuing to base legal rulings on invalid assumptions about sexual identity, courts enforce cultural norms about both the binary nature of sexual identity and what it means to be a male or female. In doing so, courts are handling sexual identity in much the same way that they once handled questions of racial identity (see, e.g., Wriggins, this volume). As was the case in race cases, courts are employing a kind of "biological essentialism" to determine who is a male and who is a female, which relies heavily on questionable medical protocols that are themselves deeply imbricated with cultural expectations.

As with race, the science of sexual difference is itself a cultural construction. Because of this, the so-called "biological indicators" of sexual identity are of questionable utility. The physical and social experience of sex and gender simply do not fit neatly into a binary categorization. As a result, when courts rely upon scientific and medical expertise to evaluate sexual difference, they necessarily play a role in the enforcement and reproduction of cultural norms about what bodies should like.

Tort law is not unique in the role that it plays in this process. Like other legal narratives, tort law narratives both reflect and contribute to broader cultural meanings. Cultural norms about sexual difference may be particularly susceptible to enforcement and reproduction in tort law, however, because of the way in which many tort doctrines operate to explicitly draw upon dominant cultural norms.

First, and most obviously, is the fact that most tort cases are tried by a jury which, in many cases is explicitly charged with determining liability on the basis of norms (see generally Hans, this volume). Most tort cases also rely on expert testimony and, under current doctrine, medical viewpoints that are consistent with professional custom and/or have been published in peer review journals are treated with extensive deference. As a practical matter, this means that, in the context of tort litigation, doctors and other medical experts become the arbiters of what constitutes sexual identity.

Finally, damages principles that focus on making the body "whole" may also play a role in encouraging a view of sexual identity in which assumptions about what is natural play a particularly important role. This is because the goal of making a victim whole is often interpreted as putting things back to their natural state. For all of these reasons, tort law may be especially vulnerable to cultural assumptions about the nature of sexual identity.

CHAPTER NINE

Whiteness, Equal Treatment, and the Valuation of Injury in Torts, 1900–1949

JENNIFER B. WRIGGINS

This chapter focuses on the relationship between U.S. tort law, race, and legal culture in the first half of the twentieth century. For purposes of this chapter, my definition of tort law is a narrow one, consisting of legal doctrine and court decisions. My idea of legal culture is based on David Nelken's concept that legal culture ranges "from facts about institutions such as the number and role of lawyers or the ways judges are appointed and controlled, to various forms of behavior such as litigation or prison rates, and at the other extreme, more nebulous aspects of ideas, values, aspirations, and mentalities" (Nelken 2004, 1). This view of culture includes informal practices, institutional features, and decision-making frameworks that contribute to how law actually operates. Legal culture overlaps with and cannot be clearly detached from the wider culture. Similarly, tort law, even as I have narrowly defined it here, is infused with culture and affects culture.

The chapter begins by highlighting glaring ways in which U.S. tort law and legal culture from 1900 to 1949 were "white." The next section shows that the whiteness of litigants and witnesses served as the default in published court decisions, and that African American people were excluded from decision-making roles in the tort system, consistent with the racism of the wider culture and the rest of the legal system. After highlighting these conspicuous facets of whiteness, the essay then turns to an important tension in tort law and legal culture. The tension is between the dominant practice of resolving tort claims on an individualized basis and the conflicting but weaker principle, which served as an undercurrent, that equal treatment of all people was important. In elucidating this tension, the text explains in general terms how the dominant practice of resolving tort claims on an individualized basis permitted some success for black tort plaintiffs, but also allowed bias to devalue those plaintiffs' claims. Finally, the essay focuses on specific manifestations of African American success and inequality in tort litigation. Looking at a variety of sources, including tort law decisions, together with cultural products such as newspaper articles and an influential book, this section pays particular attention to the justifications that some judges used to rationalize their unequal treatment of African American plaintiffs. These attempted justifications, necessary only because of the undercurrent that called for equal treatment, typically involved classifying black plaintiffs and their claims as different in kind from white plaintiffs and their claims, which meant that equal treatment was not necessary, and inferior treatment of blacks' claims was appropriate. Altogether, institutional factors such as private enforcement led to a degree of African American access and success in tort litigation, which was surprising given the racist culture and legal system of the time. However, the idea of equal treatment under law was ignored or defined in ways that meant it did not need to apply to African Americans' tort claims.

The methodological challenges posed by this inquiry are familiar. Patterns have always been difficult to see in the decentralized, multilayered, settlement-oriented U.S. tort system (Galanter 1996, 1099–1105; Saks 1992, 1154–1155, 1190). Moreover, the process by which injured people come to recognize injuries and make claims for them (or not make claims for them) is extremely complex (Blasi and Jost 2006, 1156–1159; Felstiner et al. 1980). This chapter begins serious consideration of relationships among U.S. tort law, race, and legal culture, but does not comprehensively examine all issues concerning race, torts, culture, and injury.[1]

Conspicuously White Aspects of Tort Law and Legal Culture

Tort law and legal culture were white in at least two glaring ways. First, in appellate decisions, whiteness of litigants and witnesses was the norm, unstated except when litigants or witnesses departed from that norm. Second, only white persons or persons perceived as white, were allowed to be jurors, lawyers, and judges in the torts litigation system. Exclusion of persons who were not white, except as plaintiffs, defendants, and witnesses, was a central feature of the system.[2]

The consistent cultural and linguistic practice in published tort opinions was for whiteness to serve as the default. Generally, race was not mentioned unless someone involved in the litigation, such as a plaintiff or a witness, was identified as other than white. Appellate courts generally referred to such "others" as "Negro" or "colored." Hundreds of tort opinions from all regions mention the litigant's race when the litigant is seen as colored or Negro (Welke 2001, 379–389; Wriggins 2005a, 100, 110–135).

While whiteness of plaintiffs and others was the generally unmentioned default, sometimes a plaintiff's whiteness can be inferred from the context of decisions. Language used to describe the plaintiff as well as the factual context occasionally evoked whiteness. For example, a wife described as "fragile, delicate, [and] sensitive" who was insulted by a "Negro woman" attendant employed by the railroad while sitting in the "ladies waiting room" simply had to be white, although her race was not specifically mentioned (*Gulf v. Luther* 1905). Sometimes whiteness can be inferred from spatial or other factual context, such as that of a wrongful death case in which the "decedent was in the waiting room for white passengers" when a flying timber struck and killed him (*Taylor v. Vicksburg, Shreveport & Pac. R.R.* 1922]).

Second, the torts litigation system was part of a culture founded on notions of white supremacy in which racially exclusionary practices were deeply rooted. The passage of discriminatory laws expanded during the first two decades of the twentieth century (Woodward 1974, 98). Violence against blacks by whites in the South was pervasive during the Jim Crow period (Welke 2001, 365). Lynching crested between 1900 and the New Deal. Blacks were prevented from voting and had no political power (Friedman 2002, 111–117). As Lawrence Friedman stated, describing the racial caste system, the "American system of apartheid was firmly in place" in the first half of the twentieth century (Friedman 2002, 280 and discussed at 114–122, 144–147, 280–348). Only white men had decision-making roles in the civil justice system throughout this period. The large majority of juries were all white and all male from at least 1900 through the 1950s (Colbert 1990, 75–93). Similarly, the vast majority of attorneys were white and male in the first half of the twentieth century (Smith 1993, app. 2, table 13), which ensured that judges were white and male. These are conspicuous, important ways in which tort law and legal culture were "white." These two aspects, however, only begin the inquiry into relationships among race, tort law, and legal culture.

Next, some of the ways that tort law and legal culture dealt with injury claims brought by black claimants will be explored.

The Tension Between Individualized Claim Resolution and Equal Treatment

Individualized Claim Resolution

Given the "whiteness" of tort law and legal culture, it might be surprising to learn that African American tort plaintiffs achieved some success in the torts system, winning tort cases in all regions during the first half of the twentieth century and even earlier (Welke 2001; Wriggins 2005a, at 100, n7). Various institutional factors, defined in this chapter as part of legal culture, probably provide most of the explanation for the partial success of black litigants.[3] Tort doctrines such as negligence and battery generally were racially neutral in their terms (Wriggins 2005a, 105, n26, 113, n53). At times, courts rejected parties' efforts to shape race-specific doctrinal rules. For example, one opinion rejected the notion that it was inherently negligent to employ a black mule driver (*Patterson v. Risher* 1920). Explicit statements that African American plaintiffs should be compensated less than white plaintiffs because of race were rare in the hundreds of published cases I have read in the course of this research (Wriggins 2005a, 127, n124). At the same time, treatment was not equal across the color line. It seems fair to say that black people's tort claims were often devalued relative to white people's tort claims. Some of the same institutional factors that allowed for success in tort litigation also allowed for inequality and devaluation of black plaintiffs' injury claims.

The overarching institutional factor that led to the success of black plaintiffs was the tort litigation system's commitment to individualized claim resolution. Individuals, not government actors, brought tort cases. Those cases were either settled or tried one by one. The availability of contingency fee agreements, the major mechanism by which tort cases were brought, provides part of the institutional explanation. These agreements, used since the mid-nineteenth century (Karsten 1998, 231), were a widely used method of financing litigation, in which attorneys advanced the costs of the litigation and took their fees and expenses out of the proceeds. Lawyers who worked on contingency had financial incentives to select and aggressively pursue cases that their clients were likely to win on liability and recover significant damages, whatever the race of the injured person. It seems reasonable to assume that contingency fee lawyers, who would have been white, factored in the racism of actors in the legal system in their decisions to take cases as well as in their settlement recommendations. These lawyers probably had very different motivations from government prosecutors who would have had to seek reelection by a solely white electorate. Many black clients could not have paid a lawyer's hourly fee, but were able to find representation and win tort suits. While individual tort cases against large defendants did not fundamentally challenge the racial caste system, the National Association for the Advancement of Colored People summarized some tort cases won by black plaintiffs in its magazine, *The Crisis,* suggesting that they were important statements of self-determination to many blacks at the time (Wriggins 2005a, 107, n33).

Second, liability and damages were assessed on a case-by-case basis. Juries, who generally decided tort trials, had tremendous discretion in deciding liability and assessing damages in particular cases. Doctrinal principles were supposed to be applied consistently in different cases, but facts always varied. Damages were not determined by any sort of fixed schedule, but were individualized and based in part on decision-makers' intuitive judgments. The individualized focus forced judges and juries to look closely at the facts of each individual plaintiff's injury and reach verdicts with reference to that injury. The fact that the trial setting allowed each plaintiff's case to be presented as an individual story may have helped white fact finders see it as such. Moreover, many of the defendants were railroad companies, which may have enabled plaintiffs to tap into widespread local anger at railroads for their unchecked power and the number of injuries they inflicted (Welke 2001, 99–100). These two factors, namely the availability of lawyers who would work on a contingent fee basis, and the practice of individualized claim resolution, together contributed to black plaintiffs' success in the torts system.

Equal Treatment

The same individualized focus that allowed some success for black plaintiffs also allowed tremendous inconsistency and made unequal treatment hard to detect. On the one hand, a broad basic principle of the rule of law for hundreds of years has been that everyone in the same situation should be treated the same way. According to basic ideas of formal equality, similar injuries in similar situations should produce similar liability determinations and similar compensation.

An injury to a black person that was similar to a white person's injury under comparable circumstances should result in similar liability determinations and similar damages. Also, in theory, to determine whether a particular result in a particular situation was equitable, one would look at similar situations and see if the result was the same. If the result was not the same, it was in some way unfair.

Yet, tort law's enforcement mechanisms made it very difficult to compare case results. Different juries and judges could make conflicting determinations of liability and damages on virtually identical facts. Since each injury was conceptualized as different and each person was different, the idea of rigorously comparing case outcomes to determine whether parties were treated fairly was anathema to torts. The individualized enforcement approach was in tension with the idea of equal treatment in law.[4]

However, the idea of equal treatment persisted as an undercurrent in tort law, at times looming into view and at times receding from view. The next section discusses some of the ways this tension between individualized claim resolution and equality operated, focusing particularly on the types of justifications offered by judges for their unequal treatment of black tort plaintiffs.

Applications to Tort Litigation

Damages at Trial: Reactions to Race-Based Remittitur

[I]n one sense, a colored man is just as good as a white man, for the law says he is, but he has not the same amount of injury under all circumstances that a white man would have.

(Judge Dugro, quoted in the *New York Times,* Negro Not Equal to White: Suffers Less Humiliation in False Arrest, May 22, 1909, 16)

An important example of the tension between equal treatment and individualized claim resolution was the New York case of *Griffin v. Brady,* which was notorious at the time, but has since receded into obscurity. The *New York Times* on May 22, 1909 carried the headline, "Negro Not Equal to White: Suffers Less Humiliation in False Arrest, Court Holds." George Griffin, a black Pullman porter, had sued Daniel Brady, president of Brady Brass Company, for false imprisonment damages because, he claimed, Brady had "maliciously caused his arrest on the charge of having stolen a card case containing $20, several railroad passes, and valuable papers, but the next day, when the case was investigated by a Magistrate, he was discharged" (*New York Times,* May 22, 1909, 16). The events took place in Montreal. A jury in New York found Brady liable and awarded Griffin $2,500. After the verdict, trial judge Philip Dugro told Griffin's lawyers "that he would set the verdict aside unless their client would consent to a reduction of the amount of damages to $300." This practice, known as remittitur, allows a trial judge who thinks a jury verdict is excessive to give the plaintiff a choice between a lower damages amount and a new trial (Johnson and Gunn, 2005, 185). When the plaintiff objected, the judge reduced the verdict (*New York Times* 1909, 16).

Justice Dugro's courtroom comments attracted notice. Referring to Mr. Griffin, Judge Dugro reportedly said:

> He was a porter, and while he is just as good as the President of the United States, and if he is imprisoned wrongfully he should be paid for it, it would be a bad argument to say that he is just as good in many senses. He would not be hurt just as much if put in prison as every other man would be. That depends on a man's standing, what his circumstances are, and, if he is a colored man, the fact that he is a colored man is to be considered . . . [I]n one sense, a colored man is just as good as a white man, for the law says he is, but he has not the same amount of injury under all circumstances that a white man would have. Maybe in a colored community down South, where the white man was held in great disfavor, he might be more injured, but after all that is not this sort of a community. In this sort of a community I dare say the amount of evil that would flow to the colored man from a charge like this would not be as great as it probably would be to a white man. (*New York Times* 1909, 16)

Despite these race-specific and racist statements by the judge in reducing the damage amount, this decision was affirmed by three appellate orders, none of which discussed its substance (*Griffin v. Brady* 1909, 1909, and 1910).

The trial court's decision was an example of racist legal culture affecting tort law. The judge referred to formal equality, noting that "in one sense, a colored man is just as good as a white man, for the law says he is," but then departed from it. His statement attempted to avoid the basic principle of formal equality that similar injuries should be treated similarly, by categorizing the injury to a black person caused by false imprisonment as different in kind from an injury to a (hypothetical) white person caused by the same tort. Although the defendant's actions were tortious in both situations, a different injury occurred and therefore different treatment *was* called for because of the different race of the victim in each situation. His statements about different damage amounts based on race, then, supposedly did not violate the general principle that similar injuries should be treated similarly, because the injuries were not similar.

Moreover, the decision, by tying damage amounts to group-based concepts of race and status, ignored the tort tradition that injuries should be evaluated individually. The false imprisonment tort is aimed at compensating individual victims for personal humiliation and insult. The judge's decision that this victim did not suffer as much as the jury thought he did, ignored both the purpose of this tort, and the reality that the damages for this tort are necessarily subjective (Keeton 1984, 48).

The broad response to this decision reveals much about the dynamics among legal culture, race, and tort law. Articles about the decision appeared in newspapers as far away as Oakland, California, and most were disparaging (examples include, *Oakland Tribune,* "Rights of Negro for Damages," June 1, 1909, p. 6, col. 4; *Kansas City Star,* "Court Draws a Color Line—Negroes Can't Be Damaged as much as White Men, Says a Judge," May 22, 1909, p. 9, col. 2). A *Virginia Law Register* article, later reprinted in the *Central Law Journal,* titled "A New York Court Draws The Color Line," lambasted the decision. The article stated that the court would have had to go back to the fourteenth century to find support for it, and that the plaintiff's race should have been irrelevant. Where punitive damages were at stake, as in this case, a plaintiff's "station" should not be relevant to damages, the article asserted. Highlighting regional tensions, the article sarcastically noted:

> We are exceedingly glad that this decision came from a court of justice north of the Potomac. Had it occurred in a southern state we can imagine the agony of mind that it would have cost the New York Evening Post and a few other journals of that character. We do not believe that in our Court of Appeals the court would have listened for one moment to an argument based upon the color of the suitor before it. (*Central Law Journal* 1909, 119)

And it stated that the judge had it backwards: the injury caused by false imprisonment to a porter "might be far greater than to a Vanderbilt or a Rockefeller."

One reason that Judge Dugro's statements received rather widespread attention is that by insisting that damages correspond to race and status, they so clearly deviated from the central idea that liability and damages in torts claims should be evaluated on a case-by-case basis. Moreover, by placing injuries to blacks in a different category from injuries to whites, his statements departed

from the persistent undercurrent in tort law and legal culture, that similar injuries should be treated similarly. Other trial judges, of course, may have made
similar remarks that were not reported or may have had similar thoughts that
they left unsaid. But, as the reaction to Judge Dugro's statements showed, the
tort practice that injuries should be evaluated individually, combined with the
secondary idea that similar injuries should be treated similarly, made it controversial to baldly state that the race and status of an injured person always should
determine the amount of his damages. At the same time, it is essential to remember that the New York appellate courts supported the trial judge's actions, send-
ing a powerful message that reducing damages of a black plaintiff because of his
race was acceptable. Reflecting the dynamic relationship between tort law and
legal culture, other trial judges later may have decided to follow Judge Dugro's
example and reduce black plaintiffs' damage awards for racist reasons, without
being explicit about it. The tort tradition of individualized claim resolution allowing broad judicial discretion over damage amounts made such decisions essentially unreviewable.

Appellate Analysis of Wrongful Death Values, I: The Epistemology of Life Expectancy

> I have not confidence in, and less respect for, these [mortality] tables made
> up by insurance agents, in which, of course, large allowance must be made
> for heavy commission, expenses, and profit. And this is especially true
> where colored persons are concerned.
>
> (Federal District Judge Adams, *The Saginaw and the Hamilton* 1905)

The question of how to measure the value of a life is perpetually vexing (Feinberg
2005; McClurg, 2005). When a person has been killed by a tort, part of that question often has involved making a counterfactual estimate of the length of life that
the deceased would have lived if her or his life had not been cut short. The reason
this estimate of life expectancy has been crucial in the context of wrongful death
litigation is that often the only element of damages allowed has been financial
loss, known as "pecuniary loss," to the survivors caused by the victim's death
(Dobbs 2000, 807). Once the life expectancy of a decedent who was financially
supporting survivors was estimated, lost wages could be calculated, reduced to
present value, and finally an estimate of pecuniary loss caused by the death to

the survivors could be made. Of course, it is impossible to accurately predict the length of an individual life. However, actuarial tables originally developed by insurance companies, showing the likely length of life of persons at different ages, have been statistically validated and widely used for over a hundred years (Glenn 2000).[5] Such tables, often referred to as mortality tables, have been uncontroversially used in wrongful death cases involving black as well as white decedents since the early twentieth century (Wriggins 2005a, 2006). A federal judge in 1905 refused to use such tables in a case involving the accidental deaths of eight people, six of whom were black. The judge's conclusion that the tables were invalid when applied to blacks was based on analysis by a leading proponent of what is now often termed *scientific racism*. This analysis claimed that blacks' immorality would cause them to die out. As discussed below, material from the wider culture affected the methodology used for tort damage determinations to the detriment of black plaintiffs.

The Saginaw and the Hamilton involved a collision between two boats in which both pilots were at fault. It resulted in appeals and ultimately a United States Supreme Court decision on admiralty law by Justice Holmes (*The Saginaw and the Hamilton* 1905, 1906, and 1907). The extraordinary discussion of race and damages by Federal District Judge Adams in reviewing the admiralty commissioner's opinion was not mentioned in any appellate opinions on the case. Sitting in New York, Judge Adams applied Delaware law which allowed only pecuniary loss damages. Judge Adams's opinion, considered here as an appellate case because it reviewed an admiralty commissioner's initial decision, agreed with a defendant's argument that the damage awards were too high and had been determined by the commissioner incorrectly, "based on mortality tables, and not according to Admiralty precedents." Although Judge Adams reduced all the damage awards, on average he reduced the awards for the deaths of blacks 10 percent more than the awards for the deaths of whites, and he reduced three of the awards for blacks 40 percent or more.[6]

Judge Adams agreed with the argument that mortality tables should not be used for life expectancy and damages determinations in the cases before him, quoting an earlier decision that rejected tables because they imposed certainty where there was none and included unstated amounts for expenses and commissions. Judge Adams noted that mortality tables "are very useful in insurance matters, but seem to afford little real aid in determining the duration of life in such cases as are now presented" (*The Saginaw and the Hamilton* 1905 at 913). The decision endorsed by Judge Adams went on to state: "I have no confidence in, and less respect for, these [mortality] tables made up by insurance agents, in which, of course, large allowance must be made for heavy commission, expenses, and profit." Judge Adams added, "and this is especially true where colored persons are concerned" (*The Saginaw and the Hamilton* 1905. at 914). He then quoted racially specific life expectancy tables based on census data from the influential 1896 book by Frederick L. Hoffman, *Race Traits and Tendencies of the American Negro*. These tables showed shorter life expectancies for "colored" people, and Adams concluded that they demonstrated what he called the "difference in the vitality of the two races" (*The Saginaw and the Hamilton* 1905 at 914). Finally, he concluded that mortality tables should not have been used in this case. Judge Adams instead used an intuitive, individualized method to shrink damages. He decided on amounts that simply seemed right to him, based on his impressions of facts such as how long each drowning victim would have lived if not for the drowning. His impressions resulted in more significant average reductions of damage amounts for family members of black drowning victims than for family members of white victims.

The rejection of mortality tables was based in significant part on race. Frederick Hoffman's *Race Traits and Tendencies of the American Negro* famously argued, based on statistical analysis of comparative mortality and other figures, that "immorality" was a "race trait" of blacks, and that the black population would eventually die out as a result of venereal and other diseases (Glenn 2000, 790–791; B. Hoffman 2003, 2). Hoffman argued that the "immorality and vice" (Glenn 791) of black people resulted in what Judge Adams called "the difference in the vitality of the two races" (*The Saginaw and the Hamilton* 1905 at 914). Judge Adams' conclusion, relying on Hoffman, was that the commonly used mortality tables improperly overestimated blacks' life expectancies. Hoffman is now seen as an architect of what is now often called "scientific racism," which was widespread among whites during this period (Glenn 2000, 790–791; B. Hoffman 2003, 2). A second factor in the tables' rejection was the judge's suspicion of knowledge that comes from the insurance industry as tainted and inaccurate by virtue of its association with that industry. This may have been rooted in the association between life insurance and gambling that was widespread in the nineteenth century (Zelizer, 1979, 67–73). Judge Adams articulated a gap between two types of knowledge about human mortality: the "neutral" scientific knowledge articulated by Hoffman in his book, and the "biased" scientific knowledge from insurance companies. In Judge Adams's view, Hoffman's knowledge simply trumped the insurance companies' knowledge.

Interestingly, Judge Adams did not only have a choice between standard mortality tables and individualized assessment. He could have used mortality tables divided by race based on the 1880 census data included in Hoffman's book. Blacks' life expectancies, after all, actually were shorter than whites' life expectancies (*The Saginaw and the Hamilton* 1905 at 914). Standard mortality tables would overestimate black life expectancies and provide a greater pecuniary loss amount for survivors of black decedents than black-only mortality tables would. Using black-only tables to estimate life expectancy would have made pecuniary loss calculations smaller for the black decedents because of shorter black life expectancies. Adams may have not done this because, based on Hoffman's analysis of diseases in the black population, he thought that even those tables overestimated blacks' life expectancies. Rather than use such race-specific tables, Adams used the "difference in vitality" of the races to jettison tables altogether and instead substitute his individualized assessment.

Judge Adams' decision did not attract press attention, in striking contrast to Judge Dugro's statements in *Griffin v. Brady* (1909) discussed previously. This lack of attention may perhaps be traced to the widely held acceptance of Hoffman's views, to a widespread suspicion of insurance companies, and to the consistency of Adams' approach with the institutional commitment of tort litigation to individualized adjudication. Because Judge Adams resolved the claims one by one, his predictive impressions and judgments were dispositive, and no real consistency was required. The use of that kind of individualized analysis allowed race and racism to continue to play a role in tort law that was unstated and very hard to detect or prove.

Appellate Analysis of Wrongful Death Values, II: Louisiana, Valuation, and Devaluation

To begin to interrogate the ways that race and racism in the legal culture and wider culture may have affected tort law in the form of appellate decisions, I closely examined Louisiana's wrongful death and survival civil code provision, section 2315, a version of which has been in effect since the mid-nineteenth century.[7] I also read 152 Louisiana appellate wrongful death and survival cases published between 1900 and 1949, comparing damage awards to black and white surviving family members of people killed by torts.[8] Black family members won cases for deaths of loved ones before juries and appellate courts, but the aggregate amounts awarded for deaths of blacks were much less than for deaths of whites, as discussed below.

The racist exclusion of black people from decision-making roles in the civil justice system, mentioned previously, that took place elsewhere in the United States also took place in Louisiana during this period. Twenty-six of these cases were brought by black family members; one hundred and twenty-six presumably were brought by white family members. Institutional aspects of legal culture discussed earlier, such as access to contingent fee lawyers and individualized claim adjudication, probably contributed to what success there was for black plaintiffs (Wriggins 2005a, 110–130).

These cases are particularly illuminating for beginning to explore relationships between legal culture and appellate tort law because of two features specific to Louisiana tort law during this period. First, an unusual aspect of Louisiana tort law allowed the survivors of tortiously killed family members to seek compensation for their own grief and emotional losses, as well as for the pecuniary losses typically allowed by wrongful death statutes (Dobbs 2000, 807). Second, because of Louisiana's civil law roots, appellate review included review of the facts, so that appellate courts discussed the amount of damages with more frequency and specificity than appellate courts in many other states which had common law traditions (Crawford 1994, 2). Putting these two characteristics together, Louisiana tort doctrine invited appellate courts to discuss and possibly compare amounts of damages for emotional loss and other types of harm.[9]

Wrongful death actions and survival actions are distinct but often litigated together. Wrongful death actions are aimed at recovering losses suffered by family members as a result of a decedent's tortiously caused death. By contrast, a survival action is the continuation of a tort claim after death that the decedent would have had if he had lived, "with damages that he could have recovered had he been able to sue at the moment of death" (Dobbs 2000, 805). Survival actions, then, typically include the decedent's pain and suffering. In Louisiana during this period, while relatives often brought a wrongful death claim together with a survival claim in the same lawsuit, appellate court decisions on damages often did not specify which damages were for which claim, making a resort to factual specifics of the case necessary in order to analyze many appellate decisions.

My general conclusion about race and damages is that these appellate tort cases often treated deaths of black people as worth less than deaths of white people. Comparing average and median damage awards to surviving family members by race in Louisiana in these cases, black family members received much lower awards than white family members. The average award to black family members, $3,559, was less than half the amount of the average award to white family members, $8,245, during this period (Wriggins 2005a, 118). The same was true for median awards; the median recovery for black family members, $3,200, was less than half the median award for white family members, $7,021 (Wriggins 2005a, 118).

In addition to awards being lower for deaths of black decedents, black decedents were "underrepresented" in these appellate cases relative to the black proportion of the population. As noted earlier, the number of these cases in which the decedent was identified as black was twenty-six, while in one hundred and twenty-six of these cases, the decedent was white (Wriggins 2005a, 110, n46). Cases with black decedents were only 17.1 percent of the total, while Louisiana's black population ranged from 47.1 percent in 1900 to 32 percent in 1950 (Wriggins 2005a, 112, n52). Many reasons could account for the disparity. One partial explanation lies in the incentives of the contingent fee system, coupled with the low wages and poverty of blacks in Louisiana during this period (Dethloff and Jones, 2000, 503; Rose, 1964, 68–70). The low wages and poverty of blacks in Louisiana, when combined with the law's focus on "pecuniary loss," made it likely that the death of a black family member would cause less pecuniary loss than the death of a white family member.[10] This in turn made it likely that damage awards compensating for pecuniary loss to black families would be less than pecuniary loss awards to white families. Contingency fee lawyers typically decline to take a case where the damage amount is likely to be very small. This would have been true in the first half of the twentieth century as well. In addition, cases with low damage amounts may be more likely to settle before a trial or appeal than high-damage amount cases. Thus, institutional factors such as the contingent fee system and poverty of blacks may have been factors in the apparent shortage of appellate wrongful death and survival cases involving black decedents, as well as in the much lower damage amounts that survivors of black decedents received.

Yet, the economic disempowerment of blacks and the incentives of contingent fee lawyers do not entirely explain the differences in damage amounts or other features of these decisions. The civil code provision, after all, did not limit damages to economic loss but also allowed damages for survivors' grief and the decedent's pain and suffering (Wriggins 2005a, 112, n50). One might expect decisions where pecuniary loss was small but other elements of damages were large. By and large it seems that there were not such decisions. Beyond pecuniary loss, language used in some decisions and structures of reasoning in some others both suggest a race-based devaluation of injuries to blacks may have been at work. Tort law, then, reflected the legal culture and the wider culture. Each of these aspects—language and reasoning structures—will now be briefly highlighted.

Judges' language in some cases stated negative generalizations about black people and stated that the decedent had either acted consistently with such generalizations or had departed from such generalizations (Wriggins 2005a, 127–128). However, in no case in Louisiana (or in the hundreds of wrongful death cases I have read from other states) did a judge articulate any generalization about whites and state that the decedent either acted consistently or inconsistently with that generalization. In some cases, devaluation of injury based on race was quite explicit. One of the most striking examples is found in 1910's *Blackburn v. Louisiana Railway & Navigation Co.* 1910). In that case, the Louisiana Supreme Court reduced a verdict for the mother of a thirty-one-year old brakeman from $6,210 to $1,985, stating: "Considering the well-known improvidence of the colored race, and the irregular life these colored brakemen lead, we think that upon this evidence a regular allowance of $15 per month would lean more to the side of liberality to the plaintiff than otherwise" (1910 at 869). The individualized method of claims resolution already had given the jury the opportunity to take into account whether this decedent had lived his life "improvidently" or "irregularly," or had supported his mother generously and regularly, factors which would have been relevant to determining her pecuniary loss. Here, the cultural product of negative, race-based stereotypes which categorized blacks' conduct as fundamentally different from whites' conduct, gave judges the justification for departing from damages conclusions reached by the individualized method, and then for devaluing the injury.

Decisions in some of these cases displayed a reasoning structure that determined the particular damage awards for survivors of black decedents based on the damage awards in earlier cases involving only black decedents. Putting blacks in different categories from whites, these cases used racially segregated or "black only" precedents to determine benchmarks for damage amounts, which resulted in lower compensation. The most vivid example of this is *Young v. Broussard*, a 1939 case in which a Louisiana appellate court actually overturned the trial court's judgment for the defendant, instead awarding $3,500 to the parents of Pentard Young, who had been killed by a night watchman (*Young v. Broussard* 1939]). In reaching this damage amount, the court declared:

> [I]n the [] case of *Shamburg v. Thompson, Trustee,* we affirmed an award of $3200 to the mother of a twenty two year old colored boy who was injured by the train at nine o'clock in the morning and died in the afternoon of the same day. The parents of a twenty-nine year old colored boy were allowed $6,000 for loss of love and affection, support, etc., and for the pain and suffering of the deceased in the case of *Rousseau v. Texas & Pac. R. Co., et al.* We have decided to fix the award in this case at $3500, which amount we believe to be proper under the facts and circumstances of this case. (ibid., 481)

The decision, referring to adult black males as "boys," used as precedents only cases involving damage amounts for black decedents. These "black-only" precedents involved low damage amounts, and although the same court had awarded higher damage amounts in cases involving white decedents, the court failed to cite them. Indeed, this court had decided a case three years earlier involving the death of a white man in his twenties which resulted in a higher award, but did not mention it. Rather, even while ruling in favor of the decedent's parents, the court stretched back thirteen years to a case decided by a different intermediate appellate court, involving the death of a black man in his twenties (Wriggins, 2005a, 126–127). This case, and a few others, displayed a reasoning structure that tried to impose some consistency upon damage awards, but it did so using a frame of reference that treated the race of the decedent (when the decedent was black) as the most relevant factor. This frame of reference, whether used consciously or unconsciously, treated the injury and loss caused by the death of a black man as different in kind from, and lesser than, the injury and loss caused by the death of a white man.

Conclusion

Considering the two most glaringly white features of tort law and legal culture of the United States in the first half of the twentieth century—the use of whiteness as a linguistic default in published legal opinions, and the exclusion of black people from decision-making roles in the civil justice system—one might expect that tort law and legal culture also would entirely prevent litigation success for black people injured by common torts of the day, such as railroad negligence. However, the emerging picture is more dynamic than these features would suggest. The foundational commitment to resolving claims in a decentralized, individualized fashion, which is a part of both tort law and legal culture, allowed some access and success for black plaintiffs. Yet, that same decentralized and individualized methodology allowed their claims to be treated as less valuable than whites' claims, and made it easy for the unequal treatment to escape notice. In the tort litigation process, damages amounts for black plaintiffs were at times reduced based at least in part on their race. In other words, the racism of the legal culture and wider culture affected tort law.

At the same time, the idea of equal treatment persisted as an undercurrent in legal culture and tort law. This undercurrent led some white decision makers to try to justify their race-based unequal treatment of black plaintiffs' claims. The attempted justifications ranged from a judge who claimed that the lower racial status of blacks meant that their damages were less than whites' damages, to a judge who used empirical data to conclude that his own intuition was more accurate than widely used mortality tables, to an appellate court that determined damages amounts for blacks by reference to past cases only involving blacks. These justificatory frameworks put black plaintiffs in different categories from white plaintiffs. These segregated categories reflected the segregated legal culture and the wider culture. The categories in which black plaintiffs were placed had a lower rank and lower value than the categories whites occupied, again reflecting the broader culture. Situating blacks in a different, lesser category from whites meant that equal treatment was not necessary, and in fact, inferior treatment was appropriate. These cultural frameworks powerfully justified and reinscribed the inequality of tort law.

PART IV

Issues of Risk and Responsibility

The Role of Tort Lawsuits in Reconstructing the Issue of Police Abuse in the United Kingdom

CHARLES R. EPP

"A High Court jury yesterday awarded record damages of £100,000 to a man who had cannabis planted on him by a police officer," a London newspaper reported in 1989 (Rose 1989). "The sum is nearly eight times the previous highest award in a case of this kind, and highest ever against the police. Mr. Rupert Taylor, aged 30, a BBC motor engineer, lay preacher, teetotaler and non-smoker, was arrested and planted with the drug by PC David Judd on his way to play dominos with a friend at a community centre in Notting Hill, west London. He told the court PC Judd had radically (sic) abused him saying, 'You had to open your fucking black mouth.'"

Although such a report might seem unremarkable in an American city, in Britain in the 1980s it was stunning. It was centered in a poor London ghetto long the subject of lurid press reports of "black" muggings and riots, often portrayed as contained only by heroic police action. Yet in contrast to earlier depictions, the black man entangled in the criminal justice system in this story is portrayed as innocent, the police as abusive, vulgar, and racist.

The difference—and, as we shall see, it was part of a radical shift in the legal terrain—lay in the endorsement of the man's story by a jury of ordinary Britons. For virtually the first time, a jury threw their sympathies wholeheartedly with the black victim and expressed outraged indignation against the police, punctuated by their award, in addition to £30,000 in compensatory damages, of £70,000 in exemplary (punitive) damages. Although British newspapers had previously reported a handful of damage awards and settlements involving police abuses, few had exceeded £10,000. The 1989 case pierced a symbolic £100,000 ceiling. Moreover, it opened a decade of dramatically rising numbers of lawsuits and damage awards against the police in cases in which the media portrayed the black victims of police abuse not as criminals but as innocent, honorable members of society. That change in portrayal contributed to a transformation of the public agenda on policing, shifting from a focus on black criminality and toward police misconduct, and then redefining police misconduct as the responsibility not of a few "bad apple" officers but as a systemic problem requiring institutional reform.

Britain provides a comparative perspective on debates over legal liability in the United States, highlighting several puzzles addressed in this chapter. Media coverage commonly portrays social problems as the responsibility of individuals while ignoring their systemic or structural sources: thus, such issues as the McDonald's coffee-burn incident and fast-food fat become, in the media, stories not about irresponsible corporate policy but about individuals' self-inflicted injuries and health problems (Haltom and McCann 2004; and this volume). In Britain, by contrast, media coverage began portraying police abuse as the institutional responsibility of police departments. Why? In modern government, there is a basic tension between managerial and popular approaches to policy reform and accountability: the United States, with the availability of tort liability and the jury, tips the balance a bit toward popular mechanisms of accountability, while Britain, with its insulated bureaucracies, professionalized civil service, and sharp limitations on tort liability and the jury, tips the balance in the other direction. Yet, in the 1990s, Britain experienced the wholly unexpected, a surge in pressure for more popular accountability of that most basic (and insulated) of British institutions, the bobby. Why? Perhaps most fundamentally, Britain has long represented a sharp contrast to the United States in basic matters of legal culture: where U.S. culture is suspicious of governmental power, British culture is suspicious of popular disorder, evidenced by British law's heavy penalties for "riot," a libel law that protects public figures from harsh criticisms, broad discretionary police powers to stop and search people on the street, and so on (see also Mather, this volume). Yet the welling up of lawsuits and jury decisions against the police seemed to reverse those cultural predispositions. Why?

The answer to these puzzles is that British police-accountability activists and lawyers strategically used footholds *in* British culture and law to undermine, at least temporarily, another verity of British culture and law, the managerial insulation of the police, and to bring to bear more popular mechanisms of accountability. They did so by drawing lessons from tort lawyers in the United States, particularly by mounting a long-term, strategic litigation campaign against institutional irresponsibility. But their success has lessons for American lawyers as well: it rested, more than is typical of recent American tort campaigns, on close connections with popular, nonlawyerly campaigning. In sum, this chapter, like those by Mather, Feldman, and Tanase in this volume, views neither tort law nor cultures as monolithic and unchanging, but rather as composed of multiple institutional orders that interact and mutually shape each other—and which, through those interactions, are sometimes open to unexpected change. Like Haltom and McCann (this volume), I find that a key site of interaction between tort law and culture is the mass media and its portrayal of tort claims and jury decisions.

Race and the Crisis in British Policing

Since the 1950s, the British police, according to Robert Reiner, the leading scholar of British policing, have suffered "an increasing haemorrhage of public confidence" and a "repeated cycle of scandal and reform" culminating in a "Permanent Crisis" (Reiner 2000, 59, 62, 202). Although part of the problem has always been garden-variety corruption, the current crisis reflects pervasive race discrimination by the police, resulting in a "catastrophic deterioration of relations with the black community" (Reiner 2000, 79). The crisis grew in the context of a widespread political backlash against immigration into Britain by racial minorities (Solomos 2003). The first clear evidence of the emerging problem appeared in 1958, as whites attacked West Indian and south Asian immigrants in the Notting Hill section of London and in Nottingham, ironically provoking a parliamentary debate over the dangers of "undesirable immigrants" (Solomos 2003, 53–55). By 1970, conservative politicians had blamed many urban problems, particularly crime and disorder, on minority immigrants, and the police had begun carrying out increasingly aggressive oversight of urban minority neighborhoods. Tensions between the police and black youths in one locality had escalated by 1970 to the point of "open 'warfare,'" signaling "a massive breakdown in relations between the police and the black community" (Solomos 2003, 123).

In the 1970s, as the British economy stagnated, unemployment mounted, and major urban areas sank into poverty, the mass media succumbed to hysteria about street crime attributed to black youths. In a seminal analysis, Stuart Hall and his colleagues (Hall et al. 1978) observed that portrayals of blacks and street crime reflected an affinity in policing and the media for stories of individual irresponsibility—the black mugger attacking an elderly white widow—rather than stories of structural or systemic problems. By focusing on "black muggings," Hall and his colleagues argued, the police and media created the "moral panic" as much as reflected it. The British police, the authors demonstrated, had "structured" and "amplified" the panic by deliberately targeting areas frequented by minority youths for increased surveillance and arrest. The media perpetuated the image of young black men as virtually inherently criminal, and the police then responded by engaging in increasingly aggressive policing tactics against young black men, leaving black ghettoes simmering with resentment.

That resentment boiled over in a series of major urban riots in the late 1970s and 1980s, and criticisms of the police began mounting. Careful research began to support minorities' claims that the police were disproportionately targeting them for stops and searches (Smith and Gray 1985). The tensions were exacerbated by the fact that, while the racial minority population of Britain grew significantly after the 1950s, the ranks of the police remained virtually entirely white. By the mid-1980s, racial minorities made up about 10 percent of the London population but only about 1 percent of the London police force (McKenzie and Gallagher 1989, 84–85).

At the same time, a number of high-profile Irish Republican Army (IRA) bombings cases fell apart as it became clear that they were based on police perjury, fabrication of evidence, and extraction of false confessions (Reiner 2000, 66; Walker and Starmer 1993). By the late 1980s, police relations with minorities and other marginalized groups had reached a low point.

Those complaining of police insensitivity and abuse theoretically had several options for checking and reforming the police, none very attractive or effective. *No* elected body directly controls the British police forces. In legal terms, Chief Constables (and constables in general) are "officers of the Crown" and thus have legal independence from direct control by any external agency; the common law doctrine of "constabulary independence" declares that constables are answerable only to "the law" (Clayton and Tomlinson 2004, 22–45). Although "answerable to the law" might seem to imply that the courts exercise oversight, traditionally even that check was largely unavailable. For decades, neither the courts nor the police paid any heed to the "Judges' Rules," a set of judicial guidelines governing the gathering of evidence (see, e.g., Reiner 2000, 65). Additionally, the official police complaints process until very recently lacked teeth, and few complaints resulted in discipline or prosecution of officers (Reiner 1993, 2000; Smith 2005).

In contrast to the judicial check used in the United States, Britain has traditionally relied on high-level official inquiries followed by national legislative reforms. In response to the Brixton riots, for instance, the government appointed a prominent retired judge, Lord Scarman, to conduct an inquiry. Although he concluded that growing popular resentment against heavy-handed policing techniques had contributed to the riots, he characterized the problem as a matter of controlling the behavior of a few individual police officers (Scarman 1981). Critics charged that Scarman had failed to recognize the depth of the policing problem, the broad degree of managerial responsibility for it, and the need for institutional reforms (Bowling and Phillips 2002, 9–10).

The Scarman Report, as Reiner (1991) observes, dominated the British policing agenda in the 1980s and contributed to legislative reforms favoring a typically British solution, managerial control. The Police and Criminal Evidence (PACE) Act of 1984 significantly enhanced police powers (particularly to stop and search people) but also increased national administrative oversight over the police and, for the first time, attempted to bring police practices under detailed legal regulation (Dixon 1997). PACE also created the Police Complaints Authority with authorization to supervise investigations into police misconduct (Smith 2005). Another 1985 statute created the Crown Prosecution Service (CPS) and authorized it to oversee police investigations and decisions to prosecute. The pressures for reform also strengthened several other centralizing forces, among them Her Majesty's Inspectorate of the Constabulary (HMIC), a police oversight agency under the authority of the Home Secretary (Brown 1998, 95–102).

Allegations of racially discriminatory policing deepened after the 1980s legislative reforms. A primary complaint has long been police stops and searches of persons on the street. As police use of their powers to stop and search expanded dramatically in the late 1980s, allegations of racially discriminatory stops exploded (Clayton and Tomlinson 2004, 5). In the United States, studies of "racial profiling" in law enforcement generally find that African American drivers are stopped at roughly one and a half to two times the rate at which white drivers are stopped, a disparity that generates widespread concern. In Britain, by contrast, blacks are stopped and searched at a rate fully *eight times* that of whites, almost certainly an underestimate, and a disparity that probably is increasing over time (Metropolitan Police Authority 2004; Police Complaints Authority 2004).

By the mid-1990s, many observers concluded that the managerial reforms of the 1980s had failed to reduce the level of police abuse. Scraton (1994, 102), summarizing numerous studies, observed that "the police habitually break the rules, commit unlawful acts before, during, and after questioning, and fabricate evidence." Sanders and Young (1997, 1068) observed that the police treatment of suspects who are poor, members of racial minorities, and young, "is frequently humiliating—and deliberately so." And Reiner (2000, 182) observed that after the 1980s reforms "the socially discriminatory pattern of use of police powers remains as marked as before."

Enter Tort Litigation

Tort litigation ultimately pierced the insulation protecting the police from accountability. British plaintiffs against the police have long enjoyed a structural incentive that American plaintiffs can only dream about: British chief constables are vicariously liable for the actions of their officers, thereby exposing police departments' deep pockets and creating the conditions for using tort lawsuits to press for institutional reform. Additionally, although plaintiffs have no right to a jury trial in most types of civil cases, through a quirk in British statutory law, plaintiffs have a right to a jury trial in the most common types of tort claims against the police.[1] Victims of police abuse, moreover, were increasingly drawn to tort litigation as their frustrations grew over the inefficient and insulated police complaints and disciplinary process. Nonetheless, vicarious liability, the availability of the jury in claims against the police, and a hidebound official complaints process existed for years before litigation against the police developed much momentum.

After the early 1980s, however, a developing infrastructure of support for lawsuits against the police propelled a growth in police misconduct litigation. Well-established solicitors' firms, particularly Birnberg's, long noted for its civil liberties work, helped foster the development of a police misconduct bar. Additionally, shared knowledge about how to pursue lawsuits against the police expanded with the publication, beginning in 1987, of several legal guides to police misconduct law and practice (see, e.g., Clayton and Tomlinson 2004; Harrison et al. 2005). In the early 1990s, Graham Smith, a police-accountability campaigner, and Russell Miller, a solicitor with Birnberg's, developed a database containing the names of police officers implicated in civil lawsuits or whose testimony had been found by a court to be faulty.[2] As the number of lawyers bringing actions against the police increased, several joined together to form the Police Action Lawyers Group (PALG), an organization that expanded networks among police misconduct litigators.[3] Finally, the plaintiffs in a growing number of police misconduct cases were able to obtain legal aid to cover their legal costs. This was especially critical because legally aided claims are not subject to the ordinary "loser pays" rule which allows courts to require losing litigants to pay their opponents' legal costs. Legal aid thus dramatically lowered plaintiffs' risks in lawsuits against the police.

As the support structure for police misconduct litigation developed, victims of police abuse increasingly turned to tort lawsuits as an accountability mechanism. The development originated with a lawsuit brought by the National Union of Miners (NUM) in 1985 over abuses by the police in a major 1984 strike, resulting in an unprecedented judgment of £425,000 plus legal costs (Milne 1991). As the miners' lawsuit proceeded, residents of poor east London neighborhoods complained increasingly of police abuses, particularly by officers stationed at the Stoke Newington police station. That station, which served a multiethnic inner-city neighborhood, had a troubled history dating to the 1950s when black defendants first alleged police abuse. Tensions increased dramatically in 1983 with the shotgun shooting of Colin Roach, a young black man, in the foyer of the Stoke Newington station. An inquest jury ruled the shooting a suicide, a determination disputed by many area residents, leading to widespread protests. As a journalist (Pauley 1985) later observed, the incident brought the area "close to [the] racial boiling point."

Area residents in 1987 formed the Hackney Community Defence Association to better coordinate action against police misconduct. The Hackney Association worked closely with a number of solicitors, among them Raju Bhatt, an attorney on the miners' team (Campbell 1997). Bhatt began to pursue tort lawsuits against the police, he said, after representing criminal defendants in "case after case" and developing a sense of outrage "when it was clear to all that the police had abused the defendant" but nothing was done to correct the problem beyond an occasional dismissal of charges.[4] "We faced a situation," Graham Smith, one of the organizers said, "in which there were literally two cases of police beatings per week in a small section of east London" and the police, the criminal courts, and the official oversight agencies were doing little to address the problem.[5]

In the late 1980s and early 1990s, damage awards and settlements in tort lawsuits against the police began increasing in frequency. Among the earliest

significant awards involved the case of a man who alleged that he had been un-
justifiably arrested and charged a number of times in incidents related to protests
against the police (Dyer 1988). In early December 1989, in the case discussed
at the outset of this chapter (Rose 1989), a jury gave a record damage award of
£100,000. By the spring of 1990, the new Hackney Association reported that it
was supporting at least six lawsuits against the police (Kirby 1990).

In May of 1990, the *Independent* newspaper published a letter from Graham
Smith and Martin Walker (Smith and Walker 1990, p. 18), organizers of the
Hackney Association, the first in a series of strategic efforts by the Association to
reframe media coverage of the issue. Smith and Walker argued that the problems
were systemic, requiring institutional solutions. The police, they wrote, were
"stereotyping whole sections of society." They called for "a complete reappraisal
of the criminal justice system, most particularly the role of the police."

Ongoing complaints about the Stoke Newington station exploded in 1991 into
a major scandal when an acknowledged drug dealer alleged that officers had accepted bribes (Campbell 1992a, 1992b, 1992c, 1992f). Soon other defendants alleged that Stoke Newington officers had fabricated evidence, and, under mounting pressure from an increasingly coordinated group of defense attorneys, judges
began to doubt police testimony in the cases and a Customs and Excise agency
investigation uncovered evidence of possible corruption (McCrystal 1993; Smith
1999). The allegations formed the basis for Operation Jackpot, a secret internal
police investigation begun in April 1991, which grew over the following year into
what senior Metropolitan (Met) Police Authority officers eventually called the
most serious allegations of police corruption in Britain in twenty years (Campbell
1992c; Kirby 1992). The *Guardian* broke the story in late January 1992 (Campbell
1992a, 1992b), and the revelations rocked the police station and neighborhood,
an area, as another newspaper (*Evening Standard* 1992) observed, "already boiling with anti-police sentiment and where they stage annual torch-lit marches to
commemorate the deaths of alleged victims of police violence."

In the wake of the revelations, the Hackney Association reasserted their demand for institutional reform (Campbell 1992c). "The situation in Hackney,"
stated Martin Walker of the Hackney Community Defence Association, "is completely and utterly out of control," and the group demanded a full, independent,
public inquiry (Campbell 1992a, 1992c). The Hackney Association reported that
the number of lawsuits it was supporting had grown to twenty-five (Campbell
1992c). In one such case, an elderly woman won a £50,000 damage award, a major

victory for the Hackney group (Myers and Campbell 1992). A number of lawyers who were members of the Association, in coordination with their local Member of Parliament (MP), suggested that the published allegations might be only the "tip of the iceberg," and called on the Government to bring in outside investigators (Brown 1992).

The Met soon suspended three Stoke Newington officers (Campbell 1992f, 1992h) and, by early July, the CPS was reexamining pending cases in which implicated officers had participated—but was refusing to reopen cases already resulting in convictions (Campbell 1992f, 1992h). Ultimately, it was learned that the station had secretly disbanded its drug investigation unit and reconstituted it with different officers (McCrystal 1993). The scandal reverberated through the criminal courts as well, where judges began overturning drug convictions coming out of the Stoke Newington station (Campbell 1992d, 1994a). Then, the CPS offered no evidence in seventeen pending cases, effectively admitting they were tainted, and an additional seventeen cases resulted in acquittals (Campbell 1992e), "specifically because Stoke Newington police witnesses were found to be not credible" (McCrystal 1993). "[S]omething of a siege mentality has descended" on the Stoke Newington station, another journalist (Campbell 1992g) observed, and its Chief Superintendent declined requests for further interviews.

As the official internal investigation dragged on through 1993, activists and even judges began to express frustration. A leak of the internal investigation's preliminary report in September 1993 revealed that criminal prosecution would be recommended against a small number of officers but that the Stoke Newington command structure would be cleared of responsibility (Campbell 1993). Graham Smith, of the Hackney Association, declared that the official investigations "have been found wanting time and time again. Maybe now there will be a judicial inquiry" (no title, *Guardian* 1993). Similarly, Lord Taylor of the Court of Appeal complained that "'dynamite' should be put under the Police Complaints Authority" in order to induce speedier action (Campbell 1994a). When the Met's investigators released a statement in early 1994 announcing the end of the inquiry and recommending prosecution of only ten officers, the Hackney Association replied that this number paled in comparison to the 381 complaints it had received and the eighty-three lawsuits that it was supporting against the police (*Independent* 1994). "Operation Jackpot," Graham Smith said, "has been unsatisfactory on all levels. Its terms of reference were too limited and it has taken far too long. The inquiry raises serious questions about police complaints investigations" (ibid.).

Seemingly confirming Smith's pessimistic assessment, the CPS, after a delay of nearly six months, announced criminal charges against only two officers. Smith declared, "This is an insult to the community" (Bennetto 1994b).

As jury awards and settlements in tort cases against the police continued to grow in number and size (Bennetto 1994a; Campbell 1994b; Mullin 1994), media coverage increasingly came to reflect the Hackney Association's claim that the problem was systemic. In June 1992, the widely read London entertainment magazine *Time Out* ran a weekly article on the "Stoke Newington Scandal" (Smith 1999). "The illusion of a regulated, user-friendly law enforcement vanishes," a journalist (McCrystal 1993) put it after interviewing area residents. "There are sullen reminders of 'bent' cops and disgruntled observations that nobody seems in a great hurry to do much about them." The day after the CPS announced prosecutions of only two officers, the *Guardian* published a summary of cases in which the police force had settled civil claims alleging police abuse and yet had taken no disciplinary action (Barr 1994; see also Campbell 1995a). In another story, the *Independent* reported "what could be one of the most embarrassing civil actions mounted against the Metropolitan Police," a case involving the police planting of a weapon in an attempt to justify the shooting of an unarmed, innocent jogger (Kelsey 1995). In the months following the filing of the jogger lawsuit, newspapers published a growing cascade of stories about lawsuits against the police, with the increasingly familiar refrain that "no officers had been disciplined over the incident, no CID [internal] inquiry would be held and no apology offered" (Ford 1995).

Tort lawyers won two key procedural victories in the early 1990s that contributed to the shift in media coverage. Raju Bhatt had long sought to dignify and publicize his clients' complaints, and, beginning in the late 1980s, he began using a procedure drawn from libel law in which victorious libel plaintiffs issue a "statement in open court" vindicating their reputation. In 1990, in an unreported decision, a judge granted victorious police abuse plaintiffs the right to present statements summarizing their stories.[6] Newspapers relied heavily on such statements (see, e.g., Campbell 1995c) until the Court of Appeal in 1997 sharply limited them. Additionally, in mid-July of 1994, the Judicial Committee of the House of Lords issued a landmark decision (*R v. Chief Constable ex parte Wiley* 1995) granting plaintiffs access to the official evidence in internal police investigations. "Once we had access to the record," Bhatt observed, "we saw how weak was the whole investigatory process. We could show to juries [in tort cases] that the investigations were, in fact, efforts at *mitigation*, not investigation. There were instances where investigators effectively told officers how they should answer questions in order not to substantiate the complaint."[7] Jury decisions soon began to reflect the newly available evidence.

The *Independent* newspaper in September 1995 published an unflattering portrait of the Met's responsiveness to complaints of police abuse, observing in its lead that "Scotland Yard has paid out nearly £1.5 million to settle 48 substantial court claims for assault or false imprisonment over the past two years—but has taken disciplinary action against only four officers as a result," two of whom were only "'given words of advice'" (Mills 1995).

In response, members of Parliament voiced concern. "It is quite remarkable that, despite these enormous payments," Chris Mullin, a Labour MP (and a long-time campaigner against police misconduct in an IRA bombing case), observed, "so little appears to happen to those responsible for the payout. I really think it is about time that the officers who are costing millions of pounds of taxpayers' money for their actions are called to account" (Mills 1995). More cases followed in the final months of 1995, among them an inquest jury's verdict of "unlawful killing" based on evidence that the coroner had condemned the police for an "appalling lack of instruction" in proper restraint techniques (Bennetto 1995; Campbell 1995c).

Sir Paul Condon, the Commissioner of the Metropolitan Police, upon releasing the force's annual report in 1994, had complained that solicitors were beginning to see the police as a "soft option" and "soft target" willing to easily settle lawsuits, and he declared that the Met would defend more cases in court (Bennetto 1994c).

As more cases proceeded to court, jury outrage exploded in a series of stunning verdicts. At the end of January 1996, on a "day of shame for Scotland Yard," an inquest jury turned in a verdict of unlawful killing in a case involving a neck hold (in a case in which the CPS had yet again declined to prosecute), and the Met settled a separate police abuse case for £90,000 (Mills 1996b, 1996c, 1996d). The following day, the political fallout began. Chris Mullin, the prominent Labour MP, declared: "The Metropolitan Police are paying millions each year in damages and lawyers' fees, yet the Commissioner is flatly refusing to take any action against officers whose misbehaviour is responsible for this cost to the taxpayer. The longer this goes on, the more that public confidence will be undermined" (Mills 1996b, p. 6).

Mullin's critique proved to be only the beginning of a venting of public indignation. On March 28, 1996, juries in two police abuse cases handed down awards of £64,000 and a record-breaking £220,000 (Campbell 1996b). The jury in the latter case awarded the plaintiff, Kenneth Hsu, £200,000 in punitive damages after Hsu's barrister urged:

> send a clear message to the Commissioner that the public will no longer tolerate lying, bullying, perjury and racism by officers of the Metropolitan Police. In this case a small award of damages would be greeted as a victory by the officers involved. Even a moderately large award would be greeted with relief at Streatham police station. It is only if you award damages on an unprecedented scale that you can be sure the Commissioner will be told of your award, will take note of it and will act on it. (Campbell 1996b, home section, p. 5)

"But yesterday Scotland Yard was defiant," reported the *Independent* newspaper, "saying that none of the officers would be disciplined—and that in both cases there would be an appeal against the amount of damages" (Mills 1996a, news section, p. 11). A flurry of newspaper articles followed, on the theme, as one headline put it, that "anger grows at soaring cost of police assaults" (*Independent* 1996c, news section, p. 6; see also *Independent* 1996b). "MPs and lawyers are concerned," the article observed, "that awards and settlements are now so frequent that urgent action is needed. Their greatest anxiety is that officers are rarely the subject of criminal charges or disciplinary action" (*Independent* 1996c, news section, p. 6). Sadiq Khan, Hsu's solicitor, observed that victims of police misconduct had turned to lawsuits as a last resort "because the Police Complaints Authority is so impotent" (quoted in *Independent* 1996c, news section, p. 6). In response, an embattled Met leadership maintained its defiance. Brian Hayes, deputy commissioner of the Met, declared that the agency would "'keep its nerve' in the face of civil [tort] actions" (quoted in Deane 1996, home news).

Three days later, in another case of police brutality, the Met was hit yet again with a new record jury award, £302,000, including £170,000 in exemplary damages (Ford 1996b). The Met declared that the officers involved in the case would face no further disciplinary action (Victor 1996). Four days later, a London jury awarded another man £108,000, including £45,000 in exemplary damages (*Independent* 1996a). As spring turned into summer 1996, the big damage awards kept coming, many above the previous £100,000 ceiling (Campbell 1996a; Ford 1996a; *Guardian* 1996a, 1996b; Varley 1996).

Condon, complaining that jury awards had gone "stratospheric" (Press Association 1996), ordered an appeal. The Court of Appeal heard it in *Thompson and Hsu v. Commissioner of Police,* issuing a landmark decision in early 1997. The Met asked for caps on damages, and the most noted aspect of the decision was its rate structure for damages, which capped exemplary damages at £50,000 and suggested appropriate rates for typical kinds of claims, many of which would reduce the awards by London juries. On this basis, London newspapers reported the decision as an outright victory for the Met (see, e.g., Davies 1997; Ford 1997b; Travis 1997). Ironically, the damages framework also worked to *increase* the size of awards in many outlying jurisdictions (Dixon and Smith 1998). But on other key issues the decision rejected the Met's appeal, particularly its request for effectively prohibiting exemplary damages in most cases (Dixon and Smith 1998). Lord Woolf defended juries' right to impose exemplary damages in order "to demonstrate publicly the strongest disapproval of what occurred and make it clear to the Commissioner and his force that conduct of this nature will not be tolerated by the courts" (*Thompson and Hsu,* p. 777).

Many plaintiffs' attorneys took the new rate structure and the damages cap as a death knell for litigation (see, e.g., Taylor and Deane 1996) and the 1997 decision in *Thompson and Hsu* undoubtedly closed a brief era in the history of British law. The size of awards in individual cases against the police plummeted, and eventually the Met's total annual payouts began to decline as well—and media coverage, too, declined.

Policy Reform in the Wake of the Litigation Campaign

Although relatively short-lived, the litigation campaign and the associated media coverage contributed to a dramatic shift in the policy agenda on policing. The older agenda is concisely expressed in *Winning the Race* (Her Majesty's Inspectorate of the Constabulary [HMIC] 1996/97) the first of a series of major inquiries by the HMIC into police and race relations, which, while reporting "pockets of wholly unacceptable racist policing," declared that "these comments . . . should be kept in perspective" as the police had "done as much as any other public organization" in addressing racism (HMIC 1996/97, para. 2.9 and executive summary).

By 1997, however, as litigation pressure and media coverage increased, the policy climate changed. In the summer, activist lawyers succeeded in destroying the legitimacy of the Crown Prosecution Service's long-standing refusal to bring criminal charges in cases of police abuse, leading, among other things, to an investigation of deaths in custody by the European Committee for the Prevention of Torture (Dyer 1997a, 1997b). In May of 1997, the Labour Party returned to power and placed police reform high on its domestic agenda. Chris Mullin, the long-time critic of the police, was selected as chair of Parliament's Home Affairs Committee with jurisdiction over domestic policy, including policing. Under Mullin's leadership, the Committee conducted hearings on the problem of police misconduct, recommending broad-sweeping reforms (Smith 2001, 385).

The Labour government also appointed Sir William MacPherson to head an official inquiry into the 1993 murder of Stephen Lawrence, a young black man, by white racist youths. After the initial police investigation fell apart, Lawrence's parents alleged that the police had not taken the case seriously. MacPherson's report, released in early 1999, proved to be a stunning, agenda-setting critique of British policing. In essence, he endorsed the Hackney campaigners' long-standing call for systemic policing reform. He concluded that British policing was shot through with "institutional racism," defined as "The collective failure of an organization to provide an appropriate and professional service to people because of their colour, culture, or ethnic origin" (MacPherson 1999, para. 6.34, 6.39). In sharp contrast to the Scarman Report, MacPherson dismissed the view that reform need focus only on removing a few "bad apples" or performing incremental improvements. Instead, he recommended a number of broad reforms aimed at making policing "as open and accountable as possible" (1999, para. 6.57).

The government quickly adopted legislation and national policies aimed at implementing a number of MacPherson's recommendations. In 2000, the government adopted the Race Relations (Amendment) Act, imposing on government agencies a duty to promote racial equality; a new Freedom of Information Act allowing public access to governmentally held information; a new "Ministerial Priority" increasing the level of trust of the police among minority communities, along with performance indicators of progress in this direction; new Codes of Practice governing police recording and reporting of racist incidents and investigations of racist crimes; new police training regarding race relations and cultural awareness; and so on (Home Office 2000). Whether the legislative reform agenda has changed frontline policing is a complicated matter; there is evidence both of significant change and resistance to change.

A Concluding Assessment:
The Culturally Conditioned Impact of Torts

There may be, at first, the impression that there is something very *English* about the events described in this chapter. English courts and law, as Mather (this volume) persuasively shows, have long been famous for a preference for order, stability, and respect for authority. In the area of police misconduct litigation, the necessity of obtaining legal aid in order to be shielded from the "loser pays" rule almost certainly limited the number of lawsuits. By American standards, moreover, the damage awards and settlements remained small—and yet the British press and governing officials responded as if stunned by a massive onslaught. Thus the commissioner of the Metropolitan Police said the awards had "gone stratospheric." Ultimately, after only a few years of rising damage awards, the Court of Appeal, at the request of the Commissioner, placed caps on the size of awards, thereby muzzling tort law's bite.

The American and British experiences with tort litigation against the police, however, also have much in common. In both settings, a powerful synergy has developed between tort lawsuits, the institution of the jury, and media coverage. As Haltom and McCann (2004; and this volume) demonstrate, the news media have an affinity for tort litigation, and the meaning and development of tort law is, in part, constituted by media portrayals of tort lawsuits. An individual plaintiff, graphic complaints, and money awards make compelling news.

Although, as Haltom and McCann (2004) show, the media typically do not frame issues in terms of corporate or governmental responsibility—the individual elements of stories are amplified, the underlying institutional mechanisms stripped or muffled—tort lawsuits have the potential to threaten the stability of institutionalized power. Thus, the British press, police officials, members of Parliament, and activists alike viewed awards of £100,000 (roughly $160,000 at the time) as stunning, and officials scrambled to respond. What mattered, however, was not the awards' size so much as their departure from past patterns and their significance in the battle over how to frame the issue of police accountability. The rise of the £100,000 award thus indicated that the terrain had shifted, that policing was entering a new era. The new era's defining characteristic was a collapse of public faith in the integrity of police treatment of racial minorities and the managerial system of police accountability. The clearest indicators of that collapse were juries' decisions. In case after case, juries of ordinary Britons sided with blacks complaining of police abuse, and, as time went on, juries' frustrations with a perceived lack of police responsiveness increased, resulting in rising damage awards. Litigation against the police thus achieved something unprecedented: it brought to full public view the long-held complaints by minority communities of discriminatory and abusive police action and, through detailed examination of the experiences of particular individuals, legitimated those complaints. Tort litigation, in sum, threatened the legitimacy of the policing authorities by a simple mechanism: exposing them to public embarrassment in the news media.

In the end, though, perhaps the most compelling aspect of the British policing litigation was its capacity to redefine the problem of police abuse from a conception of individual police officer responsibility (the "bad apple" syndrome) to institutional responsibility. How did policing litigation—in contrast, say, to litigation against fats in fast food—largely succeed in this endeavor? A key factor undoubtedly is the striking, vivid evidence in many police misconduct cases of *individual* irresponsibility on the tort defendant's side. To be sure, plaintiffs against the police commonly struggle to overcome a presumption that they provoked the police by their own irresponsible behavior. But, even then, there is on the defendant's side, unlike in matters of corporate policy, an individual whose actions may be exposed as vulgar, abusive, and irresponsible. Beyond that, however, policing may offer greater opportunities for attributions of organizational or systemic responsibility. In contrast to businesses in the "free market," the central ideology of professional policing—that frontline officers are managed by professional standards, departmental policies, and, ultimately, the law—provides fertile ground for a discourse of institutional responsibility for abuse. Indeed, American tort litigation against the police similarly contributed to a shift toward organizational responsibility, an argument that I develop elsewhere. Nonetheless, relatively unique elements of the British litigation campaign also contributed to the shift in public discourse. The lawsuits against the police in London grew from a coordinated campaign that combined popular mobilization and litigation. Spokespeople for the campaign, among them nonlawyer "campaigners" and solicitors, repeatedly and consistently conveyed the message that police abuses were *not* the product of individual bad apples but rather of systemic failings. The lawsuits and rising damage awards—and, ultimately, exemplary damages in several cases—indicated the message's persuasive power, and newspaper coverage followed the shift in jury decisions. In the end, it was a synergy among these elements—graphic evidence of abuse by individual officers, consistent identification by campaigners of institutional irresponsibility in regulating those officers, jury decisions, and media coverage—that generated broad institutional reforms.

The underlying problems are, by no means, resolved. The British Broadcasting Corporation in 2003 presented a documentary, *The Secret Policeman,* based on conversations among officers recorded by an undercover journalist. The tapes revealed outrageous evidence of intentional racism, and, even more troublingly, evidence that the perpetrators felt confident that they would face no sanction for their views and actions.

If the problem of racial discrimination in British policing remains deep, however, it is at least openly recognized, discussed, and framed as a matter requiring systemic reform. That shift in the agenda may be attributed, at least in part, to a tort litigation campaign.

CHAPTER ELEVEN

Lawyers and Solicitors Separated
by a Common Legal System

Anti-Tobacco Litigation in the United States and Britain

LYNN MATHER

When people take risks with a product and get sick, who is responsible? The individual risk taker? The maker of the harmful product? Or government, acting to protect the health of its citizens? Tobacco use gives pleasure, but also a high risk of illness and death. Countries vary enormously in how they deal with tobacco, and smoking rates are likewise quite different across the world. Some governments own their own tobacco companies and enjoy the resulting revenue. Others implicitly encourage private corporations who manufacture tobacco, accepting their political and economic support, and letting individuals assess public health risks themselves. Still others actively discourage tobacco use through regulation and taxation. Litigation provides another avenue for regulation.

American plaintiff lawyers have filed thousands of suits against tobacco manufacturers. Most cases lost, but there have been some enormous verdicts for plaintiffs and a massive settlement with the states for $246 billion dollars in 1998. In Britain, very few anti-tobacco suits have been filed, and only two cases have come to court, both of which lost. Why are there such differences in the patterns and results of tort litigation against tobacco in the United States and in Britain? Focusing on the role of lawyers, I explore how the structure of lawyers' fees, the organization of the legal profession, and support for political litigation express cultural values about the role of law in compensating for injury and deterring misconduct. These factors influenced the willingness of American, English, and Scottish lawyers to represent clients in suits against tobacco manufacturers and shaped the trajectories and outcomes of their cases.

Tobacco litigation provides an excellent lens for comparative research on legal cultures. The medical and public health experts as well as tobacco manufacturers in the two countries shared scientific research and defined the problem of tobacco control in somewhat similar ways. Both countries relied primarily on voluntary efforts and education to deter smoking, although Britain more aggressively used taxation for tobacco control (Berridge 2004; Rabin and Sugarman 2001). Responsibility under tort law for injuries resulting from harmful products is similar in the two countries, but the legal strategies used in the two countries were quite different. Americans rushed to court with tort claims, while the British did not.

By focusing on the role of lawyers in this chapter, I do not mean to ignore other crucial factors shaping tobacco litigation in Britain and the United States. Let me briefly note some of these. First, since compensation is a major goal of tort law, health care differences can explain the paucity of suits in Britain. Under the British comprehensive health care system, smokers suffering from lung cancer or heart disease know that their medical costs are covered. By contrast, since Americans pay for their own health care costs and a large fraction lack insurance, litigation provides a way to pay their medical bills. A second point centers on personal responsibility, the ethos that individuals should take care of themselves and accept the consequences of their own choices. This value is firmly held in both the United States and Britain and explains the skepticism toward tort litigation that is found in both societies. But the meaning of personal responsibility varies. The British traditionally balance it with faith in the government to provide social welfare and support for their citizens, while Americans combine individual responsibility with a belief in legal entitlements and rights-based remedies. Increasingly, Americans have demanded what Friedman (1985b) calls "total justice," a belief in law to protect and compensate them when things go wrong.

Third, Britain's top-down, unitary system of government contrasts with the decentralized, fragmented U.S. political system in which political power is widely dispersed through federalism and three distinct branches of government. Decentralization in the United States encourages individuals to initiate claims and articulate interests in whatever forum they can achieve the most success. Further, American state court judges, most of whom are selected by popular election, often reflect the values of their local communities in their decisions, compared to judges representing authority in the more hierarchical British judiciary (see von Benda-Beckmann, in this volume).

Finally, a jury trial is rarely allowed in civil cases in Britain, whereas the right to a jury is guaranteed by the U.S. Constitution for all types of cases. As Hans (this volume) demonstrates, juries express and reinforce cultural values of local communities and allow popular participation in governing.

Differences between health care systems, processes of compensation, centralization or decentralization of political and judicial power, and the use of juries, provide helpful context for understanding lawsuits against tobacco in these two countries. Yet the question remains, why would huge numbers of individuals suffering ill effects from smoking choose to sue cigarette makers in one country but not in another, particularly since the legal rules on risk and responsibility are similar? The very construction of a tort claim, with its attribution of blame to tobacco manufacturers for fraud and deceit about the harms of their product, depends on *lawyers* willing to articulate that tort conceptualization, *smokers* or their families willing to become legal clients in such cases, and *judicial* or *jury* verdicts to reinforce tort remedies as appropriate. The next two sections discuss what happened in the various legal attempts to hold tobacco manufacturers responsible for the illnesses of smokers in the United States and Britain. The third section compares lawyers in the two countries on how their actions made sense within their own cultural contexts, and yet how that "sense" was also sharply contested. This section provides the central theme of the chapter, namely how lawyers and solicitors articulate and enact fundamental ways of thinking about risk and responsibility.

Anti-Tobacco Litigation in the United States

After the release of scientific research on the health hazards of smoking, lawyers sought to hold cigarette makers accountable for misleading the public about the harms resulting from their product. Between the 1950s and the early 1990s, plaintiff lawyers in the United States filed more than 700 product liability lawsuits against tobacco manufacturers on behalf of smokers and the families of deceased smokers (Rice 1995). None of these suits succeeded. Tobacco manufacturers aggressively defended their product, challenging the scientific evidence and framing illness as the result of individual responsibility. Finally, in 1988, an American trial jury for the first time found a cigarette company negligent and awarded damages to the family of a deceased smoker, Rose Cipollone. An appeal in that case led to the 1992 Supreme Court decision (*Cipollone v. Liggett Group*) that federal law did not entirely preempt state legal claims against tobacco, as cigarette manufacturers had long argued, thus allowing anti-tobacco legal mobilization to proceed. Lawyers from that case, along with medical researchers and other legal experts, had already been meeting to coordinate their efforts. Annual conferences of the Tobacco Products Liability Project (TPLP) began in 1985 and provided a network of information, contacts, and support for those seeking to use legal strategies to reduce smoking rates and to hold the tobacco industry responsible for the injuries caused by smoking (Daynard 1988).

Why did antismoking advocates align with lawyers and public health experts to pursue tort litigation against tobacco manufacturers rather than, for example, making tobacco control a political campaign issue or a legislative priority? The answer harks back to Tocqueville's observation nearly two centuries ago: "Scarcely any political question arises in the United States that is not resolved, sooner or later, into a judicial question." Turning to law to resolve political problems makes a certain degree of sense within American culture. Lawyers, as America's aristocracy, have played key roles on both sides of the tobacco controversy. Lawyers for the defense had developed sophisticated tactics to shield the cigarette industry from scrutiny and liability. As a major campaign donor to both political parties and experienced in lobbying, the tobacco industry was also powerful in Congress. On the other side were plaintiff lawyers, newly flush with resources as a result of successful lawsuits over asbestos, who saw tobacco as the next injurious product to fight, and who had their own political allies.

Three different groups of lawyers initiated the last wave of litigation against tobacco during the 1990s: *government attorneys* filing claims on behalf of the states for health care reimbursement; plaintiff attorneys filing *class actions* on behalf of large groups of injured smokers; and plaintiff attorneys filing product liability suits for *individual smokers* or their families. As explained in Mather (1998), this legal mobilization received widespread media coverage as it sought to shift responsibility to the cigarette manufacturers for the cost of injury and death resulting from tobacco use. Between 1994 and the middle of 1998, the number of anti-tobacco lawsuits increased dramatically, from 73 to 807.

Government litigation began in 1994 with Mississippi's Attorney General, Mike Moore, suing to recover the health care costs that Mississippi had paid in caring for sick and dying smokers. His legal theory was unprecedented and ridiculed in the press. Moore had developed the novel idea with two law school classmates, one of whom was a successful tort lawyer who had made millions in asbestos litigation. Through coordination and advocacy, meetings with anti-tobacco lobbyists and other lawyers, and continued media coverage, attorneys general from forty other states ultimately filed their own suits against the tobacco industry. These suits resulted in settlements with four states (Mississippi, Minnesota, Florida, and Texas) for a total of $40 billion. After intense political lobbying in Congress, a failed effort at new federal legislation, and increased financial uncertainty for manufacturers, the tobacco companies and the remaining forty-six states settled the litigation by signing the Master Settlement Agreement in 1998 for $206 billion, an extraordinary sum.

Not wanting to be left out of such rewards, lawyers in the Department of Justice, encouraged by President Clinton, filed a similar claim to recover the federal government's share of health care costs, alleging the industry's violation of the Racketeer Influenced and Corrupt Organizations (RICO) Act, a federal antiracketeering law, in hiding the dangers of tobacco use from consumers. The lawsuit (*U.S. v. Philip Morris et al.*) began in September 1999, but took five years to reach a bench trial in 2004. The U.S. government had originally asked for $280 billion, but had to reduce the amount to $130 billion to comply with an appellate court ruling on the penalty calculation. During the closing arguments at trial, attorneys for the federal government further reduced the remedy they were seeking to only $10 billion, a reduction attributed to political influence of higher-ups in President Bush's administration (Fiore et al. 2005). In August 2006, Judge Gladys Kessler ruled that the tobacco companies had clearly violated racketeering laws when they conspired to mislead the public about the health hazards of smoking. That decision is currently on appeal.

Class actions provided the second line of legal attack against tobacco. Sixty lawyers experienced with suits against the asbestos industry pooled their resources, pledging $100,000 each annually to finance and file a massive class action suit (*Castano v. American Tobacco Co.*). Claiming negligence, fraud, and deceit by tobacco companies, this suit amassed *all* current and former smokers in the country to hold the companies liable for the financial costs of addiction. The federal trial judge surprised observers in 1995 and certified this "class" of nearly 100 million individuals and began planning for a massive trial. One year later a federal appeals court reversed the decision and denied certification of a class action, but the legal strategy resurfaced in class action filings at the state level. Most of these "Sons of *Castano*" suits lost, as the tobacco industry successfully challenged the use of class action status.

Plaintiff lawyers in Miami filed a different kind of class action, the *Engle v. R.J. Reynolds Tobacco Co.* case, in 1994, seeking recovery for the injuries of all Florida smokers caused by cigarette smoking. In July 2000 this case resulted in the largest jury award ever in a U.S. case, with punitive damages set at $145 billion. Six years later, the Florida Supreme Court overturned the punitive damages as excessive, but upheld the liability verdict and allowed individual suits for compensatory damages to proceed (*Engle v. Liggett Group Inc.* 2006).

Individual lawsuits against tobacco manufacturers comprise the third set of tort claims. After hundreds of trials in which juries effectively blamed the smokers for their own health problems due to their choice to smoke ("assumption of risk," as the defense argued), new information emerged that changed the cultural and legal landscape. Plaintiff lawyers obtained damaging internal industry documents through discovery. Evidence about the industry's knowledge of addiction, nicotine manipulation in products, and cover-up of scientific evidence persuaded some juries to hold cigarette manufacturers responsible. But plaintiff victories at jury trial, such as *Carter v. Brown & Williamson* in 1996, were overturned on appeal. The tobacco companies could point with pride to *their* track record—still far more wins than losses with juries and a much better appellate record as well.

Nevertheless, tort lawyers have continued to sue on behalf of individual smokers, taking advantage of lessons learned from earlier cases and sharing evidence obtained in discovery. Trial outcomes have reflected the regional variation in smoking and in attitudes toward tort litigation. Juries on the West Coast (where smoking rates are lowest), for example, have been more skeptical of tobacco's arguments about individual responsibility than have juries in the Midwest. In two multimillion dollar verdicts, *Boeken v. Philip Morris Inc.* (2001) in California, and a 1999 verdict in *Williams v. Philip Morris et al.* (2002) in Oregon, juries explicitly rejected Philip Morris's defense that it had already paid enough through the state settlements. In March 2006 the U.S. Supreme Court declined to hear Philip Morris's appeal in the *Boeken* case, thus leaving the $82 million jury award intact (including $76 million in punitive damages).

The U.S. Supreme Court intervened, however, in the *Williams* case. An Oregon jury awarded the family of lung cancer victim Jesse Williams over $800,000 in compensatory damages and $79.5 million in punitive damages, the largest award ever in Oregon. On appeal, lawyers for Philip Morris used the *Williams* case to pursue the broader issue of federal constitutional limits on punitive damages. The U.S. Supreme Court in *Philip Morris et al. v. Williams* (2003) ordered the Oregon Supreme Court to reconsider its judgment in light of the 2003 ruling of *State Farm v. Campbell*. That decision held that although punitive damages "are aimed at deterrence and retribution," the due process clause prohibits punishment that is "grossly excessive or arbitrary." Guideposts for determining acceptable damage awards include the reprehensibility of the defendant's misconduct and the disparity between the harm suffered and the punitive damages. The Court suggested that punitive damage awards should not ordinarily be more than nine times greater than compensatory damages. Punitive damages in *Williams* were nearly 100 times greater but the Oregon Supreme Court refused to reduce the award in 2006 and again in 2008. In a scathing opinion against Philip Morris, the Oregon court recounted the decades of deceit and fraud that justified the jury's verdict on damages:

> There can be no dispute that Philip Morris's conduct was extraordinarily reprehensible. Philip Morris knew that smoking caused serious and sometimes fatal disease, but it nevertheless spread false or misleading information to suggest to the public that doubts remained about that issue. It deliberately did so to keep smokers smoking, knowing that it was putting the smokers' health and lives at risk, and it continued to do so for nearly half a century. (*Williams v. Philip Morris et al.* 2006 at 1177)

One year later, however, in February 2007, the U.S. Supreme Court overturned that Oregon ruling. The U.S. Supreme Court's five to four decision in *Philip Morris v. Williams* (2007) rested on a narrow holding about how the trial jury reached its verdict and the factors they considered, rather than on the more fundamental question of excessiveness of the verdict. In January 2008, the Oregon Supreme Court in *Williams v. Philip Morris et al.* (2008) responded to the higher court by reinstating the punitive damage award and expressly relying on independent state law to justify its ruling, a judgment that Phillip Morris appealed. The U.S. Supreme Court agreed to hear the case for a third time and a ruling is expected in 2009.

Tobacco manufacturers now argue that they are paying the states through the Master Settlement Agreement and cooperating with government to protect public health and stop teenage smoking. This turnaround has not deterred plaintiff lawyers from continuing to file new cases for individual plaintiffs, but it has helped to shift public attitudes, including those of juries. In contrast to the media coverage of the 1990s, which for a brief period ostracized "Big Tobacco" (Mather

1998), more recent news reporting depicts greedy lawyers as the villains (Haltom and McCann 2004).

Plaintiff lawyers and attorneys general in the United States acted as policy entrepreneurs for tobacco control, seeking to hold the industry responsible through document discovery, advocacy in the press and at trial, and alliances with politicians and public health groups. Cigarette manufacturers and their counsel responded with campaigns for tort reform and ads about the profits lawyers made from lawsuits and the value of individual choice and responsibility. Many plaintiff lawyers turned from tobacco to suits against other dangerous products such as lead paint, guns, and junk food (see Haltom and McCann, this volume). Some lawyers kept their sights on tobacco but expanded their horizons overseas to help mobilize international public health concerns. Thus, American lawyers have taken their understanding of tort law to the World Health Organization (WHO) where they passed the "tobacco-free initiative" in 2002. As the WHO Web site notes, "Used properly, the law can help transform the paradigms of tobacco control, awaken public outrage, strengthen public policies and redress injuries." What we see then is a transnational expansion of U.S. style legal strategies for tobacco control.

Anti-Tobacco Litigation in Britain

In Britain the story was somewhat different. Public health experts and government officials defined the tobacco control policies through education, regulation, and taxation. Tort lawyers were nearly invisible. Smokers generally accepted their illnesses as their own responsibility. Anti-tobacco interests lobbied for stronger regulation but the government's 1992 White Paper stopped short of banning tobacco advertisements. The idea of suing manufacturers was virtually unknown. There were two cases, however, quite similar to those filed in the United States. *Hodgson et al. v. Imperial Tobacco and Gallaher,* a multiparty case in England, lasted nearly seven years and finally collapsed in 1999 without reaching a trial, and *McTear v. Imperial Tobacco,* an individual plaintiff action that began in 1993 in Scotland and ended after trial with the judge ruling against McTear in 2005. The difficulties that plaintiff lawyers faced in each of these cases illustrate the much narrower space of tort law in Britain for addressing tobacco-related injuries.

For several decades, a small number of plaintiff law firms in Britain had expanded their work to address injuries resulting from disasters such as airline crashes, or from defective or harmful products such as thalidomide or pollution. Such multiparty or group litigation was relatively new and more restrictive than class action litigation in the United States during the 1990s (Day, Balen, and McCool 1995). This difference in legal rules also reflected Britain's more proactive policies of government taking responsibility for large-scale injuries, in comparison to the individually filed legal claims in the United States (Kagan 2001; Kritzer 1996).

In the case of tobacco, several English solicitors (lawyers) saw the potential for using multiparty actions to hold tobacco manufacturers responsible for smokers' injuries. These solicitors had traveled to the United States for meetings of trial lawyers engaged in lawsuits against the cigarette industry. They returned with legal tactics and reams of information to use in test case litigation in Britain. Given permission to advertise for clients under 1984 Law Society rules (Day, Balen, and McCool 1995), one English law firm placed newspaper advertisements inviting people to discuss issues of ill health and smoking (see Figure 11.1).

Following advertisements such as this during the early 1990s, at one meeting in Liverpool, "nearly 200 potential plaintiffs suffering from smoking related illnesses" showed up (Albright 1997, 364). John Barrie Hodgson, a heavy smoker who had recently been diagnosed with lung cancer, attended one of these meetings and agreed to file suit. He became the lead plaintiff in the group claim, *Hodgson et al. v. Imperial Tobacco and Gallaher*. Solicitor Martyn Day began pretrial work on the case in 1992. A crucial goal for the solicitors was to obtain funding to be able to pursue the case. Since English solicitors are prohibited from working on a contingent fee basis, the law firm turned to government-funded legal aid for assistance. At first the firm's applications were refused, but the solicitors persisted through several more hearings and appeals.

In 1995, the Legal Aid Board "finally agreed to grant legal aid, ruling that the tobacco plaintiffs had 'reasonable grounds for taking proceedings' against the tobacco companies" (Albright 1997, 370). This meant that the British government would be underwriting the costs of suing the two biggest tobacco companies in Britain. Given the sharp cutbacks in the government's budget for legal aid, the high expenses anticipated for the *Hodgson* trial, and the political and controversial nature of the litigation, few were surprised when the Legal Aid Board changed its mind the following year, and withdrew aid to the plaintiffs in the

SMOKING & ILLNESSES

We act for a number of clients who have suffered serious injuries

which have led to permanent ill health, pain and disability. The

initial diagnosis suggests that smoking may well have caused or, at

least, aggravated their conditions.

If you believe that you are similarly affected we may be able to

help you recover damages by way of compensation.

Call now for a free initial consultation.

Graham Leigh, Pfeffer & Co.

SOLICITORS

FIGURE 11.1   Smoking and Legal Compensation for Illnesses (from Day, Balen, and McCool 1995: 295; contact information omitted)

case. The High Court denied the appeal on the Board's ruling in 1996, and legal aid was not obtained.

Although denial of legal aid seemed to present an insurmountable financial obstacle, a new legal development encouraged Martyn Day to continue with the case. In 1995, Parliament passed an act to permit "conditional fee agreements" (CFAs) in many areas of the law. Under the new CFA system, a lawyer could represent a client on a "no win, no fee" basis. In September 1996, the law firm of Leigh Day agreed to take the *Hodgson* case, "the first large-scale product liability case to be taken on a conditional fee basis since such fees were introduced in 1995" (Howells 1998, 696).

Both the British conditional fee agreement and the American contingency fee encourage lawyers to represent clients in cases with some chance at success, and the clients do not need to pay their lawyers at the outset. Under both arrangements, clients pay their lawyers only if they obtain a successful verdict or settlement. But there is a huge difference between the two systems. The contingency fee allows lawyers to obtain a percentage of any damages won by the client, whereas the amount of the conditional fee is determined by the solicitors' hourly fee plus an "uplift" not to exceed twice the agreed-upon hourly fee. The potential rewards for lawyers under a contingency fee are thus far greater than under a conditional fee.

Britain's "loser pays" rule also explains why funding was so important in this case. Under this system, "unsuccessful plaintiffs are liable for defendant's costs," so that "losing plaintiffs must fund their adversary's defense in addition to absorbing their own legal costs" (Rogers 1998, 228). If nothing else, this loser pays rule "creates a massive disincentive to litigate . . . especially in expensive group action litigation" (Rogers 1998, 228). This disincentive of having to pay the defendants' costs in the event of loss becomes especially apparent in suits against a defendant as wealthy as the tobacco corporations.

Nevertheless, some solicitors are willing to work on the conditional fee basis. As Martyn Day himself put it in discussing the tobacco cases, "it is a serious risk for the firm but we feel strongly that these are good cases and if we do not take them on we would be saying that the English legal system is incapable of giving these people a fair hearing" (Albright 1997, 375). The firm of Leigh Day filed the initial writ in the *Hodgson* case in the fall of 1996. The suit claimed that the smokers contracted lung cancer "as a result of their smoking . . . [and] that their cancers were caused by the negligence and/or breach of statutory duties of the two companies in their manufacture and distribution of cigarettes" (Tobacco Industry Litigation Reporter 1996).

In 1997, the Labor Party won a decisive electoral victory and, for the first time in two decades, controlled the House of Commons. The Labor government immediately announced it would pursue a ban on tobacco advertising as well as create a comprehensive tobacco control program. Now that the government was taking stronger action to curb tobacco, some felt that the lawyers should abandon their case, as the issues were ultimately political not legal ones.

Martyn Day turned to the newly emerging documents from the American litigation to use in evidence in the *Hodgson* litigation. Internal tobacco industry memos, damaging scientific reports, correspondence, and marketing studies all became public as a result of the discovery and trials in the United States. This information provided "a huge boost to plaintiffs' lawyers in countries as far-flung as Australia, Britain, Canada, Ireland and Israel" (Karlen and Van Voris 1998,

A7; and see Daynard, Bates, and Francey 2000). Besides the American lawyers, British solicitors were the heaviest users of the document depositories, one of which was located in Guilford, England, and held millions of pages of records from British American Tobacco.

Procedural issues consumed the early months of the *Hodgson* case and then the claimants' case received a mortal blow with a pretrial ruling in 1999. Trial judge Michael Wright ruled that most of the claimants involved in the group action could not sue because they had exceeded the three-year period of limitations. The risks of continuing the litigation for the few remaining were too great and the case was over. To save their clients from paying the tobacco companies' huge legal costs, plaintiffs' lawyers agreed to two terms. First, they agreed not to sue Gallaher or Imperial again until 2008 and not to sue other tobacco firms for five years. Second, they agreed not to reveal any of the evidence they had uncovered (Farrell 2000, B20). "Lawyer Martyn Day . . . said that balancing the ruling 'against the massive costs involved, we had to advise the plaintiffs to pull out'" (*National Law Journal* 1999, A16). As it was, the Leigh Day firm had expended £2.5 million in fees and payments to experts (Farrell 2000, B20). Undaunted, Day wrote recently that "as the years count down to the end of my period in purdah," he will continue to explore ways to bring new claims against the British tobacco industry (Day 2006, 5).

Commenting bitterly on the demise of the *Hodgson* suit, one solicitor said, "isn't it convenient for a court to find that the plaintiffs had the requisite knowledge more than three years before they started proceedings? It stops the litigation . . . and the system is not even put to the test" (Barr 1999, 252). Other observers were less sympathetic to the plaintiffs and thought all along that litigation was inappropriate, that smokers should accept personal responsibility, and that the firm was wrong to use conditional fees to push the boundaries of law by instigating tort litigation against corporate defendants.

While the *Hodgson* suit was wending its way through the English courts, the case of *McTear v. Imperial Tobacco* began in Scotland. Alfred McTear, a heavy smoker with lung cancer, initiated litigation in 1992. His wife continued the suit after Alfred died in 1993. Glasgow solicitor Cameron Fyfe represented McTear and took his claim seven times to the Legal Aid Board; each time the case was denied government funding (Davis 2005). Somewhat like Martyn Day, Fyfe has a reputation as an unusual lawyer, eager to take on new social and political causes and to use group litigation to do so. His firm had 160 other clients ready to join a multiparty case against the tobacco companies, depending on the outcome of McTear's suit (Davis 2005). As in the *Hodgson* case, the judgment in *McTear* would send an important signal to other potential litigants and solicitors.

McTear's firm worked gratis for twelve years on the suit and received very little support, even from Scottish health boards (Davis 2005). The local representatives of Action on Smoking and Health (ASH), Scotland's antismoking group, contributed some help but the plaintiff's firm was totally outmatched by the estimated 10 million pounds spent by Imperial Tobacco in its defense (Davis 2005). After the trial concluded in Edinburgh, Lord Nimmo Smith took fifteen months to write his opinion. The verdict was a total loss for the plaintiff. The judge released his judgment of over 600 pages on May 31, 2005—World No Tobacco Day, as observers wryly noted.

The judge acknowledged the vast disparity in resources between the two sides in the case but wrote that the case faced fundamental problems that could not have been solved by additional resources. Alfred McTear began smoking with the knowledge that there were health risks involved, and therefore, as Imperial Tobacco argued, the company was not responsible for the consequences of the plaintiff's choice to smoke. Lord Nimmo Smith reiterated the importance of self-determination in law, writing that adults "have the responsibility of making reasonable choices, not least on matters affecting his or her safety, health and welfare. This approach is fundamental to the workings of our society . . . There is no duty to save people from themselves . . . the responsibility is theirs alone" (¶7.178–79). Even further, and in stark contrast to the U.S. judgments on tobacco, the Scottish judge rejected epidemiological evidence on the link between cigarette smoking and lung cancer, writing that "epidemiology cannot be used to establish causation in any individual case" (Friedman and Daynard 2007, 5).

In his lengthy decision, the trial judge refuted every argument made by the plaintiff. The judge even commented that the medical expert witnesses for McTear lacked credibility because they were connected to the advocacy group ASH, and hence "were clearly committed to the anti-smoking cause; and no doubt for this reason were prepared to give evidence gratis. . . . By contrast, all the expert witnesses for Imperial Tobacco charged fees for their services" making their testimony more credible (¶5.18). Predictably, comments on the verdict were divided, but an article in *New Statesman* noted that, "medical and legal professionals' criticism of the sweeping judgment was surprisingly muted" (Davis 2005). Some commentators also pointed out McTear himself was not so sympathetic a claimant—yes, he was the father of three and only forty-eight years old when he died, but he "had a troubled past and had been to prison" (Davis 2005).

In sum, although several British solicitors attempted litigation against tobacco manufacturers for injuries to smokers, only two cases made it to court. One ended without trial and the other resulted in a complete victory for the defense. Solicitors' strategies of using tort claims to obtain compensation for harms caused by the tobacco industry's fraud, misrepresentation, failure to warn, or other misconduct, did not succeed in England or Scotland.

Lawyers and Solicitors as Conduits for Culture

Why were so many lawsuits filed against cigarette companies in the United States, and with some significant proplaintiff results, but in Britain only two court cases were filed, *Hodgson* and *McTear,* both of which were unsuccessful? To answer this question, I have focussed on the role of lawyers and solicitors. How do lawyers think about which problems or injuries make viable cases? How does the way lawyers are paid for their work affect their views about tort claims and their legal strategies? What social networks or institutional mechanisms reinforce the relation between law and politics?

First, consider the financial incentives and disincentives lawyers face in thinking about whether to file a risky lawsuit such as one against tobacco companies. The financial calculus to support legal mobilization discourages litigation for change in Britain. The British rule that a losing plaintiff must pay the costs of the defense creates a significant obstacle for solicitors thinking about commencing high-risk litigation, particularly if not funded by legal aid. Although Britain now has legal insurance ostensibly "to eliminate . . . risk for plaintiffs litigating cases on a conditional fee basis," that insurance does not apply to tobacco liability cases (Albright 1997, 375; and see Howells 1998). Consequently, plaintiffs who sue tobacco manufacturers and lose must be prepared to fund their adversary's defense. By contrast, U.S. plaintiff lawyers who lose a case must absorb only their legal and court costs, not the costs of their opponents. "This point is of crucial importance in tobacco cases where the discrepancy in resources between the defendant tobacco companies and the litigants is so great" (Sirabionian 2005, 503).

While British solicitors face larger potential costs, American tort lawyers see greater possible gains due to the contingency fee, which provides lawyers a percentage of any winnings. American lawyers who participated in the state settlements, or in some of the highly successful class actions, for example, made *billions* of dollars as a percentage of the final settlement. And indeed some of these lawyers used the largesse they amassed in asbestos litigation to fund the even riskier suits over tobacco. But the conditional fee in Britain does not allow such great rewards for the solicitors. And in fact the no-win, no-fee basis can discourage them from putting together risky or innovative claims. Clarification of the CFAs in the 1999 Civil Procedure Rules, may have helped, according to one British solicitor (Care 2000). But if not, the legal support structure for legal mobilization (especially financing) proves critical not only for pursuit of individual legal rights (Epp 1998) but also for private law claims for damages caused by negligence or defective products. Rewards for British solicitors even with the new conditional fees remain substantially smaller than those for their American counterparts.

Most important, the difference in fee structure affects more than lawyers' economic calculations about whether to accept a lawsuit. The structure also affects how lawyers think about assessing cases and about the culture of claiming (see Trautner 2006). Is the case a good one or not? Britain's heavy reliance on legal aid reinforces the notion that there is an objective assessment of *merit* in cases. That is, some cases have merit and deserve representation and others do not. The fact that the Legal Aid Board rejected the claims of Hodgson and McTear was perceived not as a political judgment, but instead as an objective comment about the quality of the cases. By contrast, the contingency fee system in the United States reinforces a more "contingent" and malleable sense of who deserves representation and what constitutes a "good" case. Individual lawyers in the United States are encouraged to make that determination themselves, rather than having a centralized government body like the Legal Aid Board decide.

Further, without punitive damages the financial rewards for plaintiffs are far less in Britain. Such awards involved billions of dollars in the United States. Although the *Engle* award was overturned, the *Boeken* (California) and *Williams* (Oregon) awards still stand as powerful cultural statements placing responsibility for harm on the tobacco companies. The awards constitute financial, as well as moral, victories for plaintiff lawyers due to the share of the award they will receive through contingency fees. During the height of the state litigation in the late 1990s, "punitive damages have been called 'the lever that brought the tobacco companies to the bargaining table'" (Rogers 1998, 218). Britain has a very narrow range of cases in which exemplary or punitive damages can be awarded (see Epp, this volume). The British find it quite bizarre that individual lawyers would share in such large damage awards. Since punitive damages reflect punishment within the civil justice system, awards should go to the government and victims, not their legal advocates. Even Martyn Day, "Britain's contemporary anti-tobacco crusader" (Rogers 1998, 199) refers to such compensation for American lawyers as "obscene profits" (Day 2006).

Second, differences in procedural rules governing tort proceedings reflect cultural values. Federal rules on group actions in the United States have been far more generous in what constitutes a "class" than are the British rules defining "multi-party actions." Lawyers in the United States have relied extensively on class actions to aggregate claims in cases such as race and sexual discrimination, toxic waste, and product liability. The rules (until recent cutbacks) have encouraged U.S. lawyers to think about group cases not only as a financial inducement for litigation but also as a way to make a political statement and challenge corporate power.

Another rule difference that affected the *McTear* case was the more stringent evidentiary requirement in Scotland that prevented lawyers from introducing the massive documentary evidence on industry misconduct that had been so effective in the U.S. litigation. According to McTear's lawyer, such evidence can only be used if a witness is brought to court to authenticate each document and the plaintiff lacked the resources to bring in such witnesses (Friedman and Daynard 2007).

Third, how does the organization of the legal profession affect lawyers' interest in litigating over tobacco and their ability to succeed? Britain's lawyers are less specialized and organized around particular areas of practice than are those in the United States. Britain does have the Association of Personal Injury Lawyers, but it is not as strong an advocacy group as, for example, the American Association for Justice, formerly the Association of Trial Lawyers of America. The few solicitors who filed tort claims against tobacco were encouraged by American lawyers at conferences in the United States, not by their British peers. The U.S. plaintiff bar has developed an elaborate support system for lawyers engaged in different kinds of litigation, including sharing of information, ideas, and documents, and regular meetings. Such coordination was especially apparent in the tobacco litigation. See, for example, the pooling of resources from different plaintiff firms in the *Castano* class action, or the TPLP Web site that advertised "*Boeken* Trial in a Box," a carefully selected and organized package of key tobacco industry documents used in the *Boeken v. Philip Morris* trial in California.

In the *McTear* case, American observers find it surprising that his solicitor would have taken such an unsympathetic plaintiff for a test case. Such action shows "no understanding of politics of litigation; it violates Plaintiffs Lawyering 101" (Daniels 2006), referring to the widely shared knowledge in the American bar about how to select clients to maximize success in litigation. The McTear case was taken for this litigation because, according to solicitor Cameron Fyfe, it "was the only one that was both ripe for adjudication and had a plaintiff willing to be the first 'test case'" (Friedman and Daynard 2007, 5). That a plaintiff lawyer would pursue test case litigation with a client who had a prison record underscores the conventional British legal perspective, which lacks "a tradition of thinking about litigation in that way" (Flood 2006).

Fourth, British solicitors and American lawyers have different abilities to mobilize favorable media coverage for their cases. In the United States it is not uncommon to see lawyers giving press conferences or speaking to the media about ongoing litigation. Attorneys general for the states regularly issued press releases about their suits against the tobacco companies in order to garner political support in their states and show themselves as crusaders for public health. Some private plaintiff lawyers think quite strategically about speaking to the press and succeed at it, although most lack the institutional support to spin their cases successfully and as a result lose the battle for public opinion (Haltom and McCann 2004). By contrast, British lawyers are prohibited from talking to the press during litigation. It is considered inappropriate professional conduct. The divided legal profession in Britain also limited the ability of lawyers to act as policy entrepreneurs. The solicitors do the work for a case, gathering evidence and preparing it for trial. But then the actual advocacy has traditionally rested with the barrister. This division splits the voice and may diminish the effectiveness of lawyers to speak out even after trial. Barristers no longer have exclusive advocacy rights before the English high court, however, as the result of contentious struggle during the 1990s (Abel 2003).

Change in the English legal profession during 1990s points to a crucial aspect of legal culture. Culture is not static and monolithic, but instead contains multiple and often conflicting strands. Moreover, as we have seen through the tobacco litigation, legal cultures should not be thought of as independent entities. While multiparty actions and conditional fees in Britain show borrowing from the United States, sharp restrictions in government funding of legal aid and other civil justice reforms in Britain reflect concerns about public costs and lawyers' greed. Similarly, in the United States, tort reformers have reduced punitive damages through legislative caps and constitutional limits through appellate lawmaking.

Conclusion

An individual smoker diagnosed with lung cancer does not automatically turn to tort claims for compensation and damages. The response to injury depends on the cultural context and the available normative frameworks for thinking about it. Such frameworks include, for example, personal responsibility ("It was my fault for continuing to smoke"), fate ("illness happens—no one is to blame"), or the legal responsibility of the cigarette maker ("It's their fault for lying about the harms and addictiveness of cigarettes"). The cultural values that encourage people to choose among these frameworks are constituted in part by law. In particular, lawyers and solicitors are crucial in articulating and communicating the meaning of the illness and the locus of responsibility. The early successes of several U.S. plaintiff lawyers in gathering damaging evidence through pretrial discovery and persuading juries to hold tobacco manufacturers liable opened the window of tort remedies for smoking-related illnesses. Judicial decisions upholding those verdicts also sent a message that tort law could play a role in finding fault and assigning blame in tobacco cases. But of course the framework of individual responsibility also continues to be widely accepted. The process of locating the appropriate fault line in tobacco litigation occurs through arguments in trials, lawyers' advice to clients about whether to file claims, judicial and jury decisions, and responses to legal actions from the media and the community.

Certain institutional practices in the United States facilitated the lawsuits filed by plaintiff lawyers against tobacco manufacturers: a fee structure that encourages lawyers to take risks with relatively low danger of loss; the possibility of enormous gains through punitive damages and the amassing of class action suits; a community of specialized plaintiff-oriented lawyers to share information and reinforce particular legal strategies; and the ability of lawyers to act as spokespersons for their causes in the media as well as in the courtroom. Solicitors in Britain adopted the litigation strategies of U.S. lawyers in filing the *Hodgson* and

McTear cases against cigarette manufacturers, and the legal rules on fault were similar, but the results were not the same. Even with some borrowing of the U.S. style practices, such as Britain's new multiparty actions and conditional fees, the tort framework was rejected for tobacco-related injuries.

Most important, the legal rules and institutional structures affecting lawyers and solicitors reflect and reinforce underlying cultural values in the two countries. It is naïve to think that a rule change alone, such as the introduction of conditional fees in Britain, will mean that "it is likely only a matter of time before [tobacco] verdicts similar to those handed down in U.S. courts are handed down in the United Kingdom" (Sirabionian 2005, 505). Although there are voices in Britain advocating greater use of litigation to address issues of public policy, the dominant cultural values there still discourage what is seen as the peculiarly American reliance on law and courts. And indeed, even in the United States, the cultural values surrounding the role of litigation in policy making remain in flux.

CHAPTER TWELVE

Suing Doctors in Japan

Structure, Culture, and the Rise of Malpractice Litigation

ERIC A. FELDMAN

This chapter examines conflict over medical malpractice claims in Japan, and uses it as a lens through which to view the relationship between tort law and its social, economic, and political context. Allegations of medical malpractice in Japan have been rising rapidly. What explains the increasing willingness of people who believe that they are victims of medical malpractice to sue? And what (if anything) does the upswing in malpractice litigation suggest about the changing role and importance of the legal system in the lives of the Japanese people?

The relationship between law and society in Japan has long been the source of scholarly speculation, and occasionally the topic of serious academic analysis (Cole 2007; Feldman 2007). The two most widely held points-of-view are dramatically different. One suggests that Japanese culture (rarely defined but generally assumed to encompass social values, norms of behavior, and modes of interpersonal interaction) places a high premium on the preservation of social harmony and the avoidance of open conflict (Kawashima 1963). In that view, the language of law is subordinate to the power of social integration and leads people to forego lawsuits. The other explanation for Japan's low litigation rates posits a more structural cause; namely that the elite has created barriers to inhibit access to the legal system and limit the extent to which courts can be a potent force of social change (Haley 1978; Upham 1987). Among the most important of those barriers are constraints on the number of licensed attorneys, the imposition of high case filing fees, a slow and costly civil litigation process, and limited damage awards (Haley 1978).

Medical malpractice litigation provides an ideal opportunity to reexamine these conflicting theories about the relationship between law and society in Japan. Over the past several decades, particularly the past ten years, medical malpractice lawsuits have increased rapidly.[1] The numbers are small, but the rates of increase are not. From only 102 malpractice claims filed in Japanese courts in 1970 the number escalated tenfold to 1,003 in 2003; in the decade between 1992 and 2002 claims grew by almost 150 percent from 371 to 906. To what extent does this support the view that cultural constraints to litigation have softened over the past decades? Does it suggest that structural barriers previously inhibiting access to the formal legal system have been reconfigured?

Unlike most analyses of litigation in Japan that examine its relative infrequency, this chapter focuses on the growing frequency of medical malpractice litigation and offers an explanation for its cause and consequences. It claims that more malpractice suits are reaching the courts for both cultural and structural reasons. First, formidable structural barriers to civil litigation have been softened, some that affect all civil cases and others specific to medical malpractice. The increasing number of lawyers, for example, makes it easier for potential plaintiffs to find attorneys, and the creation of a new expert witness system expedites malpractice suits. Second, these structural changes have occurred in, and are intertwined with, a broader social and political climate that is increasingly fertile ground for the escalating rates of malpractice claiming. An overall decrease in trust placed in medical elites, for example, and media coverage that highlights malfeasant doctors, have created an atmosphere in which malpractice litigation is increasingly attractive.

The consequence and broader significance of the rise in medical malpractice claims, although speculative, is far-reaching. The interaction of structural changes that facilitate the use of the courts, and broader sociopolitical changes that reinforce the attractiveness of litigation, could well cause the number of medical malpractice lawsuits to continue to rise. Although that interaction is difficult to document, it is relatively easy to describe. The creation of specialized medical courts and the increasing availability of attorneys, for example, underscore the legitimacy of seeking legal advice and the acceptability of formalizing one's grievances into lawsuits. As the demand for attorneys grows and more claims are filed, a greater number of lawyers will be attracted to medical malpractice as a field of expertise, and courts will accommodate the growing caseload. Further, the rise in medical malpractice claims highlights a significant departure from the government's long-standing approach to tort-related claiming, when it effectively shut the door to tort litigation. Potential litigants faced such daunting institutional barriers to suing that they had little choice but to resolve their claims through alternative channels. Ultimately, people came to see themselves as preferring extrajudicial solutions to formal legal institutions. Now, through a number of loosely related reforms, the government is loosening and lessening the barriers to the courts by, for example, licensing additional lawyers, creating new court procedures that have led to shorter trials, streamlining the process for recruiting expert witnesses, and designating specialized courts to resolve medical malpractice lawsuits. Whereas a rise in the incidence of tort-based litigation was once a catalyst to the creation of alternatives means of dispute resolution or administrative compensation systems, medical malpractice litigants are now promised a faster, more narrowly tailored legal process that makes suing increasingly attractive.[2] What this demonstrates is a new legitimacy for litigation and an increasingly important place for law in the lives of Japanese citizens. Such a claim is difficult to empirically support; the data and observations offered in this chapter outline the argument and begin to build the case.

Medical Malpractice in Japan: The Escalation of Litigation

As indicated earlier, the frequency of medical malpractice litigation has changed dramatically over the past several decades, as illustrated in Table 12.1. In 1970, there were only 102 new malpractice cases filed in Japan. That number increased to 310 in 1980, varied between 196 and 381 from 1980 to 1992, and then began to climb, reaching 795 new filings in 2000 and 1,110 in 2004 before dropping slightly the next two years.[3] The backlog of malpractice cases also steadily rose from the early 1990s thorough 2004, leading to a growing concern about whether courts are able to resolve malpractice claims in a timely manner.[4] And for the first time, in 2000 and 2001, there were more medical malpractice cases resolved through litigation than court-supervised mediation, and in some instances plaintiffs had joined forces by aggregating their claims.[5] Finally, the number of cases brought against government owned/operated hospitals also increased in the late 1990s and early 2000s, a category of cases that directly affects the state's financial well-being and reputation (*Daily Yomiuri* 2003b). Compared to the overall increase in the rate of civil litigation in Japan since the late 1980s—a rise of approximately 29 percent in District Court filings, the bulk of it

TABLE 12.1
Medical Malpractice Claims in Japan, 1992–2006

Year	# new claims	# pending claims	# disposed claims	% settled (wakai)	% judicial decisions
1992	371	1257	364	——	——
1993	442	1352	347	——	——
1994	506	1466	392	——	——
1995	488	1528	426	46.5	40.4
1996	575	1603	500	51.8	35.4
1997	597	1673	527	52.8	36.6
1998	632	1723	582	49.0	39.9
1999	678	1832	569	46.9	40.4
2000	795	1936	691	45.9	44.1
2001	824	2038	722	44.0	46.3
2002	906	2075	869	43.8	44.4
2003	1003	2043	1035	49.1	39.2
2004	1110	2149	1004	46.1	40.3
2005	999	2086	1062	49.8	37.7
2006	913	1860	1139	53.3	35.3

SOURCE: See Supreme Court of Japan (2005a).

involving bad loans and debt collection—the rise of medical malpractice litigation is dramatic.[6]

Added to the increase in civil litigation, there has also been a rise in police reports alleging malpractice.[7] Article 21 of the Medical Act (*Ishi-hō*) imposes a duty on physicians to notify the police when they observe what they believe is a "suspicious" death (Yoshida et al. 2005). The exact criteria for what counts as "suspicious" are unclear, and a number of medical societies have struggled to define the types of cases that should trigger the reporting requirement. In April 2004, the Supreme Court issued a ruling in a widely reported case involving a hospital error and subsequent cover-up that challenged the reporting requirement as a violation of the right against self-incrimination. The court affirmed the duty to report, but failed to clarify the types of cases that must be reported. The notoriety of that case drew attention to the rapid escalation of police reports, which went from 21 cases in 1997, to 124 in 2000, to 248 in 2003. In short, the number of newly filed medical malpractice litigation cases has increased quickly in Japan, the backlog of pending cases is much larger than in the past, and deaths that may be the result of malpractice have a greater likelihood of being reported to the police. Along a number of important dimensions, the relations between doctors and patients are more "legalized" than they were just a decade ago.[8] The rapid rate of increase raises the possibility that medical malpractice litigation could continue unabated, and poses questions about why such litigation has become more common and how its increase should and could be managed.

Japan's Law of Negligence, the Civil Litigation System, and How It Is Changing

Those who believe they have been injured as the result of a medical error can pursue a legal remedy under the substantive law of torts (*fuhō kōi*).[9] Tort law in Japan, unlike the plethora of conflicting rules one finds in different U.S. states, is codified and national, and the basic legal principle underlying tort-related harms is stated in Article 709 of the Civil Code. Based on the nineteenth-century German law of accidents, the Article states that "A person who has intentionally or negligently infringed any right of others, or legally protected interest of others, shall be liable to compensate any damages resulting in consequence." As in American tort law, the central elements of a malpractice claim brought under Article 709 are the establishment of a duty of care (*chūi gimu no teido*), evidence that the duty was breached (*ihan*), a causal link (*inga kankei*) between the breach and the harm, and damages (*songai baisho*). The crux of a malpractice case is generally the identification of the applicable standard of care, the determination of whether the defendant provider met the standard, and the analysis of the causal relationship between the defendant's actions and the plaintiff's injuries.

A great deal depends upon how the standard of care is defined, which party must bear the burden of proving to the court that the defendant did or did not exercise due care, and which party is required to show that the defendant's actions did or did not cause the plaintiff's injury. The standard of care in Japanese malpractice cases is determined with reference to national rather than local practice (Nishino 2000, 106). With regard to the burden of proof (*shōmei sekinin*), Japanese courts treat medical malpractice just like other tort claims, and they require plaintiffs to prove the central elements of their allegations.[10] As Japanese academic commentary on the burden of proof in malpractice claims uniformly asserts, the burden of proof falls on plaintiffs, and interviews with judges and malpractice attorneys confirm that plaintiffs are required to establish the prima facie elements of their claims. Only after they have done so must defendants argue that they met the standard of care, or that their actions did not cause the alleged harm.[11] In short, by requiring plaintiffs to bear the burden of proof in medical malpractice cases, Japanese courts effectively limit the number of plaintiffs' malpractice claims that can succeed.

In addition to the specific legal elements of tort malpractice cases, several long-standing features of the Japanese legal system have a significant bearing on the initiation and resolution of medical malpractice claims, and changes to some of those features appear to be a factor in the increasing prevalence of malpractice litigation. For many years, for example, the compensation of attorneys was regulated by the Japan Bar Association. Although the association's fee schedule formally has been abolished, it is still a reasonable guide, since many lawyers continue to bill clients in accordance with the guidelines.[12] With the fee schedule formally eliminated (the bar association argued that it was a restraint on trade), attorneys are now free to impose contingency fees. Some have reduced their retainers and added a 20 percent contingency fee, but relatively few have eliminated up-front payments by plaintiffs and moved to an exclusively 30 percent contingency fee arrangement. The ability to pursue malpractice claims less expensively is likely to increase the number of potential malpractice claimants. Its impact on attorneys is less clear. Shifting some of the financial risk of medical malpractice claims to attorneys may decrease their willingness to handle such cases. But it could also attract risk-taking attorneys who would not have otherwise worked in the tort law or malpractice area but now see it as an attractive practice area.

In addition to a retainer, plaintiffs have long been required to pay a case filing fee (*tesūryō*) to the court. The fee is based on the amount of the claimed damages and is determined as shown in Table 12.2 (Wada and Maeda 2001, 142).

The filing fee, along with the retainer, requires a significant investment by plaintiffs who want to bring malpractice cases. It is particularly difficult for those who are young and of modest means, who are the most likely to sue over so-called "bad baby" cases—those that involve a child born with a serious neurological, physical, or intellectual impairment. In the United States, such cases are particularly attractive to attorneys and often lead to generous jury awards. But in Japan, even though cases involving impaired newborns represent some of the highest court-awarded damages in the malpractice area,[13] the number of such cases that reach the courts is reduced because new parents, generally in their late twenties or early thirties, are unable to afford the approximately US$40,000 needed to initiate a US$1 million case. So far, no changes have been made to the filing fee requirement, and it remains a strong disincentive to litigation.

TABLE 12.2
Case Filing Fees Paid by Plaintiffs

Damages sought by plaintiff:	Amount paid to the court:
Less than ¥300,000	¥500 for each ¥50,000
¥300,000 to ¥1 million	¥400 for each ¥50,000
¥1 million to ¥3 million	¥700 for each ¥100,000
¥3 million to ¥10 million	¥1000 for each ¥200,000
¥10 million to ¥100 million	¥1000 for each ¥250,000
¥100 million to ¥1 billion	¥3000 for each ¥1 million
Over ¥1 billion	¥10,000 for each ¥5 million

SOURCE: Wada and Maeda (2001: 142).

Likewise, another disincentive to litigation is the determination of damages in Japanese civil litigation. There are no juries in civil cases, which eliminates at least some of the uncertainty experienced by parties to medical malpractice claims in the United States.[14] Moreover, damage calculations by Japanese courts result in awards both modest and predictable (Leflar and Iwata 2005, 200). No punitive damages are permitted in Japan, and cases that might lead to such damages in the United States are generally handled by Japanese criminal law.[15] Compensatory damages as well as payments for pain and suffering in medical malpractice closely follow those for personal injuries that result from automobile accidents. Both types of damages are determined with reference to what is colloquially known as the "Red Book," a bright red guide to traffic accident harms published annually by one of Tokyo's lawyers' associations (*Tokyo San Bengoshi-gai Kōtsū Jiko Shori Iinkai* 2002). The Red Book contains hundreds of traffic accident diagrams that help courts and insurance adjusters evaluate the cause of and responsibility for particular types of crashes, as well as actuarial tables that provide guidelines and illustrations for the calculation of damages. They include "active" damages (*sekyoku songai*), such as the cost of hospitalization, massage, visits to hot springs, and the like, and "passive" damages (*shōkyoku songai*), that refer to losses like missed salary (ibid., 1–56). The Red Book also offers a relatively simple approach to pain and suffering damages (*isharyo*), providing a matrix that takes into account the type of injury, the length of hospitalization, as well as the age, gender, and wage-earning status of the plaintiff, among other factors (ibid., 57–72). Unlike the individualized and highly variable pain and suffering damages in U.S. tort litigation, in Japan the reliance on a standard set of factors leads to a modest variance between the lowest and highest payments. Because

TABLE 12.3
Number of Licensed Attorneys and
Total Population of Japan

Year	# Attorneys	Population of Japan
1960	6321	94,301,623
1965	7082	99,209,137
1970	8478	104,665,171
1975	10,115	111,939,643
1980	11,441	117,060,396
1985	12,604	121,048,923
1990	13,800	123,611,167
1995	15,108	125,570,246
2000	17,126	126,925,843
2005	21,185	127,760,000

SOURCE: See Japan Bar Association (2006); Statistics Bureau, Ministry of
Internal Affairs and Communications.

plaintiffs' demands for damages are likely to approximate those suggested by the
Red Book, payments in medical malpractice cases in Japan are more predictable
and more modest than in the United States. As a result, plaintiffs are reluctant to
invest in significant retainers and filing fees when winning their case leads to a
limited payout, perhaps one they could have negotiated outside of court.

Another structural factor that contributes to the increase in malpractice litigation is the growing number of attorneys willing to take malpractice cases. In
part, the availability of attorneys is a consequence of the contraction of other
types of legal work in the 1990s, particularly real estate, which kept many solo
practitioners busy during the 1980's economic boom. In addition, a generation
of lawyers who came of age during the 1960s and embraced medical malpractice
work as part of a belief in patients' rights has reached full maturity (Feldman
1997). They have successfully passed on their commitment to representing plaintiffs in malpractice cases to an increasing number of younger attorneys, some of
whom now have their own practices, and others who work in firms but do pro
bono work on behalf of people who feel they are victims of medical accidents
(Leflar and Iwata 2005, 201n46). In fact, there appears to be a correlation between the increase in the total number of attorneys in Japan and rising rates of
medical malpractice claims. As shown in Table 12.3, the number of attorneys in
Japan has been steadily increasing since 1960, and between 1990 and 2005 the
lawyer population increased more than 50 percent, whereas the overall population grew by less than 5 percent.

TABLE 12.4
Number of Licensed Female Attorneys
in Japan

Year	# Female Attorneys
1960	42
1965	79
1970	179
1975	299
1980	420
1985	587
1990	766
1995	996
2000	1530
2005	2648

SOURCE: See Japan Bar Association (2006).

Even more dramatic is the increase in the number of women licensed to practice law (Table 12.4). Not only do they often find it difficult or unattractive to work in traditional firms; for some, medical malpractice has a special appeal. Women are generally the primary caregivers in Japanese households and are more likely to have frequent (and potentially negative) interactions with the health care system. This may lead them to make medical malpractice their professional focus.[16]

In a variety of ways, therefore, the structure of the Japanese legal profession and the substance of Japanese tort law affect the frequency and outcomes of malpractice lawsuits.[17] Although none of the factors described are targeted specifically at medical malpractice litigation, each has an impact on malpractice lawsuits, and certain recent changes to them appear to be altering both the rate of malpractice filings and how they are resolved.

Reforming Medical Malpractice Litigation:
The Pace and Accuracy of Justice

Of equal or perhaps greater importance, several structural changes were recently implemented that are aimed directly at two issues of particular importance to medical malpractice litigants: (1) the length of time it takes for claims to be resolved and (2) the accuracy of court judgments that deal with technical scientific and medical issues. William Gladstone's maxim that "justice delayed is justice denied" has particular salience in Japan. The languid pace of trials, in which cases are scheduled to be heard discontinuously (e.g., one day each month)

TABLE 12.5

Length of Time Between the Filing and Final Judgment of Malpractice Cases
and Civil Cases in District Courts, 1994–2006 (in months)

Year	Medical malpractice cases	All civil cases
1994	41.4	9.8
1995	38.8	10.1
1996	37.0	10.2
1997	36.3	10.0
1998	35.1	9.3
1999	34.5	9.2
2000	35.6	8.8
2001	32.6	8.5
2002	30.9	8.3
2003	27.7	8.2
2004	27.3	8.3
2005	26.9	8.4
2006	25.1	7.8

SOURCE: Supreme Court of Japan (2005b).

rather than from start to finish, has long been identified as one reason why Japanese plaintiffs find litigation an unsatisfying approach to conflict resolution. Justice officials and others involved in Japan's legal reform activities, acutely aware of such concerns, made the acceleration of court proceedings a reform priority. But speed has the potential to work at cross-purposes with accuracy, particularly in cases that require detailed scientific or medical knowledge. It is perhaps not surprising, therefore, that two recent changes bearing directly on medical malpractice—the development of a new system for calling expert witnesses and the creation of specialized medical courts—are targeted at speeding up malpractice trials and ensuring that judgments in such cases are as accurate as possible.

Data on the pace of civil justice underscore the view that the infrequency of medical malpractice litigation might in part be the result of the length of time it takes courts to resolve malpractice claims. As illustrated in Table 12.5, between 1994 and 2006 such claims took far longer to resolve than other civil claims. Although the pace of resolving both malpractice and nonmalpractice claims has gotten faster over that period, dramatically so in the case of malpractice, in 2006 it still took an average of 25.1 months for the usual malpractice case to move from filing to final judgment in the district courts (the first-resort trial court for such cases), and far longer for cases that were appealed.

The fact that a typical malpractice case takes more than three times longer than a civil case to be resolved increasingly came to be seen as an unfair barrier to malpractice litigants. Indeed, the government's Justice System Reform Council, which has since 1999 been at the forefront of reforming Japan's legal system to make it more accessible to its citizens, has taken a particular interest in accelerating the pace of civil claims generally, and malpractice specifically. In its politically influential 2001 report, it advocated the implementation of a variety of changes that would improve the processing of civil claims, and cut in half the amount of time it takes to resolve medical malpractice conflicts. Two significant reforms have taken aim at those goals: (1) the creation of a new type of expert witness system and (2) specialized courts (Justice System Reform Council 2001).

Reforming the Expert Witness System

Japan's expert witness system, similar to those of France and Germany, is set out in Article 212 of the Code of Civil Procedure.[18] The primary function of experts in Japan is service to the court, generally consisting of a panel of three judges. Parties may also hire their own experts. Experts are generally identified as predisposed toward plaintiffs or defendants, and in Japan many more are available to defendants.

Until recently, in malpractice and other claims, parties who believed they needed expert testimony submitted a motion to the court and, if the presiding judge agreed, the court would contact the appropriate experts.[19] It took on average 133.3 days for an expert to be successfully recruited, a delay that resulted in part from the lack of a single, simple procedure for expert identification. Courts sometimes asked medical societies or academic medical departments for recommendations but doing so was generally a ten-month process (Murata 2000; Tokyo District Court 2000). Parties could submit a list of potential experts to the court, but the opposing party was allowed to vet them, which was time consuming. Many experts, once identified, refused to advise courts on medical issues, the result of medical hierarchy and paternalism (Sakamoto 2002, 201). Senior physicians occupy the top of carefully crafted pyramids of power, and classmates, members of the same professional organizations, co-workers, and others with professional or personal ties were reluctant to get involved in cases that may make them adversaries. Financial considerations rarely offered a sufficient incentive to overcome such reluctance. The cost of expertise varied with the complexity of a case, but was generally between 300,000 and 500,000 yen, and almost never over one million yen (*Tokyo Chihō Saibansho Iryō Soshō Taisaku*

Iinkai 2003, 43). Once a court secured the participation of an expert, the fee was paid to the court by the party that initially requested expert involvement. It was ultimately paid by the losing party.

After experts agreed to serve and take an oath, the court provided them with pleadings and other relevant legal and medical documents, and requested either a written or (less frequently) an oral report. Parties could submit written questions and seek clarification of written reports. They can also cross-examine experts who gave their reports orally. Experts who provided false testimony were subject to imprisonment for up to ten years (Criminal Code, Article 171).

The "Conference" Approach

On January 8, 2003, the Tokyo District Court invited three physicians to discuss the merits of a malpractice claim involving a patient who underwent a jaw operation and died of heart failure (Asahi Shimbun, 2003).[20] The architects of this new "conference" method (*tōron hōshiki ni yoru kantei*) of consulting medical experts cite several advantages over the current system, including convenience (experts may convene via closed circuit television rather than traveling to the courthouse) (*Nikkei Shinbun* 2002), speed (experts will have only two months to review medical charts, and conferences are limited to a single day),[21] and objectivity (bringing several experts together may reduce their tendency to defend the actions of other medical providers). In addition, experts prepare only a single page of notes prior to a conference. This makes it much more difficult for the parties to offer a detailed (and potentially aggressive) rebuttal. For those who avoid serving as expert witnesses because they do not want to be subjected to withering cross-examination, the new system should provide some welcome relief.[22]

Expert Commissioners

The most innovative and controversial reform involving experts is the creation of a group of special court advisors. As stated by the Judicial System Reform Council, "study should be given . . . to the manner in which new systems for expert participation in litigation should be introduced, in which non-lawyer experts in each specialized field become involved in all or part of trials, from the standpoint of their own specialized expertise, as expert commissioners (*senmon iin*) to support judges."[23] Such experts will be called directly by the court, and will assist in identifying and analyzing disputed issues, facilitating settlement, rendering opinions on technical issues, and evaluating evidence, among other functions. In contrast to traditional expert witnesses, expert commissioners will work exclusively as advisors to the court, and their opinions will not be considered formal evidence at trial. For this new system to succeed, it will have to overcome the view held by some members of the plaintiff's bar that physicians and other medical experts will almost inevitably internalize a prodefense bias (Asashi Shimbun, 2002). Otherwise, plaintiffs' attorneys are likely to oppose any form of expert involvement in medical malpractice cases that does not depend upon their explicit approval of every expert involved in a case.

Creating Specialized Medical Malpractice Courts

In addition to the focus on how outside experts can assist courts, there has been a simultaneous effort to help sitting judges understand and assess the input of experts. Most civil cases are randomly assigned. The Tokyo District Court, for example, has fifty divisions, each staffed by a panel of three judges. Filed cases are assigned to a division that is responsible for the case until it is settled or is tried. Instead of randomly assigning medical malpractice cases, several of Japan's most important courts—including the district courts in Tokyo, Osaka, Nagoya, and Chiba—have recently created "consolidation divisions" (*shūchūbu*), that specialize in malpractice claims.[24] Since 2001, for example, four of the fifty divisions of the Tokyo District Court have been assigned all malpractice cases (approximately 200 per year, as shown in Table 12.6). The hope is that judges in those divisions will acquire expertise that better enables them to handle technical medical issues.[25] In some cases that means they will have the ability to themselves identify and engage with experts, and in other cases use their acquired expertise to comprehend and decide malpractice claims

An analysis of the Tokyo District Court's *shūchūbu* that looks at 228 cases disposed of after October 1, 2002, shows that 36 percent (82 cases) were decided by the court's specialized judges, and 127 (55.7 percent) were settled through mediation (Yamada and Ogawa 2004, 17, 26). Of the 228 cases decided by a judge, plaintiffs won 40.2 percent (82 of 228) and lost 59.8 percent (49 of 228) (ibid., 26). Moreover, cases handled by the medical court appear to proceed far more rapidly than malpractice cases channeled through the regular court system, with 35 percent of them disposed of within one year; the average case takes less than seventeen months. This makes them ten months faster than the national average (ibid., 26). Each of the four specialized medical divisions receives an average of three to five new cases each month.

TABLE 12.6
Tokyo District Court, Specialized Medical Court (*shūchūbu*), 2001–2007

Year	# new claims	# pending clams	# disposed claims
2001	126	162	22
2002	192	256	98
2003	180	262	164
2004	218	334	154
2005	195	337	191
2006	194	294	238
2007	201	280	215

SOURCE: Cases were accepted by the Specialized Medical Court beginning in April 2001.
Data from 2004–2007 provided by Judge Keiko Mitsuyoshi; pdf on file with author.

Despite the effort to facilitate the involvement of experts in malpractice cases and create specialized medical courts, some judges and commentators argue that courts should decide a wide array of such cases without consulting experts (Yamana and Ōshima 2003, 19). Judge Fukuda Takahisa of the Tokyo District Court, for example, points out that the Internet has enabled individuals to learn a great deal about medical issues, and notes that expert opinions almost always conflict. Consequently, he believes that judges should be proactive in learning about medical issues and trust their own judgment. Suzuki Toshihiro, a prominent plaintiff's attorney, agrees that attorneys and judges can often rely on their own understanding of the medical issues when determining whether malpractice occurred (*Mainichi Shimbun* 2002). In short, at the same time that specialized courts have become operational and judges are working to facilitate the participation of experts in medical cases, some influential legal elites are claiming that such expertise is overrated and should play a less prominent role in medical malpractice cases.

Exogenous Influences on the Rise of Malpractice Lawsuits

In addition to the structural aspects of the civil litigation system that have affected malpractice, there is a set of factors exogenous to the legal system that is particularly relevant to the rise in malpractice claims. First, the increasing number of people who are taking their medical providers to court is at least in part a result of the erosion of public trust in elites generally, and physicians in particular. Public opinion surveys on such matters can be unreliable, but the available data support the conclusion that public trust in doctors has been declining.

When a 1978 survey by the *Yomiuri Shimbun* newspaper, for example, asked patients about their level of trust in doctors, 21 percent said they had a high level of trust, and 68.2 percent said they had a moderate degree of trust, with only 6.8 percent expressing some distrust, and .8 percent saying they don't trust doctors at all ("*Iryō ni Kansuru Yoron Chōsa*" 2005). A decade later, in 1988, a survey by the *Asahi Shinbun* newspaper found that the 21 percent of people responded positively to the statement "I don't really trust my doctor" (*amari shinrai shiteinai*); that number dropped to 20 percent in 1992, but increased to 28 percent in 1996 and 30 percent in 2000, and settled at 26 percent in 2002.[26] That trend was underscored by a 2003 *Yomiuri Shimbun* newspaper survey of 3,000 people showing that 77 percent were very or somewhat anxious about being the victim of medical malpractice. Overall, the surveys reveal a gradual but clear decrease in trust and increase in distrust that is particularly dramatic among those between the ages of twenty and forty.

Hospital administrators have gotten the message, and have been experimenting with different ways of regaining the allegiance of patients. Some have started to talk about patients as "customers," and offer services that until recently would have been unthinkable, like Shizuoka Prefecture's Seirei Hamamatsu General Hospital. It employs several doorwomen to greet patients, open their car doors, and treat them like they were entering a luxury hotel (Tsukahara 2004). To some extent, the erosion of trust has been fueled by the media and its intensive coverage of providers who have engaged in outrageous conduct (subjecting the wrong patients to high-risk procedures, altering medical records to cover up evidence of mistakes, etc.), triggering public criticism of the medical system (Leflar and Iwata 2005). From this perspective, increases in malpractice litigation reflect a change in how people regard medical practitioners, and elites more generally, who are no longer perceived as atop a rigid social hierarchy that makes them immune from legal attack.

Second, the financial needs of victims may be growing because of a retrenchment in benefits offered through national health care and other parts of the social welfare system. With higher co-pays resulting in higher out-of-pocket health care costs, those with injuries that they believe were caused by negligent medical care may be more likely to sue in order to recoup their expenses. The tendency is exacerbated by Japan's "lost decade" of economic stagnation in the 1990s; people are being asked to bear greater health care costs at a time when they have less money than they had ten years earlier (Kuroyanagi 2005).

Third, as briefly mentioned earlier, media coverage of medical malpractice litigation has brought public attention to suing doctors. Both lawyers and patients, as well as judges, government officials, and others, are influenced by the media. In the late 1990s, media coverage of malpractice cases soared. A database that tracks stories in Japan's leading newspapers indicates that in 1990 there were only 161 stories about malpractice; that jumped to 413 in 1997, 1,258 in 1999, and between 2,000 and 3,000 since (Kodama 2007, 73, figure 2). The increase was marked by a large number of stories written about a number of now-notorious medical mishaps, like a mix-up involving two patients who received the wrong surgery (the lung patient received heart surgery, and vice versa) and the cover-up of a mistake involving a faulty artificial heart-lung machine (Kawabata 2006). In addition, litigation brought by hemophiliacs against both the Ministry of Health, Labor and Welfare and pharmaceutical companies in the 1990s created a political scandal that was widely viewed as an example of how innocent and helpless people are mistreated at the hands of the medical establishment (and was instrumental to the success of the lawsuit and settlement of hepatitis C claims in 2007) (Feldman 2000). Such stories depict medical malpractice litigation as a morally just cause, not the impecunious scheming of greedy parties, and pique the interest of the general public as well as attorneys and potential claimants.

Interestingly, at least from the perspective of the United States, criticism of overly generous awards to plaintiffs, spiraling insurance premiums, greedy plaintiffs' attorneys, or increases in claiming that lead to undeserving lawsuits are virtually unknown in Japan. When this criticism is expressed—like when a Deputy Minister of Health, Labor, and Welfare exclaimed that there are "growing numbers of money hungry weirdoes trying to get rich by blaming the medical world"—the outburst led to demands for his resignation, not a groundswell of support (*Mainichi Daily News* 2003). According to the vast majority of media accounts, therefore, the rising rate of malpractice claims reflects a growing number of medical accidents, not illegitimate lawsuits, insurance company gauging, or ambulance-chasing attorneys.[27]

In sum, together with structural changes (previously discussed in the sections "Japan's Law of Negligence, the Civil Litigation System, and How It Is Changing" and "Reforming Medical Malpractice Litigation: The Pace and Accuracy of Justice") that have affected the frequency of medical malpractice litigation, there are a variety of exogenous factors that have contributed to (and been affected by) the rise in malpractice claiming. A cycle has emerged in which more malpractice litigation triggers more media coverage of underperforming physicians; more media coverage negatively influences the public's view of elites; a lower regard for elites, combined with fewer barriers to litigation, contributes to the willingness of people to sue. The result is both an increase in the number of malpractice claims and a weakening of whatever normative barriers may have inhibited litigation. As structural impediments to litigation are lifted, cultural constraints are weakened as well, and what occurs is both a rise in litigation rates and a changed view of litigation. The relatively small number of medical malpractice claims suggests caution in using them as the basis for a broad claim about law and society in Japan. Nonetheless, if one views the trend in malpractice litigation as indicative of what is occurring in other areas of civil litigation—and the aggregate data reported by Ginsberg and Hoetker offers some support for that view—it appears that an important shift is occurring in the role of tort law in the lives of Japanese citizens (Ginsburg and Hoetker 2006).

A New Era of Japanese Tort Law: The Lure of the Courts

It is easy to imagine the many ways in which Japanese legal and political elites could have utilized tried-and-true methods to ensure that patient complaints about substandard medical care would rarely end up in court. They could have raised filing fees; made it more difficult to hire experts to testify about the standard of care; randomly assigned malpractice cases to judges with little experience handling technical medical matters, thus ensuring delay; created attractive alternative dispute resolution mechanisms that were fast, cheap, and generous; placed tighter limits on damages; and more. One need not look far to find examples of state-created barriers to tort-based litigation that channel potential litigants away from the courts toward extrajudicial forms of redress. That has been a favored way of handling conflict, and it may well have been an effective way of handling the rise in malpractice lawsuits.

When the number of claims relating to automobile accidents began to escalate in the post–World War II era, for example, the government passed legislation in 1955 that required all vehicle owners to carry a minimum level of insurance (30 million yen by the early 1990s), and stipulated that they were liable for all damages unless they could prove that (1) they were not negligent; (2) a third party, or the accident victim, was negligent; and (3) the owner's car was not defective. To collect, parties followed a finely grained procedure under which they first consulted with a government traffic accident counselor, an insurance company representative, or a member of the bar association; the claim was evaluated; and payment was tendered. If parties were displeased with the settlement, they would go to a Traffic Accident Dispute Resolution Center. Claims over auto accidents ended up in court for two reasons: (1) if complainants were unhappy about the settlement resolution or (2) initially demanded more of a payout than insurance would cover. In effect, the law channeled disputes through an administrative process that rejected the negligence standard and instead held vehicle owners strictly liable for auto accident-related harms. The result was a system in which most accident victims would recover, while imposing limited transaction costs and providing modest, capped damages. Disgruntled accident victims could always go to court and rely on traditional tort principles, but they had to accept a significantly lower likelihood of recovery (and higher adjudication costs) than for administratively processed claims.

Disputes over environmental harms also illustrate how tort claims have been channeled away from the courts. In a series of cases brought to the courts in the 1960s and early 1970s, plaintiffs relied on tort law principles and achieved a number of significant political and legal victories. As a consequence, the government created an extrajudicial mechanism to divert cases from the courts. Under the 1973 "Law for the Compensation of Pollution Related Health Injury," claimants can collect damages without proving a causal link between the existence of a pollutant and the emergence of health harms. In place of causation, claimants are permitted to show the administrators of the compensation fund (in the Ministry of Health, Labor, and Welfare) that there is a statistical correlation between a particular disease and a particular type of pollution. The showing is based on epidemiological data that relieves claimants of the burden of proving specific causation as long as they can establish a general correlation between the discharge of the allegedly polluting substance and the outbreak of disease. As a result, those who consider themselves victims of environmental pollution generally rely on nontort rules and seek damages from the bureaucratically managed compensation system rather than through torts and courts.

Auto accidents and environmental harms are hardly the only areas in which personal injury compensation has been diverted away from the courts.[28] Although it is difficult to precisely identify the government's motivations for creating extrajudicial, nontort remedies for certain personal injuries, one can make certain observations about the consequences of such an approach. For one, it is clear that the reliance on extrajudicial approaches to personal harms has limited the number of cases brought to the courts and made the government a crucial actor in the processing and resolution of tort-related claims (Upham 1987). In addition, administrative schemes in Japan have taken one of the goals of U.S. tort law—compensation—and made it the foundation of its system for managing accidental injuries. The U.S. experience, in contrast, has relatively few administrative compensation schemes, and litigation of personal injuries is far more common.

In the area of medical malpractice as well, extrajudicial dispute resolution and compensation has been one way of managing injuries caused by malpractice, especially the Japan Medical Association's (JMA) liability claims management system.[29] More than half of Japanese physicians are members of the JMA, and most of them purchase membership bundled with malpractice insurance (Kōmi 1990). The JMA's malpractice insurance is priced at less than US$1,000/year, regardless of practice area, and includes coverage of approximately US$1 million/year with a US$10,000 deductible.[30] Physicians with JMA insurance who believe that they have harmed a patient as a result of malpractice can notify the local JMA office, which will investigate the incident and, in three to twelve months, either dismiss the claim or offer compensation. Payments are generally modest, with the largest recorded payment US$1.3 million. Since the JMA system is overseen by a mix of JMA officials and insurance company employees, there is no public reporting requirement and thus little available data on the frequency or typical disposition of claims.[31] In fact, the system is only minimally publicized, and it is not clear how well informed patients are about its existence.

The JMA's extrajudicial dispute resolution mechanism has kept at least some cases away from the courts, thereby sidestepping the costs of litigation and providing compensation in certain relatively clear cases where judges would be likely to find in favor of plaintiffs.[32] One might have imagined that the government, cognizant of the rising number of malpractice suits, would have tried to build on the JMA system. Doing so may have enabled it to keep the courts out of the malpractice business, so that disgruntled patients would resolve their grievances in a less adversarial and public way. But that is not how the state responded. Instead, a patchwork of government initiatives—some targeted generally at better enabling the business community to resolve disputes through the courts, and others aimed specifically at medical malpractice litigation—have made courts far more accessible and attractive to aggrieved patients than in the past. What this suggests, this chapter has argued, is a fundamental shift away from efforts to limit recourse to the courts, a shift that is both the result of and a continuing cause of new structural configurations and sociopolitical dispositions. No longer does the state simply slam the door on tort litigation by making courts particularly cumbersome and expensive. No longer do potential litigants face such daunting institutional barriers to suing that they have little choice but to resolve their claims through alternative channels. Instead, in the face of a rising tide of malpractice claims, the government has crafted a set of structural solutions that are at odds with its long-standing posture toward tort-based conflict. In doing so, it has eliminated many (but not all) of the impediments to using the courts to manage personal injury claims that have been the subject of so much attention by legal scholars.[33]

Changes in the relationship between law and society, however, do not occur in a vacuum; they are responsive to, and indeed a product of, economic trends, political opportunities, and social values. This chapter has thus emphasized not only structural changes in Japanese civil litigation, but also the sociopolitical context of the changes surrounding the emergence and resolution of medical malpractice claims, particularly the growing negative perception of medical and other elites. Just as legal rules and procedures have reshaped Japan's medical malpractice system, so too has the cultural context of that system been altered. It is difficult, perhaps impossible, to say whether changes in law triggered or trailed the broader social changes in which they are embedded. The more important observation is that the two are closely intertwined and that a careful examination of conflicts over medical malpractice reveals their interdependence.

Broad economic and political factors were crucial to laying the groundwork of legal reform. The 1990s were a period of economic malaise in Japan, and Prime Minister Koizumi staked much of his political capital on administrative, political, and legal reform. Indeed, the changes one observes in medical malpractice coincide with a more general embrace of legal reform.[34] For almost a decade (and most powerfully since the late 1990s), the banner of "*shihō kaikaku*" (legal/judicial reform) has been waved by the Ministry of Justice, Japanese Federation of Bar Associations, Ministry of Education, Secretariat of the Supreme Court, legal academics, and others, who have come together on a variety of blue-ribbon panels to propose and implement a wide array of changes to Japan's legal system.

Some have been targeted at specific areas of legal procedure, like the new Code of Civil Procedure; some have created laws where none had previously existed, such as the Freedom of Information Act and the law governing nonprofit organizations; still others are aimed at the legal profession, particularly the restructuring of legal education. Medical malpractice litigation was hardly the prime mover of these many reforms, although it was important to some of them, like those involving the expert witness system. The high visibility of malpractice is the result of it becoming a "test case," offering reformers an opportunity to publicly demonstrate the concrete impact of far-ranging (and often ambiguous) new legal institutions. For policy makers who want evidence of their commitment to improving the pace of civil justice, for example, the acceleration of the resolution of medical malpractice trials offers a rough-and-ready guide. So the Japanese government's new embrace of formal legal mechanisms is particularly visible in the area of medical malpractice, but it is surely not the only area of rapid change.

It is tempting to observe the legal changes surrounding medical malpractice in Japan and conclude that they are yet another example of Japan's alleged tendency to become more like the United States (Sasao et al. 2006).[35] At least some of the recent changes surrounding tort law and malpractice litigation in Japan do seem to provide some evidence of "convergence" with the United States and perhaps a more general "global" convergence. Those include a reliance on the formal legal process as a reasonable venue for the airing and resolving of malpractice claims, a willingness to train more attorneys to represent parties in malpractice cases, and experimentation with specialized courts and the expert witness system. On the other hand, significant differences remain between the tort systems of Japan and the United States, namely the possibility of high-pain-and-suffering awards in the United States, the existence of punitive damages, true contingency fee billing, the availability of juries, and more, that sharply differentiate the management of medical malpractice claims in the United States from that in Japan.

The changes described in this chapter, therefore, ought not to be mistaken for what some have called the "Americanization" of Japanese law (Keleman and Sibbitt 2002).[36] There is no compelling evidence that the Japanese tort system is converging with the U.S. tort regime, and much to suggest that the area of medical malpractice in Japan is characterized by structural and social features that will continue to distinguish it from U.S.-style malpractice litigation. Instead, what is occurring in Japan is an example of the complex interplay of formal legal rules and procedures with economic, political, and social factors that frame their existence, creating a symbiotic relationship in which structure and culture affect and are affected by each other. The result is a shift in the importance of tort law and a changed social context in which it operates. As the legal rules and procedures governing medical malpractice claims change, so too does the society in which they are embedded, laying the foundation for yet another stage in the long relationship between tort law and society.

CHAPTER THIRTEEN

The Role of the Judiciary in Asbestos Injury Compensation in Japan

TAKAO TANASE

Landscapes of Asbestos Litigation

Asbestos and asbestos products have caused grave health hazards on an unprecedented scale worldwide. In addition to workers in factories using asbestos products, nearby residents as well as consumers and inhabitants of buildings containing asbestos have also been affected. According to a prediction made in the United States, asbestos exposure will have produced some 130,000 cases of mesothelioma and 300,000 cases of cancer during the period of 1965 to 2030 (Carroll et al. 2005, 16). In Japan, it is forecast that asbestos will be responsible for 100,000 cases of mesothelioma and twice that number of cancer cases.

This massive victimization has tested the capability of the legal system to respond. In the United States, by 2002, asbestos litigation resulted in the payment of $70 billion in compensation; but only $30 billion of this amount were allocated to the victims, while the rest was consumed by lawyers' fees (Carroll et al. 2005, 88). It is well known that tort litigation requires high transactions costs, but still this number is staggering. Is it really impossible to pay proper injury compensation without spending such enormous fees?

In Japan, asbestos-related injuries are compensated mainly through workers' compensation. Awards are reasonably generous, providing compensation of 80 percent of a person's salary for absence from work as well as a lump-sum payment and survivor annuity upon the death of the victim.

Furthermore, worker's compensation is not an exclusive remedy as it is in the United States, and workers can sue the employer for damages while retaining such payments. Therefore, to avoid unnecessary litigation, most of the major corporations in Japan have agreements with company unions to pay for damages if workers get injury compensation. These agreements provide compensation for pain and suffering, which is not covered by worker's compensation, and are typically in the amount of 20–30 million yen in cases involving fatal injuries.

Japanese worker's compensation also differs from that of the United States in that it is administered by the national government. Dues are collected from all industries according to a formula set by administrative rules, and each claim is processed directly by the government bureaucracy. In this way, the costs of compensating such massive occupational injuries as asbestos-related diseases are diffused throughout entire industries, and workers do not have to face the risk that a particular company will be unable to pay due to bankruptcy.

The Japanese system does, however, have a weakness of its own. Since workers usually do not get legal assistance when they file for compensation, claims for unknown or novel occupational diseases are rarely pushed hard. In 2005 the Kubota Company, formerly Japan's largest asbestos producer, suddenly announced that seventy-nine of its workers had died of mesothelioma and lung cancer, and three nearby residents suffered the illnesses.[1] The news shocked Japan, and the media reported the extent of asbestos exposure and injuries with a dire prediction of more deaths to follow. Because of this heightened awareness, other workers nationwide and the relatives of deceased workers started to file claims. Previously only 10 percent of known mesothelioma patients in Japan had filed claims, but after 2005 the number suddenly jumped, and now most of the work-related mesothelioma patients get compensation. The lung cancer patients understandably have more difficulty, but they fair better than before, too.[2]

Thus, before 2005, the Japanese system was efficient in paying compensation to asbestos victims, but it featured a substantial "error cost" in that it left a large population of workers uncompensated. To rectify the inadvertence after 2005, the government initiated various measures such as relaxing the standard of proof and reaching out to potential victims of asbestos-related illnesses. A new compensation program was also instituted in 2006 to give deceased relatives who failed to file workers' compensation within the five-year statute of limitations an annuity plus a lump sum payment. The program also covers asbestos victims who cannot claim worker's compensation. These are individuals who have contracted mesothelioma or lung cancer with certain symptomatic signs of asbestos exposure but do not have, or cannot prove, a history of exposure in asbestos-contaminated factories. Although they are not eligible for workers' compensation, they are paid 100,000 yen per month plus 3 million yen in case of death. The program is centrally managed by the government and jointly funded by the government and the industry as a whole.[3]

This is the compensation system currently in place in Japan to address asbestos injuries. Although it appears that everything is well organized and the problems of compensation are now properly addressed, victims are in fact not wholly satisfied with the system, and there are discernable efforts underway to destabilize it. The major opposition comes from the victims and the labor unions supporting them. They argue that the new compensation system to supplement workers' compensation is too narrow in permitting compensation only in cases of mesothelioma and lung cancer with clear evidence of asbestos causation.[4] They contend, for example, that lung cancer patients with pleural plaque still encounter a high rejection rate. Asbestosis and other pulmonary diseases are not compensated at all. Second, they argue that payments by this new compensation program are unacceptably low and should be equal to those paid by worker's compensation. Furthermore, even if workers receive workers' compensation for asbestos injuries, they are not given additional payments for pain and suffering unless they are full-time employees of major corporations. In theory, they could sue for tort damages on top of worker's compensation, but this is difficult especially for unorganized workers, such as independent contractors who migrate from one workplace to another.

The critics of the asbestos compensation system use a slogan, "redress the damages without a crack," meaning that every victim is equally entitled to full compensation. This slogan may be universally accepted as an ideal, but in real life it has proved impossible to provide both full compensation and equal compensation. When these two objectives are not met at the same time, philosophies of constructing the compensation/tort system tend to diverge, emphasizing one of the two objectives over the other. While in the United States the ideal of full compensation is stressed because of its connection to the goal of individual justice, in Japan equal justice has more resonance among the people because of its connection to the goal of collective justice. Thus, equal justice has served as the foundation for compensation in Japanese asbestos cases.

In addition to pressing their claims in the context of ordinary political campaigns, victim groups and allied lawyers have initiated two major lawsuits, one in Osaka and one in Tokyo, both suing the government for negligence. Under

Japanese law, the government may be held liable if its office inflicts damages negligently in wielding its power. There is no sovereign immunity, and the concept of negligence is interpreted to include the "strongly unreasonable non-enforcement of the law."[5] Not particular named individuals, but the whole administration can be held accountable for a disaster caused by lax governmental enforcement. In the asbestos area, the Ministry of Labor issued many regulations over the years, but critics contend that the regulations were ineffective to forestall a disaster that was well known and predictable from the experiences of other countries. They suggest that the government was so committed to the process of economic development that it refrained from taking necessary measures to protect Japanese workers.

If the courts find for the plaintiffs in these lawsuits and hold the government liable for asbestos injuries, the compensation system will be affected significantly. As every victim, regardless of the site where he or she was exposed to asbestos, can potentially sue the government for not regulating the risk properly, a victory for the plaintiffs would be equivalent to establishing a national compensation system for all asbestos victims. But this, of course, assumes that one or a few big lawsuits can determine liability and that the government will comply fully with their outcomes. There must be some mechanism to enable this courts-and-government coordination.

Even if liability is clearly established, however, the issue of setting criteria to determine the eligible victims still remains. The compensation system requires criteria that are objective and easy to handle. The criteria established as a ministerial ordinance in compliance with court decisions must be honored by the parties and should be beyond court challenges as much as possible. When the government is held liable for the injury in a mass tort case, most often it is only a partial liability with the government paying a portion of damages and the rest being borne by the industry. The asbestos manufacturers would still have to be held responsible for any compensation beyond worker's compensation.

Does this mean that Japanese workers would be required to sue the manufacturers for damages individually as in the United States? The answer is clearly "no." So far there are fewer than twenty asbestos cases, and it is unlikely there will be a sudden increase of future cases. It is therefore safe to say that in Japan a small number of lawsuits determine the course of compensation for mass injuries such as asbestos-related diseases, including the liability of manufactures. The current system of compensation may be destabilized if plaintiffs end up winning

the major lawsuits now being litigated, but this would lead at most to the establishment of another system of compensation and not to a wholesale reliance on
the strategy of litigation.

If that is the case, then how is it possible for such a small number of cases to
determine the fate of compensation nationwide in Japan? To answer this question, I will first describe in detail one prototypical case in which the litigation of
a mass tort action resulted in the creation of a new framework for compensation
in Japan. That was the SMON case, brought in the early 1970s.

Scarcity of Lawsuits

SMON is an acronym for subacute myelo optico neuropathy. In 1967 a large
number of patients complaining of specific neurological symptoms, such as un-
explained diarrhea and visual dysfunction, were found within specific areas. The
Ministry of Health and Welfare established an investigating committee made up
of medical experts, and the committee issued a finding that SMON was a side
effect caused by chinoform, a medicine widely prescribed for a broad range of in-
testinal disorders. There were, however, some scientists who disputed the finding
and advocated further studies. Legal scholars were also divided as to whether the
pharmaceutical company could be held liable for selling chinoform, which had
been approved by the Ministry and sold for a long time as a common medicine.

In this climate of massive health hazards and of lingering doubts, litigation
was begun in 1971. At first, only a small number of plaintiffs filed suit. The number of plaintiffs gradually increased, however, and further suits were filed in
courts in various regions of the country. Eventually, the SMON cases became the
most extensive ever litigated in Japan. One consolidated case before the Tokyo
District Court featured 2,000 plaintiffs, and more than 5,000 plaintiffs appeared
altogether in twenty-seven district courts nationwide.

After five and a half years' proceedings,[6] the Tokyo District Court issued an
advisory opinion, explaining in detail how it had reached a judgment on the
issue of liability and on the payment schedule for plaintiffs who had different
degrees of impairment. Issuing an advisory opinion of this kind was quite unusual, but the court considered it necessary to prod the parties into negotiating
a settlement, for the plaintiffs demanded not just a payment but an acknowledg-
ment of responsibility on the part of both the pharmaceutical company and the
Ministry. The company had insisted that the disease was caused by an unknown

virus and denied responsibility. The government refuted the liability as a matter of law. Although the advisory opinion was clear on the defendants' liability and made specific findings of fault, some plaintiffs were still adamant in establishing liability beyond dispute and rejected the settlement offer. Nevertheless, this opinion cleared the way for other courts to follow the lead and make similar judgments for the plaintiffs. Within a year, nine major district court judgments were handed down, and all of them not only found for the plaintiffs but awarded damages similar to the formula set forth in the Tokyo District Court's advisory opinion.

While these lawsuits were unfolding, the plaintiffs in all the pending cases in Japan formed a national organization, called the National SMON Conference, and conducted negotiations with the government at the same time that they were holding sit-ins in front of the Ministry building and other protest events. Finally, in September 1979, an agreement was reached between the victims, the pharmaceutical company, and the government. The agreement (called *kakuninsho*, a written affirmation) provides for a monthly health care allowance of 30,000 yen, nursing care expenses for seriously ill victims, and other costs, in addition to compensation granted by the court. The health care allowance itself accounted for 25 percent of the average compensation allowed for all victims. The plaintiff's glossary called these additional allowances "permanent measures for victim redress." The lead counsel for the plaintiffs explained this expression as follows, "Restitution is the most highly preferred remedy for damages. As human injuries cannot be compensated by money, the culpable parties should provide medical expenses, nursing-care services, as well as rehabilitation facilities to alleviate the pain and help the victims to return to their daily lives as much as possible." The lawsuit, he added, represented the struggle of the SMON victims to regain the "human rights robbed of them" and the right to "live humanly."[7]

The Director of the Pharmaceutical Affairs Bureau of the Ministry of Health and Welfare testified in the Diet on the agreement with the SMON National Conference and said, "If there are victims other than those participating in the lawsuits, we encourage them to file suits. The MHW will handle them quickly." That is, a de facto administrative compensation system was established by pledging payment to all victims according to the settlement formula stipulated in the agreement.

Other mass tort cases in Japan culminated in a similar settlement pattern. Depending on the nature of exposure, access to political movements, and the specific issues raised in each case, they followed slightly different paths before arriving at a final conclusion. But in all of these cases there is a discernable pattern, which I call a "scarcity of trials." That is, when a major catastrophic event occurs and many victims are harmed as a result, one or a few major lawsuits are brought, sometimes with hundreds of plaintiffs in a single case. The litigation takes several years to conclude, but if the courts find for plaintiffs or announce the contours of settlements, the parties along with the government proceed to negotiate a global settlement. The settlement includes those victims who did not participate in the litigation and even victims who have not yet manifested symptoms. In short, the final outcome is the establishment of a system of government-run compensation.

How can such a cost-saving resolution of mass torts be possible in Japan? I will describe the mechanism that enables global settlements to arise as the result of only a few lawsuits by focusing on three major actors, namely the court, the lawyers, and the public administration.

Courts

The primary factor contributing to the scarcity of trials is the organization of the court itself. There are relatively few courts in Japan, and they are nationally unified under one Supreme Court. The Japanese court actively adopts joinder proceedings and treats separate cases that have been joined as if they were actually single cases. Consolidating cases in this fashion is considered to be not only necessary for the defense to reduce its burden to answer the complaints, but also a way to do justice to the plaintiffs by rendering a uniform decision. This policy significantly affects lawyers' strategies as well. In the United States, where jury trials are the norm, too much consolidation would create a risk that the fate of an entire group of victims and the industry might be determined by a single jury.[8] In Japan, however, a panel of three professional judges renders a decision after intensive hearings and with a detailed explanation of the reasoning behind the decision. Quite often a judgment in a difficult case, such as the SMON litigation, becomes book-like in length. Inevitably, the lawyers representing the victims have to consolidate their efforts to win a decisive victory in such a case.

A mammoth joinder proceeding has its own difficulty. Sufficient trial time cannot be allocated to examine individual damages and causation. In the SMON litigation, only a small number of victims representing different levels of severity were selected and examined carefully. The court then devised an injury classification and payment schedule for each category of injuries. All individual plaintiffs were assigned to a category solely on the basis of their medical records. This expedited procedure for handling individual damages is actually identical to the one used in administrative compensation systems. The court in mass joinder cases copies this approach, partly inadvertently, but without qualms or contestation from the parties. In this process, we can see the smooth transition from court judgment to an administrative scheme of compensation.

On the other hand, when it comes to issues of liability, the courts pour in abundant resources. In the SMON litigation, all nine courts of first instance spent five to six years before rendering judgments. The opinions, especially that of the Tokyo District Court, contained detailed examinations of the testimony of expert witnesses and relevant medical literatures. Legal scholars commented on them as though they were a medical book. The judges were determined to bring closure to these legal battles, which had generated nationwide interest.

The fact that the Japanese judiciary is organized centrally and hierarchically also contributes to the scarcity of trials. Not only does the Supreme Court have ultimate authority over the interpretation of law nationally, but also decisions of major courts, such as the Tokyo and Osaka district courts, carry much weight in forging a consensus among all the courts of Japan. The courts are implicitly coordinated horizontally as well as vertically. Ideally, the courts should speak with one voice in Japan, and they often do.[9]

Lawyers

Lawyers, too, play an important role in bringing about global settlements in Japan. Since the contingent fee system does not exist in Japan, lawyers usually charge down payments when they are retained. This creates some hardship for people without means, especially for victims who have lost their earning capacity due to their illness or injury. Thus, in situations such as the SMON cases, most victims are unable to retain lawyers on their own, and lawyers undertake the case without being paid initially.[10] In Japan, this style of lawyering is common in cases in which lawyers work for common people who have been deprived of their "rights as humans." It is termed "work with a *te-bento*," meaning "to bring one's own lunch to work." The image matches very well the identity that Japanese cause lawyers typically embrace.

This type of lawyer identity has roots in the history of Japan's modernization. In the late nineteenth century, when Japan built a nation state to match the Western powers, it adopted a model of the modern absolutist state with a strong bureaucracy at the center. The adoption of this model affected the judicial system. A bureaucratic judiciary was placed in the center and the lawyers at the periphery. This power structure was apparent in various aspects of the judiciary before World War II, and it was also reinforced by a division within the legal profession. As the Emperor was at the pinnacle of state power, judges and prosecutors were called *zaicho,* meaning "being in the Emperor's Court," while private lawyers were *zaiya,* "being in the field." In terms of their practice, the lawyers were effectively barred from the government-business-military complex, that is, from the power elites, and had to find their clients among the common people. Naturally, these lawyers identified themselves as "being with the people," with a connotation that the people were powerless, or worse oppressed by the powerful, and that the lawyers had to fight with them against the deprivation of their rights.

The absolutist state was dismantled after World War II, but the fundamental makeup of the prewar political structure remains. A strong bureaucracy with the characteristics of neutrality and professionalism is at the center of government, and the centrally organized judiciary continues to command authority within the judicial system. The view of the judges being in the center aligned with the power and lawyers being in the field aligned with the common people persists even now. An idealized image of "lawyers working for the people" may have some appeal in the United States, too, but in Japan, this image has stronger overtones of struggles for political power, and it also has a more official status having been enshrined in the first article of Japan's Law of Lawyers: "Lawyers have a mission of defending fundamental human rights and achieving social justice."[11] The fact that more than 1,000 attorneys participated in the SMON lawsuits with *te-bento*—no remuneration—attests to the appeal of this mission statement to Japanese lawyers.

These public-spirited lawyers formed a large-scale counsel team in each court and then had periodic contacts with each other to share information and to devise the best common strategy. Witnesses that proved to be effective in one trial were used in other courts as well, and the effect was almost like having one national trial held in several sites concurrently. This sharing of information and strategy was also necessitated by the fact that lawyers can participate in such nonprofit litigation only as a part-time contribution. They must continue their

daily practices to maintain their law offices. It is also significant that these lawyers share a view of lawyering as involving fights against the power of government alliances. This sense of mission breeds solidarity among them and helps
them work as one body. Furthermore, since they view the litigation as a struggle
of the common people to condemn the government and business for the callous disregard of human rights, the lawyers participating in lawsuits such as the
SMON cases are willing to go to the streets with the victims to demand remedial
measures and a compensation system.

Public Administration

The third important actor that contributes to achieving global settlements is
the public administration. In the United States, damage claims against the government for regulatory failures are not allowed in principle. Injuries caused by
exposure to toxic substance or dangerous pharmaceuticals are considered to be
the responsibilities of the companies involved. It is generally assumed that public money should not be spent for compensation, except in rare cases in which
there are public interest reasons to do so.[12] Also, although the notion of sovereign immunity has historical roots in English common law, its rationale in the
American context now lies in the belief in democracy. The administration can be
held accountable through various political channels and through administrative
legal actions. Assuming that these mechanisms work satisfactorily, providing
additional avenues through damage suits is not only unnecessary but might even
over-deter officials from exercising necessary discretion. Also, considering the
financial burden, it is the people who pay the damage awards if the Government
is held liable. When the case involves mass injuries and mandates huge damage
awards, this political consideration has to enter into the liability assessment. The
power to assess the state indemnity, therefore, has to remain in the hands of the
people who are the ultimate sovereign. In short, a greater unity between the government and the people is assumed to exist in the United States to the extent that
the people are believed to be capable of effectively controlling the government
and to bear the burden through taxation regarding what the government spends.
This is sovereign immunity in a modern sense.

The Japanese think about these issues differently. To be able to sue the government for regulatory failures in cases like SMON—or asbestos—is very important
in order for the people to hold the government accountable. In fact, state indem-

nification suits have played a significant role in Japanese judicial history. In the SMON litigation as well, the plaintiffs stressed the importance of the suit against the government.

Initially many held the view that the government could not be held accountable, as the disease was thought to be of some unknown epidemic and the Ministry of Health and Welfare itself had organized the investigating committee to find the cause. But plaintiffs' lawyers found overseas documents that had, at an earlier stage, indicated the risk of neuropathy caused by chinoform. These documents proved, the lawyers argued, that the Ministry could have foreseen the consequences of allowing the drug to be sold as a common medicine. If the government had taken active measures to protect public safety and to gather information thoroughly before granting permission to manufacture and market the drug, a large-scale injury would not have occurred. The courts agreed with this contention.

It is interesting to note that here particular officials were not held individually liable for violating the law, and instead the entire Ministry was held liable for not taking an active role. The court found that the Ministry had failed to revise the relevant laws and regulations to ensure the safety of medicines. Citing the fact that in the United States the drug in question had been withdrawn from the list of approved nonprescription drugs ten years earlier, the court chided the Japanese administration for its laxity in overseeing the safety of medicine. This technique of citing the stringent regulations in the United States or Europe and then criticizing the Japanese government for not meeting the international standard is quite common in Japan.[13]

A similar pattern is evident in the aftermath of the Kubota Corporation's announcement of massive-scale asbestos injuries among its workers and nearby residents. The newspapers argued in their editorials that the government should bear responsibility, alleging that while other countries had already banned asbestos the administration in Japan had hesitated to do so for fear of slowing the economy. One newspaper observed that it was "the same pattern as the HIV-contaminated blood scandal" and cited the case of HIV infection via unheated blood products in which the government was faulted. It was still fresh in people's minds.

By contrast, in the United States there were hardly any arguments that the American government should be held liable for health hazards caused by asbestos.[14] In Japan, at least in the eyes of the people, the government is always implicated in large-scale injuries caused by toxic substances or medicines. I argue that behind these attributions of responsibility to the government lies the characteristic view of Japanese political structure as dividing the people from the government, with the former oppressed by the latter. It is a resentment of the people vis-à-vis the power of government, and to the extent that this view reflects political reality, it functions to equalize the power imbalance. State indemnification suits serve as a mechanism for democracy in Japan.

Ironically, this invocation of the administration as a culpable party in mass tort cases also enables the government to play a decisive role in shaping global settlements. In the SMON case, the government was held liable for the payment of damages, which in the advisory opinion of the Tokyo District Court were set at 30 percent of the total award. Beyond this judgment, however, the government and the pharmaceutical company together agreed to pay the same amount to other victims who were not plaintiffs. This decision concerning the scope of the global settlement reflects an underlying assumption that the government is expected to treat the people equally, and if it pays damages to some it must offer the same to others who are equally qualified. This norm of equal treatment, coupled with the efficiency requirement in administration, led ultimately to the standardization of payments. The courts in the SMON cases observed these norms and practices scrupulously, and thus there was a smooth transition from the litigation phase of the SMON cases to the administrative phase.

Culture of Compensation

By considering the three types of actors involved, we now understand better how a scheme of compensation for mass torts in Japan is made possible by only a few lawsuits. Even though the major asbestos lawsuits are still underway, and we do not yet know the results, we can be sure that the litigation will not open the floodgates for a torrent of similar lawsuits, as occurred in the United States. Instead, they will probably close the gates either to renew the compensation scheme or simply to maintain the status quo of existing compensation for asbestos-related injuries.

Why is such a distinctive form of closure possible in Japan and not in the United States? The history of late modernization in Japanese society is certainly part of the reason, as analyzed in the previous section. But European countries that achieved modernization much earlier than Japan nevertheless show a similar inclination to devise compensation schemes for mass injuries. Ignoring for a moment the concrete differences and making only a rough approximation, we can identify a divide between Europe and Japan on the one hand and the United States on the other in terms of the prominence of a strong bureaucracy in state management. The career path of social elites is particularly revealing in this regard. In Europe and Japan, but not in the United States, the public bureaucracy recruits the brightest university graduates and then places them later in their careers as top executives and statesmen.

The mechanism to achieve the scarcity of litigation operates with this bureaucratic state as a background. Courts and lawyers are also organized so that they have secure places in it. Political scientists describe the policy-making processes in this bureaucracy-centered political structure as "corporatism." The defining characteristic of corporatism is that policy is made through negotiations at the top between the national bureaucracy and the national organizations of interest groups. This set of arrangements fits perfectly with the way in which compensation is negotiated in mass-injury cases. Courts are horizontally coordinated so that one capital letter "Judgment" is produced. Lawyers, often numbering hundreds or more, come together to form a national organization, or a loosely coordinated network. Plaintiffs, too, form a social movement-like organization at the national level. In the SMON cases, only one corporation was involved, but in other cases more than a few corporations are named as defendants. Yet even in these instances, the companies are somehow coordinated among themselves, and they negotiate informally with the Ministry of Health and Welfare to present a uniform position on settlements. Out of these organizations and national-level movements, and through negotiations, a global settlement is created after the court decisions. This process could be termed *legal corporatism*.

The search for an explanation may lead observers to dig further. History and political structure truly are determinants of how mass-injury cases are handled in the judicial system. I have suggested that particular historical events, such as the late modernization in Japan or the existence of absolutist monarchs, had lasting effects on subsequent events via the makeup of political structure in the modern Japanese state. Yet, those historical incidents themselves had antecedent events; and, looking in the other direction, the resulting political structure may be constantly modified by subsequent events. There is no end in the causal chains and in the workings of destabilizing forces. Especially in this age of globalism, novel and important destabilizing forces might be found at work in the Japanese system.

Then, there must be a theme to work through the fortuity in history or the contingency in destabilizing forces and to make out a unique identity of the society. Historical events or particular circumstances facing the system do not directly affect the way the system works. They are always mediated by local interpretation and by the conscription of institutional imagination. It is therefore worthwhile to probe this underlying layer of meanings, which is a culture in the broad sense.

To understand how culture can enable a particular approach to tort compensation, imagine how Americans would react to the proposal to introduce legal corporatism in their society. The majority would certainly worry about the concentration of power in the state. They would probably concur, moreover, that the courts should not be nationally coordinated to produce a consensual "Judgment." The plaintiffs' lawyers could properly coordinate their efforts, but it is unlikely they would unite to work for a single scheme of compensation. Most Americans would also be likely to see it as an abuse of power for the public administration to intervene in essentially private disputes between pharmaceutical companies and victims over the matter of compensation.

On the other hand, tort reforms are heatedly debated in the United States, and many Americans have no qualms about looking to the legislature to restrain or, on different occasions, to encourage private tort suits. For asbestos litigation, there were many attempts in the U.S. Congress to establish a national compensation scheme which would provide that, once compensation became available, tort suits would be prohibited. In such proposals, the government does indeed seem to intervene in private suits and to institute compensation with the force of the state. Yet these interventions are only regulations from the outside. The essential character of tort suits would remain intact whenever they could still be brought, and lawsuits would remain entirely distinct from global compensation schemes.

In Japan, however, there are no regulations on tort litigation from the outside. Parties choose freely between compensation schemes or tort suits. In the case of workers' compensation, claimants are able to sue on top of the compensation they receive from the system. But this does not lead to wholesale litigation on a scale matching the mass injuries. Since features amenable to compensation systems are embedded in tort litigation, compensation follows without restricting the bringing of lawsuits.

Conclusion

There are two competing schemes to address the problem of mass injuries: judiciary/tort-damages and administration/compensation. In the United States, the first of these two approaches—tort law litigated in courts—is at the core, and it is curtailed or replaced by the second—compensation by administration— only when litigation creates serious problems. In Japan, the second approach is the archetype, and what begins as tort litigation becomes subtly transformed to articulate better with the goals of a general system of compensation. This point is well illustrated in a remark made by an organizer for the Tokyo-based state indemnification suit: "Litigation is necessary to make compensation available without litigation."[15]

At bottom, then, what different underlying existential worlds can be found in societies electing one of these two divergent schemes? Although torts have changed significantly from the old days, with the advent of insurance, enterprise liability, and "total justice," I submit that tort law still retains at its core the notion of individual liability. The culpable person should pay damages, and, as a matter of right, the injured person should get restitution. No further state intervention is needed other than the provisions of the law and the guarantee that the injured shall have a day in court. Empowerment of plaintiffs by contingent fees, punitive damages, and the sympathetic jury are all contemporary ingredients of this scheme. Even scary stories of a flood of asbestos lawsuits which have "run amok"[16] do not destroy the belief in its fundamental legitimacy.

What, then, is the situation in Japan? Even though the same notion of individual justice is sometimes extolled, especially in the formal discourse of lawyers, in the daily lives of the Japanese people the notion of interdependence holds sway. It comes from the view that we, as vulnerable persons, are dependent on one another. A general reliance upon others is the constitutive principle of Japanese society, ideally allowing the individual to rely on others' respect for one's right without actually claiming a right. Once this tacit expectation of "they wouldn't make us troubled" is betrayed, however, as in mass injuries caused by not properly caring for ordinary people, major lawsuits are commenced, and the media start to carry the news of plaintiffs' sufferings. People watch these lawsuits unfold like a drama. They share the anger of those who have been betrayed. In the end, the courts authoritatively declare the wrongs of the government and the corporations, and formal apologies are made so that all can return to their normal social lives. In Japan, the system for paying compensation to all victims—an ideal of equal and collective justice—is an important ingredient of the normal. We see in mass torts the reenactment of this same ritual to confirm what we are as Japanese.

PART V

Causation, Duty, and Obligation

Discourses of Causation in Injury Cases

Exploring Thai and American Legal Cultures

DAVID M. ENGEL

An old friend who lived in Thailand for a number of years told me a true story he heard on a recent visit there.[1] The story concerned a traditional healer in Northern Thailand who was known to have the ability to see far into the past and future. A woman with cancer went to him to learn the cause of her affliction. The healer meditated and saw into the woman's previous life when she had been a food vendor. In her former existence, the woman had severely beaten three other food sellers, creating a burden of bad karma that was being discharged in her current life and had caused her illness. What could she do? The healer again used his vision to see that the food seller's former victims had also been reincarnated as women living nearby. Go to see them, urged the healer. Beg their forgiveness. And so the woman with cancer sought out each of these three total strangers, presented them with gifts, and apologized for wrongs she had committed in a former life. None of the women thought this was strange. All understood that the chain of cause and effect could stretch back across years and lifetimes. After she made amends, the woman's cancer went into remission.

This chapter explores discourses of causation in tort law and in everyday life.[2] Familiar, culturally based explanations of the causation of injuries and illness may differ significantly from formal legal concepts and usages. In this chapter, I suggest that an analysis of such differences can help us understand how ordinary people perceive tort law and how tort law functions in society. The discussion that follows is comparative, juxtaposing two very different societies—Thailand and the United States. In both settings, social and cultural changes have brought new understandings of causation with important implications for the invocation and administration of tort law. The chapter concludes with general observations about the relationship between popular belief systems, concepts of injury and responsibility, and the future of tort law.

The story with which this chapter begins, concerning the Thai woman with cancer, illustrates the salience of discourses about causation that are widely shared among ordinary people yet are not recognized by the law. The idea that this woman's illness was caused by her own misdeeds in a former life is immediately understandable to and widely shared by most Thais, and that is why the three "victims" she approached were not surprised by the apology proffered to them by a total stranger. Yet the same Thai lawyers and judges who might understand and retell such stories to their friends in private would nevertheless consider this kind of causal explanation completely inappropriate—perhaps even absurd—if it were raised within the framework of Thai tort law. Obviously, cancer may have many causes and does not necessarily arise from tortious behavior, but it is not unusual for American tort litigants to characterize cancer as an injury caused by the misconduct of pharmaceutical manufacturers or producers of toxic substances or dangerous consumer products. Such lawsuits are, however, extremely rare in Thailand. Although there are many reasons for this difference, the rarity of tort litigation in Thailand appears to be related at some level to the distinctive discourse of causation that predominates in Thai culture outside of the courtroom, linking illness or injury to the misdeeds of the victim. The connection between popular understandings of causation and the use—or nonuse—of tort law is a central concern in the discussion that follows.

Causation and the Intersection of Tort Law and "Community Norms"

As every first-year law student knows, causation is a key element in tort litigation, connecting the conduct of the defendant to the injury suffered by the plaintiff (see, e.g., Dobbs 2000, 405; Epstein 1999, 248; Keeton 1984, 263–265). Without proof of a causal connection, it is usually said, the plaintiff's claim must fail no matter how serious the harm or how egregious the defendant's misdeeds. American judges and legal commentators typically view the establishment of a causal link between conduct and injury as a matter of factual (as opposed to legal) inquiry: Did the defendant, in effect, push over the first domino and initiate a sequence of events that led to the plaintiff's misfortune? In the Anglo American system, such factual determinations are deemed particularly appropriate for the jury, since jurors are considered best able to apply commonsense, community-based concepts and thought processes in determining whether causation has been proved.

One of the most insightful essays about causation in American tort law was written fifty-three years ago by Wex Malone. In an article titled "Ruminations on Cause-In-Fact" (1956), Malone made two points that are especially relevant to this chapter. First, he criticized the assumption that causation is simply a factual determination free of the policy concerns that are so prominent in other aspects of tort law. Malone suggests that the issue of causation is actually a crucial site of tension between judge and jury. Judges, according to Malone, have plausible linguistic formulae that can justify either deference to the jury or its complete exclusion from the determination of causation. The judge's choice depends on considerations of policy, although such considerations may be hidden from view. Judges may block the jury's application of community norms and values when they conclude that legal or social policy should prevail over culturally based perspectives on causation.[3] For this reason, a thoughtful analysis of causation in tort law will allow us to perceive points of conflict between tort law and its broader cultural context.

Malone's second point is that people do not draw causal inferences in the way we usually assume. Humans—including judges and jurors as well as litigants and lawyers—do not reason from a finding of causation to a conclusion about responsibility but in reverse fashion from a general theory of responsibility to a finding of causation. In Malone's words, causation "is merely an acceptable deduction from evidential facts. All deductions are drawn purposively—that is to say, they are drawn for a reason" (1956, 62; see also Scales, this volume). Any injury can be explained in varying ways by applying radically different causal frameworks, and the selection of one framework over the other depends on one's purpose in asking the question of causation. Malone offers one example: "Where a doctor and a judge both seek to answer the same question of simple cause, the answers given may be different because their respective interpretations of cause are colored by the purpose to which each puts that word" (1956, 63).

Writing as he did more than a half century ago, Malone did not take this second insight as far as we might today. The reasoning process he described—from ideas of what we should do about injuries to ideas about what causes them—goes far beyond the different perspectives of a doctor and a judge in a trial. Such causal reasoning can be found in every social context and is not confined to the courtroom. When ordinary people experience injuries, their interpretive process may begin with ideas about risk and responsibility in society and move from there to a search for causal explanations that are consonant with those ideas. If they believe, for example, that individuals should assume responsibility for most injuries they suffer, then they may conclude that the harm was caused by the injury victim herself, by fate, or by God. If they believe that large corporations should assume greater responsibility for the social ills associated with their activities, they may conclude that injuries or illnesses were caused by consumer products or toxic substances in the environment. This construction of causal explanations is quite different from what is usually assumed: that an injured person will analyze causation in a purely inductive fashion and will conclude that law is relevant only when a factual examination of the causal chain discloses that the injury at one end is connected to a prior tortious act at the other. If causal inferences arise in a quite different way, if the starting point is actually a set of widely shared assumptions about responsibility for illness and injury in society, then a cultural analysis of causation may help us understand generally how injured people perceive the relevance and the irrelevance of tort law.

Causation in Thailand: Ghosts, Karma, and the Law

Both of Malone's points shed light on my friend's anecdote about the Thai woman with cancer. First, as I have suggested, the story points to a deep tension between legal concepts of causation used by lawyers and judges and those found in the broader culture. Causal accounts of this kind are very familiar in Thailand and are immediately understood and probably accepted by most listeners, yet they have no place within the formal Thai legal system. The traditional healer's explanation is completely inconsistent with the pleadings and oral arguments of any Thai tort case I encountered in my fieldwork.[4] Second, the story illustrates the process of reasoning backward from a theory about the nature of risk and responsibility in human society to the identification of a specific cause. In this story, Buddhist beliefs about karma provide the starting point. Karma is a religious-based theory of causation that associates events in one's life with the meritorious and nonmeritorious acts one has performed in the past. An individual's store of merit—or lack thereof—can produce either fortune or misfortune. Sometimes karma operates in very specific ways to produce injuries or illness. Harming the leg of an animal, for example, can cause one's own leg to be broken (Engel 2005, 485). Similarly, in my friend's story, the woman suffered from brain cancer, and the traditional healer told her that in her former life she had injured the heads of her fellow food sellers. Even when karma operates in more general ways, it represents an inescapable law of cause and effect that sooner or later dispenses justice. The root cause of illness and injury is the prior action of the person who suffers them.

The karmic theory of causation has several distinctive features, especially when considered in relation to tort law. First, it expands the temporal span between cause and injury. Rather than viewing injuries in terms of events immediately leading to an accident, as tort law tends to do, karmic explanations identify causes that may have occurred years before or even in a previous lifetime. Second, as we have seen, karmic explanations tend to locate the root cause of injuries in the conduct of the injured person, and they interpret behavior by another party, even negligent, reckless, or intentional behavior, as secondary to the past misdeeds of the victim herself. Indeed, the other party's negligence may be viewed as a product of the injured person's own karma and therefore part of the causal dynamic the victim herself set in motion. Finally, causal explanations based on karma are, in Malone's terms, *purposive* in that they carry with them a set of assumptions about the proper way to respond to injuries. From a Buddhist perspective, the *purpose* that should guide an injury victim is not necessarily to obtain a damage award from the other party but to add to one's store of merit through forgiveness and compassion in order to correct the karmic imbalance that led to misfortune in the first place.

The Thai injury victims whom I interviewed[5] tended to offer multiple causal explanations when asked why they had been harmed. Karma was always among the most important and led them to conclude that their suffering was caused by something they had done wrong, either to another human or animal or to the defendant herself in her current incarnation or in a previous lifetime. In addition to karma, injury victims usually mentioned several other causal factors. Some interviewees referred to negligence—their own and that of another person. Many pointed to the intervention of malevolent ghosts, who come into existence after an abnormal or violent death. These ghosts are the spirits of deceased persons that linger at the spot of an "abnormal death" (*taai hoong*). Because of the circumstances of their death, the spirits cannot continue on their cycle of death and rebirth without first taking the life of a passer-by who can replace them. If these ghosts do not actually kill people who come near, they may succeed in inflicting serious injuries. Some interviewees stressed one or another of these causal factors, but most mentioned combinations of them as contributing to their injury. In their discussion, they would shift easily from one causal framework to another without any apparent sense of inconsistency. Nevertheless, self-blame was a predominant theme and the workings of karma were all-pervasive.

Consider, for example, the case of Thiphaa, a thirty-eight year-old rice and vegetable farmer who was injured when she and her husband were struck by a drunk driver while riding their motorcycle loaded with goods to sell at the market. Among the multiple causes of her mishap, Thiphaa first mentions that she failed to heed warning signs that often presage an accident: her husband had a bad headache, he spoke with uncharacteristic rudeness to a stranger, and their daughter made unusual requests for food just before they left. Second, although the other driver admitted that he had driven recklessly while drunk, Thiphaa believed that her husband had also caused the accident by speeding. A third cause was a ghost associated with the slaughterhouse near the road where the accident occurred. Because Buddhism teaches that it is sinful to kill even an animal, malevolent ghosts are likely to be found in the vicinity of slaughterhouses. When the other driver told Thiphaa and her husband that he turned in front of them because he did not see them coming, the people at the scene of the accident said, "Oh, it's happened again. The ghosts blocked the view." Thiphaa acknowledges the existence of the ghosts, and she believes their role was confirmed when her grandmother consulted a spirit medium after the accident, but she thinks that the causal contribution of the ghosts was limited because they did not impair her husband's vision, only that of the oncoming driver.

Although contributory negligence and ghosts were important causal explanations, Thiphaa thought the most important cause of her accident was karma. She and her husband were injured because of their own past actions. They could not be sure what those actions were, but she knew that as farmers they must have inadvertently taken the lives of other living creatures. In Thiphaa's words:

> What we did follows us into the present . . . We worked in the vegetable fields. We tilled the soil and uprooted the plants, and we may have harmed insects or other creatures. It seems that our fate[6] attached itself to us without our knowing it . . . Those insects didn't die, but we didn't see them. We caused them some injury . . . Those creatures, whatever they were, we injured them without killing them. Then we left them alone. That bad karma attached itself to us.

If their own karma caused the injury, then it would have been inappropriate to respond with an aggressive insistence upon compensation from the other driver. The ideal response was to behave virtuously and magnanimously when reaping what were, after all, the consequences of their own misdeeds. Indeed, an overly assertive demand for compensation might only make matters worse. Several interviewees told me that the injurer may have harmed them in this life, but in a previous life they must have harmed the injurer. If they failed to respond with mercy and forgiveness this time around, then in future lives the two of them would continue to take turns injuring one another into eternity. One young father was even afraid that, if he pursued injury compensation from a negligent teenage girl, his bad karma could return to harm his own young daughter when she became a teenager.

Since karma ultimately fixed responsibility on Thiphaa and her husband, it was not surprising that they readily agreed to accept no more than a token payment from the other driver and never considered invoking the law. Although they lost nearly 30,000 baht in medical and travel costs and income, the other driver was poor and they felt sorry for him. He offered to pay 4,800 baht but in the end was able to scrape up only 3,000 baht (about US$75), which they accepted out of a feeling of compassion. Because of their belief in the karmic origins of misfortune, generosity and compassion seemed to them the preferable response.

Although many of the interviewees listed negligence among the causes of their injury, both their own negligence and that of the other party, most of them believed that the causal contributions of ghosts and karma were more important. Karmic causal analysis did not in itself lead injured persons to the conclusion that the injurer must be compelled to pay compensation. Nevertheless, the interviewees maintained that within traditional Thai society it was always expected that injurers would compensate their victims because of village-level beliefs that the injurer's conduct had offended the community of humans and guardian spirits (see Engel 2005). In the past, therefore, injurers were required to pay for the victim's expenses and, just as importantly, the cost of ceremonies to restore equilibrium and harmony to the village. Failure to do so would put the entire community at risk, and thus everyone had a stake in compelling the injurer to pay. Interviewees suggested, however, that with the breakdown of village society and with the enormous increase in highway accidents involving individuals from different villages, community pressure on injurers has diminished. Furthermore, new kinds of injuries have become more common as the result of an exponential increase in the number of motorcycles and cars as well as the establishment of new industrial plants, and such injuries are not readily perceived as affronts to a particular community.

In the past, the failure to pay traditional forms of compensation could occasionally lead to legal action. The injured person sometimes brought a tort action or a private criminal suit,[7] which would be withdrawn as soon as an amount of compensation pegged to traditional remedies was offered. Tort litigation was infrequent, but when it did occur it could be seen as legitimate because of its close association with traditional remedies. The court of first instance in the official Thai legal system was a court of last resort for Thai customary law. Nowadays, however, the traditional remedial systems rarely function effectively, or at least that is the view offered by my interviewees. Courts do not serve as the ultimate sanction for refusing to accede to the wishes of the community, since the community and its remediation practices are now less important than in the past. The causal explanations that place ultimate blame on the victims themselves now acquire even greater significance than before, and those who suffer injuries usually do no more than consult the spirit medium, present offerings to ghosts, and perform various ceremonies to make merit and to strengthen their karma and good fortune.

Injury narratives in contemporary Thailand suggest that causal explanations nowadays tend to reinforce the assumption that injured persons should take responsibility for themselves. Records of tort litigation are consistent with this emergent view of causation in Thai culture. My investigation of tort cases filed in the Chiangmai Provincial Court suggests that litigation is even more disfavored today than it was in the past. The number of tort cases per thousand population in the 1990s was about the same as the number filed in the 1960s and 1970s, although the number of potentially tortious injuries per capita had almost certainly increased by a very substantial amount.[8] Nowadays it is likely that far more people suffer injuries from highway or industrial accidents than they did twenty or thirty years ago, yet the quantity of tort litigation has not increased. In effect, therefore, the steady rate of tort litigation per capita suggests that it is much less likely that injury victims in Thailand today will turn to tort law.

A closer look at one of the relatively rare injury cases that was actually litigated in Chiangmai reveals a causal narrative that is dramatically different from the narratives I obtained from my interviewees. This case illustrates the gaping disconnect between concepts of causation found in the Thai courts and in society as a whole. In an unremarkable personal injury case brought in 1993 by a woman named Rampha Sekajan against a man named Sakda Inthakaew, we find only the briefest mention of causation and no reference at all to ghosts or karma. According to the pleadings, the defendant drove a large ten-wheel truck full of rocks for road construction work. The plaintiff was a passenger in a pickup truck driven by her husband. Her vehicle came to a stop at an intersection and then proceeded to cross the highway. Other oncoming traffic slowed to let them across, but, according to the pleadings, the defendant drove carelessly without taking the precautions that a reasonable person in his situation would observe. He drove at a high speed, passing other vehicles on the highway that had slowed down. When the defendant got to the intersection, the plaintiff's truck was half-way across the road, but the defendant was unable to stop his large vehicle in time, "which was the *cause* of the death of Mr. Warakan Sekajan and the bodily injuries received by the plaintiff."

That is the extent of the causal explanation offered in the formal complaint. The plaintiff's own courtroom testimony was equally laconic in its treatment of causation: "As our car began to turn right onto the [highway], the ten wheel truck driven by the defendant came from the direction of the airport, passing other vehicles that had slowed to make way for us. He struck the truck driven by my husband near the driver's side door. I was knocked unconscious. The defendant's ten wheel truck was speeding and the driver was not being careful." In her testimony, however, the plaintiff goes on to mention a detail omitted by her lawyer in the formal complaint. She states that she later returned to the scene of the accident and saw that the defendant's truck had dragged her vehicle off the road about 30 meters and had collided with two motorcycles, a telephone relay box, the bathroom of a nearby house, and a tamarind tree.

This last detail is revealing. Many interviewees explained the cause of their injuries in terms of ghosts near the highway, and ghosts typically dwell in trees. The plaintiff's mention of a tamarind tree in the path of the defendant's truck raises the possibility that she believes the tree to be inhabited by ghosts who obscured the defendant's vision or caused him to lose control of his truck. No mention of ghosts appears in the plaintiff's courtroom testimony, however, nor are they mentioned anywhere in the court documents. Equally conspicuous by its absence is the discourse of karma.

It is not surprising that the causal narratives offered by injured persons in everyday life differ so strikingly from the causal narratives presented in court. As Wex Malone (1956, 62) observed, causation "is merely an acceptable deduction from evidential facts. All deductions are drawn purposively—that is to say, they are drawn for a reason." There is no reason—no valid *purpose*—in the context of formal Thai tort litigation to draw causal deductions that involve ghosts or karma, even though they may be among the most significant causal explanations that the plaintiff might offer in other social contexts. In a court of law, the only "purpose" of proving causation is to establish the responsibility of a negligent defendant to compensate an injured plaintiff. Discussion of causes that may be more important to the parties outside of court would not be productive in the courtroom. Everyone involved in the litigation is therefore careful to exclude from the legal process any mention of the causal explanations that may be most important in Thai culture.

What are the implications for a system of tort law in which legal concepts of causation diverge dramatically from concepts that are found in the broader culture? I have suggested that there appears to be a general decline in the use and even the awareness of Thai tort law. In Thailand, legal and community-based ideas about causation seem to be traveling down very different paths. Although tort litigation was never a popular option, it was available when negotiation of a traditional remedy at the village level proved impossible. Litigation was, to paraphrase Clausewitz on war, merely the continuation of negotiations by other means, and it usually concluded with a settlement calibrated to the remedies familiar in village society. Law was not seen to be at odds with community-based belief systems but was the ultimate sanction for failing to adhere to them.

Nowadays, however, village-level practices and remedies are becoming dim memories of a distant past. There are few viable customary mechanisms for compelling the payment of compensation to an injured person. In the absence of an effective customary system of remediation, injured persons understand themselves to be faced with a choice between legal action and adherence to Buddhist principles of forgiveness and compassion. Evidence from case files and hospital interviews suggests that these individuals generally choose religion over tort law. The growing belief that people should take responsibility for their own injury costs and that tort law is, even more than before, an irrelevancy, stems from familiar causal explanations that pervade contemporary Thai society and ultimately lead back to the injured person.

Discourses of Causation in America

The preceding discussion of causation in Thailand illustrates Wex Malone's insight that causation can become a site of tension between tort law and social or cultural norms and practices. The clash between legal and community-based concepts of causation in Thailand helps explain why tort law has become a more remote and unappealing option for injury victims. What might a similar study of causation in the United States reveal? I am not aware of research that asks injured Americans to reflect on what caused their misfortune and what responses seem most appropriate and efficacious in light of their understandings of causation. Nevertheless, research on American tort law frequently offers indirect evidence that causation is understood quite differently among legal professionals and among ordinary people in American society. One dramatic example is provided by the history of Bendectin cases litigated in the 1980s and 1990s.

As described by Sanders (1998), jurors in the Bendectin drug cases consistently expressed a more expansive view of causation and of legal responsibility than tort law allowed. The Bendectin cases involved children with so-called "limb reduction" birth defects whose mothers had taken the drug during pregnancy to combat morning sickness. As Sanders (1998, 2) points out, "the precise cause of most [birth] defects is unknown" and only 3 to 5 percent can be causally connected to the mother's exposure to toxic substances such as prescription drugs. Nevertheless, the plaintiffs in the Bendectin cases believed that their children had been harmed by the negligence of Bendectin's manufacturer, Merrell Dow Pharmaceuticals, Inc., and half of the juries that were permitted to deliberate in these cases agreed with the plaintiffs' theory of causation. Yet, as Sanders describes in his book, only a single appellate court sustained a jury finding that Bendectin caused birth defects.[9] As these tort cases worked their way through the American legal system, the appellate courts reached a consensus on tort law causation as it was to be applied in the Bendectin cases and issued a series of rulings that denied the jury the opportunity to apply its own potentially more expansive views. Apparently judges, plaintiffs, and jurors were thinking about causation in very different ways.

The theory of causation applied by appellate court judges in the Bendectin cases is clear enough. Their opinions display an increasingly enthusiastic endorsement of scientific analyses of causation in cases involving exposure to potentially dangerous drugs. Following the standard articulated by the United States Supreme Court in *Daubert v. Merrell Dow Pharmaceuticals, Inc.* (1993, 590; quoted in Sanders 1998, 153) the courts in the later Bendectin cases required that expert testimony on causation must be based on evidence acquired through the "methods and procedures of science." They concluded that the plaintiffs' theories of causation were scientifically unsound—because of failure to address properly the concept of "relative risk" and because of what the courts viewed as the inherent weaknesses of epidemiological studies to establish causation (Sanders 1998, 179–180). Absent evidence of causation that satisfied these criteria, the appellate courts concluded that the Bendectin claims should simply be dismissed.

Yet half the juries that were allowed to consider the Bendectin cases apparently viewed causation quite differently, and their views did not change over time. In Sanders' words: "There is but one place where the Bendectin controversy continues unabated: in the jury room. The four Bendectin trials that have taken place since 1990 have resulted in one defense verdict, one hung jury, and two plaintiff verdicts. The juries who returned plaintiff verdicts awarded damages of $33.75 million and $19.2 million in compensatory and punitive damages" (1998, 185).

The appellate courts that "choked off this litigation" (Sanders 1998, 185) were clearly concerned that the jurors might apply some alternative, unscientific views about causation if they were given the chance. What might these views be? If jurors who found for the plaintiffs did not base their causal analyses on the "methods and procedures of science," what did they base them on? Were they merely ignorant? Were they bamboozled by unsound expert testimony? Or were they reflecting a different set of understandings about causation that were culturally familiar to them yet excluded from the legal system—much like the discourse of karma that was banished from Thai courtrooms?

As Wex Malone (1956) observed, causation is not an objectively observable fact of nature but is the product of reasoning backwards from a general theory of injury and responsibility, a "purposive" deduction about the source of harm the plaintiff has suffered. What theories of risk and responsibility are most familiar to ordinary Americans? Might these theories help explain why jurors, who are drawn from the community, may view causation differently from judges? Might they explain why injured persons sometimes hold views about their entitlement to compensation that are significantly broader or narrower than the rules of tort law?

In my own study of a rural American community in the 1980s (Engel 1984; Greenhouse et al. 1994), I found that theories about responsibility for injuries varied significantly from one social group to another yet rarely resembled the black-letter rules of tort law. In "Sander County," a rapidly changing midwestern community, newcomers—most of whom were industrial workers and ethnic minorities—often assumed that their injuries should be compensated by the business enterprise that launched the injurious activity, regardless of the fault of either party. But old-timers in this town, who were mostly farmers or small-business owners, had very different views. They expressed a strong ethic of self-sufficiency and a dislike for those who sought to convert their injuries into dollars. Not only did the old-timers consider a stoic response more honorable, but they also assumed that injured people could frequently be blamed for their own mishaps—a "purposive" deduction about causation that flowed from a broader theory of what should be done about injuries in society. The view of risk and responsibility shared among longtime residents led them to the conclusion that the primary and most important *cause* of injuries was usually a lack of care by the injured person. Such views of causation correspond loosely to the Thai assumption that injury victims cause their own misfortune by past misdeeds that create bad karma.

Three features of these discourses of causation in Sander County stand out. First, the discourses were variable and contested, even in this relatively small and self-contained social setting. Second, the views of newcomers and of long-time residents seldom corresponded to the concepts of causation found in the American legal system. Newcomers held quite broad views about responsibility to pay compensation, even when it was unclear that any negligent act by another party had led to the injury. Old-timers tended to view all injuries in terms of the carelessness of the injured person without close attention to the possible misconduct of anyone else. Neither perspective resembled the analysis of causation and responsibility that American tort law requires. Third, the discourses of causation in the American setting were not only pluralistic but ostensibly secular. Although many of the interviewees were religiously observant, they differed from their Thai counterparts in that they seldom framed their causal explanations in explicitly religious terms drawn from sacred texts or teachings.

The absence of an explicitly religious discourse of causation in Sander County should not, however, obscure a possible connection between the American and Thai settings. Even an overtly secular framing of causation and responsibility for injury may suggest a form of popular religion or moral philosophy that corresponds to the Thai belief in karma and spirits. Consider, for example, Bergstrom's (1992) study of accident litigation in New York City from 1870 to 1910. Bergstrom argues that a sharp increase in tort litigation at the turn of the twentieth century occurred in part because of a popular reconceptualization of causation. Previously, Bergstrom contends, New Yorkers had viewed accidents as inevitable and their own suffering as fate—a view not too different from that of Thai Buddhists. According to Bergstrom, however, by 1910 New Yorkers tended to adopt a broader concept of causation and searched for more remote causes originating in human misdeeds. Bergstrom associates this shift with a "great surge in society's sense of duty to others . . . a moral regeneration" (1992, 182). Injured people increasingly eschewed a stoic self-help philosophy and viewed their suffering in terms of the obligations citizens owed one another in an "interdependent" society: "In so doing, they defined anew the 'inevitable' event as a compensable injury, conceiving it as the cause and responsibility of someone else" (1992, 175).

In Bergstrom's account, changing cultural concepts of causation came into conflict with the more rigid legal definitions. Although these popular concepts were expressed in secular terms, they resonated with moralistic concerns about human relationships and interpersonal obligations. The law, however, tended to deny the causal connection that New Yorkers increasingly perceived and rejected the growing societal belief that injurers should assume responsibility for a broader range of accidental injuries. Judges and lawyers imagined themselves to be insulated from the moral imperatives that Bergstrom characterizes as increasingly important to New Yorkers at the turn of the twentieth century.

Other researchers have perceived a similar moralistic framing of the causation issue among ordinary Americans who are involved in injury cases. Feigenson (2000), for example, argues that juries in injury cases reduce complex, systemic causal situations to simplified, individualized morality plays with good guys and bad guys. He calls these morality plays "melodramas" and contends that such belief-based framing of injury cases becomes more common as society becomes more technologically advanced: "(T)hrough popular melodramas people seek to reaffirm moral order in a confusing world . . . (A)t least some aspects of common-sense thinking about accidents also display a reassuring fantasy of justice that denies some of the causally messy realities of life" (2000, 225–226).

Feigenson (2000, 190) notes specifically that the Bendectin cases probably pitted a moralistic view of causation against the scientific version that the appellate courts eventually endorsed. More broadly, his analysis suggests that a religious-like sensibility accounts for the framing of causation questions by laypersons, including those who serve on juries, although the discourse of causation they employ is, unlike the popular Thai discourse described above, desacralized. Sunstein et al. (2002) suggest that this tendency may be widespread: "The substitution of *everyday morality* for legal standards, documented here, might well be a pervasive phenomenon in the legal system" (75).

Few scholars have examined how ordinary people in American society think about the causation of injuries. In the absence of more extensive research, we can only speculate that secularized but moralistic discourses of causation have indeed become widespread in American society and that they may manifest themselves in distinctive forms—such as the opposing discourses of individual responsibility and of interdependence—which significantly affect injured persons' decisions to bring tort actions and jurors' evaluation of such cases when they are litigated.

Haltom and McCann (2004 and in this volume), convincingly demonstrate how the mass media, through selective and distorted depictions of injury cases, reinforce an "individualist ethic" that makes tort claimants appear greedy, irrational, and antisocial (see also Greenhouse et al. 1994). Jain (2006) suggests that American legal culture narrows popular understanding of injuries and their causation, leading to the common perception that each injury is an isolated event with its own causal history, a view that obscures broader patterns of personal injury that might lead to quite different conclusions about who should take responsibility for the victims of predictable "accidents" (see also Scales, this volume). Sterling and Reichman (this volume) show how changing standards of tort liability reflect transformations in societal concepts of responsibility for accidental injuries. Yet these studies of societal views about risk and responsibility also acknowledge that no single discourse of causation prevails in our society. Even in the mass media, theories of individual responsibility often clash with theories of interdependence or enterprise responsibility similar to those described by Bergstrom in turn-of-the-century New York.

Although these popular discourses of causation are typically presented as secular in character, a few commentators have addressed the explicitly religious framing of causation issues in American tort cases. Their observations are suggestive for our comparisons of the United States and Thailand, but unfortunately they presume a radically simplified view of what counts for religion in American society and of who is "devout." Cook (2004), for example, assumes that devout Christians uniformly endorse the ethic of individual responsibility and therefore adopt a *narrower* view of causation than that of American tort law. He argues that a "faith-based view" of causation in tort cases would attribute injuries to God's plan rather than human action, except in situations where the defendant clearly sinned by choosing to disobey God. Cook's view is shared by Beisner (1991), who writes:

> one can see a clear correlation between the growth of government as provider and the deterioration of belief in the providence of God. That trend makes citizens imagine that the state can make everything right, can salve their wounds, can restore all their losses. So long as that view prevails, people will seek relief from all their troubles at the bar of justice, not at the fountain of God's grace. But to the extent that people regain faith in God's providential care over them, they will be less likely to seek relief through litigation.

The views expressed by Cook and Beisner find their counterparts in the publication *ATLA's Litigating Tort Cases.* David Wenner's (2003) chapter on "Juror Bias" in that publication advises that so-called "personal responsibility" jurors tend to be biased in favor of defendants. Such jurors tend to have "strong religious beliefs" that lead them to conclude that most injuries are not caused, fundamentally, by defendants: "(T)hese jurors believe that what happened to plaintiff is God's will or part of some divine plan, and the whole matter is preordained. The jurors often believe the rewards come in the next life or heaven. A belief like this renders moot and makes it unnecessary to file a lawsuit" (§35:19, 33). Wenner advises plaintiffs' attorneys to attempt to identify these pro-defendant jurors at voir dire by asking about their religious beliefs in relation to tort actions (§35:23, 45). Not surprisingly, the Republican Study Committee (December 2003) jumped on Wenner's recommendation with a press release claiming, "Trial Lawyers Don't Want Religious Jurors," and asking, "Is ATLA saying that one way to 'strengthen America's civil justice system' is to keep religious people who believe in traditional values and personal responsibility off of juries?"

Cook, Beisner, and the Republican Study Committee share the assumption that religiosity in American society (by which they appear to mean primarily born-again Christianity) leads inevitably to a view of causation based on the ethic of individual responsibility, and to some extent Wenner concurs. Accordingly, they all contend that religiosity (as they conceive it) is opposed to the use of tort law to obtain compensation for injuries that are, in the most basic sense, the fault of the injured person. Although we may question their analysis, these studies do make it apparent that explicitly religious discourses of injury causation in the United States can bear a surprisingly close resemblance to the desacralized morality of individual responsibility described in my study of Sander County and by Haltom and McCann and Scales in this volume. All of these studies strongly suggest that discourses of causation in the United States tend to be mor-ally charged and highly concerned with issues of individual responsibility versus interdependence and enterprise obligations toward those who suffer illness or injury. Discourses of causation, whatever their valence, provide a vantage point outside the tort law system from which ordinary people may view injuries, risk, and responsibility, and may deploy concepts that are quite different from those that are used by lawyers and judges. In this sense, the multifarious, contentious, and mostly secular discourses of causation in American legal culture may turn out to be surprisingly similar to the relatively homogeneous and more explicitly religious discourses of ghosts and karma in contemporary Thailand.

Conclusion

This exploration of Thai and American legal cultures demonstrates, as Wex Malone suggested more than fifty years ago, that a close consideration of the issue of causation can enhance understanding of the interaction between legal doctrine and popular beliefs and practices. In Thailand, rapid social change has contributed to a distinctive discourse of causation that draws on concepts of karma as well as the ubiquitous interventions of ghosts and spirits into human affairs. Although spirit belief systems formerly provided a mechanism for com-pensating injury victims, the weakening of village-level customary law has led many injury victims to abandon any thought of pursuing a remedy and to justify their decision in terms of their own karma. They view this explicitly religious discourse of causation as opposed to what they understand as legal discourse, which allows no space for karmic explanations of injury causation. Further, they believe that the filing of a tort claim will merely increase one's bad karma and will perpetuate suffering rather than address its root cause. Thus, an analysis of injury causation in Thai legal culture enriches understanding of why tort law has come to seem even more remote and alien to injury victims than it was in the past and why it appears to be used even less frequently than before. It helps us to see how tort law and popular beliefs and practices in Thailand have shaped one another over time and produced some of the most distinctive features of Thai legal culture.

Although ethnographic research on this topic is sparse in the American con-text, I have suggested that there may be some striking similarities to the situation in Thailand. In the United States, as in Thailand, there are indications (such as the Bendectin litigation) of a divergence between concepts of causation within the official tort law system and concepts that are familiar to laypersons. Evidence from several studies suggests the prevalence of morally charged discourses of causation in American culture, generally expressed in secular terms but occasionally explicitly religious. Such discourses appear to be varied and contested, sometimes supporting an expansive view of compensation for injured persons and sometimes supporting a restrictive view. In either case, it appears that these widespread discourses of causation differ substantially from tort law doctrine, explaining why Wex Malone could characterize the issue of causation as a site of tension between judge and juror.

If, as suggested in the Introduction to this volume, tort law infuses and is infused by cultural meaning, research on causation may help to reveal tort law more clearly as a phenomenon of legal culture. In both Thailand and the United States, prevalent discourses of causation affect the ways in which tort law is perceived and used—or avoided—by ordinary people. These patterns of perception, use, and nonuse of tort law affect the vitality and direction of the law itself; and the development of the law, in turn, continually shapes popular perceptions and practices. In the American context, the institution of the trial jury ensures that lay understandings of causation continually play a part in the legal evaluation of causal claims—up to the point where a judge declares the jury's findings impermissible. In the Thai context, the tort law system is more insulated from cultural discourses of causation, yet popular perceptions seem to have affected tort law in Thailand by diminishing its role in the handling of most injury cases. In both societies, and perhaps elsewhere in the world, the study of causation may prove to be a particularly rewarding means to understand tort law and cultural practice.

CHAPTER FIFTEEN

"Nobody Broke It, It Just Broke"

Causation as an Instrument of Obfuscation and Oppression

ANN SCALES

The title of this chapter refers to a Swahili language-teaching exercise that a friend experienced in Tanzania. It goes like this. One speaker asks a question, "who broke it?" Another speaker responds, "nobody broke it, it just broke." My friend, who grew up in England, was struck by the contrast between her own habits of assigning responsibility with the apparent comfort among Swahili speakers with things just breaking for no apparent reason. She went on to narrate how this linguistic insight conformed to her other experiences of living in Tanzania. She took some solace in being in a society where people did not always feel compelled, in her words, to impose linear explanations upon the world.

The Swahili-learning story is about variability in perceptions of causation. As David Engel's work much more fully illustrates (Engel 2005, and this volume), perceptions of causation are matters of cultural and theological habits. Every culture has varying stories of causation and responsibility. I think these are essentially human stories, the need for which emerges from the form of consciousness that humans, perhaps uniquely, exhibit. They are stories of origins, stories of beginnings, connections, and ends, stories of possibilities beyond present experience, the possibilities for wholeness within, or transcendence of, this mortal coil. They can also be stories of oppression and greed.

I want to tell a specific chapter in the story of causation, one having to do with gender oppression in the U.S. torts system. Of course, it is not only women who have lost out. Like every other legal institution, the torts system has disproportionately disadvantaged the groups who were already subject to a range of historical disadvantages. Jennifer Wriggins's work focuses directly, for example, on tort law's devaluation of injuries to African Americans (Wriggins 2005a, and this volume).

Disadvantage occurs differently for different groups. I investigate how the torts system functions as a means of social control of women qua women, and whether it might be an agent of gynocide. I conclude that in this society women are being asked to accept a corporate version of "nobody broke it, it just broke," without investigation of or participation in how causal notions have increasingly become uncertain, and without any meaningful contest as to who should bear the burden of that uncertainty.

We need to understand various aspects of cultural contingency in causal notions. In a recent article, David Engel (2005) recounted a story from a woman in Northern Thailand named Buajan who had been struck by a car while standing at a roadside food stand. She was comfortable in applying various metaphysics of causation to explain her experience. Familiar to a Western point of view, she included the driver's negligence in swerving toward her and her own (self-assessed) negligence in failing to watch for the oncoming car. But Buajan's understanding of her injury also included the influence of a ghost residing in a tree near which she was hit, and matters of karma. As Engel notes, Buajan "unself-consciously" shifted from one explanatory narrative to another (Engel 2005, 409), including invisible forces, mystical forces, and deterministic forces.

Buajan is more than a mouthpiece for her culture. Nonetheless, her narrative incorporates identifiably Buddhist notions: ideas of causal flexibility, an allowance and reverence for forces beyond human control, and a consequent nonlinearity in explanations of events. At the same time that she expresses a notion of the temporal contours of the immediate controversy, she conveys how her injury is connected to the eternal, and even how it illustrates the illusory nature of time.

That point of view on the causes of injuries diverges from the point of view we learn in the United States, in at least four interrelated ways. First, Western stories of origins, of beginnings and ends, are linear and "scientific," or more accurately, scientistic. Ontological fuzziness is reason to discredit any explanation. For a tort plaintiff to refer to the ghosts in the tree would essentially be to capitulate to the directed verdict.

Second, Americans have never really been comfortable with multiple causation. The relatively recent acceptance of comparative negligence does not contradict the historical habit. Consider that a majority of states have developed some version of "modified" comparative negligence, whereby a plaintiff recovers nothing at some probabilistic point. In Colorado, for example, a plaintiff can recover a proportionate share of her damages, but takes nothing if the trier of fact finds that her responsibility is as great as or greater than the defendant's. We're still stuck in an either/or ontological regime.

Third, that atomism of our causal habits tends to the presumption that events are disconnected. The 2006 pornographic murders of little girls in Colorado and Pennsylvania gave rise, for example, to condemnation of the availability of firearms (*New York Times* 2006), but almost no exploration of whether the murders were ordinary expressions of male dominance and/or militaristic violence. The preferred explanation is that these were "freakishly gratuitous acts of malice" (Shriver 2006), just inexplicable isolated incidents.

Fourth, and perhaps most important, tort narratives in this country are not "unself-conscious." Everyone in the discussions that gave rise to this volume emphasized that the "narrative of personal responsibility" in tort discourses has diminished other important considerations. Our culture fixates upon self-accountability, self-determination, and self-control. I'm shoulder to shoulder with the social critics who recognize the "fetish of subjectivity" as a trap (Jacoby 1975). Tort plaintiffs always have blame turned upon them. It is a central aspect of hegemonic power to get victims to blame themselves.

These four aspects of Western causal habits are a veritable menu for defense lawyers in tort cases. It can't be proved that our client caused it; too many forces contributed to the problem, so our client can't be held liable; what happened here is disconnected to other alleged incidents of our client's harm doing; and the plaintiff brought it upon herself, by being and acting like a woman.

Causation

Causation falls into the category that I call "intractable questions" (Scales 2006, 47–62). Western metaphysics has always been nervous about causation. Different philosophers tried different approaches, but it was the Scottish empiricist David Hume, who, in the mid-eighteenth century, provided the only explanation that no one can really get beyond: causation is just a matter of habitual inference. To associate a specific alleged cause with a specific alleged effect is crucial to human survival. It is a very useful habit that we rely upon thousands of times each day, but we cannot ever, not even in a single simple instance such as relying on gravity or hitting a billiard ball, absolutely logically prove that such a thing as causation even exists. Thus, *any* causal question depends upon an analysis of habits of inference.

For Westerners, those habits depend (at least in theory) upon empirical observations: how close do an alleged cause and an alleged effect have to be to each other in time for us to infer a causal relationship? How close do they need to be in space? How often must the alleged effect follow the alleged cause for us to say that what was a mere association, a mere correlation, should be promoted to the category of *causation*?

In U.S. legal culture, causation has been the justifying glue that sticks a defendant to a plaintiff. Causation particularizes the injury by singling out this plaintiff; wrongdoing particularizes this defendant against the background of the totality of the injury's causes (Weinreb 1983, 38). The requirement of factual causation is expressed as a matter of the ideal of "corrective justice," and anything beyond that—usually called "distributive justice"—is portrayed as irrefutably irrational. For example, in the first diethylstilbestrol (DES) case, shifting the burden of proof on causation and imposing "market share liability" on defendants, California Justice Richardson in dissent argued that the majority's decision defied the laws of geometry: "if you hit the square peg hard and often enough the round holes will really become square, although you may splinter the board in the process" (*Sindell v. Abbott Laboratories* 1980: 940). Dig his position: anyone who had a view of the situation different than his had to be both crazy and irresponsible.

Toxic Torts

Western causal rigidity is exemplified in toxic tort litigation. The DES cases are one kind of milestone for women in that field, but unusual in that the DES harms are always related to a "signature disease" firmly associated with DES exposure. That is not so for most toxic torts. In federal toxic tort litigation in recent years, consolidated after the U.S. Supreme Court's decision in *Daubert v. Merrill-Dow Pharmaceuticals* (1993), judges have systematically excluded plaintiffs' expert testimonies on causation, specifically on whether various sorts of products are capable of causing the sorts of injuries that the plaintiffs exhibit. The persistent bugaboo in all of this has been the *effective* requirement that plaintiffs produce epidemiological evidence on the causation element.

I underscore the word *effective* because judges like to pretend that they are not pretending to be scientists. It is commonplace for judges to say that epidemiological evidence is not *required* for the plaintiff to meet her preliminary burden, but then to hold that the plaintiff has not met her burden because she has not produced sufficient epidemiological evidence. For example, in one of the leading cases in the silicone breast implant litigation, the federal judge in Colorado saw no problem in uttering the following two statements within the same opinion: "This is not to say that epidemiological studies are required in this type of tort action . . . Therefore, epidemiological studies are necessary to determine the cause and effect between breast implants and allegedly associated diseases" (*In re Breast Implants Litigation* 1998: 1228, 1224). I've read the opinion a dozen times, and still don't find any reason for the contradiction, except for the judge's unexamined confidence in his own rationality.

Moreover, assuming there is epidemiological evidence available in these toxic tort cases, that evidence has to have certain features and minimum "scientific" results even for a jury to hear about it. That story has already been told many times (Berger 1997, 2128; Conway-Jones 2003; Eligman, Kim, and Biklen 2003; Finley 1999; Scales 2006; Wagner 1997, 778). Plaintiffs can't achieve epidemiological studies by themselves, epidemiology is not the be all and end all of causal inquiry, and the courts—by and large—have turned their "gatekeeping" function into more of a "search and destroy" mission. Most real epidemiologists think it is nonsense. Nonetheless, most juries will not get to make the determination of the weight of scientific evidence, so militaristic has the federal judiciary become in its gatekeeping post.

I won't rehearse the literature on corrective versus distributive justice in tort law, except to endorse the notion that both exist along an accepted continuum in decision making (Bronaugh, Barton, and Keren-Paz 2003). My point here is simply this: given the ontological status of causation—as the exercise of mere habit—*every* causal judgment is some version of redistributive justice. Everything depends on what a society's habits of inference are, how habits are learned, and whose habits are enforced as legal rules. In Catharine MacKinnon's classic observation, every rule is already an affirmative action program for somebody (MacKinnon 1989, 224).

Justice demands clarity about those habits. Clarity would also be the result of giving up on the graven worship of quasi-science, of embracing the coherence theory of [legal] truth, and asking, following the late Lon Fuller, "toward what end is this activity directed?" (Fuller and Perdue 1936–1937, 52). The very purposes of U.S. tort law are up for grabs.

The scientism, what we might call the quasi-empiricism of the toxic torts regime, is the worst kind of positivism. These judges think they are empiricists, relying on what defense lawyers tell them are the coolest and most rational methodological models. Indeed, it is the very complexity of the models that has exacerbated the danger of positivism in causation decisions. It does make one wonder about the head trip in deciding what "is" is. This is the power I have previously called "epistemological privilege." I've argued that measurement of it should be a regularized evidentiary principle in all kinds of cases (Scales 2006, 107–111).

Empiricism and Feminism

As this chapter is my first foray into the world of "Law and Society," this would be the place to pose a few questions about empiricism itself. I suppose that I am a Law and Society person, if the point of that identification is to endorse the generation of data and analyses to inform legal discussions and to suggest legal directions. That is essential to the realization of the promise of the Legal Realism of the 1930s. All of the competing jurisprudential schools—from Law and Economics on the right to radical feminist queer race theories on the left—claim to be inheritors of the Realist tradition. I am one of the claimants. With due respect to all concerned, however, I find discussions of methodologies pointless in themselves, and the perpetual demonstration of the "co-constitutive" nature of law and culture to be noncontroversial. Toward what end is this activity directed?

In my view, the greatest achievement of legal feminism worldwide has been to expose and explore the nature of harms to women that, for whatever sad reasons, hadn't been seen before. A big part of the feminist contribution has been empirical. Feminist social scientists, both male and female, have explicated cause and effect, or at least systematic effects of bad attitudes, for several decades and in many contexts. I am proud, for example, of my colleagues Nancy Reichman and Joyce Sterling (Reichman and Sterling 2004a, 2004b) who have done fabulous work regarding the lack of women in legal hierarchies. Such research explains, over and over again, the real benefits and burdens in social arrangements. That work *does* something.

Yet, empiricism for empiricism's sake is problematic for feminists, for at least three reasons. First, women are not believed. When a hegemonic structure is confronted with a story of injustice, the first response always is, "it didn't happen." Feminist activists and litigators are used to this. Shakespeare's Isabella in *Measure for Measure,* when asked to exchange sex for justice, intoned: "To whom shall I complain? Did I tell this, [w]ho would believe me? O perilous mouths!" (Shakespeare 1604(?): Act III, Scene IV). What happened to Isabella is no different from what happened to Anita Hill, or to countless unnamed sisters who do not report crimes or demand damages on the utterly justifiable ground that speaking out will make their lives worse. In Colorado, after the rape charges against basketball hero Kobe Bryant were dismissed, rape reports went down. Was that because potential perpetrators learned their lesson and desisted from their proclivities? Or was it because there *were* rapes, but the victims desisted from reporting them?

Second, when speaking truth to power, empirical evidence never seems to be good enough. Put another way, how often do points have to be proven? The University of Denver College of Law sponsored a conference on domestic violence, particularly on the question of accountability for domestic violence in light of the 2005 decision of the United States Supreme Court in *Town of Castle Rock v. Gonzales* (2005). That case held that a woman had "no protected interest," and therefore that there were no federal civil consequences for police failure—during a ten-hour window of opportunity—to enforce a restraining order. Never mind that the woman's ex-husband murdered their three daughters in front of the police station. The experts who gathered at the University of Denver College of Law in March 2006 didn't need more proof, didn't believe that the problem was the lack of methodologically significant studies. We can study our heads off. It makes no difference without serious commitment to eliminating physical abuse of women.

This notion was illuminated by two comments during the discussions leading to this volume. One participant asked how many times anyone had to prove that tort law disadvantages women and people of color. It has been done. Does doing it indefinitely make anything different? Another participant, clearly thinking out loud, suggested an incoherency in U.S. legal consciousness. In this era of victim impact statements in court, in this time of vehement public revenge, crime victims are put on a pedestal, yet tort victims are reviled. The women in the room reminded him that it depends on what sort of crime victim you are. If you are a victim of an alleged rape, for example, your special status could consist in having your perhaps-too-sexy panties passed up and down the lines of jurors (Heller 1991). If that's the pedestal, I'm certain that rape victims would prefer to step down.

Third, if we do prove the harms to women as women, we're marginalized as practitioners of "victimology" (Minow 1993; Volpp 1996). Victimology has become an unfortunate part of public discourse, and it requires deep interrogation. The oft-cited instance of tort plaintiffs out of control is the case of Stella Liebeck, who sued McDonalds because she was burned by their coffee. Though she won the case, McDonalds won the public relations war on behalf of all corporate defendants, because most accounts of that case left out the facts. Those facts included McDonalds' intentional overheating of coffee as a marketing strategy, McDonalds' knowledge of prior injuries to consumers, and McDonalds' lying about its expectations of consumer behavior (Gerlin 1994). The plaintiff in that case was a 78-year-old woman, and contrary to popular accounts, it was not her but her grandson who was driving the car. He had stopped to allow his grandmother to add sugar and cream to her coffee. While she attempted to pry the plastic lid off the cup, the coffee spilled, seriously burning her thighs and genitals. The New Mexico court reduced the punitive damages award (calculated as the profit on two days of McDonalds' coffee sales) by 75 percent.

Other contributors to this volume have fully demonstrated media distortions of basic facts in Ms. Liebeck's case (McCann, Haltom, and Bloom 2001; Haltom and McCann 2004, 183–206). That is one ball of string. But we should, in Mari Matsuda's words, ask the next question. Was the judge comfortable in reducing the punitive damages award because Ms. Liebeck's thighs and genitals were no longer sexually desirable or socially valuable?

I see the Liebeck case as a kind of rape narrative. The experts on the media coverage borrow directly from rape discourse in noting that Ms. Liebeck was "victimized twice" (McCann, Haltom, and Bloom 2001, 175). The defense lawyer objected to the admission of evidence of earlier burns from her client's coffee by stating, "[f]irst person accounts of sundry women whose nether regions have been scorched by McDonald's coffee might well be worthy of Oprah . . . But they have no place in a court of law" (McCann, Haltom, and Bloom 2001, 128). That depersonalization ("sundry women"), that reduction of women to bodily parts and derision of those parts ("nether regions"), and trivialization of injury (jurisdiction only in the court of Oprah) are ingredients in most rape stories. Two other rape-like aspects are present: she asked for it (everybody knows that coffee burns, just as everyone knows the deserved result of wearing a short skirt), and it is easy to cry "burn." Conversely, we can understand the vilification of male tort victims like the Fast Food man as the feminization, thus trivialization, of them (see Haltom and McCann this volume, surveying press characterizations of a fast-food plaintiff as "lazy, indulgent, greedy, undisciplined, exploitive, given to blaming others for own failures").

Tort Law and Women Loathing

From its inception, products liability law was about resisting the disempowerment of consumers. Recall that in the concurring opinion that started the products ball rolling, California Justice Roger Traynor stated (*Escola v. Coca-Cola Bottling Company* 1944: 467):

> As handicrafts have been replaced by mass production with its great markets and transportation facilities, the close relationship between the producer and consumer of a product has been altered. The consumer no longer has means or skill enough to investigate for himself the soundness of a product . . . and his erstwhile vigilance has been lulled by the steady efforts of manufacturers to build up confidence by advertising and marketing devices such as trade-marks . . . The manufacturer's obligation to the consumer must keep pace with the changing relationship between them.

In this, I regard Justice Traynor as the Martin Luther of jurists, the enemy of enforced distance between power and those dependent upon it. Justice Traynor would not be happy with recent retrenchments in products liability law, such as the demise of the "consumer expectation" test in favor of risk-utility analyses that tend to reinforce the paternalism of corporate power.

I am comfortable in comparing Justice Traynor to a theologian because of the theological underpinning to the specific tort injuries—pharmaceutical harms in the context of women's reproductive lives—on which I focus. That is, just as the theological background in David Engel's recounting of Buajan's story is the Buddhism practiced in northern Thailand, the theological background for women's experience in the U.S. tort system is the story of creation in the book of Genesis.

Eve was made from Adam's rib (Genesis 2:22), hence an afterthought, and only a partial man. In addition, Eve and her descendants have an unequal relationship to God. She deserves no better. There was only one command in Paradise: to refrain from eating of the fruit of the tree of knowledge of good and evil (Genesis 2:17). Eve blew it in a way understood as a sexual transgression. She can't be trusted not to disobey. It has henceforth been righteous for the law to act forcefully and comprehensively to control women, particularly in their sexual and reproductive lives. To be a woman is to occupy a continually enforced distance from authority and authoritative decision making, whether that authority is God, the state, or corporate pharmaceutical manufacturers. Finally, here is God's admonition to Eve about her reproductive status: "I will greatly multiply your pain in childbirth, in pain you shall bring forth children; yet your desire shall be for your husband, and he shall rule over you" (Genesis 3:16). It is almost impolite these days to mention this Biblical imperative, but one notices that the law has incorporated it—at least when convenient. The economy required women to be able to work throughout pregnancy and childbirth. A lactation-suppressant such as Parlodel, for example, might be heretical, but it kept many new mothers at work, harm to them and to God's wishes notwithstanding.

Various scholars, notably Martha Chamallas and Lucinda Finley, have proven again and again how tort law is complicit in the control of women, in part by trivialization of our injuries. Part of what they and others have shown is that health care in the United States discriminates against women in all manner of ways. This is painfully obvious in the area of pharmaceutical products. As a biological matter, women have different health needs than men, but that answers nothing. The biological differences only restate the questions of who is in charge and who will be put at what level of risk. As one trade association Web site puts it, "[w]omen's continuum of healthcare needs makes them a *more lucrative marketing target* than men" (Lead Discovery, Ltd. 2006) (emphasis added).

Women are a gold mine for drug companies. For example, all kinds of hugely profitable "mood-altering" drugs are disproportionately prescribed to women. Women are disproportionately represented among the elderly, who are more often in need of medications, particularly pain medications, and among nursing home and mental health facility residents, who are routinely drugged into stupors (Ilminen 2001). The late great Andrea Dworkin forcefully described the deployment of pharmaceutical might against females (Dworkin 1983, 158–159):

The solution to female emotional excess, whether expressed by the woman—appropriately by her lights—or hallucinated by the male doctor, is keeping women calm or numb or asleep with drugs. The dulling of the female mind is neither feared nor noticed; nor is the loss of vitality or independence. The female is valued for how she looks . . . and for domestic, sex, and reproductive work, none of which requires that she be alert . . . Thirty-six million women can be tranquilized in a year and the nation does not notice it, does not miss their energy, creativity, wit, intellect, passion, commitment—so much are these women worth.

In this chapter, I focus just on causation issues involving the "girl drugs," the drugs that derive from the imperative to govern women's unruly bodies, particularly their necessary but messy reproductive capabilities. Here are a few of the greatest hits:

Thalidomide (antimorning sickness)
DES (antimiscarriage)
Bendectin (antimorning sickness)
Dalkon Shield IUD
Copper-7 IUD
High-estrogen dosage oral contraceptives
High-dosage patch contraceptives (Ortho-Evra patch)
Super absorbent and scented tampons
Silicone breast implants
Parlodel (to suppress lactation)
Hormone replacement therapies

For all of these (with the exceptions of Thalidomide, which was never marketed in the United States, and tampons, which are not considered to be drugs), the manufacturers in question did not test their products adequately prior to Food and Drug Administration (FDA) approval, failed to impart information to regulators and doctors when potential problems emerged (both pre- and post-marketing), and did not undertake further research in response to adverse information (at least not until forced by litigation). *Then,* with the exception of DES (for which there was a signature disease), the causation requirement has tended to foreclose tort recovery for plaintiffs.

I am not saying that women should always avoid girl drugs. There *has* been better living through chemistry, and as an inhabitant of a female body, I have benefited from that. Moreover, I am not claiming that women are absolutely numerically disproportionately harmed by medical products. I *am* claiming this: The girl drugs are killers of women and their children. Drug companies who make and market them are exploiting sex inequality, specifically women's inequality to men.[1] The failure to test such drugs adequately, and the consistent failure to inform women of the risks of these drugs, cannot be understood as other than the cavalier use of women's bodies as profitable test grounds for which no one will be held accountable. It is sex discrimination.

It is ironic that Viagra, one of the few blockbuster drugs specifically developed for and marketed to men, may be the occasion for exposure and regulation of gender specificity in commercialized health care. Viagra is sometimes prescribed to women, but has not been particularly effective (so it is not the pharmaceutical holy grail: the prescription drug that increases female sexual desire). Viagra has caused reexamination of the system because it, like most of the medications and devices for women that I listed earlier, would ordinarily be understood as a "lifestyle drug."

Lifestyle drug is such a telling term, but not capable of exact definition. The idea originates in insurance lingo, whereby matters that are "medically necessary" are covered, but "nontherapeutic" treatments are not. Thus, contrary to popular lawyerly belief, the first Viagra case was brought neither by women seeking insurance coverage for girl drugs nor by men injured by Viagra. Rather, the first Viagra case was bought by a class of male plaintiffs against an insurance company that refused to cover Viagra. Their argument was that the company was denying a product "vital to human existence" (Hayden 1999, 180). It was soon thereafter that women began to demand coverage of contraception under health insurance policies, arguing that women's control of their sexual and reproductive lives is not a "lifestyle" choice, but is life itself for most women. I'm sorry to say that it has taken injuries associated with Viagra (most prominently, vision problems) to make the sex specificity of risk imposition a big deal. I hope that decision makers will take a close look at the "female maladies" (a redundancy, in the Biblical worldview) and therapies that have given rise to so much toxic tort litigation.

In addition to all of this—the theology and history that make women expendable—women are relatively poor. As Martha Chamallas has discussed, corporate defendants are perfectly well aware that if you're going to hurt somebody, it is way better to hurt poor people, because that will diminish what is often otherwise the largest element of economic damages, their future earning capacity (Chamallas 2005). Women will be discriminated against again by now-prevalent caps on noneconomic and punitive damages (Cady 1997; Finley 2004).

Taking Sex Oppression Seriously

There are all manner of problems with the U.S. tort system, starting with the oft-observed fact that the tort system is an incredibly inefficient and spotty form of health insurance. Indeed, because the United States is the only industrialized country that does not provide universal health insurance, the tort system bears numerous burdens—financial and symbolic—that it doesn't have to bear in other countries. In Canada, for example, due to the availability of universal health care, many tort victims will have neither need nor inclination to sue (Chamallas 2005; Kritzer, Bogart, and Vidmar 1991). In the United States, persons hurt by drugs, depending on whether they have health coverage and the generosity of that coverage, may have no choice but to sue drug companies even to get close to breaking even.

In the U.S. pharmaceutical world, there is also an astonishing "back-loading" of risk. The FDA has virtually disappeared, except in its enforcement of the George W. Bush administration's political and religious priorities. The years' long delay of approval for over-the-counter emergency contraception is an outrage, but just the outrage du jour (Kaufmann 2006).

The facts are that, when it counts, the FDA requires minimal preapproval testing of drugs, has no meaningful oversight regarding the completeness or truthfulness of data presented to it by pharmaceutical companies, and has minimal "post market surveillance" powers that are rarely and slowly used. Further, consumers cannot bring a claim for "fraud on the FDA" (*Buckman v. Plaintiffs' Legal Committee* 2001). The all-too-common result is that drugs come to market too easily, manufacturers have no incentive to conduct thorough testing of their products at any time, no consumer can stop them, and thousands of people can be killed or hurt before the government gets around to doing anything about it.

Moreover, as of January 2006 and with far too little notice, the FDA decided that its pronouncements on drug safety preempted state law actions against drug manufacturers. The twisted part of the pronouncement is how in the preliminary rule the FDA didn't mention preemption, so it didn't solicit certain kinds of salient comments, and it sure enough didn't get them, so it didn't have to ask for them. Here is what the regulation says: "Although the proposed rule did not propose to preempt state law, it did solicit comment on product liability issues. FDA received no comments on the proposed rule from State and local government entities."

It takes ages for the damage of such self-righteousness to be undone. The idea, propagated by the framers of the Restatement Third of Torts, that states' common law may be obsolete, and that the FDA can effectively take over the regulation of drug safety, has become a cruel joke. In the "cruel joke" department, remember that if a plaintiff sues the drug manufacturer, she effectively has to produce artificially high results in epidemiological studies to succeed, a kind of investigation that is both far more extensive and far more expensive than anything the manufacturer had to produce to the FDA before the manufacturer started producing, marketing, and making profits from those same drugs. And anything the manufacturer *did disclose* about possible risks of a product, including explanations for taking a product off the market, as a matter of law will *not* be sufficient for that plaintiff to show that the defendant caused her injuries. It is an extreme understatement to note that the present system creates incentives on the part of drug manufacturers to have *no idea and not to care* what the consequences of their actions will be (Berger 1997, 2119; Wagner 1997). That, to me is a good definition of "privilege," epistemological and otherwise.

In response to the problems inherent in toxic tort litigation, various scholars and judges have proposed different alternatives. Some commentators want to beef up the regulatory oversight of drug companies and/or add criminal penalties for drug companies' failures to follow safety testing requirements. Some of the proposals have to do with the creation of new institutions, such as science courts. There is considerable support for reducing recoveries based upon the probability of causation (Wagner 1997).

If we have to have causation at all, I am most attracted to the proposals that advocate burden shifting to defendants on the question of causation as a means of encouraging more thorough testing of drugs and placing the onus of causal uncertainty on those who make the profits. Margaret Berger, for example, proposes that a plaintiff prove:

(a) a manufacturer's failure adequately to test or to reveal information relevant to assessing potential risks,

(b) her exposure to the manufacturer's product;

(c) her ill health consistent with an untested-for or undisclosed risk; and

(d) damages.

Thus, the plaintiff's *prima facie* case is proved. Then:

(a) the burden shifts to the defendant to show that there is no general causation, i.e. that the sort of harm plaintiff suffered could not possibly be caused by exposure to its product,

OR

(b) damages will be reduced by the amount(s) to which defendant shows the plaintiff's harms to be attributable to other causes (Berger 1997, 2144).

Berger explains that her proposal is a logical extension of other measures courts have taken to relax proof requirements when plaintiffs cannot establish causation (Berger 1997, 2124), and that it is in fact an amalgam of the claiming provisions under Judge Jack Weinstein's Agent Orange settlement and the Johns-Manville asbestos bankruptcy trust (Berger 1997, 2151).

Berger has joined with Aaron Twerski in a more recent proposal, which would seem to go further in eliminating causation. They would understand the pharmaceutical tort as a failure of informed consent (Berger and Twerski 2005). If a plaintiff took a drug (or underwent a treatment) without understanding the risks, and if such a risk befell her, and if she can show that a reasonable patient wouldn't have undertaken the treatment with knowledge of the risks, then she would have a cause of action against those responsible for failing to discover and inform her of the risks. Berger and Twerski make no commitment about what damages should be available in such an action, but I would urge that they be the same as in an ordinary medical malpractice informed consent case; they should include everything.

I applaud these proposals as far as they go, but would note two major problems. First, though Berger titles her groundbreaking 1997 piece "Eliminating General Causation," both her proposals reincorporate the requirement insofar as the plaintiff has to show that a defendant manufacturer should have identified some *particular risk to which she was later subject*. Because a plaintiff will have to prove what should have been discovered, the burdens of uncertainty still fall largely on plaintiffs (Golanski 2003).

Second, and of more cosmic importance, the notion of isolating causes in toxic and environmental torts is archaic. If it is true that 80 percent of chemicals now in use have never been assessed for any sort of risks (Wagner 1997), the world has become a toxic soup. Risks are exponentially increased by other unknown and perhaps unknowable risks. The ontological status of causal claims can only become shakier. When we know this, it is unconscionable to pretend that we don't.[2] It is, moreover, unconscionable to allow the myth of causation to continue to be a corporate hiding place. On some ontological level, it may be true that "nobody broke it, it just broke." But the law cannot allow risk-profiteers to disappear into uncertainty.

Equality: If Not This, Then What?

Martha Chamallas argues that certain tort doctrines and practices in tort litigation should be understood as Equal Protection violations (Chamallas 2005, and this volume). I hope that we will all work on that. Among present obstacles, perhaps most daunting is the requirement that the plaintiff show that the defendant intentionally discriminated against her on a prohibited basis, as mandated by the wrongheaded and paranoid case of *Washington v. Davis* (1976). Thus, it is not enough for, say, the FDA or a pharmaceutical manufacturer merely to *know* that their negligent actions might be particularly devastating to women. The plaintiff has to show that such defendants intended to discriminate on the basis of sex. It doesn't have to be that way. Canada, for example, has done away with the intent requirement in constitutional equality cases, and the foundations of that republic have not yet crumbled (*Andrews v. Law Society of British Columbia* 1989). While it is not clear how far Canada will go in eliminating de facto sex discrimination (*Symes v. Her Majesty the Queen* 1993), the Ontario Court has held that it is unconstitutional sex discrimination for expert witnesses to be allowed to rely upon sex-based actuarial tables in calculating damages awards (*Walker v. Richie* 2005; see also Adjin-Tettey 2004). That aspect of the case is not at issue in the appeal pending before the Canadian Supreme Court.

Of course, it would be ideal if the United States understood discriminatory trade practices and governmental licensure as matters of pressing constitutional urgency. In the meantime, however, there is nothing stopping legislatures and courts from attempting to remedy the rampant sex discrimination in tort law. I would like to see an enactment that would establish harms done to women by pharmaceutical actors as civil rights violations. We have a range of emergent remedies that constitute the building blocks for such an enactment.

Consider, for example, the wide variety of "hate crimes" statutes, recognizing that ordinary crimes are more reprehensible when perpetrated for discriminatory reasons. Moreover, a number of states have provided civil remedies for such hate crimes, and some states provide civil remedies for such actions even if they are not otherwise crimes (see sources collected at Agyemang 2006, 965 nn234–238). Though most states limit the underlying conduct to instances of "intimidation" or "harassment," other sorts of conduct could be added, or intimidation and harassment could be interpreted to include pharmaceutical practices that are predatory on women's health. Further, the discriminatory causation (often called "motivation") that informs the notion of hate crimes (and civil remedies for hate crimes) is less than the discriminatory animus required in Equal Protection cases. The hate crimes models recognize the criticality of bias, intentional or not, in social conduct.

Add to that foundation consumer fraud provisions from various states. These allow civil actions when it can be shown that a consumer would not have bought the drug if she had known of the risks or the defendant's inadequate investigation or reporting of risks. Such statutes are beginning to be interpreted to allow class-based relief when insurers bring the claims on behalf of their insureds (*International Union of Operating Engineers Local No. 68 Welfare Fund v. Merck & Co.* 2006). The consumer fraud models get past the general causation requirement in toxic torts. They require reimbursement of the costs of drugs, and often, statutorily mandated damage multipliers. In the consumer fraud context, individual plaintiffs do not ordinarily recover their individual damages. But a legislature could change that, too.

The actual drafting of statutory remedies for pharmacological gynocide will have to wait for a later time, but here would be the structure: (1) if a manufacturer targets a drug to women as women, or to men as men, (2) and that manufacturer conducted insufficient, misleading, or undisclosed premarket testing (defined as that which a reasonable consumer would want investigated, and upon which their consumption would depend), then (3) manufacturers would at the very least be forced to disgorge their profits. Damage multipliers would enact the principle of hate crimes recoveries and would also avoid costly litigation of the constitutionality of punitive damage awards. And there is no necessary reason why a legislature could not also require the payment of individual damages for violations of the statute. I will work on it. I do not claim that such a statute would be perfect, but it might get defendants off the comfy dime of exploiting women's health needs *and* causal uncertainty simultaneously.

Whatever works. The notion that "nobody broke it, it just broke" is marvelous grist for academic consideration of cultural variation. However, the law must oppose the corporate appropriation of causal uncertainty in this culture where linear causation has been the norm, but where the edges of the norm are fraying with obscene profits on one side and obscene group-based injuries on the other. We've learned that there are other ways to think about causation. We can and must think about it differently. A happy instance of the Western metaphysical celebration of agency is a can-do attitude. The exemplar of that metaphysic was Sir Francis Bacon. Now is the time to embrace his admonition: things that have never been done will never be done unless we embrace methods that have never been tried.

CHAPTER SIXTEEN

The Cultural Agenda of Tort Litigation

Constructing Responsibility in the Rocky Mountain Frontier

JOYCE STERLING AND NANCY REICHMAN

Legal historians debate whether the tort system at the turn of the twentieth century was a compensation system for victims or simply a system built to provide economic subsidy for emerging industry (Friedman 2005, 356–357; Friedman and Russell 1990; Horowitz, 1977; Schwartz 1981b, 1989). Friedman's 2005 findings that most plaintiffs who filed a legal claim in Alameda County, California, in the late nineteenth century were either turned away with no compensation or with very small amounts of damages supports the conclusion that the tort system created an economic subsidy for industrial development.

Our chapter suggests that the subsidy debate as it has been argued to date may be too narrowly construed and consequently miss the important cultural dimensions of tort litigation, irrespective of the actual resources that are distributed. Tort law performs an important cultural function by "creating" meanings for dutiful relationships, risky situations, and attributions of blame for "accidents." Tort law reflexively constructs the meaning of accidental events by organizing injury claims, defining wrongs that may be subject to legal remedies, and transforming everyday accounts of mishap into legal claims of responsibility. Successful tort claims transform accidents from "acts of god," beyond anyone's control, to socially or personally responsible events. No longer a matter of fate, injuries are the consequence of accountable, social action.

> The fundamental concepts of tort law—negligence, fault, reasonableness, responsibility, blame—are not out there in nature, immutable, etched in stone ready to be plucked whole from the tree of life. Rather, these concepts and the theories or doctrines that

give them meaning are socially constructed, moveable boundaries. Indeed, it would be hard to find a better set of indirect, unobtrusive measures of changing values that can be gained from the evolution of tort law in modern times. (Polisar and Wildavsky 1989, 142)

On the one hand, the act of bringing suit can *reflect* popular conceptions of obligation, relationship, causation, and responsibility. Personal injury claims are the products of "culturally conditioned ideas of what constitutes an injury and how conflicts over injuries should be handled" (Engel 1984, 554). Bergstrom (1992, 184), for example, found that New Yorkers filed more personal injury claims in New York City between 1870 and 1910 despite fewer wins and smaller damage awards because of changing popular conceptions of responsibility and blame and a new way of thinking about the relationship between man and machine. New Yorkers "increasingly refused to bear the burden [of accidents] themselves" replacing the "'rugged individualism' principle of personal responsibility with social responsibility regardless of fault" (ibid., 176). In Engel's (c. 1984) Sander County the resort to court to handle claims of personal injury was infrequent and typically a consequence of social distance between the parties and a changing sense of community obligations (Engel 1984). In his chapter in this volume, Engel compares his Sander County study to his study of Thai tort victims. His analysis emphasizes how religious understanding of accidents and fate affect interpretations of causation.

On the other hand, court outcomes can help *create* meaning for accidental events, creating new definitions of obligation, relationship, causation, and responsibility that feed back into popular conceptions of fault and legal responsibility. It is in this later sense that we argue that tort law can take the form of a cultural subsidy around accidents creating important symbols of stability and rationality that, in Denver, encouraged continued community development despite the harsh realities of frontier living.

To explore the relationship between court outcomes and culture, we considered the disposition of claims brought against two different kinds of transportation defendants, railroads and tramways in the city of Denver between 1862 and 1917. Given the importance of both defendants to the development of Denver, the subsidy thesis suggests that plaintiffs would receive little or no recovery for injuries they suffered while acting within the spheres of these two defendants and that tort outcomes would be similar for both classes of defendants. They were not. Although plaintiffs did not often recover for injuries, as the subsidy theorists suggest, the picture was a bit more mixed. Railroad accident victims who sued the railroad for compensation for their injuries typically found their cases dismissed. When the courts resolved cases, either through trial verdicts or judgments, injured victims recovered. The story with respect to injury claims against local tramways is a bit different. A smaller percentage of cases were dismissed. Far more cases were settled. And, once again, when the court was involved in resolution of the cases, injured plaintiffs prevailed. To understand these different outcomes and in particular the different rates of dismissal and settlement, we turn to differences in the cultural significance of each form of transportation and the social meaning of blame attached to accidents that occurred in their paths.

Denver's Railroads and Tramways

Some writers have suggested that western states can be understood best as colonies of the eastern states. If so, Denver is certainly one of the colonial cities (Abbott et al. 1982). The "Queen City," as she was known, became a conduit for capital from the East, providing credit and transportation to the outlying frontier. It was not always so. Before the rails reached Denver in 1879, the city was stagnating. However, in the decade after the rails arrived, the population increased by sevenfold (Noel 1996, 68). "Almost overnight the train depot replaced the stage office as the nucleus of the city" (Noel 1996, 68). Raw materials from outlying areas flowed through Denver on their way back toward eastern consumption (Dorsett and McCarthy 1986) and with them brought a new sense of cosmopolitanism.

Denverites' support for the railroads was ambivalent, at best. A majority of railroads operating in Colorado were owned by outside capitalists (Dorsett and McCarthy 1986, 60–61), a mixed blessing for Denverites who, on the one hand, depended on outside capital to fuel regional growth and, on the other, sought to create their own "native" power elite. The ambivalent relationship between Denver and the railroads had an impact on the Colorado constitutional convention in 1875–76 as it took up the issue of how best to regulate them: "Many saw the destiny of the new state at stake: either the people would rule Colorado by having the power to regulate the railroads and keep service and rates in check, or the railroads would run Colorado . . . Sponsors of the constitution asserted Colorado must do nothing to frighten away eastern capital" (Goodstein 2003, 90). As the newly formed state began to assert itself, however, local elites began to push back. In 1884, Governor Evans resolved:

> Whereas these industries are being greatly crippled and some of them utterly destroyed by the blighting effects of railroad extortion and railroad discrimination, be it resolved: that we earnestly request the good citizens, the businessmen and the capitalists of all of the cities and towns of Colorado to associate themselves into Boards of Trade or Chambers of Commerce for the promotion of their local interests and for general cooperation in advancing the interests and protecting the rights of all parts of the state (Denver Chamber of Commerce n.d.).

In short, the meaning of railroads for citizens of Denver can be best captured by the term *necessary evil*. Railroads occupied an important, almost sacred, role in the city's development. As a national icon, railroads represented the frontier and the possibilities of rugged individualism that brought new citizens to seek their fortunes in the city on the plains. Locally, they were the source of life—the lifelines to the civilizing East, without which the city would not, indeed could not, exist, Yet, despite their best efforts, Denver's elite exerted little control over the railroads and their owners, not in the courts, legislatures, or boardrooms. The railroad, an iconic image of frontier America, was an untouchable force of city formation.

If the story of railroads is one of local elites subservient to outsider interests, the story of tramways is one of internal struggles for control. Controversies about, and lawsuits over, the tramway franchise were ongoing during the period (Goodstein 2003, 60), capturing among other things questions of ownership and the right to occupy the city streets. The Denver City Tramway Company was organized by Denver's founding fathers John Evans, William Byers, and Roger W. Woodbury. The first streetcar line, the Denver Horse Railroad Company was constructed in 1871. By 1890, Denver claimed to have one of the most extensive cable car networks in the country (Leonard and Noel 1990, 35–39, 54–57).

> Streetcar operations were vital. Very few residents owned horses. Upkeep and stabling for these animals was extremely expensive. Even the rich usually depended on streetcars to get them to and from their jobs. Hopping on the trolley was the prime means of visiting a park, going to church, or attending a play. (Goodstein 2003, 273)

While railroads connected Denver to the cultures of the coasts, tramways were central to the "suburbanization" and growth of the city, allowing Denver's elites to build and live outside of the city limits. "A nickel fare and a fifteen minute ride transported Denverites from the saloon-filled city to dry suburbs" (Noel 1996, 70).

In sum, if railroads were sacred, tramways were clearly profane. Denver's tramways were locally owned; their operations were a part of routine conflicts about city governance.

Accidents and Injuries

Railroads and tramways created new kinds of troubles for Denver's citizens. The metal monster's destructive power brought both progress and disaster to the developing American landscape. By the end of the nineteenth century, railroads and streetcars had become a major source of accidents (Friedman, 1987, 367).

Some of Denver's citizens harmed by these transportation entities evoked the law of torts to seek compensation for their injuries. Many did not. The findings of coroners' juries may play a role here. When called upon, the court system responded by allocating blame and creating accounts of responsibility. But, interestingly, the same behavior, for example, being hit while crossing the tracks, evoked a different level of response depending on whether it was a railroad train or a tramway that caused the accidents. Clearly, instrumentality was a factor. The metal monster was not the same machine as the tramway. Arguably (and argue tort lawyers did), trains were harder to stop than tramcars. However, we suggest that the cultural meaning of these two forms of transportation made a difference as well and helps to explain the different and often contradictory responses to claims of injury.

Accidents occurred on the rails because "shit happens" or, later, because an employee did not do his job correctly; the railroad, itself, often was untouchable. Accidents on the tramways were far more contested. In some cases, plaintiffs prevailed. In many they did not. But unlike the railroad victims, tramway victims could often count on their "day in court." Two cases illustrate this difference. In 1916 the parents of a nineteen-year-old male killed crossing railroad tracks in Denver brought suit in Denver District Court for wrongful death (*Headley et al. v. Denver & Rio Grande Railroad Company* 1915: 500). The trial court accepted the defense of the railroad without allowing the jury to decide whether the plaintiff observed his duty of due care before crossing the tracks (ibid., 502–505). The accident happened at a known railroad crossing situated at the intersection of four railroad tracks owned by the defendant. Several safety measures were in place to protect the crossing. An automatic signal bell was in place to ring when a train was within 500 feet of the crossing, although the bell was out of order and had not been working for over a week before the accident. City ordinances limited the maximum speed of trains at this point to twenty miles per hour. On the day of the accident, Headley was riding his bicycle to work as he did every morning, attempting to cross the rails at his usual spot. Train No. 1 traveling south at about twenty-five or thirty miles per hour passed the plaintiff as he began to cross. Immediately, the "Uncle Sam" passed going northbound. According to witnesses, the plaintiff had crossed the southbound track and was beginning to cross between the two tracks when he turned the wheel quickly to avoid the oncoming train. He then appeared to hit an object, fell from the bike, and was killed by the "Uncle Sam" train. The defendant in the case acknowledged both the broken signal bell and the train's excessive rate of speed, but they argued that Mr. Headley did not "stop, look and listen" as was required. The Supreme Court upheld the trial court decision to give the defendant a directed verdict, referring to both Colorado case law and case law from other states to support its decision.

The justices appeared to be far more responsive to cases involving the tramway. On October 17, 1890, Nesbit, a conductor on a streetcar owned by the Denver Tramway Company, fell to the ground while collecting fares and was run over by the streetcar, seriously and permanently injuring his foot and ankle. The train was traveling between twelve and fourteen miles per hour. Mr. Nesbit testified:

> I was passing from the motor to the trailer in order to collect a fare or fares, and I had hold with my right hand of the hand rail of the motor car, and I swung around in the usual way to catch hold of the hand rail of the trailer car and thus transfer my hold. I came in contact with the hand rail of the trailer car, and thought I had it for the instant, but just as I was transferring my hold the motor gave a sudden bound up and threw my hand so high I missed the trailer and fell. (*Denver Tramway Co. v. Nesbit* 1896: 409)

Since some streetcars were equipped with "lifeguards" or "fenders' designed to prevent a conductor's foot from passing on to the track, Mr. Nesbitt claimed, the lack of such device on his car was clearly negligence. The trial court found for the plaintiff. The Supreme Court reversed and remanded for a new hearing. Although ultimately the plaintiff failed to recover, the trial court judge's decision not to direct a verdict at the outset suggests that the trial courts were willing to offer a day in court to individuals injured by the tramways and, thus, a forum for debating the issues of risk and responsibility.

In the following section we examine records of the Denver Trial Court and the Colorado Supreme Court to consider how accident victims were treated by both and to learn more about the narratives of blame applied to different kinds of defendants.

Constructing Responsibility in the Courts

The recognition of a duty owed is a fundamental element of tort law without which recovery would be impossible. At its core, the concept of duty defines a social relationship of obligation and accountability. An obligated party is asked to account for and then compensate/remedy an injury incurred by another. Being hit by a train when you cross the tracks can be viewed as just another reminder that "shit happens." Ann Scales in this volume characterizes blame for torts as a generalized state—"Nobody broke it, it just broke." Or, it can be recognized as the consequence of negligence by a train conductor who failed to provide the appropriate signal. Often, the physical act is the same. However, what the act means and the obligation of the parties to take care can change depending on cultural understandings about relationships, risk, and responsibility. In railroad cases, the concept of responsibility was fixed and determined elsewhere in case law from other states. In tramway cases, the response was both more fluid and inconsistent, an outcome of local debates.

We examined cases filed in Denver District Court every fifth year from 1862 through 1917. The year 1862 marked the beginning of the court system in Denver, and 1917 the nation's entry into World War I and a recognized break in Denver's history. Most importantly, the period of our study captures Colorado's transformation from a territory to a state and Denver's development from a small frontier community to a sophisticated metropolitan center. The Registers of Action for Denver District Court, the upper-level trial court in Colorado, provide the baseline data. Unfortunately, these registers do not contain damage amounts for the tort cases. Since the number of cases heard in the trial courts was relatively low in the first four sample years of the study, we collected every case file for those years (1862–77). For the remaining sample years, a 20 percent sample (every fifth case) was assembled to document the court's business. We collected the total population of tort cases for the sample years in our study (N = 1,519). We reviewed railroad and tramway cases decided by the Colorado Supreme Court between 1883 and 1917 (n = 48). The Supreme Court was the court directly above the trial courts for a number of years in our sample. The first Court of Appeals was established in 1891 and abolished fourteen years later (1905). The Court of Appeals was reestablished in 1911 only to be disbanded again in 1915. It was not re-formed until 1970.

The Role of Tort in the Business of the Trial Court

Overall, tort claims comprise about 10 percent of all claims filed in civil court. Although it is certain that bringing a lawsuit was an option for only a small fraction of injuries, Denver courts heard proportionately more tort claims and tort claims were a more stable feature of court dockets than comparable jurisdictions. (See Friedman and Russell's [1990] analysis of Alameda County, California.)

As expected from the analysis of other jurisdictions, defendants prevailed overall. Nearly half of the cases were disposed of by dismissal. Sixteen percent of tort actions resulted in a settlement, indicating that victims may have recovered something. Approximately 11 percent of the tort actions resulted in a trial, equally divided between bench and jury trials. When a court agreed to hear a case, injured victims were more likely to be winners. Of the plaintiffs whose cases were heard by a judge or jury, 65.8 percent received an award, a finding that appears contrary to the findings of many of the longitudinal litigation studies. Defaults were rare in tort actions.

Looking at tort actions as a whole, our findings are consistent with Friedman and Russell's (1990, 313) conclusion that the system for attributing blame and compensation for injury was an obstacle course, indeed, and certainly no *norm* of collective responsibility for injury.

Railroads and Tramways as Tort Defendants

Railroads and tramways had a destructive impact on citizens' health, and as their activities increased they became a significant part of the docket (Figure 16.1).

Overall, tramway plaintiffs were more successful getting the attention of the court whether they left with compensation or not. Tramway cases were less likely to be dismissed and more likely to go to trial than railroad cases (Table 16.1). Nearly a third of the tramway cases were settled, while only 11 percent of railroad cases were similarly disposed as small victories for the plaintiffs. Railroad plaintiffs more easily side stepped contests over their responsibility; a greater

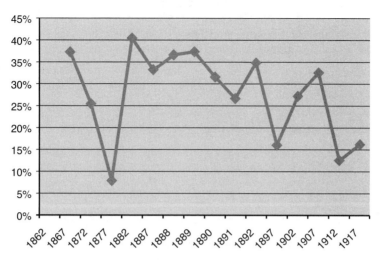

FIGURE 16.1 Percentage of Tort Cases Involving Transportation
Defendants (original data are with the authors)

SOURCE: Original data are with the authors.

TABLE 16.1
Tort Litigation in Denver Trial Courts, 1862–1917:
Disposition of Cases Against Railroads and Tramways

	Railroads		Tramways	
Dismissal	35%		23%	
		58		32
Judgment	17%		19%	
		28		27
Trial	11%		15%	
		18		22
Settlement	16%		39%	
		27		56
Other	22%		3%	
		36		5
Total		167		142

SOURCE: Original data are with the authors.

percentage of tramway cases went to some kind of trial. At trial, plaintiffs and
defendants were equally likely to win (Table 16.2), although as we discuss below,
railroad "wins" for the plaintiff often were reversed on appeal. Judgments were
more likely to be resolved in favor of plaintiffs in cases against both railroads and
tramways.

Plaintiffs injured by the tramway were both more likely to get a full hearing
in the trial court, and they were more likely to be upheld at the Supreme Court.

TABLE 16.2
Winners of Judgments and Trials in Cases Against Railroads and
Tramways: Denver Trial Courts, 1862–1917

		Railroads	Tramways
Judgment			
	Plaintiff Wins	63%	70%
	Defendant Wins	37%	30%
	n=	27	27
Trial			
	Plaintiff Wins	50%	55%
	Defendant Wins	50%	45%
	n=	18	22

SOURCE: Original data are with the authors.

Fifty-four percent (7) of tramway plaintiffs and only 24 percent (8) of railroad plaintiffs won affirmation of their trial court victories on appeal. Defendants in railroad accidents were affirmed 9 percent (3) of the time, and they were able to reverse trial court decisions for plaintiffs in 15 percent (5) of the cases. There were no decisions reversing and holding for the plaintiff. Railroad and tramway accident cases that were appealed were equally likely to be sent back to the trial court for new trials.

The Supreme Court opinions are particularly useful for understanding the cultural determinants and implications of differential treatment of railroad and tramway accidents. Unlike modern appellate opinions, the nineteenth-century opinions tended to focus and argue about the "facts" presented by both the plaintiffs and defendants. "What happened?" was rehashed in the opinions that included substantial trial testimony from plaintiffs, witnesses, and defendants. To further factual arguments, the Court examined photographs of accident sites and maps of accidents as well as testimony from the trial record. Opinions, after the turn of the nineteenth century, included dissents, reflecting strong disagreements with the majority's version of the facts as well as questions of law.

Railroad companies were absolved of responsibility often, even with clear evidence of the defendants' bad acts. In those cases, the court ignored or disregarded the negligence of the defendant and instead shifted its focus on the behavior of the plaintiffs, who were required to prove that they did not contribute in any way to their own injury. A daunting task. By shifting the burden in this way, the Supreme Court justices did two things. First, they created a subsidy for the railroads, allowing them to operate without the threat of financial consequence for their behavior (the classic subsidy argument). Second, they provided support for the ideology of the rugged individualism of westward expansion. Individuals were asked to accept both the opportunities and personal responsibilities associated with entrepreneurial activities. Accidents that occurred on the railroads were bad luck, and individuals who suffered such bad luck were left to manage on their own.

The situation was far different in the tramway cases. Although the injuries were similar (e.g., being hit by a car when crossing a track or becoming injured when coupling or decoupling two cars), justices engaged the question of mutual obligation or the relative negligence of the parties. The bad acts of the tramway companies were considered part of the calculus and not simply disregarded. Again, the effect was twofold. To be sure, the courts often acted in ways that supported the financial interests of the tramways (subsidy). By engaging the issue of mutual responsibility, justices also promoted and fostered ongoing, often contested, relationships between the tramways and the citizens of Denver. Subsidy was considered alongside the needs to create a sense of community and mutual obligation.

Work Accidents

Thirty-three percent of work accident cases heard by the Supreme Court involved employee-employer relationships. Often the decision turned on whether the relationship could be classified as constituting that of a "fellow servant." Despite the existence of doctrine that could absolve employers of responsibility for injuries suffered by their employees, Denver trial courts often resisted the wholesale adoption of "eastern" law and continued to award damages to those employees. These trial court outcomes were appealed as a matter of course. The fellow servant rule was upheld virtually wholesale when the case involved the railroad. The rule was far more contested, tweaked, or ignored when the work accident happened on a tramway.

In *Colorado Central v. Martin* (1884), the Court barred recovery by constructing a narrative of status that allowed supervisors to be conceptualized as equal to those who worked for them, that is, fellow servants. Threatened by attack from train robbers, the Colorado Central decided to provide guns on the train for the defense of employees and passengers traveling between Denver and Cheyenne. On one trip, the baggage master forgot to take the ammunition out of the guns. As they were being reloaded onto the train after a brief stop, one of the shot guns accidentally exploded and injured the conductor, Martin. The trial court found for Martin. In its opinion, the Supreme Court acknowledged the duty of the railroad company toward its employees, particularly when carrying dangerous weapons. But rather than attributing blame to the railroad for not providing safe procedures for carrying weapons, the Court reasoned that the conductor and the baggage master should be viewed as fellow servants. The Supreme Court reversed the trial court's decision for the plaintiff and exonerated the railroad company from liability.

The court opinion in an employee injury case involving the Denver Tramway (*Denver Tramway Co. v. Jennie Crumbaugh* 1897) tells a different story. Crumbaugh, a conductor for the Tramway Company, was killed while working on a tramway line in North Denver. After he finished his run for the day, Crumbaugh was on the ground attaching the wire that reversed the trolley position so it would be ready for the next conductor on its return trip. Another tram car, the No. 110, operated by the same company, was standing on the same track approximately eight feet away prepared to start in the opposite direction. After sounding two bells, the conductor on the No. 110 applied the electrical switch to begin moving the car forward. However, the switch was out of repair, causing the electricity to operate in reverse. The car backed down upon Crumbaugh and crushed him to death between the bumpers of the two cars. The electric reverse switch and the brake on the No. 110 car had been out of repair for some time before this incident, but had been declared fixed when brought to the track by Mr. Truitt, an employee of the company. Although the Tramway Company argued that Truitt was a co-employee with Crumbaugh and he rather than the company should be liable for the death of the plaintiff, the trial court found for the plaintiff. The decision was upheld on appeal. Ignoring the negligent behavior of other employees, the Court relied on the "safe-tool" exception, which required employers to provide safe machinery for their employees, and held the company responsible for not fulfilling their obligation to have cars that operated properly.

Disenchanted with court decisions in favor of industries, especially the railroads, the Colorado state legislature attempted to broaden definitions of liability through passage of Employer Liability Acts in Colorado in 1893, 1901, and 1911, each version an effort to clarify the meaning of the Act. Despite the legislation, plaintiffs injured by railroads continued to lose at the trial courts, and they continued to appeal. In each case, the Supreme Court reversed the trial court decision and remanded for a new trial. We found no similar Supreme Court cases involving workplace injuries by tramway employees. Without access to the full records of trial court cases, we can only speculate about their absence. It well may be that tramway plaintiffs prevailed at the trial court and tramway corporations (being locally owned) did not fight the trial court decisions. Tramway companies may have been more likely to settle their cases. Or perhaps tramway plaintiffs were less likely to appeal if they lost at the trial courts. No matter which of these explanations is supported by the empirical evidence, the absence of appeals of plaintiff victories in cases brought by tramway employees suggests the legal system responded differently when the injured worker was employed by a tramway rather than by a railroad company.

Stop, Look, and Listen: The Case of Traveler Accidents

A number of accidents occurred when individuals attempted to cross rail tracks or were unaware of the approach of a tramway. In tort terminology, we refer to these legally constructed relationships as trespasser/licensee. When these accidents involved railroads, they evoked the citizens' duty when crossing tracks to "stop, look, and listen." Over time, the risk of crossing railroad tracks changed from simply crossing (a more or less fixed risk of travel) to being misled about safety (a behavioral risk). Legal doctrine defined the duties of plaintiffs and defendants as ones of mutual obligations to consider safety. However, when deciding railroad cases Supreme Court judges placed the overwhelming burden on the injured parties to prove that they did not contribute to their injury through their own negligence. Railroads had few obligations to establish that they met their duty of care toward those needing to cross railroad tracks.

In *Nucci v. Colorado and Southern Railway Co.* (1917), Mr. Nucci sued the railroad for injuries sustained when he was hit by a train while crossing the tracks with his team of horses and wagon. Mr. Nucci was driving his wagon parallel to the track when he decided to cross. The highway was on a downgrade, so at the point where Mr. Nucci had to cross, there were cottonwood trees and willows, and he testified that they obstructed the view of the track. The trial court dismissed the plaintiff's claim. At issue on appeal was Nucci's distance from the track and whether it was sufficient to check to see if a train was coming down the track. Unlike any other case we considered, the Supreme Court published the plaintiff's testimony and evidence, including a picture of the site of the accident, within the majority opinion. Despite repeated questioning, Mr. Nucci maintained that, "About thirty yards from the track I stopped my horses and looked and listened to see if a train was coming. The whistle did not blow, or the bell ring. I neither saw nor heard a train. I did not see the train coming. I was in the middle of the track when the train struck me" (584). The railroad company admitted that they never rang their bell or blew their horn. Nor did they come to a complete stop as was required by statute. Together, these actions constituted "negligence per se" and the defendant admitted its negligence. Nevertheless, the defendant claimed, the accident was caused more by the plaintiff's actions than their own. The Supreme Court sitting en banc affirmed the decision of the trial court to dismiss the plaintiff's claim. Three justices dissented, arguing that the majority failed to fairly weigh the mutual obligations of the parties. The majority opinion reflected the view that railroads deserved the benefit of the doubt, if not full subsidization of their ever-increasing accidents.

The decision making in *Denver Tramway v. Wright* (1909) stands in marked contrast to the railroad-crossing accidents. Tramways were equally deadly to travelers in Denver, but in particular to pedestrians or travelers on bicycles who shared the streets with the tramcars. Mr. Wright was riding his bicycle on a bikeway that ran between two tram lines. About two feet west of and parallel to the east tram track, Mr. Wright was hit from behind by a tramway, dragged another 100 feet, and killed. The trial court record indicated that the tramway failed to ring its bell or slow the car down until the car actually hit Wright. At the conclusion of trial testimony, the defendant moved for a directed verdict that was denied. Unlike the railroad case, the court recognized the mutual obligations of the parties and found for the plaintiff. The case was appealed. The Supreme Court opinion never mentioned anything like the "stop, look, and listen" admonition of the railroad crossing accidents. According to the majority opinion in the Wright case, a duty to regulate the speed of the train and sound a bell rested with the defendant. The case for the plaintiff was upheld on appeal.

Similar to Wright, in *Philbin v. Denver City Tramway* (1906), the court recognized a difference between street tramways and the "metal monster," the steam railway. In their opinion the Court states that:

> It is the duty of a traveler to look out for himself and to exercise such ordinary care as would be exercised by reasonable persons under attendant circumstances, but the duty imposed upon persons crossing a steam railway track to stop, look and listen, is not rigidly applied to persons traveling a street used by a street railway. (Ibid.)

The perception, real or imagined, that tramways were better able to regulate their speed than railroads appears to have been a consideration for the court. But the ruling also demanded a lower level of accountability. Railroad and tramway accidents occurred on the same downtown Denver streets filled with pedestrians, vehicles, horse-drawn wagons, and wheelmen, but the court held railroads and tramways to different standards of care.

Passenger Accidents

The Supreme Court's responses to appeals of cases involving passenger injuries continued to distinguish the responsibilities of different transportation entities and their relationship to those who traveled on them. Five passenger cases involving railroads and four involving tramways were considered by the Colorado Supreme Court during the period of our sample.

Mr. Percy McGeorge was a passenger on the Colorado & Southern Railway. As the train was rounding a curve, it encountered a dirt slide that had come down upon the track. The train hit the dirt slide. The sudden shock to the train threw the plaintiff, who was then standing, across the car seats and seriously injured him. McGeorge complained that his injury was caused by negligence on the part of the defendant for not maintaining its roadbed. In response, the defendant claimed that the injury was due to an "unavoidable accident, alleging in substance that the approximate and efficient cause of the injury was the result of an act of God, unforeseeable and irresistible" (*Colorado & Southern Railway Co. v. McGeorge* 1909). At the trial court, the plaintiff won a jury verdict and judgment. Upon appeal, the question for the Court focused on the definition of the defendant's duty toward the plaintiff as a passenger. At issue were two contradictory jury instructions given upon the conclusion of evidence entered in the case. In one instruction the jury was bound to hold the railroad responsible for *any degree of negligence* found (ibid., 747). In a second instruction the jury was told that the railroad company was to be held to a reasonable degree of care for a common carrier to conduct its business. As long as the railroad acted reasonably, then accidents due to problems on the roadbed, tracks, and so forth were not recoverable for plaintiffs (ibid., 747). The Supreme Court turned to similar cases from other states and held that the lesser standard prevailed. The Court reversed the decision of the trial court and remanded for a new hearing where, given their decision, a victory for the defendant seemed certain. Arguably, the fact that the Court chose the pro-defendant instruction reinforced the still "sacred" status of the railroads.

Again, decisions in the appeals of tramway cases evoked a different concept of obligation. In these cases, the Courts found that tramway companies had a duty to the passengers who traveled with them. In *Denver Tramway Co. v. Ann Owens* (1894), the plaintiff rang the bell to signal the conductor to stop the car so that she could exit. As she stepped off the platform of the car, there was a violent jolt and she was thrown to the ground and severely injured. The gripman contended that the plaintiff did not ring the bell until he was past the stop and he assumed that she wanted to get off there. At both trial and appeal, the acts of the plaintiff were contested. Did the plaintiff attempt to step off the car prior to it coming to a complete stop? Witnesses could not offer definitive proof for either version of the story. The uncertainties of the case resulted in five separate jury trials. In three of the five trials, the jury found for the plaintiff. The appellate court affirmed Miss Owens's trial court victory. Their decision was clear that the burden in the tramway accident fell squarely on the shoulders of the tramway company, rather than on the conduct of the plaintiff.

The Cultural Agenda of Tort Litigation

Employing historical data for the period 1862–1917, the picture of the emerging western city of Denver shows that tort litigation in the trial courts overall supported defendants in both railroad and tramway accidents. These findings are similar to those in the longitudinal litigation of court literature. But we find patterns in the railway and tramway cases that complicate the usual story: tramway cases were more likely to be resolved by settlement than railroad cases (suggesting at least a small victory for plaintiffs); tramway cases were less likely to be dismissed than railroad cases (dismissals being seen as a victory for defendants); if plaintiffs went to trial, they were more likely to be winners in these lawsuits; if railroad victims won at trial, they were more likely to be overturned on appeal than tramway victims.

Our analysis of the Supreme Court cases used the detailed illustrations from court opinions for more narrative information. These data showed that on the one hand, railroad defendants were more likely to be absolved of responsibility, even when evidence of negligence was presented to the court; the Court relied on use of the fellow-servant rule to avoid liability more frequently in the railroad cases than in tramway accidents. On the other hand, the Court was more likely to recognize mutual obligation between tramways and their injured workers, pedestrians, and passengers, and plaintiffs in tramway cases were more likely to be upheld on appeal than plaintiffs in railroad accidents.

The differential outcomes of similar types of injury claims brought against railroad and tramways bring into relief the cultural significance of these two actors and the scripted roles each played in community development. Time after time, the Colorado Supreme Court released railroad companies from their obligations to citizens even when there was adequate legal justification to hold them accountable. In railroad accidents the Supreme Court usually placed responsibility for accidents squarely on the shoulders of plaintiffs. The Court's decisions promoted the railroads as sacred, an entity not to be challenged or disrespected, and removed them from responsibility for their effects on community life. Railroad companies were given license to be distant and to disengage from dialogue about community norms, roles, and responsibilities. Tramways, on the other hand, were required to account for their actions. A similar license to operate with impunity was not awarded to tramways. Although tramway companies were sometimes absolved of their responsibility for accidents, the mutual obligations of plaintiffs and defendants were nearly always part of the debate. Often in these cases, the court weighed the obligations of "both" parties and directly engaged questions about interdependence and community obligations and responsibilities in the developing city.

Two "cultural" factors appeared to influence the Court's differential response to railroad and tramway responsibilities to citizens in the developing city. These include the risky relations between parties and the risky places occupied by their transportation machinery.

Conclusion

The confluence of national and legal norms created a foundation for cultural development in a growing community. Our analysis points out how the courts constructed a cultural agenda within tort litigation that furthered the development of the new western city of Denver.

The Denver data support the conclusions of subsidy put forth by Friedman, Friedman and Russell, and others. The picture of tort litigation in early Denver suggests that "subsidy" is much more complex than simply economic subsidy. It may include cultural agendas that were equally important in the building of western cities. Denver has battled the stereotyped visions of the frontier from its earliest days to the present, most significantly the stereotyped visions of a Wild West. The newcomers to this emerging western city pushed for a vision of law and order. Replicating the legal culture of the East appeared to be one means of achieving order and stability and creating new sets of relationships between citizens and local representatives of the emerging transportation industry.

The trial courts construction of "causation" and "responsibility" in railroad and tramway cases reflected the cultural agenda of rugged individualism and an orderly city that lay at the heart of Denver's campaign for citizens, although the courts differed in their treatment of each. The construction of standards of care and notions of individual responsibility distinguished plaintiffs in the railroad cases from those in the tramway cases. Railroads were often absolved of responsibility for their accidents while tramways were found to have mutual responsibility for accidents that occurred on their lines. These differences reflect the court's perception of liability that shaped and was shaped by definitions of risky relations and risky places.

The impact of social distance between plaintiffs and defendants and the attribution of responsibility that attaches to social distance can be characterized by classifying the defendants as insiders or outsiders. In his classic account of disputing in Sander County, Engel (1984) found that the handful of personal injury cases "shared a common feature: the parties were separated by either geographic or social distance that could not be bridged by any conflict resolution process short of litigation" (Engel 1984, 567). Community "insiders" avoided courts and relied on informal resolution of their disputes, while "outsiders" employed the formal processes of the courts.

The railroad companies operating in Denver were owned, in large measure, by eastern financiers with no personal ties to the city or to the accident victims who made claims against them. Along with their financial capital, the railroad corporations brought outsider norms and values that they expected to be honored by the local legal system (e.g., the established use of the "fellow-servant rule" in other states protecting these outsider entrepreneurial corporations from liability). Tramways, on the other hand, were locally owned and operated. Tramway owners were "city builders" and part of the local community. Those injured by the tramways were closer at least geographically, if not socially, to the tramway owners.

The dynamic of social distance operated a bit differently in Denver trial courts at the turn of the twentieth century than in Sander County at the later part of the century. Although our study of court cases does not address the issues of court avoidance, higher rates of settlement at the trial courts for cases involving the tramway insiders seem consistent with Engel's findings from Sander County. Cases involving parties that shared geographical and social space were more likely to be resolved without evoking the full formal legal process. As cases progressed through the legal system, that is, having passed some sort of disputing threshold, the shared geographic and social space generated greater issue engagement than cases where there was more distance between the parties. In contrast, the interests of railroad outsiders were protected by formal and often pro forma application of "the law." Fearful that liability decisions against railroad corporations could be interpreted as hostility toward the necessary influx of financial capital to the community, the courts avoided the issues and applied whatever defensive rules were at hand. So, in an interesting twist to Engel, we find that the courts did not engage when the claims were made against outsiders, but rather accepted their claims wholesale most of the time. Once inside the legal system, tramway "insiders" were more likely to be taken to task by the courts than railroad "outsiders." Unlike in Sander County, everyone in Denver could be classified as a newcomer, in some sense. The courts did not have to mediate between the old and the new. Instead, the courts became an important forum where the very sense of community and norms of obligation could be established in the first place.

Both railroad and tramway accidents occurred on Denver's public streets. Traffic was not well organized as found on modern thoroughfares, and citizens were maimed crossing railroad tracks and tramway lines alike. The Court, however, constructed different meanings for the "public" spaces occupied by railroads and tramways.

> The difference between the rights of steam railways and street railways is marked and unquestioned, although in many respects somewhat similar. The distinguishing difference is in the exclusiveness of the right of a steam railway company to occupy its track as against all other persons or modes of locomotion. The street railway, however, occupies the surface of the highway subject to the common use not only of the balance of the road, but also for that part covered with the tracks by either the pedestrian or the driver of a vehicle. The cases are not entirely agreed in their description of the easement enjoyed by the transportation company. It is always conceded not to be exclusive, but is generally held to be superior . . . All the courts agree, however, that there

still remains with the pedestrian, the users of vehicles and of horses, the old right which they always enjoyed—to use all of the King's highway at their pleasure and for their convenience. (*Davidson v. Denver Tramway Co.* 1894)

Thus, the meaning of public space appeared to depend less on objective conditions of the space, for example, frequency of contact with citizens, proximity of the railroads and tramways to the pedestrians, and the amount of congestion, and more on who was operating within that space. The quote above and the reception of courts to the railroads when they were sued for crossing accidents, suggest that the railroads were given priority or the "right of way" to their space. Although both railroads and tramways operated on city streets, only tramways were required by the courts to acknowledge that they shared the space with other entities and traffic. Railroads were granted primary access to the space occupied by their tracks, even though the tracks were often laid on city streets with significant pedestrian and vehicular traffic. Priority use of these public spaces was denied to tramways, while it was granted to railroads.

The priority of the railroad public space meant that those who came into contact with railroad space operated at their own risk. Individuals who crossed the tracks were responsible for their own fate. The sacred character of the railroad remained intact. Railroad liability for accidents was rare. Indeed, railroads frequently avoided the costs of trial by winning at the pleading stage. Accidents involving tramways, entities with recognized responsibilities for sharing space with others, was a different matter altogether. Courts more frequently hashed out questions of liability and held tramways responsible.

In this chapter, we have suggested that early disparities in outcomes of railroad and tramway cases should be examined within a broader cultural framework that analyzes the risky relations between workers and transportation companies, the risky places shared between pedestrians and railway traffic, and the risky cargo when carrying passengers on the rails. It is this analysis that points to the status of railroads as sacred and tramways as profane in the eyes of the Denver courts. Expanding on the cultural propositions suggested by Engel in this volume, we suggest that tort law emerges not just from an interpretation of the facts of an accident, but from the social context and cultural understandings of accidents and risk found outside the law.

Reference Matter

Acknowledgments

We would like to thank the extraordinary group of authors who faithfully answered our call for this collective project and produced such excellent and innovative chapters. David Engel wishes to thank his longtime faculty secretary at the University at Buffalo Law School, Dawn Fenneman, for her invaluable support. Michael McCann thanks Jennifer Fredette, his graduate student assistant at the University of Washington, who helped in various ways throughout the project, including managing the Web site. The two of us also thank the University of Denver Sturm College of Law for hosting a conference in April 2006 that brought our group together for the first conversation that ultimately led to this book.

Notes

Introduction

1. Our conception of legal practice heeds David Nelken's insightful argument in Chapter One that studies of culture should focus on both meaning and behavior, on both who we are and what we do.

2. American Law Institute (1998).

Chapter One

1. See Nelken, 2004, and now Nelken 2005 and 2007.

2. An important cultural variable is how far, in places other than the United States, the same corrective, distributive, and retributive aims are pursued by a comparable branch of private law or distributed among other types of law or regulation.

3. But relevant empirical studies of tort law may be difficult to find even in the local languages. The lack of such research is of course itself evidence of cultural differences.

4. My comments on Italian law are derived from discussions with lawyers, judges, and law professors as well as interviews carried out in southern Italy.

5. But looking to the state does not mean welcoming the nanny state. My wife, a left-leaning Italian judge, finds it amusing that imported champagne bottles have warnings on them about the danger of opening the corks without due care.

6. The last Berlusconi government on the final day of office passed a law in response to lobbies of road accident victims, increasing from 30 percent to 50 percent the advance on expected compensation—provided there were grave indications of responsibility—and extended this beyond cases where "special need" could be shown.

7. In other work, Feldman has sought to show that there are other situations in which Japan makes more use of (tort) law than other industrial countries.

8. Preliminary interviews were conducted with a lawyer, an insurance agent, a loss fixer, an auto repairman (whose role is not marginal), someone running an agency

for dealing with car accident cases, and someone who had been involved in a motor accident.

9. Engel shows that there is nothing inevitable about the rise in car ownership leading to more tort cases. But in so doing he confirms the value of treating legal culture as a crucial intervening factor.

Chapter Two

1. Cotterrell (1995, 235) also notes the "uncertain scope of community."

Chapter Three

I am grateful to Niketa Kulkarni and Jay Krishnan for their collaboration in providing important components of this essay and to Neil Bjorkman for research assistance.

1. During this era, the *All-India Reporter* occupied a position roughly analogous to the West System of law reporters in the United States as the most widely used and often-cited nationwide set of law reports. Before Independence it reported judgments of the High Courts and Courts of the Judicial Commissioners of the various provinces of British India, as well as the decisions of the Privy Council of the House of Lords in cases from India. Since Independence, it reports the judgments of the Supreme Court and the High Courts in each state. These are the only courts whose judgments are published and become part of the accessible body of precedent. The *All-India Reporter* does not publish every case that appears in the official reports or in local series of law reports.

2. We worried about comparing British India with the Republic of India, since the latter includes the former Princely States and omits the parts of British India that became Pakistan and (eventually) Bangladesh. Amid all the boundary changes of component units, only one major unit remained unchanged, the United Provinces, later renamed the State of Uttar Pradesh. Fortunately I was able to find data for Uttar Pradesh from 1903 onward, and the same trends are evident.

3. This must be qualified by some adjustment for the decreasing percentage of adults in the population. But more important was the creation of tribunals outside the regular courts and the creating of original jurisdiction in the higher courts to hear claims for violations of the Constitution's chapter of Fundamental Rights.

4. A sunk cost auction is a game, often used as a business school exercise, in which some good (say a million rupees) is awarded to the highest bidder, but the person who bids the second-highest amount also must pay the amount he bid. Thus even if the opponent's last bid exceeds one million, there is an incentive to bid just a bit more in order to reduce one's loss by the value of the prize, but then the opponent is presented with a similar incentive, ad infinitum. In practice, the game ends when one party runs out of money or grows indifferent to the possibility of reducing the loss by the prize amount. For a discussion of this concept see Hadfield (2000, 980–982).

5. For an analysis of the failure to seek legal remedy in an incident in which over three hundred were killed after drinking poisonous liquor, see Manor (1993).

Chapter Four

Thank you to Youngjae Lee and John Witt for comments on an earlier draft. This chapter benefited from discussion at Fordham Law School and at the faculty of law of Bar Ilan University.

1. For an exception, see *Ard v. Ard* 1982 (lifting the traditional parental immunity only to the extent of the available liability insurance).

2. Of note to insurance scholars, the article was adapted from her master's thesis written under the direction of Edwin Patterson.

3. See www.law.uconn/library/ilc/fiction.htm (portal to the insurance fiction collection).

4. Of note, liability insurance contracts generally do not cover fines or penalties that are assessed by civil authorities, either. The relationship of civil fines and penalties to the tort-crime boundary is a topic for future work.

5. See, e.g., *State Farm Mut. Auto. Ins. Co. v. Wertz* 1995.

6. See, e.g., *Ambassador v. Montes* 1978.

7. Sharkey 2005 reports that it is a "minority" position recognized in only nine U.S. states and, in most of those states, vicariously assessed punitive damages are insurable. See Baker 1998b for an explanation of how large corporations are able to obtain offshore insurance that indemnifies the corporation for punitive damages assessed in jurisdictions in which such insurance is contrary to public policy.

8. A possible exception, discussed in Wriggins 2001, might be crime-torts in which the perpetrator believes that the victim will share the liability insurance proceeds with the perpetrator. As Wriggins discusses, this is a possible concern in the domestic violence context.

9. In cases involving intentional harm, the usual rule prohibiting insurance companies from subrogating against their own insureds does not apply. See, e.g., *Ambassador Ins. Co. v. Montes* 1978.

10. The one obvious exception is drunk driving, because the overwhelmingly compensatory purpose of compulsory automobile liability insurance has prevented automobile insurance companies from putting drunk driving exclusions in their policies (Schermer 2004). The divorce context may be another significant exception to this generalization. Apparently, tort claims arising out of spousal abuse are not uncommon in the divorce context, particularly when there are significant assets in the spousal estate or held separately by the husband (see Ellman and Sugarman 1996). Thank you to Anne Dailey for bringing this to my attention.

11. In that case, Ambassador Insurance Company asked the New Jersey courts to declare that it had no duty to defend or pay for a wrongful death claim. The claim arose

out of a crime for which Ambassador's policyholder was convicted and sent to prison: he burned down a building in the middle of the night knowing that his tenants were inside. The trial court agreed with Ambassador that liability insurance did not cover that claim and granted summary judgment. When the landlord appealed, however, it became clear that the insurance policy in the official record did not contain an intentional harm exclusion, and the landlord argued for reversal on that ground. The appellate court rejected the landlord's contract-based argument and, like the late nineteenth-century court decisions that McNeely reviewed, held that no explicit exclusion was necessary because liability insurance for intentional harm is against public policy. On further appeal, the New Jersey Supreme Court reversed, as McNeely would have predicted, on the grounds that the policy did not contain an explicit contract provision excluding claims arising out of intentional harm. The court used this unusual situation to state emphatically that liability insurance for intentional harm does not violate public policy because the proceeds of the insurance policy go to the victim, not the criminal. Moreover, as the court explained, this insurance would not create a dangerous incentive because the liability insurance company would be free to bring a subrogation action against the policyholder to recoup the money it had paid to the victim. (The fact that, as a practical matter, the insurance company would be unlikely to bring an action against a criminal sitting in jail has no bearing on the question of incentives: if the defendant has no assets and no insurance, the victim would be equally unlikely to bring an action.)

12. *Allstate Ins. Co. v. Malec* 1986.

13. I should be clear that an insurer may not be able to unilaterally adopt the pay-and-then-subrogate approach, for reasons sketched in Baker (2008, 437–438). In short, few people would choose to purchase a more expensive liability insurance policy that authorized the insurance company to pay the victim and then pursue them, so cheaper policies with an intentional harm exclusion can be expected to dominate the market. But a state legislature or insurance regulator could easily solve that problem by requiring all liability insurance policies in a specified market to be structured in this way. To those who object that the pay-and-then-subrogate approach would be impractical, I point to the automobile insurance market. Automobile liability policies generally contain intentional harm exclusions, but uninsured motorists (UM) coverage typically steps in to fill the gap, and the insurance company that issued the UM policy is permitted to subrogate against the tortfeasor. This approach is even more unwieldy than what I am suggesting (because two different liability insurance companies are involved), but it achieves essentially the same end (cf. Wriggins [2001] arguing for using the uninsured motorists approach to compensate victims of domestic violence).

14. As of fall 2008, Allstate is the largest U.S. homeowners' insurer to include this exclusion. State Farm (among others) does not ordinarily use such an exclusion.

15. The two exceptions to this morally objectionable situation in the United States today are the same two fields that McNeely mentioned in 1941: crimes at work and crimes

involving automobiles. If an employer intentionally injures a worker, the worker not only gets to collect workers compensation benefits, but also gets to bring a tort action against the employer (despite the fact that, ordinarily, workers compensation precludes tort claims against the employer). The automobile insurance situation is a bit more complicated (reflecting the fact that automobile insurance never completed the transformation to a victim compensation fund that McNeely predicted), but victims of intentional harm usually are able to recover: if the driver's insurer does not have to pay, the victim's uninsured motorists' insurer usually will have to pay (Schermer 2004).

16. Directors' and officers' insurance defines the operative terms "claim" and "defense expenses" broadly enough to include criminal defense costs (e.g., Executive Risk Indemnity 1996).

17. Medical liability insurance provides ongoing criminal defense cost coverage for "criminal charges against an Insured Person arising out of the rendering of or failure to render Medical Services" (e.g., Executive Risk Indemnity 1998).

18. The NRA's liability insurance policy promises to reimburse criminal defense costs in cases involving self-defense, as long as the charges eventually are dropped or there is an acquittal. See http://www.locktonrisk.com/nrains/selfdefense.asp (last visited December 2, 2007).

Chapter Five

An earlier version of this chapter was presented at a conference on "The Cultural Foundations of Tort Law," Sturm College of Law, University of Denver, April 7–8, 2006. I am indebted to David Engel and Michael McCann for organizing a stimulating conference and for their suggestions for revision of my early efforts. I also thank my colleagues Jim Henderson and Kevin Clermont for their extraordinarily helpful comments about the tort and civil procedure matters raised in the early draft. I thank Amanda Stevens for research assistance.

Chapter Six

The coding for this chapter was conducted by an extremely diligent and talented group of undergraduates—Maegen Beattie, Kelsey McCarthy, Kiersten Weinberger, Ryan McCord, Keith Hiatt, Sidney Lewis, Colleen Melody, Michael Pope, and Terra Stewart—and supervised by Ph.D. candidate Shauna Fisher, who contributed in many ways. We thank all of them, and especially Shauna. We also appreciate the funding from a generous National Science Foundation grant SES-0451207.

1. For example, while dismissing the initial claims of attorneys on behalf of several children against McDonald's, Judge Robert Sweet urged a revision of the pleadings in terms so pungent that they must have whetted the food fighters' appetites: "Chicken Mc-Nuggets, rather than being merely chicken fried in a pan, are a Frankenstein creation

of various elements not utilized by the home cook . . . Chicken McNuggets, while seemingly a healthier option than McDonalds hamburgers because they have 'chicken' in their names, actually contain twice the fat per ounce as a hamburger. It is at least a question of fact as to whether a reasonable consumer would know—without recourse to the McDonalds website—that a Chicken McNugget contained so many ingredients other than chicken and provided twice the fat of a hamburger" (http://banzhaf.net/obesitylinks).

Then, after being equally critical of the hidden dangers of McDonald's french fries, the judge concluded (perhaps aware of his pun): "If plaintiffs were able to flesh out this argument in an amended complaint, it may establish that the dangers of McDonalds' products were not commonly well known and thus that McDonalds had a duty towards its customers" (htpp://banzhaf.net/obesitylinks).

2. An even more dramatic example of demonstrated virtue and public sacrifice is provided by Harish Bharti, a Banzhaf protégé living in Seattle who led the legal campaign for Hindu vegetarians against McDonald's misrepresentation of their beef-enhanced french fries (Bharti 2002)

3. We searched "LexisNexis Academic" under "General News" and in "Major Newspapers." For "Litigation Articles" we deployed the search string "(obesity OR obese) AND (fast food) AND (litig! OR lawsuit OR sue!) in 'Headlines, First Paragraphs, Terms.'" We did *not* search for those key terms in the entire texts of newspaper articles. Our search string for "Non-Litigation Articles" was "(obesity OR obese) AND (fast food) in 'Headlines, First Paragraphs, Terms.'" However, we qualified the search with the third condition "AND NOT (litig! OR lawsuit OR sue!) in 'Full Text' rather than 'Headlines, First Paragraphs, Terms.'" Coders detected but *six* lawsuits mentioned in the "Non-Litigation" sample.

4. Future texts will compare and contrast media coverage in the United States with coverage of U.S. cases in Canada, Australia, and the United Kingdom.

5. A missing value for journalistic "mode" (that is, episodic, thematic, editorial, or unclassified newspaper articles) reduced the number in the Litigation Sample by one article.

6. If "Plaintiffs and Defendants Share Responsibility," "Corporate Duplicity," "Attorneys' Fees or Motives," and "Public Costs" are excluded, the remaining frames detected constitute about 82 percent of all themes coded. Inclusion of "Plaintiffs and Defendants Share Responsibility" would drive the total invocations of responsibility to about 87 percent of all themes coded. Of course, "Corporate Duplicity" may be taken to be assignment of blame or culpability beyond mere responsibility, in which case almost 95 percent of the coded themes concerned responsibility, accountability, or culpability.

7. Although attributions of "Corporate Duplicity" occur far more often (both by columnar percentages and absolute numbers) in "Litigation" stories than in "Non-Litigation" stories, the relationship of that frame to attributions of responsibility is hardly unambiguous. We are not certain how to articulate responsibility with the "Attorneys' Fees or

Motives" frame because reasonable analysts will differ in "unpacking" that theme. Almost seven out of every ten references to lawyers' motivations or billings were found in articles that invoked litigation and tobacco, so that frame strikes us as mostly a reply to the conduct of tobacco litigation.

8. Broken down by the nature of the article—episodic, thematic, editorial, or other (see www.lawslore.info/ for more definition of "other" articles)—these patterns are complexified.

9. Coders also assessed the explicitness or intensity of the description, which yielded a five-point scale ranging from very negative assessments to very positive assessments. For Table 6.2 we simplified presentation of those data in a tripartite scheme.

10. The rank-order correlation (Spearman's) between Litigation and Non-Litigation Samples was 0.56.

11. Critser's well-known article (2000) and book (2004) emphasize the class issue. However, his analysis focuses on class-based consumption patterns, arguably contributing to the stigmatization of lower income citizens as undisciplined and irresponsible, rather than on the class-based politics of production, which much litigation strives to identify. Our anecdotal evidence suggests that scientific experts did a better job of raising issues about targeted low-income, minority, and youthful publics.

12. While we do not develop the point here, studies of mass-media coverage of legal disputes provide a useful mode of comparative research between and among different polities, different historical epochs, and different subcultures.

Chapter Eight

Portions of this chapter first appeared in *The Columbia Journal of Gender and Law* (Bloom 2005).

Chapter Nine

Thanks to David Engel, Michael McCann, and the participants in the Cultural Foundations of Tort Law Conference. Many thanks to David Goldman, Zachary Brandmeir, Joshua Scott, Erin Krause, Jenni Hebert, and Jeremy LeStage, for research assistance. Thanks to David Achtenberg, Martha Chamallas, George Chauncey, William Corbett, Zanita Fenton, Rachel Godsil, James Hackney, Jr., Duncan Kennedy, Lois Lupica, and Deborah Tuerkheimer for reviewing drafts of sections of this essay. Thanks to Dean Peter Pitegoff, Dean Colleen Khoury, the University of Maine School of Law, and the University of Southern Maine for research funding for this project. The Boston University School of Law Faculty, the Northeastern University School of Law Faculty, the University of Maine School of Law Faculty, and the Ohio State-Moritz School of Law Faculty provided very useful comments at faculty workshop presentations. I also have benefited from discussions with Mary Bonauto, Margaret Burnham, Joseph Glannon, James Hackney, Jr.,

Jenni Hebert, Keith Hylton, Randall Kennedy, Vaishali Mamgain, Martha McCluskey, Katharine Silbaugh, Deirdre Smith, Barbara Welke, and John Fabian Witt. Thanks to the librarians at the New York Historical Society and the Garbrecht Law Library at the University of Maine School of Law. Parts of this essay were originally published in vol. 49, issue 1 of "Torts, Race, and the Value of Injury, 1900–1949," *Howard Law Journal* 99 (2005)

1. More discussion of issues in this chapter is found in Wriggins, 2005a, 2005b, and 2005c, and more will be found in Martha Chamallas and Jennifer B. Wriggins, "The Measure of Injury: Race, Gender, and the Law of Torts," forthcoming 2009, from New York University Press.

2. The term *black* used in the chapter refers to African American people and others identified in cases as "Negro" or "colored." Occasionally the term *African American* is used in such contexts. The term *white* refers to Caucasian people and those perceived or identified as white. This chapter's focus on issues involving blacks and whites is not to suggest that such issues comprise the entire subject of race and torts (Espinoza and Harris 1997; Perea et al. 2000). The cases discussed in this chapter do not deal with situations where racial identification is at issue. This chapter does not discuss issues of racial identification, skin color gradations or social construction that scholarship has begun to address (Gross 1998; Haney Lopez 1994; Harris 1993; Jones 2000; Sharfstein 2003).

3. The fact that some cases were brought and won by African American plaintiffs should not lead one to forget the equally, and possibly more, significant cases that probably were not brought. Part of the story about race and torts in the first half of the twentieth century is how the torts system did not provide remedies for much racially influenced or motivated tortious (and criminal) harm such as lynching. *Lynching* has been defined by Randall Kennedy as "a killing done by several people acting in concert outside the legal process to punish a person perceived to have violated a law or custom" (Kennedy 1997, 42–49). Almost three-quarters of reported U.S. lynchings between 1882 and 1969 were of black victims (ibid., 42). Lynching was rarely prosecuted criminally (ibid., 42), and tort lawsuits seeking compensation for lynching also seem to have been very rare (Chadbourn 1933, 78–80, 119). Second, tort suits were doubtless never filed for countless acts by whites toward African Americans, such as assaults and batteries that were tortious.

4. Moreover, in a society divided by racial caste, questions arise about what constitutes a "similar" injury to a black or white person (Wriggins 2005c).

5. Not only is it impossible to accurately predict the length of an individual's life, but life expectancies vary over groups, as shown in a recent study that found differences in life expectancy by race, gender, and geography (Murray et al., 2006). The question of how finely grained statistics should be to use for predictive purposes raises many broad policy points (Austin 1983; Chamallas 2005; Feinberg 2004, 31; Glenn 2000).

6. One of the two awards for the deaths of white people was reduced by 20 percent. The award for the death of the other white person was reduced by 35 percent; this was

for a forty-two-year-old white man who had been in poor health. Reductions in awards for the deaths of black people ranged from 29 percent to 43 percent (*The Saginaw and the Hamilton* 1905, 914–915).

7. It is referred to as a civil code provision rather than a statute because Louisiana is a civil code state. Much of its law derived initially from French law rather than common law. Acts passed by its legislature are commonly referenced in this way rather than as statutes (Friedman 1985, 171–173).

8. For the discussion in this section, all reported Louisiana wrongful death and survival cases with Westlaw key numbers 117k95-99 from 1900–1949 were reviewed and included in a database (Wriggins 2005a, 110 n46). The key numbers covered the following areas under the general heading of "death actions"; measure and amount of damages, in general (k95), statutory limits (k96), discretion of jury (k97), inadequate damages (k98), and excessive damages (k99). Computer searches such as "colored & tort" and "Negro & tort" and similar searches have also been done in the Louisiana cases database, and when a case indicated a decedent was black, that case was included in the database (Wriggins 2005d). These cases were generally brought under earlier versions of Louisiana Civil Code 2315 (2005).

9. Since U.S. tort law and legal culture were decentralized, with much variation between states, definitive generalizations as to the role of race in legal culture in other states at this stage would be premature.

10. There are surprisingly few readily available data about personal income in the first half of the twentieth century. The first census to incorporate data about income was in 1939. Census data from 1939 showed that white male workers earned approximately twice as much as males of other races (U.S. Census Bureau, 1975, 297, Series G, 189–204).

Chapter Ten

The research reported in this chapter was supported by a grant from the General Research Fund of the University of Kansas. I am grateful to several participants in the history told here for giving generously of their time and knowledge, particularly Graham Smith, Raju Bhatt, Tony Murphy, Russell Miller, Sarah Ricca, Stephen Cragg, John Wadham, David Hamilton, and John Beggs. Any remaining errors are mine.

1. Plaintiffs may request jury trials when alleging malicious prosecution and false imprisonment (which are typically combined into a single action with the third common claim, assault. See Section 69(1) of the Supreme Court Act 1981; Section 66(3) of the County Courts Act 1984 contains identical provisions. For discussion see Clayton and Tomlinson 2004, pp. 107–108.

2. Interview, Graham Smith, Nottingham, England, June 4, 2004. Interview, Russell Miller, June 2, 2004. See also Campbell 1995b.

3. Interview, Sarah Ricca, convener of PALG, London, May 17, 2004.

4. Interview, Raju Bhatt, London, May 26, 2004.

5. Interview, Graham Smith, Nottingham, England, June 4, 2004.

6. Interview, Raju Bhatt, London, May 26, 2004.

7. Interview, Raju Bhatt, London, May 26, 2004.

Chapter Eleven

I am grateful for the comments and suggestions from Ozzie Ayascue, Stephen Daniels, David Engel, John Flood, Herbert Kritzer, Michael McCann, and Alan Paterson. Thanks also to Nichole Dragone, Jesika Gonzalez, and Jason Maxwell Spitalnick for valuable research assistance. Earlier versions of this chapter were presented at the American Political Science Association meetings in 2000 and the Socio Legal Studies Association meetings in 2006.

Chapter Twelve

The research and writing of this chapter was supported in part by a University of Pennsylvania Law School Faculty Summer Research Grant. I am grateful to Robert Leflar, Craig Martin, and Frank Upham for their comments on an earlier draft of this chapter, to Alison Stein for outstanding editorial assistance, to Timothy Van Dulm for his professional research help, and to many friends and colleagues in Japan, especially Kawabata Yoshiharu and Kodama Yasushi.

1. As claims have escalated so too has the public debate, with the media, medical and legal organizations, elected officials, bureaucrats, and others debating the cause of the escalation and what (if anything) should be done in response. See, for example, Feld (2006).

2. Milhaupt and West (2004, 241) also observe "increased legalization" in their study of Japanese corporate governance, noting that "the role of lawyers in the Japanese economy, and in society generally, will continue to increase."

3. See Supreme Court of Japan (2005b).

4. Ibid. Cases primarily involve internal medicine (approximately 25 percent of all cases), surgery (~20 percent), and obstetrics (15 percent). See Supreme Court of Japan (2005c).

5. For example, over two dozen families of patients who were injured by heart operations at Tokyo Women's Medical University Hospital created the Higaisha Renrakukai and filed both civil and criminal charges (*Daily Yomiuri* 2003a).

6. Ginsburg and Hoetker (2006), argue that the relatively modest overall increase in litigation rates (compared to medical malpractice) since the 1980s is evidence for the importance of institutional, not cultural, barriers to litigation.

7. For a discussion of the role of criminal law in medical malpractice litigation in Japan, see Leflar and Iwata (2005).

8. In comparison to the United States, the incidence of medical malpractice litigation in Japan is modest. In 2002, there were approximately 250,000 physicians in Japan (population 127 million), 159,131 working in hospitals and 90,443 in clinics, who received a total of 606,399,536 outpatient office visits (an average of almost 5 annual visits/person), and made almost 14 million hospital admissions (*Kōsei Tōkei Yōran* 2002). In the United States that same year, there were 853,000 physicians, a population of almost 290 million, 1,083,500,000 outpatient visits (3.74 annual visits/person), and close to 34 million hospital admissions. Based on that data, one might expect a malpractice rate in the United States two to four times higher than that in Japan. In fact, there were more malpractice cases filed in Philadelphia in 2000, 2001, and 2002 than in all of Japan (http://www.courts.state.pa.us/ Search/Default.htm?&q=medical%20malpractice%20filings%20philadelphia&t=-480).

9. Medical malpractice claims can be brought under tort or contract law, and frequently lawsuits include both claims. Ultimately, the legal question is identical—did the provider satisfy the duty of care, and if not did the provider's breach cause the plaintiff's injuries? See Ramseyer and Nakazato (1999, 67–68). Practical differences include a three-year statute of limitations for tort claims versus ten years for contract claims, and differences in damage awards.

10. For a discussion of standards of proof in civil and common law jurisdictions, see Clermont (2004, 263, 264), who argues that in civil cases Japanese courts require proof "to a high probability similar to beyond a reasonable doubt." See also Taniguchi (1997, 767). Obtaining evidence in malpractice cases can be difficult. The JMA has successfully fought a law that would give patients the right to see their medical records. The Medical Practitioners Law (Ishi-hō) requires that physicians create and store charts, but only for five years, and it lacks sanctions for the alteration of patients' records. In 2003, the Japanese Diet passed the *Kojin Jyōhō Hogo ni Kansuru Hōritsu* (Personal Information Protection Law), Law #57, May 30, 2003. Although it did not address the issue of access to medical records, the Ministry of Health, Labor, and Welfare issued interpretive guidelines that specified the conditions under which patients in government-operated medical facilities could access their medical records. See *Koseirōdōshō, Iryō-Kaigo Kankei Jigyōsha ni Okeru Kojin Jyōhō no Tekisetsuna Toriatsukai no tame no Gaidorain* (Guidelines for the Management of Personal Information by Employees of Medical and Elderly Care Facilities), December 24, 2004. Many patients remain unable to access their records.

11. See, for example, Nomi (1999, 29), describing how plaintiffs in medical malpractice cases "must prove that the doctor's conduct fell below the level of the standard established by law." A different view is expressed by Ramseyer and Nakazato (1999, 67), who claim that "courts deliberately switch the burden" and impose it on tort defendants (rather than plaintiffs), who must demonstrate that they met the standard of care or that their actions did not cause the plaintiffs' harms.

12. In malpractice (and other civil) cases, according to the guidelines, plaintiffs cover their attorney's out-of-pocket costs and pay a retainer. In cases where plaintiffs are seeking less than ¥3,000,000, they pay a retainer of 8 percent; between ¥3,000,000 and ¥30,000,000, the retainer is 5 percent; between ¥30,000,000 and ¥300,000.000, plaintiffs pay 3 percent, and over ¥300,000.000, the fee is 2 percent. In addition to the retainer, attorneys could (and often did) add a 30 percent premium to the fee, and if they won the case they would double the initial retainer.

13. The initial payments in malpractice cases steadily decrease as a plaintiff's age increases, a function of the decrease in damages that are requested in claims. For plaintiffs between ages zero to nineteen, the average sum of attorney retainer and filing fees is ¥3,149,119; between ages twenty to thirty-nine, ¥2,297,272; for those between ages forty and fifty-nine, ¥2,280,118; and for those between ages sixty to seventy-nine, ¥1,876,676 (Wada and Maeda 2001, 143).

14. See Ramseyer (1988) for a discussion of the predictability of Japanese courts. For an analysis of using juries in malpractice cases, see Kawabata (2000, 27, 30–31).

15. For a thorough discussion of the criminal law approach to medical malpractice in Japan, see Leflar and Iwata (2005).

16. Another group that may become central to malpractice litigation in Japan is physicians who matriculate at one of Japan's new postgraduate law schools. At one school (Omiya Law School) ten of eighty first-year students in 2004 had medical degrees. Attorneys with specialized medical knowledge are likely to be attracted to legal practice that builds on their unique skills.

17. Demographic changes may also play a role; and it is possible that elderly individuals with time and money are more likely to sue.

18. In France and Germany, judges can select individuals from a list of possible experts that is assembled annually by the court; no such list exists in Japan.

19. Between 1989 and 1998, experts were used in 22.5 percent of medical malpractice cases, and plaintiff's chances of prevailing in malpractice litigation that involves experts increases from 29.9 percent to 39.1 percent (Sakamoto et al. 2002, 200).

20. As of November 2003, the Tokyo District Court has only used the conference method on four occasions.

21. In the current system, a single expert may take many months, or even a year, to render an opinion.

22. See Yamamoto (2000). Under recent amendments to the Code of Civil Procedure, experts first present their views, followed by questions from the judge, then the party requesting an expert, and finally the other party.

23. American courts have also experimented with scientific advisors (Rabin 2000). Ōshima (2003).

24. A detailed discussion of consolidation bureaus can be found in *Tokyo Chihō Saibansho Iryō Soshō Taisaku Iinkai* (2003).

25. Judges are regularly rotated; few postings last more than five years, and many are only three. To acquire a useful degree of medical expertise and use it in medical cases, judges will probably need more time than is possible under the current system of judicial administration.

26. See Nakamura (2000). The 2002 survey data are from "Zenkoku Yoron Chōsa Shōhō" (Detailed Report of the National Public Opinion Survey).

27. Regulators have undertaken a number of initiatives targeted at reducing the frequency of medical errors. Officials have created a mandatory accident reporting system, for example, that is managed by the Japan Council for Quality Health Care (2005). The Japan Board of Medical Societies has also set up a reporting system and is developing guidelines for disciplining doctors who have been convicted in criminal malpractice cases (*Daily Yomiuri* 2005b). The government has sought to eliminate poorly performing doctors by beefing up the Medical Ethics Council, a ten-member group dominated by doctors and former Ministry bureaucrats. The Council's narrow mandate only allows it to discipline physicians (1) charged with professional negligence that results in death; (2) convicted of a criminal offense, or (3) who misappropriate funds by fraudulently submitting claims for government reimbursement. Since 1971, it has revoked only sixty licenses, none due to malpractice. To improve the Council's performance, the Ministry has charged it with meeting four times per year (rather than two), and appointed new members trained in law and journalism (*Mainichi Shimbun* 2003). Finally, there are various efforts underway to improve the performance of physicians. The Japan Board of Medical Specialties announced in early 2005 that it was considering the creation of a licensing system that would be linked to the reporting of medical accidents, the Ministry of Health, Labor and Welfare is considering a revision to the Medical Practitioner's Law (Ishi-hō) that would require the retraining of physicians who commit medical errors (*Daily Yomiuri* 2005a), and the Japan Medical Association is requiring providers who have been the subject of more than three medical malpractice complaints to undergo retraining (Nihon Ishikai 2005).

28. Conflicts over injuries involving pharmaceutical products are another example. The seminal dispute in this area involved a group of people suffering from a neurological disorder called subacute myelo-optico neuropathy, or SMON. As a direct consequence of a Kanazawa District Court decision, in 1979 the Ministry of Health, Labor and Welfare created the Adverse Drug Reaction Fund (ADRF, also known as Drug Side-Effects Injuries Relief and Research Promotion Fund Act, and Relief Fund for Injuries Caused by the Side Effects of Medicines), administered by the government but financed through contributions by the pharmaceutical industry. All claims are evaluated by a group that operates under the auspices of the Ministry, and payments cover medical expenses, nursing expenses, a living allowance, and a pension or a lump sum to surviving family members. By 1995, for example, 1,714 thalidomide-related claims had been paid, for a total of

4.7 billion yen (over US$40 million). Other related funds, like the Inoculation Act of 1948, amended in 1977, provide avenues of redress for children who suffer from the side effects of compulsory vaccination.

29. Japan's approach differs from U.S.-style medical screening panels in numerous ways (the JMA process is started by a physician, the insurance company plays a central role, and screening occurs before cases are filed). See Macchiaroli (1989–90).

30. In contrast, the mean medical liability insurance premium in the United States in 2000 was $18,400, and for ob/gyn it was $39,200. See U.S. Census Bureau, Statistical Abstract of the United States: 2004–2005, p. 109. According to officials at Tokio Marine, Japan's largest insurance carrier, the company makes little or no profit on malpractice insurance. Instead, such insurance is a loss leader, enabling the company to sell physicians other profitable insurance products, like home and auto insurance. In fact, the cost of insuring a typical Mercedes in Tokyo is ten times the cost of malpractice insurance. The JMA also supports low malpractice insurance rates, which it believes help to boost JMA membership.

31. The one published study of the JMA's liability claims management system indicates that it handles 400 claims/year, but the data is old and impossible to verify. See Nakajima et al. (2001) and Nihon Ishikai (2001).

32. The lack of juries in Japan, and the professionalized judiciary, make Japanese courts relatively more predictable than those in the United States. See Ramseyer (1988).

33. There is of course nothing irreversible about this shift; old impediments to litigation may in the future be resuscitated or new ones could be created.

34. Just as one of Tokyo's local city councils has promoted a new smoke-free sidewalks policy under a banner that proclaims that social relations once structured by informal manners are now governed by formal rules (*maana kara, ruuru e*), the government more generally has expended a tremendous amount of energy since the late 1990s promoting the idea that the rule of law needs to be strengthened, and people need to be legally empowered. It is difficult to measure the degree to which such rhetoric shapes consciousness and changed consciousness influences the willingness to litigate. But there is some empirical support for the claim that rates of litigation are increasing across the board, and the new rhetoric of legal reform at least suggests a greater willingness to portray litigation as a social good than has previously been the case.

35. Sasao et al. (2006): "the situation [regarding medical malpractice litigation] in Japan is gradually becoming more like that in the United States." See also Keleman and Sibbitt (2002).

36. A somewhat stronger case can be made that malpractice law in Japan has become increasingly similar to that in Canada and the United Kingdom, where pain and suffering awards are lower than in the United States, punitive damages and juries are uncommon, and contingency fees are of recent origin.

Chapter Thirteen

1. All major newspapers carried the news next morning, on June 30, 2005.

2. In 2003, while there were 878 deaths from mesothelioma, only 85 of them got workers' compensation. But, in 2006, 1,006 mesothelioma and 790 lung cancer patients received the compensation: http://www.mhlw.go.jp/houdou/2007/05/h0525-2.html (checked on 06/06/2007).

3. An annual budget for the fund is 9 billion yen (approximately $US90 million), and the government (national and local) contributes 18 percent and the rest is borne by the industry as a whole (*Asahi Shinbun,* August 30, 2006).

4. Only when the symptomatic evidence of asbestos scars in the lung tells that the chance to contract lung cancer has been elevated by a factor of two or more can he or she get compensation.

5. The most recent Supreme Court decision (April 27, 2004) regarding this state indemnity arising out of the inadequate regulations was the Chikuho Jinpai (pneumoconiosis in Chikuho coal mine) case. The Court found that, "Before the Pneumoconiosis Law was passed in 1960, most of the coal mines failed to use the wet drills, and caused the miners to contract the pneumoconiosis. As the wet drills had been known to be effective in preventing the disease already in the middle of 1950's, and as the Ministry of Trade and Industry was mandated to regulate the industry for the workers' safety, the nonfeasance that the Ministry failed to have revised the Ministerial ordinance earlier than 1960 to supervise the industry to use the wet drills is "strongly unreasonable (non)exercise of its power beyond the permissible discretion."

6. In Japan, the hearings are not clearly divided between the pleadings and the trial, and the trial consists of a series of testimonies usually held once every month or two.

7. This expression is very common and has a wide appeal to the people in Japan. In a national opinion survey I conducted in 2005, the respondents were asked to choose the most important human rights that Japanese society had to protect among the following: (1) the right not to be discriminated against, (2) the right to be protected from the abuse of the police, (3) the right to criticize the government freely, (4) the right to live humanly. The results were (1) 18 percent, (2) 7 percent, (3) 11 percent, and (4) 63 percent. See Tanase (2007b, 271).

8. This concern is explicitly mentioned in denying a class action in mass tort cases. "One jury, consisting of six persons will hold the fate of an industry in the palm of its hand. This jury may disagree with twelve of the previous thirteen juries—and hurl the industry into bankruptcy . . . But it need not be tolerated when the alternative exists of submitting an issue to multiple juries constituting in the aggregate a much larger and more diverse sample of decision-makers" (*In re Rhone-Poulenc Rorer, Inc.* 1995).

9. This idea of the Supreme Court speaking in one voice is reflected in the anonymity of individual judges. In a small pilot study I conducted at Kyoto University (Tanase

1987, 47), the law students were asked to write down the names of the Supreme Court justices they knew. More than half of them could not recollect any name at all, and among those who could recollect, the majority knew only one, and a few knew only three of fifteen incumbent justices.

10. Besides the retainer fee which is paid initially, Japanese lawyers typically receive the contingent fees when the case successfully concludes. But, the amount is relatively low, 10 to 15 percent of the award. So, in the SMON case, as in other mass-tort cases, the fee was not enough to sustain the lawyers' practices. Especially considering the number of lawyers involved, the length of the proceedings, and the amount of total awards, entrepreneurial lawyers have no place in such mass-injury cases.

11. Compare this with the first article of American Bar Association Model Rules of Professional Conduct, "A lawyer shall provide competent representation to a client" (Rule 1.1).

12. Typically, when the national compensation system is established, with or without government money being used, the public reason is mainly to forestall the litigation and consequent financial burdens so that otherwise useful activities are not hindered. The typical example is the establishment of the Vaccination Compensation system with the waiver of indemnity rights against the pharmaceutical companies.

13. This political rhetoric is typical in late modernization. When the government tried to modernize Japan in the late nineteenth century, it had to borrow the framework of European nations, and the modernization was meant to catch up to the already modernized Europe, the wrongs found in Japan were attributed to the gap with Europe. See Tanase (2001, 187).

14. Interestingly, however, when people in United States were asked (telephone survey; sample 1,013, in 2007) whether they agree with the following statement, "Should people be allowed to sue the government for failing to regulate materials that are known to be hazardous, such as asbestos?" the majority said (1)Yes: 70 percent, and (2) No: 24 percent (the rest, didn't know). Those who said "yes" tended to be more politically liberal and critical of the social hierarchy. They were also less punitive than those who said "no." See Tanase (2007a, 126).

15. I heard this remark at the International Asbestos Conference, organized by Ban Asbestos Network Japan, and held in Yokohama on November 23–24, 2007.

16. Such a story is abundant even in academic treatises of asbestos litigation. See, for example, Hensler (2002, 1899) and Stengel (2006, 223).

Chapter Fourteen

1. Thanks to John Grima for sharing this story with me and for helping me to interpret its significance. For their helpful comments on this article, thanks to Jaruwan Engel, Michael McCann, and Winnifred Sullivan.

2. *Discourse* here refers to widely shared patterns of thinking and speaking that shape perceptions and constrain assumptions about the "of course" nature of the social world.

3. Referring to jurors' conceptions of causation as "culturally based" is my own gloss on Malone, who does not use these terms.

4. My research on injuries in Thailand had two aspects. First, I retrieved and photo-copied every injury case litigated over a six-year period in the Chiangmai Provincial Court. Chiangmai is the name of a major province located in northern Thailand as well as the province's capital city. The city is the largest in the northern region, but much of the province is still rural. Litigation activity in the Provincial Court therefore reflected the conflicts and concerns of the residents of a major city as well as of the village society that surrounds it. The second aspect of my research involved extended, in-depth interviews with numerous Chiangmai residents, including thirty-five individuals who had been ad-mitted to one of Chiangmai's largest hospitals for treatment following serious accidents involving some type of interaction with another person. I conducted these interviews in Thai and attempted to learn about the causal explanations offered by individuals from a broad variety of social backgrounds. By locating a group of interviewees at a hospital, I was able to discuss injuries and causation with people who had not necessarily had any contact with the legal system. As it turned out, none of them viewed their injuries in terms of tort law, and none consulted an attorney. Their indifference to the law was paral-leled by the data I obtained from my research in the courthouse, where I found, surpris-ingly, that tort law appeared to play an even smaller role in relation to injuries than had been the case when I conducted similar research in Thailand twenty-five years earlier. For a more detailed explanation of my conclusion that there has been a net decrease in tort litigation per injury in Chiangmai from the mid-1960s to the present, see Engel (2005).

5. See description of fieldwork supra note 4.

6. Thiphaa uses the term *khraaw khrô,* or "fate," rather than *kam* (karma). Although Keyes (1977, 117) suggests that Thais consider fate to operate on different principles from karma and to exert its influence without regard to past misdeeds, it is apparent from Thiphaa's narrative and from many others I collected that fate can also be understood in terms of karmic laws of cause and effect. Most interviewees in this study used fate and karma interchangeably or paired together as "*khrô-kam.*"

7. In Thailand, as in some other civil law countries, the injured person has the right to prosecute a criminal case either by himself or in cooperation with the public prosecutor.

8. Reliable statistics on accident rates in Thailand over time do not exist. Since most injuries treated in the hospital are caused by highway accidents, however, the number of registered motor vehicles serves as a credible indirect measure of accident rates. In 1965, according to the annual *Statistical Reports of Changwat Chiangmai, National Statistical Office, Office of the Prime Minister, Thailand,* there were 8,740 registered motor vehicles in Chiangmai Province. In that year, 0.081 tort cases per 1,000 population were litigated in the Chiangmai Provincial Court. By 1997, there were 677,123 registered motor vehicles

but only 0.125 tort cases per 1,000 population. The number of motor vehicles had increased by a factor of 77. Presumably the number of accidents had also increased substantially, yet the tort litigation rate had remained almost the same over more than three decades. Furthermore, most of the tort cases litigated in 1997 were property damage claims. Only 9 cases involved personal injuries. See, generally, Engel (2005, 497).

9. *Oxendine v. Merrell Dow Pharmaceuticals, Inc.* (1986), discussed by Sanders (1998, 153).

Chapter Fifteen

1. Conversely, steroid use disproportionately affects young men. I do not directly address that problem because steroids are not commonly *prescribed* drugs (particularly not for bodybuilding). However, the sex discrimination remedies that I suggest later in this chapter should apply to any sex-specific pharmaceutical problem where the substance oppressively contributes to gender conformity.

2. In the case brought against the EPA for injuries suffered (or to be suffered) from exposure to toxins released from the collapse of the World Trade Center on September 11, 2001, Judge Deborah A. Batts refused to grant immunity to former EPA Secretary Christine Todd Whitman. The judge said the Secretary's reassurance to New Yorkers soon after the event that it was safe to return to their homes and offices was "conscience shocking" (*Benzman v. Whitman* 2006: 18).

Bibliography

Abbott, Carl, Stephen J. Leonard, and David McComb. 1994 (Rev). *Colorado: A History of the Centennial State*. Niwot: University Press of Colorado.

Abel, Richard L. 2003. *English Lawyers between Market and State*. New York: Oxford University Press.

Abraham, Kenneth. 2008. *The Liability Century*. Cambridge, MA: Harvard University Press.

Abrams, Kathyrn. 1994. "Title VII and the Complex Female Subject." *Michigan Law Review* 92:2479.

Acharyya, Bijay Kisor. 1914. *Codification in British India*. Calcutta: Banerji.

Adjin-Tettey, Elizabeth. 2004. "Replicating and Perpetuating Inequalities in Personal Injury Claims Through Female-Specific Contingencies." *McGill Law Journal* 49:309.

Agyemang, Tracy. 2006. "Reconceptualizing Child Sexual Exploitation as a Bias Crime Under the PROTECT Act." *Cardozo Journal of Law and Gender* 12:937.

Albertson, Stephanie, Erin Farley, and Valerie P. Hans. 2004. "Jury Decision Making," in *Encyclopedia of Applied Psychology,* Vol. 2, Charles Spielberger, ed. Oxford, UK: Elsevier Ltd.

Albright, Audra A. 1997. "Could This Be the Last Gasp? England's First Case Against the British Tobacco Industry." *Temple International and Comparative Law Journal* 11:363.

Allen, Charlotte. 1994. "Jurisprudence of Breasts." *Stanford Law and Policy Review* 5:83.

Allen, Ronald J., and Michael S. Pardo. 2003. "The Myth of the Law-Fact Distinction." *Northwestern University Law Review* 97:1769.

American Association of Pediatrics ("AAP") Policy. 2000. "Evaluation of the Newborn with Developmental Anomalies of the External Genitalia." *Pediatrics.* 106:138.

American Law Institute, 1965. *Restatement of Torts 2d*. St. Paul, MN: American Law Institute Publishers.

American Law Institute. 1998. *Restatement Third, Torts: Products Liability.* St. Paul, MN: American Law Institute Publishers.

Asahi Shimbun. 2002."In Applying Expert Testimony, Proceed with Care." (July 11).

Asahi Shimbun. 2003. "Ishi 3-nin, Tōron Hōshiki de Kantei" (With 3 physicians, a conference method of experts). Evening edition (January 8).

Associated Press. 2004. "Working Poor Face Higher Obesity Rate: Unhealthy Food is Cheaper, Easier to Obtain." Available online at http://www.msnbc.msn.com/ib/4440827/.

Austin, Regina. 1983. "The Insurance Classification Controversy." *University of Pennsylvania Law Review* 131:517.

Austin, Regina. 1988. "Employer Abuse, Worker Resistance, and the Tort of Infliction of Mental Distress." *Stanford Law Review* 41:1.

Austin, Regina. 1989. "Sapphire Bound." *Wisconsin Law Review* 1989:540.

Baker, Tom. 1995. "Constructing the Insurance Relationship: Sales Stories, Claims Stories and Insurance Contract Damages." *Texas Law Review* 72:1395.

Baker, Tom. 1996. "On the Genealogy of Moral Hazard." *Texas Law Review* 75:237.

Baker, Tom. 1998a. "Transforming Punishment Into Compensation: In the Shadow of Punitive Damages." *Wisconsin Law Review* 1998:211.

Baker, Tom. 1998b. "Reconsidering Insurance for Punitive Damages." *Wisconsin Law Review* 1998:101.

Baker, Tom. 2001. "Blood Money, New Money and the Moral Economy of Tort Law in Action." *Law & Society Review* 35:275.

Baker, Tom. 2005. *The Medical Malpractice Myth.* Chicago: University of Chicago Press.

Baker, Tom. 2006. "Liability Insurance as Tort Regulation: Six Ways that Liability Insurance Shapes Tort Law in Action." *Connecticut Insurance Law Journal* 12:1.

Baker, Tom. 2008. *Insurance Law and Policy: Cases Materials and Problems* (2nd edition). New York: Aspen Publishers.

Baker, Tom, and Sean S. Griffith. 2009. "How the Merits Matter: D&O Insurance and Settlements in Securities Class Actions." *University of Pennsylvania Law Review* 157: 755–836.

Balsara, S. D. 1970. "Law of Torts." *Annual Survey of Indian Law* 7:310.

Banzhaf III, John F. 2002. "Who Should Pay for Obesity?" *San Francisco Daily Journal* (February 4). Available online at http://banzhaf.net/docs.whopay.html.

Banzhaf III, John F. 2004. "Jurors Will Hold Fast Food Companies Liable for Obesity—Surveys Support For Plaintiffs Same in Obesity and Tobacco Cases." Accessed March 3, 2004, at http://banzhaf.net/obesitylinks.

Barr, Emily. 1994. "Fair Cop?" *Guardian* (July 28).

Barr, Robert. 1999. "Of Bananas, Tobacco, and Denning." *Solicitors Journal* 12 March: 252.

Bartlett, Katharine T. 1994. "Only Girls Wear Barettes: Dress and Appearance Standards, Community Norms, and Workplace Equality." *Michigan Law Review* 92:2541.

Bearak, Barry. 2000, "In India, The Wheels of Justice Hardly Move." *New York Times,* June 1, at A1.

Becker, Gary S. 1968. "Crime and Punishment: An Economic Approach." *Journal of Political Economy* 76:169.

Beisner, E. Calvin. 1991. "Restoring Sanity to Our Tort System." Accessed April 10, 2008, at http://www.reformed.org/webfiles/antithesis/index.html?mainframe=/webfiles/antithesis/v2n3/ant_v2n3_tort.html.

Bell, John. 2001. *French Legal Cultures.* Cambridge: Cambridge University Press.

Ben-Asher, Noa. 2006. "The Necessity of Sex Change: A Struggle for Intersex and Transsex Liberties." *Harvard Journal of Law & Gender* 29:51.

Bennetto, Jason. 1994a. "Police Pay £33,000 Over Assault Claim." *Independent* (July 26).

Bennetto, Jason. 1994b. "Two Face Charges in Drugs Row Inquiry." *Independent* (July 27).

Bennetto, Jason. 1994c. "Met Chief Attacks Lawyers." *Independent* (August 2).

Bennetto, Jason. 1995. "Verdict Opens Way for Action Against Officers." *Independent* (November 11).

Berger, Margaret A. 1997. "Eliminating General Causation: Notes Toward a New Theory of Justice and Toxic Torts." *Columbia Law Review* 97:2117.

Berger, Margaret A. 2005. "What Has a Decade of *Daubert* Wrought?" *American Journal of Public Health* 95:S59.

Berger, Margaret A., and Twerski, Aaron D. 2005. "Uncertainty and Informed Choice: Unmasking *Daubert.*" *Michigan Law Review* 104:257.

Bergstrom, Randolph E. 1992. *Courting Danger: Injury and Law in New York City, 1870–1910.* Ithaca, NY: Cornell University Press.

Bernstein, Anita. 1997. "Treating Sexual Harassment with Respect." *Harvard Law Review* 111:445.

Berridge, Virginia. 2004. "Militants, Manufacturers, and Governments: Postwar Smoking Policy in the United Kingdom," in *Unfiltered: Conflicts over Tobacco Policy and Public Health,* E. A. Feldman and R. Bayer, eds. Cambridge, MA: Harvard University Press.

Bharti, Harish. 2002. "Interview with Harish Bharti Regarding Victory." Available online at http://hbharti.com/h_bharti_mcd/interview_03_02.htm.

Black, Bernard S., Brian R. Cheffins, and Michael Klausner. 2006. "Outside Director Liability." *Stanford Law Review* 58:1055.

Blackless, Melanie, Anthony Charuvastra, Amanda Derryck, Anne Fausto-Sterling, Karl Lauzanne, and Ellen Lee. 2000. "How Sexually Dimorphic Are We? Review and Synthesis." *American Journal of Human Biology* 12:151.

Blankenburg, Ehrhard 1997. "Civil Litigation Rates as Indicators for Legal Culture," in *Comparing Legal Cultures,* David Nelken, ed. Aldershot, UK: Dartmouth.

Blankenburg, Ehrhard, and Freek Bruinsma. 1994 *Dutch Legal Culture* (2nd edition). Boston, MA: Deventer.

Blasi, Gary, and John T. Jost. 2006. "System Justification Theory and Research: Implications for Law, Legal Advocacy and Social Justice." *California Law Review* 94:1119.

Bloom, Anne. 2005. "Rupture, Leakage, and Reconstruction: The Body as a Site for the Enforcement and Reproduction of Sex-Based Legal Norms in the Breast Implant Controversy." *Columbia Journal of Gender and Law* 14:85.

Boot, Max. 1998. *Out of Order: Arrogance, Corruption, and Incompetence on the Bench.* New York: Basic Books.

Bora, Pranab. 1996. "A Man-Made Horror." *India Today* (January 15).

Bowling, Ben, and Coretta Phillips. 2002. *Racism, Crime and Justice.* New York: Longman.

Bragge, Lily. 2005. "Choosing the Right Gender." *The Age.* (February 1, 2005). Accessed October 20, 2007, at http://www.theage.com.au/articles/2005/01/31/1107020318710.html#.

Brickey, Kathleen F. 2006. "In Enron's Wake: Corporate Executives on Trial." *Journal of Criminal Law and Criminology* 96:397.

British Broadcasting Corporation. 2003. "The Secret Policeman." Documentary program, BBC 1. Oct. 21.

Bronaugh, Richard, Peter Barton, and Tsachi Keren-Paz. 2003. "An Inquiry Into the Merits of Redistribution Through Tort Law: Rejecting the Claim of Randomness." *Canadian Journal of Law and Jurisprudence* 16:91.

Brown, Arthur. 1998. *Police Governance in England and Wales.* London: Cavendish.

Brown, Colin. 1992. "Inquiry into Police May Affect Appeals." *Independent* (June 24).

Brownell, Kelly D., and Katherine Battle Horgen. 2003. *Food Fight: The Inside Story of the Food Industry, America's Obesity Crisis, and What We Can Do About It.* New York: McGraw-Hill.

Bureau of the Census. 1975. Historical Statistics of the United States 297, Series G.

Burns, John F. 1995. "As Fire's Toll Exceeds 400, Indians Seek Bodies of Kin." *New York Times* (December 25).

Butler, Judith. 1993. *Bodies That Matter.* New York: Routledge.

Cadden, Joan. 1993. *Meanings of Sex Difference in the Middle Ages: Medicine, Science, and Culture.* New York: Cambridge University Press.

Cady, Troy L. 1997. "Disadvantaging the Disadvantaged: The Discriminatory Effects of Punitive Damages Caps." *Hofstra Law Review* 25:1005.

Cain, Maureen. 2000. "Orientalism, Occidentalism and the Sociology of Crime." *British Journal of Criminology* 40:239.

Caldwell, Paulette A. 1991. "A Hair Piece: Perspectives on the Intersection of Race and Gender." *Duke Law Journal* 1991:365.

Campbell, Duncan. 1992a. "Disquiet Dogs Community Police Station." *Guardian* (January 31).

Campbell, Duncan. 1992b. "Police Suspected of Drugs Dealing." *Guardian* (January 3).

Campbell, Duncan. 1992c. "Thirty Officers are Named as Group Seeks Judicial Inquiry into Policing." *Guardian* (February 8).

Campbell, Duncan. 1992d. "Four Cleared of Police Drug 'Fit-Ups." *Guardian* (March 3).

Campbell, Duncan. 1992e. "DPP Gets New File on Police Station." *Guardian* (March 24).

Campbell, Duncan. 1992f. "Two Suspended After Police Inquiry." *Guardian* (June 24).

Campbell, Duncan.1992g. "Drug Arrest Put Police in the Front Line." *Guardian* (July 11).

Campbell, Duncan. 1992h. "Police Suspend Third Officer." *Guardian* (September 11).

Campbell, Duncan. 1993. "Police Station Cleared of Organized Drug-Dealing." *Guardian* (September 16).

Campbell, Duncan. 1994a. "Corruption Claims 'the Worst in 20 Years.'" *Guardian* (February 4).

Campbell, Duncan. 1994b. "Police Damages for Attack Victim." *Guardian* (July 5).

Campbell, Duncan. 1995a. "Violent Arrest in Poll Tax Riot Costs Met £30,000." *Guardian* (January 13).

Campbell, Duncan. 1995b. "Base Data," *Guardian* (March 28).

Campbell, Duncan. 1995c. "Police to Pay for Drugs Lies: Victim of Fabricated Evidence and Malicious Prosecution Accepts £76,000." *Guardian* (December 12).

Campbell, Duncan. 1996a. "Met Pays £150,000 after Assault on Kurd Refugees." *Guardian* (June 14).

Campbell, Duncan. 1996b. "Police Must Pay Record Damages." *Guardian* (March 29).

Campbell, Duncan. 1997. "Spotlight/Guardian Libel Case: Fighting for Truth on the Front Line." *Guardian* (February 8).

Carbado, Devon, and Mitu Gulati. 2000. "Working Identity." *Cornell Law Review* 85:1259.

Care, Alan. 2000. "Smoking Can Seriously Damage Your Litigation." *Independent* (May 30).

Carroll, Stephen J., Deborah R. Hensler, Jennifer Gross, Elizabeth M. Sloss, Matthias Schonlau, Allan Abrahamse, and J. Scott Ashwood. 2005. *Asbestos Litigation*. Santa Monica, CA: Rand Institute for Civil Justice.

Case, Mary Ann. 1995. "Disaggregating Gender from Sex and Sexual Orientation: The Effeminate Man in the Law and Feminist Jurisprudence." *Yale Law Journal* 105:31.

Central Law Journal. 1909. "A New York Court Draws The Color Line." *Central Law Journal* 69:118.

Chadbourn, James H. 1933. *Lynching and the Law*. New York: Johnson Reprint Co.

Chakravarty, Sayantan. 2003. "Uphaar Case: Pay a Price," *India Today* (May 5), at 44.

Chamallas, Martha. 1992. "Feminist Constructions of Objectivity: Multiple Perspectives in Sexual and Racial Harassment Litigation." *Texas Journal of Women and the Law* 1:95.

Chamallas, Martha. 2005. "Civil Rights in Ordinary Torts Cases: Race, Gender, and the Calculation of Economic Loss." *Loyola of Los Angeles Law Review* 38:1435.

Chamallas, Martha, and Jennifer B. Wriggins. Forthcoming 2009. *The Measure of Injury: Race, Gender and the Law of Torts*. New York: New York University Press.

Chase, Oscar. 2005. *Law, Culture, and Ritual: Disputing Systems in Cross-Cultural Context*. New York: New York University Press.

Chiarloni, Sergio. 1999. "Civil Justice and its Paradoxes: An Italian Perspective," in *Civil Justice in Crisis: Comparative Perspectives of Civil Procedure*, A.A.S. Zuckerman, ed. New York: Oxford University Press.

Chodesh, Hiram, Stephen Mayo, A. M. Ahmadi, and Abhishek M. Singhvi. 1997–98. "Indian Civil Justice Reform: Limitation and Preservation of the Adversarial Process." *New York University Journal of International Law and Politics* 30:1.

Clayton, Richard, and Hugh Tomlinson. 2004. *Civil Actions Against the Police*. London: Thomson/Sweet & Maxwell.

Clermont, Kevin M. 2004. "Standards of Proof in Japan and the United States." *Cornell International Law Journal* 37:263.

Clifford, James, and Marcus, George. 1986. *Writing Culture: The Poetics and Politics of Ethnography*. Berkeley: University of California Press.

CNN American Morning with Paula Zahn. 2002. "Lawsuit Trying to Prove Fast Food Chains Responsible For Making Us Fat." (July 26).

Colapinto, John. 2000. *As Nature Made Him: The Boy Who Was Raised as Girl*. New York: HarperCollins.

Colbert, Douglas L. 1990. "Challenging the Challenge: Thirteenth Amendment as a Prohibition Against the Racial Use of Peremptory Challenges." *Cornell Law Review* 76:1.

Cole, Anthony. 2007. "Commercial Arbitration in Japan: Contributions to the Debate on Japanese 'Non-Litigiousness.'" *New York University Journal of International Law and Politics (JILP)* 40:29.

Coleman, Brady. 2004. "Pragmatism's Insult: The Growing Interdisciplinary Challenge to American Harassment Jurisprudence." *Employee Rights and Employment Policy Journal* 8:239.

Collins, Cindy. 1997. "Product Liability . . . Bristol-Myers Squibb the Latest Winner in Breast Implant Controversy." *Inside Litigation* 10:11.

Coniff, Ruth. 1997. "It's All in Your Head." *The Stranger* (May 29).

Conley, John M., and William M. O'Barr. 1990. *Rules versus Relationships: The Ethnography of Legal Discourse*. Chicago, IL: University of Chicago Press.

Conway-Jones, Danielle. 2003. "Factual Causation in Toxic Tort Litigation: A Philosophical View of Proof and Uncertainty in Uncertain Disciplines." *University of Richmond Law Review* 35:875.

Cook, Douglas H. 2004. "A Faith-Based Perspective on Tort Causation." *Saint Thomas Law Review* 16:455.

Coombe, Rosemary J. 2000. "Contingent Articulations: A Critical Studies of Law," in *Law in the Domains of Culture*, Austin Sarat and Thomas Kearns, eds. Ann Arbor: University of Michigan Press.

Cotterrell, Roger. 1995. *Law's Community: Legal Theory in Sociological Perspective.* Oxford, UK: Clarendon Press.

Cotterrell, Roger. 1997. "Invoking Legal Culture: Debates and Dissents: The Concept of Legal Culture," in *Comparing Legal Cultures,* David Nelken, ed. Aldershot, UK: Dartmouth.

Cover, Robert M. 1983. "The Supreme Court, 1982 Term–Foreword: Nomos and Narrative." *Harvard Law Review* 97:4.

Crawford, William E. 1994. "Life on a Federal Island in a Civilian Sea." *Mississippi College Law Review* 15:1.

Crenshaw, Kimberle, 1992. "Race, Gender and Sexual Harassment." *Southern California Law Review* 65:1467.

Critser, Greg. 2000. "Let Them Eat Fat: The Heavy Truths About American Obesity." *Harper's* 100. (March).

Critser, Greg. 2004. *Fat Land: How Americans Became the Fattest People in the World.* Boston, MA: Houghton Mifflin.

Daily Yomiuri. 2003a. "Report: 32 Malpractice Suits Filed During 9-month Period" (January 11).

Daily Yomiuri. 2003b. "Patients' Families to Sue Hospital over Malpractice" (July 21).

Daily Yomiuri. 2005a. "Health Ministry Plans to Retrain Incompetent Docs" (February 21).

Daily Yomiuri. 2005b. "Specialists Group to Tackle Malpractice" (March 23).

Daniels, Stephen. 2006. Personal interview. Chicago IL. April 2, 2006.

Daniels, Stephen, and Joanne Martin. 1995. *Civil Juries and the Politics of Reform.* Evanston, IL: Northwestern University Press.

Daniels, Stephen, and Joanne Martin. 1998. "Punitive Damages, Change, and the Politics of Ideas: Defining Public Policy Problems." *Wisconsin Law Review* 1998:71.

Davies, Patricia Wynn. 1997. "Judges Curtail Juries' Ability to Punish Police Curbed by Court." *Independent* (February 20).

Davis, Stephen. 2005. "Smoke Screen." *New Statesman* (July 27).

Day, Martyn. 2006. "Tobacco Litigation." *Journal of Personal Injury Law* 1:1.

Day, Martyn, Paul Balen, and Geraldine McCool. 1995. *Multi-Party Actions.* London: Legal Action Group.

Daynard, Richard A. 1988. "Tobacco Liability Litigation as a Cancer Control Strategy." *Journal of the National Cancer Institute* 80:9.

Daynard, Richard A., Clive Bates, and Neil Franccey. 2000. "Tobacco Litigation Worldwide." *British Medical Journal* (BMJ.com online serial) (January 8).

Deane, John. 1996. "Civil Actions Will Not Deflect Police." *Press Association* (April 23).

Debroy, Bibek. 2002. "Losing a World Record." *Far Eastern Economic* (February 14).

Denver Chamber of Commerce. WH1216, Western History Collection, The Denver Public Library.

Desai, D. A. 1981. "Role and Structure of the Legal Profession." *Journal of the Bar Council of India* 8:112.

Dethloff, Henry C., and Robert R. Jones. 2000. "Race Relations in Louisiana, 1877–1898," in *XI The African-American Experience in Louisiana, Part B: From the Civil War to Jim Crow,* The Louisiana Purchase Bicentennial Series in Louisiana History, Charles Vincent, ed. Lafayette: Center for Louisiana Studies.

Dezalay, Yves, and Bryant Garth 1996. *Dealing in Virtue.* Chicago: University of Chicago Press.

Dhavan, Rajeev. 2003. "The Uphaar Case." *The Hindu* (May 2).

Diamond, Shari Seidman, and Neil Vidmar. 2001. "Jury Room Ruminations on Forbidden Topics." *Virginia Law Review* 87:1857.

Diamond, Shari Seidman, Neil Vidmar, Mary Rose, Leslie Ellis, and Beth Murphy. 2003. "Juror Discussions During Civil Trials: Studying an Arizona Innovation." *Arizona Law Review* 45:1.

Dingwall, Robert, and Emilie Cloatre. 2006. "Vanishing Trials? An English Perspective." *Journal of Dispute Resolution* 22:51.

Dixon, Bill, and Graham Smith. 1998. "Laying Down the Law: The Police, the Courts and Legal Accountability." *International Journal of the Sociology of Law* 26:419.

Dixon, David. 1997. *Law in Policing: Legal Regulation and Police Practices.* Oxford, UK: Oxford University Press.

Dobbs, Dan B. 2000. *The Law of Torts.* St. Paul, MN: West Group.

Dorsett, Lyle W., and Michael McCarthy. 1986. *The Queen City: A History of Denver* (2nd edition). Boulder, CO: Pruett Publishing Company.

Dudas, Jeffrey. 2003. "Rights, Resentment, and Social Change: Treaty Rights in Contemporary America." Doctoral Dissertation, University of Washington.

Dworkin, Andrea. 1983. *Right Wing Women.* New York: Perigee Books.

Dyer, Clare. 1988. "Police Agree to 20,000 Pounds Arrests Deal." *Guardian* (November 21).

Dyer, Clare. 1997a. "Custody Deaths Provoke European Inquiry." *Guardian* (September 8).

Dyer, Clare. 1997b. "DPP Loses Final Say on Deaths in Custody." *Guardian* (July 29).

Ehrenreich, Rosa. 1999. "Dignity and Discrimination: Toward A Pluralistic Understanding of Workplace Harassment." *Georgetown Law Journal* 88: 1.

Eidsmore, Daniel C., and Pamela K. Edwards. 1998/99. "Home Liability Coverage: Does the Criminal Acts Exclusion Work Where the 'Expected or Intended' Exclusion Failed?" *Connecticut Insurance Law Journal* 5:707.

Eisenberg, Theodore, Paula L. Hannaford-Agor, Valerie P. Hans, Nicole L. Waters, G. Thomas Munsterman, Stewart J. Schwab, and Martin T. Wells. 2005. "Judge-Jury Agreement in Criminal Cases: A Partial Replication of Kalven and Zeisel's *The American Jury.*" *Journal of Empirical Legal Studies* 2:171.

Eligman, David, Joyce Kim, and Molly Biklen. 2003. "Proving Causation: The Use and Abuse of Medical and Scientific Evidence Inside the Courtroom—An Epidemiologist's Critique of the Judicial Interpretation of the *Daubert* Ruling." *Food and Drug Law Journal* 58:223.

Ellman, Ira Mark, and Stephen D. Sugarman. 1996. "Spousal Emotional Abuse as a Tort?" *Maryland Law Review* 55:1268.

Ellsworth, Phoebe. 1989. "Are Twelve Heads Better than One?" *Law & Contemporary Problems* 52:205.

Engel, David M. 1984. "The Oven-Bird's Song: Insiders, Outsiders, and Personal Injuries in an American Community." *Law & Society Review* 18:551.

Engel, David M. 2005. "Globalization and the Decline of Legal Consciousness: Torts, Ghosts, and Karma in Thailand." *Law & Social Inquiry* 30:469.

Epp, Charles R. 1998. *The Rights Revolution.* Chicago, IL: University of Chicago Press.

Epstein, Richard A. 1999. *Torts.* Gaithersburg, MD: Aspen Law & Business.

Ericson, Richard, Aaron Doyle, and Dean Barry. 2003. *Insurance as Governance.* Toronto: University of Toronto Press.

Espinoza, Leslie, and Angela P. Harris. 1997. "Afterward: Embracing the Tar-Baby: Lat-Crit Theory and the Sticky Mess of Race." *California Law Review.* 85:1585.

Eugenides, Jeffrey. 2002. *Middlesex.* New York: Picador.

Evening Standard. 1992. "Drugs, Denials, and the Ghosts Who Won't Go Away." (February 3).

Ewald, Francois. 1991. "Insurance and Risk," in *The Foucault Effect: Studies in Governmentality,* G. Burchell et al. eds. Chicago, IL: University of Chicago Press.

Ewick, Patricia, and Susan S. Silbey. 1998. *The Common Place of Law: Stories from Everyday Life.* Chicago, IL: University of Chicago Press.

Executive Risk Indemnity, Inc. 1996. Broad Form Directors and Officers' Liability Insurance Policy. Simsbury, CT.

Executive Risk Indemnity, Inc. 1998. "Medical Practitioners Professional Liability and Legal Defense Reimbursement Policy." Simsbury, CT.

Fact Finding Mission. 2004. *Reports: Surviving Bhopal.* Available online at http://www.bhopalffm.org.

Farrell, Sean. 2000. "U.K. Group Actions Don't Pay Like U.S. Class Actions." *National Law Journal* (July 10), at B20.

Feigenson, Neal. 2000. *Legal Blame: How Jurors Think and Talk about Accidents.* Washington, DC: American Psychological Association.

Feinberg, Kenneth R. 2005. *What Is a Life Worth?: The Unprecedented Effort to Compensate Victims of 9/11.* New York: Public Affairs.

Feld, Andrew. 2006. "Culture and Medical Malpractice: Lessons from Japan. Is the "Reluctant Plaintiff"a Myth?" *American Journal of Gastroenterology* 101:1949.

Feldman, Eric A. 1997. "Patients' Rights, Citizen's Movements, and Japanese Legal Culture," in *Comparing Legal Cultures,* David Nelkin, ed. Aldershot, UK: Dartmouth.

Feldman, Eric A. 2000. "Blood Justice: Courts, Conflict, and Compensation in Japan, France and the United States." *Law and Society Review* 34:651.

Feldman, Eric A. 2007. "Law, Culture, and Conflict: Dispute Resolution in Postwar Japan," in *Law in Japan: A Turning Point,* Daniel H. Foote, ed. Seattle: University of Washington Press.

Felstiner, William L. F., et al. 1980. "The Emergence and Transformation of Disputes: Naming, Blaming, and Claiming." *Law and Society Review* 15:631.

Field, Richard H., Benjamin Kaplan, and Kevin M. Clermont. 2007. *Materials for a Basic Course in Civil Procedure* (9th edition). New York: Foundation Press.

Field, Stewart, and David Nelken. 2007. "Early Intervention and the Cultures of Youth Justice: A Comparison of Italy and Wales," in *European Ways of Law,* Volkmar Gessner and David Nelken, eds. Oxford, UK: Hart.

Finkel, Norman J. 1995. *Commonsense Justice: Jurors' Notions of the Law.* Cambridge, MA: Harvard University Press.

Finley, Lucinda M. 1997. "Female Trouble: The Implications of Tort Reform for Women." *Tennessee Law Review* 64:847.

Finley, Lucinda M. 1999. "Guarding the Gate to the Courthouse: How Trial Judges Are Using Their Evidentiary Screening Role to Remake the Tort Causation Rules." *DePaul Law Review* 49:335.

Finley, Lucinda M. 2004. "The Hidden Victims of Tort Reform: Women, Children, and the Elderly." *Emory Law Journal* 53:1263.

Fiore, Michael C., Paula A. Keller, and Timothy B. Baker. 2005. "The Justice Department's Case against the Tobacco Companies." *New England Journal of Medicine* (September 8) 353:972.

Fisk, Catherine L. 2001. "Humiliation at Work." *William & Mary Journal of Women & Law* 8:73.

Flood, John. 2006. Personal Interview. Stirling, Scotland, March 29, 2006.

Ford, Richard. 1995. "Racial Arrest Victim Wins Police Damages." *Times* (March 17).

Ford, Richard. 1996a. "Victim of Beating by Police Wins £125,000." *Times* (July 19).

Ford, Richard. 1997b. "Court Limits Exemplary Damages Against Police." *Times* (February 20).

Ford, Richard. 1996b. "Policeman's Victim Awarded a Record £302,000 for Attack." *Times* (April 27).

Franke, Katherine, 1997. "What's Wrong With Sexual Harassment?" *Stanford Law Review* 49:691.

Friedman, Jonathan. 1994. *Cultural Identity and Global Process.* London: Sage.

Friedman, Lawrence M. 1985a. *A History of American Law* (2nd edition). New York: Simon & Schuster.

Friedman, Lawrence M. 1985b. *Total Justice.* New York: Russell Sage.

Friedman, Lawrence M. 1987. "Civil Wrongs: Personal Injury Law in the Late 19th Century." *American Bar Foundation Research Journal* 1987:351.

Friedman, Lawrence M. 1990. *The Republic of Choice: Law, Society and Culture.* Cambridge, MA: Harvard University Press.

Friedman, Lawrence. 1994. "Is there a Modern Legal Culture?" *Ratio Juris* 7:117. Friedman, Lawrence M. 1997. "The Concept of Legal Culture: A Reply," in *Comparing Legal Cultures,* David Nelken, ed. Aldershot, UK: Dartmouth.

Friedman, Lawrence M. 2002. *American Law in the Twentieth Century.* New Haven, CT: Yale University Press.

Friedman, Lawrence M. 2005. *History of American Law* (3rd edition). New York: Simon and Schuster.

Friedman, Lawrence M., and Jack Ladinsky. 1967. "Social Change and the Law of Industrial Accidents." *Columbia Law Review,* 67:50.

Friedman, Lawrence M., and Robert Percival. 1976. "A Tale of Two Courts: Litigation in Alameda and San Benito Counties." *Law and Society Review* 10:267.

Friedman, Lawrence M., and Thomas Russell. 1990. "More Civil Wrongs: Personal Injury Litigation, 1901–1910." *American Journal of Legal History* 34:295.

Friedman, Lissy C., and Richard A. Daynard. 2007. "Scottish Court Dismisses a Historic Smoker's Suit." *Tobacco Control* 16:4.

Fuller, Lon L., and William R. Perdue, Jr. 1936–1937. "The Reliance Interest in Contract Damages: I." *Yale Law Journal* 46:52.

Galanter, Marc. 1968. "The Displacement of Traditional Law in Modern India." 24 *Journal of Social Issues* 24:65.

Galanter, Marc. 1983. "Reading the Landscape of Disputes: What We Know and Don't Know (And Think We Know) about Our Allegedly Contentious and Litigious Society." *UCLA Law Review* 31:4.

Galanter, Marc. 1996. "Real World Torts: An Antidote to Anecdote." *Maryland Law Review* 55:1093.

Galanter, Marc. 1998. "An Oil Strike in Hell: Contemporary Legends about the Civil Justice System." *Arizona Law Review* 40:717.

Galanter, Marc. 2001. "Contract in Court, or Almost Everything You May or May Not Want to Know about Contract Litigation." *Wisconsin Law Review* 2001: 577.

Galanter, Marc. 2002. "Law's Elusive Promise: Learning from Bhopal," in *Transnational Legal Processes: Globalization and Power Disparities,* Michael Likosky, ed. London: Butterworths.

Galanter, Marc. 2004a. "Bread for the Poor, Access to Justice and the Rights of the Needy in India." *Hastings Law Review* 55:789.

Galanter, Marc. 2004b. "The Vanishing Trial: An Examination of Trials and Related Matters in Federal and State Courts." *Journal of Empirical Legal Studies* 3:459.

Galanter, Marc. 2005. *Lowering the Bar: Lawyer Jokes and Legal Culture.* Madison: University of Wisconsin Press.

Galanter, Marc. 2007. "Everyday Law" (unpublished manuscript on file with the author).

Galanter, Marc, and Jay Krishnan. 2003. "Debased Informalism: Lok Adalats and Legal Rights in Modern India," in *Beyond Common Knowledge: Empirical Approaches to the Rule of Law,* Erik G. Jensen and Thomas C. Heller, eds. Stanford, CA: Stanford University Press.

Galanter, Marc, and Jayanth Krishnan. 2004. "Bread for the Poor, Access to Justice and the Rights of the Needy in India." *Hastings Law Review* 55:789.

Galanter, Marc, and David Luban. 1993. "Poetic Justice: Punitive Damages and Legal Pluralism." *American University Law Review* 42:1393.

Garapon, Antoine. 1995. "French Legal Culture and the Shock of Globalization." *Social and Legal Studies* 4:493.

Gardner, David. 2000. "Weighed Down by an Old Economy." *Financial Times,* 31 (Oct. 17).

Garland, David. 2000. *The Culture of Control.* Oxford, UK: Oxford University Press.

Geertz, Clifford. 1973. "Thick Description: Towards an Interpretive Theory of Culture," in Clifford Geertz, *The Interpretation of Culture.* New York: Basic Books.

Geertz, Clifford. 1983. *Local Knowledge: Further Essays in Interpretive Anthropology.* New York: Basic Books.

Gergen, Mark, 1996. "A Grudging Defense of the Role of Collateral Torts in Wrongful Termination Litigation." *Texas Law Review* 74:1709.

Gerlin, Andrea, 1994. "A Matter of Degree." *Wall Street Journal* (September 1).

Gertner, Nancy, and Judith H. Mizner. 1997. *The Law of Juries.* Little Falls, NJ: Glasser Legalworks.

Gessner, Volkmar, Armin Hoeland, and Varga Casba (eds). 1996. *European Legal Cultures.* Aldershot, UK: Dartmouth.

Gilles, Stephen. 2006. "The Judgment Proof Society." *Washington and Lee Law Review* 63:603.

Ginsburg, Tom, and Glenn Hoetker. 2006. "The Unreluctant Litigant? An Empirical Analysis of Japan's Turn to Litigation." *Journal of Legal Studies* 35:31.

Givelber, Daniel. 1982. "The Right to Minimum Social Decency and the Limits of Evenhandedness: Intentional Infliction of Mental Distress by Outrageous Conduct." *Columbia Law Review* 82:52.

Gladwell, Malcolm. 1992. "FDA Will Allow Limited Use of Silicone-Gel Breast Implants." *The Washington Post* (April 17).

Gledhill, A. 1951. *The Republic of India: The Development of its Laws and Constitution.* London: Stevens.

Glenn, Brian. 2000. "The Shifting Rhetoric of Insurance Denial." *Law & Society Review* 34:779.

Golanski, Alani. 2003. "General Causation at the Crossroads in Toxic Tort Cases." *Pennsylvania State Law Review* 108:479.

Goodstein, Phil. 2003. *Denver From the Bottom Up: From Sand Creek to Ludlow*. Denver, CO: New Social Publications.

Government of India. 1925. *Civil Justice Committee 1924–25 Report*. Calcutta: Government of India.

Grattet, Ryken. 1997. "Sociological Perspectives on Legal Change: The Role of the Legal Field in the Transformation of the CommonLaw of Industrial Accidents." *Social Science History* 21:359.

Gray, Steven. 2005. "At Fast-Food Chains, Era of the Giant Burger (Plus Bacon) Is Here." *Wall Street Journal* (January 27).

Green, Leon. 1956–1957. "Jury Trial and Proximate Cause." *Texas Law Review* 35:357.

Greene, Edie, and Brian H. Bornstein. 2003. *Determining Damages: The Psychology of Jury Awards*. Washington, DC: American Psychological Association.

Greenhouse, Carol J., Barbara Yngvesson, and David M. Engel. 1994. *Law and Community in Three American Towns*. Ithaca, NY: Cornell University Press.

Gross, Ariela J. 1998. "Litigating Whiteness: Trials of Racial Determination in the Nineteenth-Century South." *Yale Law Journal*. 108:109.

Guardian 1993. (No title.) (London) (November 8).

Guardian. 1996a. "Man Wins £27,500 After Police Assault." (July 12).

Guardian. 1996b. "Protester Gets £30,000." (July 25).

Guthrie, Chris, Jeffrey J. Rachlinski, and Andrew J. Wistrich. 2001. "Inside the Judicial Mind." *Cornell Law Review* 86:777.

Hadfield, Gillian K. 2000. "The Price of Law: How the Market for Lawyers Distorts the Judicial System." *Michigan Law Review* 98:953.

Halarnkar, Samar, and Sayantan Chakravarty. 1997. "Tickets to Hell." *India Today* (June 30), at 30.

Haley, John. 1978. "The Myth of the Reluctant Litigant." *Journal of Japanese Studies* 4:359–390.

Hall, Stuart, Chas Critcher, Tony Jefferson, John Clarke, and Brian Roberts. 1978. *Policing the Crisis: Mugging, the State, and Law and Order*. New York: Holmes and Meier.

Haltom, William, and Michael McCann. 2004. *Distorting the Law: Politics, Media, and the Litigation Crisis*. Chicago, IL: University of Chicago Press.

Hamilton, V. Lee, and Joe Sanders. 1992. *Everyday Justice: Responsibility and the Individual in Japan and the United States*. New Haven, CT: Yale University Press.

Hampton, Jean. 1992. "Correcting Harms Versus Righting Wrongs: The Goal of Retribution." *UCLA Law Review* 39:1659.

Haney Lopez, Ian F. 1994. "The Social Construction of Race: Some Observations on Illusion, Fabrication and Choice." *Harvard Civil Rights-Civil Liberties Law Review* 29:1.

Hannaford, Paula L., Valerie P. Hans, and G. Thomas Munsterman. 2000. "Permitting Jury Discussions During Trial: Impact of the Arizona Reform." *Law & Human Behavior* 24:359.

Hans, Valerie P. 1998. "The Illusions and Realities of Jurors' Treatment of Corporate Defendants." *DePaul Law Review* 48:327.

Hans, Valerie P. 2000. *Business on Trial: The Civil Jury and Corporate Responsibility.* New Haven, CT: Yale University Press.

Harding, Andrew. 2001. "Comparative Law and Legal Transplantation in South East Asia," in *Adapting Legal Cultures,* David Nelken and Johannes Feest, eds. Oxford, UK: Hart.

Harding, Andrew, and Elsin Orucu (eds). 2002. *Comparative Law for the 21st Century.* Amsterdam: Kluwer.

Harris, Cheryl J. 1993. "Whiteness as Property." *Harvard Law Review* 106:1709.

Harrison, John, Stephen Cragg, and Heather Williams. 2005. *Police Misconduct: Legal Remedies* (4th edition). London: Legal Action Group.

Hart, H.L.A. 1968. *Punishment and Responsibility: Essays on the Philosophy of Law.* Oxford, UK: Oxford University Press.

Hayden, Lisa A. 1999. "Gender Discrimination Within the Reproductive Health Care System." *Journal of Law and Health* 13:171.

Hayden, Robert M. 1991. "The Cultural Logic of a Political Crisis: Common Sense, Hegemony, and the Great American Liability Insurance Famine of 1986," in *Studies in Law, Politics, and Society,* Austin Sarat and Susan S. Silbey, eds. Greenwich, CT: JAI Press.

Hebert, L. Camille, 2001. "Sexual Harassment as Discrimination "Because of . . . Sex": Have We Come Full Circle?" *Ohio Northern University Law Review* 27:439.

Hegde, Sasheej. 1987. "Limits to Reform: A Critique of the Contemporary Discourse to Judicial Reform in India." *Journal of the Indian Law Institute* 29:153.

Heimer, Carol. 1985. *Reactive Risk and Rational Action: Managing Moral Hazard in Insurance Contracts.* Berkeley: University of California Press.

Heller, Janice. 1991. "Lawyers Lash Out at Moira Lasch; Colleagues Blast Prosecutor's Tactics in Smith Trial." *New Jersey Law Journal* (December 23).

Henderson, James A. 2005. "Managing the Negligence Concept: Respect for the Rule of Law," in *Exploring Tort Law,* M. Stuart Madden, ed. New York: Cambridge University Press.

Hensler, Deborah R. 2002. "As Time Goes By: Asbestos Litigation After *Amchem* and *Ortiz.*" *Texas Law Review* 80:1899.

Her Majesty's Inspectorate of the Constabulary. 1996/97. *Winning the Race: Policing Plural Communities.* London: HMSO.

Hermer, Laura. 2002. "Paradigms Revised: Intersex Children, Bioethics & the Law." *Annals of Health Law* 11:195.

Heuer, Larry, and Steven D. Penrod. 1994. "Trial Complexity: A Field Investigation of Its Meaning and Its Effects." *Law and Human Behavior* 18:29.

Heyderbrand, Wolf. 2001. "Globalization and the Rule of Law at the End of the 20th Century," in *Social Processes and Patterns of Legal Control: European Yearbook of Sociology of Law,* Alberto Febbrajo, David Nelken, and Vittorio Olgiati, eds. Milan: Giufre.

Higginbotham, Patrick. 2002. "So Why Do We Call Them Trial Courts?" *Southern Methodist University Law Review* 55:1405.

Higgins, Marguerite. 2003. "Advocates Meet to Plan Big Mac Attack on Fat." *The Washington Times.* 6/22. Available online at http://banzhaf.net/docs/wtmeet1.html.

Hindu. 1997. "India National Thermal Power Corp Stir on as Mishap Toll Goes Up." (May 13), at 6.

Hindu. 1989. "Toll Rises to Four in Railway Station Stampede" (March 21), at 9.

Hindu. 2002. "Deadline to Wrap Up Uphaar Trial" (April 5).

Hindu. 2005. "Court Orders Ex-gratia Payment to a Patient" (July 14).

Hindustan Times. 1989. "Bhopal Gas Settlement: Govt Justifies Amount" (March 8).

Hindustan Times. 2007. "Court wants Uphaar Case to Move Faster" (May 18).

Hoffman, Beatrix. 2003. "Scientific Racism, Insurance, and Opposition to the Welfare State: Federick L. Hoffman's Transatlantic Journey." *Journal of the Gilded Age and Progressive Era* 2:2. Available online at www.historycooperative.org/journals/jga/2.2/hoffman/html.

Holmes, Oliver Wendell. 1887. *The Common Law.* London: Macmillan.

Home Office. 2000. *Stephen Lawrence Inquiry—Home Secretary's Action Plan: First Annual Report on Progress.* London: Home Office.

Horowitz, Morton. 1977. *The Transformation of American Law: 1780–1860.* Cambridge, MA: Harvard University Press.

Howard, Philip K. 1994. *The Death of Common Sense: How Law is Suffocating America.* New York: Random House.

Howells, Geraint. 1998. "Tobacco Litigation in the U.S.: Its Impact in The United Kingdom." *Southern Illinois Law Journal* 22:693.

Huber, Peter. 1988. *Liability: The Legal Revolution and Its Consequences.* New York: Basic Books.

Hunter, William. 1897. *Annals of Rural Bengal.* London: Smith, Elder and Company.

Huntley, Jill E., and Mark Costanzo. 2003. "Sexual Harassment Stories: Testing a Story-Mediated Model of Juror Decision-Making in Civil Litigation." *Law and Human Behavior* 27:29.

Ilminen, Gary R. 2001. "Drug Misuse, Overuse Common in Nursing Homes, Report Says." *NurseWeek* (Sept. 27). Available online at www.nurseweek.com/industrypulse/drugs.

Independent. 1994. "Police Could Face Criminal Charges After Drugs Inquiry." (Feb. 4).

Independent. 1996a. "Police to Pay Man £108,000 Damages." (April 30).

Independent. 1996b. "Thuggery in Uniform." (March 31).

Independent. 1996c. "Anger Grows At Soaring Cost of Police Assaults." (March 30).

Indo-Asian News Service. 2008. "Ansal's Bail Plea Rejected, to Spend Diwali in Jail." (Oct. 23).

"Iryō ni Kansuru Yoron Chōsa." 2005. Accessed July 21, 2005, at http://www8.cao.go.jp/survey/s47/S48-02-47-15.html.

Jacoby, Russell. 1975. *Social Amnesia: A Critique of Conformist Psychology from Adler to Laing*. Boston, MA: Beacon Press.

Jagannadha Rao, M. 1997. "Need for More ADR Centres and Training for Lawyers and Personnel," in *Alternative Dispute Resolution: What Is It and How It Works*, P. C. Rao and William Sheffield, eds. Delhi: Universal Law Publications.

Jain, M. P. 1966. *Outlines of Indian Legal History*. Bombay: N.M. Tripathi.

Jain, Sarah S. Lochlann. 2006. *Injury: The Politics of Product Design and Safety Law in the United States*. Princeton, NJ: Princeton University Press.

Japan Bar Association. 2006. Accessed March 22, 2007, at www.nichibenren.or.jp/jp/katsudo/toukei/suii2.html.

Japan Council for Quality Health Care (JCQHC). 2005. Accessed March 22, 2007, at http://jcqhc.or.jp/html/english/about_jcqhc.htm.

Jettinghoff, Alex. 2001. "State Formation and Legal Change: On the Impact of International Politics," in *Adapting Legal Culture*, David Nelken and Johannes Feest, eds. Oxford, UK: Hart Publishing.

Johnson, David. 2002. *The Japanese Way of Justice*. Oxford, UK: Oxford University Press.

Johnson, Vincent, and Alan Gunn. 2005. *Studies in American Tort Law* (3rd edition). Durham, NC: Carolina Academic Press.

Jones, Trina. 2000. "Shades of Brown: The Law of Skin Color." *Duke Law Journal* 49:1487.

Justice System Reform Council. 2001. "Recommendations of the Justice System Reform Council: For a Justice System to Support Japan in the 21st Century." Accessed March 22, 2007, at www.kantei.go.jp/foreign/judiciary/2001/0612report.html.

Kagan, Robert. 2001. *Adversarial Legalism: The American Way of Law*. Cambridge, MA: Harvard University Press.

Kagan, Robert. 2007. "American and European Ways of Law: Six Entrenched Differences," in *European Ways of Law*, Volkmar Gessner and David Nelken, eds. Oxford, UK: Hart Publishing.

Kahan, Dan, David Hoffman, and Don Braman. In press. "Whose Eyes Are You Going to Believe? *Scott v. Harris* and the Perils of Cognitive Illiberalism." *Harvard Law Review* 122.

Kalven, Harry, Jr., and Hans Zeisel. 1966. *The American Jury*. Boston, MA: Little, Brown & Co.

Kalven, Harry, Jr. 1964. "The Dignity of the Civil Jury." *Virginia Law Review* 50:1055.

Kamir, Orit. 2006. *Framed: Women in Law and Film*. Durham, NC, and London: Duke University Press.

Kansas City Star. 1909. "Court Draws a Color Line—Negroes Can't Be Damaged as Much as White Men, Says a Judge" (May 22), p. 9, col. 2.

Karlen, Josh, and Bob Van Voris. 1998. "Web Fuels Suits Against Tobacco Worldwide." *National Law Journal* (March 30).

Karsten, Peter. 1998. "Enabling the Poor to Have Their Day in Court: The Sanctioning of Contingency Fee Contracts, A History to 1940." *DePaul Law Review* 47:231.

Kassebaum, Gene. 1989. "ADR in India: The Lok Adalat as an Alternative to Court Litigation of Personal Injury and Criminal Cases in South India" (unpublished manuscript on file with author).

Kaufman, Marc. 2006. "Plan B Battles Embroil States." *Washington Post* (February 27).

Kaur, Naunidhi. 2003. "Of Profit Motive and Negligence." *Frontline*, 20(10), May 10–23.

Kawabata, Yoshiharu. 2000. "Shimin no Shihō no Jitsugen no tame ni Hōsō-Ichigen, Bai-Sanshin Seido to Kokumin Shuken," 5 *Gakujutsu no Dōkō* 27.

Kawabata, Yoshiharu. 2006. "Health-Related Litigation and its Reforms in Japan Through the Eyes of Practitioner." Presented at the Symposium on Health and Justice in Asia, Dickinson College (April).

Kawashima, Takeyoshi. 1963. "Dispute Resolution in Contemporary Japan," in *Law in Japan: the Legal Order in a Changing Society,* Arthur von Mehren, ed. Cambridge, MA: Harvard University Press.

Keeton, W. Page (general editor), Dan B. Dobbs, Robert E. Keeton, and David G. Owen. 1984. *Prosser and Keeton on Torts* (5th edition). St. Paul, MN: West Publishing Co.

Keleman, R. Dan, and Eric C. Sibbitt. 2002. "The Americanization of Japanese Law." *University of Pennsylvania Journal of International Economic Law* 223:69.

Kelsey, Tim. 1995. "Shot Jogger Sues After Bungled Stake-Out." *Independent* (February 1).

Kennedy, Randall. 1997. *Race, Crime, and the Law.* New York: Pantheon.

Kerr, Norbert L., Robert J. MacCoun, and Geoffrey P. Kramer. 1996. "Bias in Judgment: Comparing Individuals and Groups," *Psychological Review* 103: 687.

Kersh, Rogan, and James Morone. 2002. "How the Personal Becomes Political: Prohibitions, Public Health, and Obesity." *Studies in American Political Development* 16:162.

Kessler, David A. 1992. "The Basis of the FDA's Decision on Breast Implants." *New England Journal of Medicine* 326:1713.

Keyes, Charles F. 1977. *The Golden Peninsula: Culture and Adaptation in Mainland Southeast Asia.* New York: Macmillan Publishing Co., Inc.

Kirby, Terry, 1992. "Policeman Received Pounds 1,000 Drugs Wage." *Independent* (July 11).

Kirby, Terry. 1990. "Policing the Police: Elderly Couple are Living in Fear After Attack by Officers." *Independent* (April 30).

Kirkland, Anna. 2008. *Fat Rights: Dilemmas of Difference and Personhood.* New York: New York University Press.

Kodama, Yasushi. 2007. "Iryō Anzen: How Safe is Enough?" 1339 *Jurist* 67 (August).

Kōmi, Masakatsu. 2000. "Symposium, Iryō Kago Soshō no Shinri ni tsuite" 1023 *Hanrei Times* (April), p. 24.

Koppelman, Andrew, 1996. *Antidiscrimination Law and Social Equality.* New Haven, CT: Yale University Press.

Kōsei Tōkei Yōran (Directory of Public Health Statutes). 2002. Accessed April 14, 2008, at http://wwwdbtk.mhlw.go.jp/toukei/youran/data16k/2-47.xls.

Kritzer, Herbert M. 1996. "Courts, Justice, and Politics in England," in *Courts, Law, and Politics in Comparative Perspective*, H. M. Kritzer et al., eds. New Haven, CT: Yale University Press.

Kritzer, Herbert M., W. A. Bogart, and Neil Vidmar. 1991. "The Aftermath of Injury: Cultural Factors in Compensation Seeking in Canada and the United States." *Law and Society Review* 25:499.

Kuper, Adam. 1999. *Culture: The Anthropologist's Account*. Cambridge, MA: Harvard University Press.

Kuroyanagi, Tatsuo. 2001. "Senmon Soshō no Kantei ni Tsuite." 120 *Hō no Shihai* 78–83 (January).

Kuroyanagi Tatsuo. 2005. Interview (on file with author). July. Tokyo, Japan.

Kurtz, Michelle. 2000. "Lesbian Wedding Allowed in Texas by Gender Loophole." Cox News Service (September 7, 2000). *Seattle Post-Intelligencer.*

Laquer, Thomas. 1990. *Making Sex: Body and Gender form the Greeks to Freud*. Cambridge, MA: Harvard University Press.

Lead Discovery, Ltd. 2006. Accessed April 4, 2006, at http://www.leaddiscovery.co.uk/reports/The%20Women's%20Health%20Outlook%20to%202008%20-%20Market%20and%20pipeline%20analysis% 20of%20major%20female%20disorders.html.

Leflar, Robert B., and Futoshi Iwata. 2005. "Medical Error as Reportable Event, as Tort, as Crime: A Transpacific Comparison." *Widener Law Review* 12:189.

Lempert, Richard O. 1981–1982. "Civil Juries and Complex Cases: Let's Not Rush to Judgment." *Michigan Law Review* 80:68.

Lempert, Richard. 1993. "Civil Juries and Complex Cases: Taking Stock after Twelve Years," in *Verdict: Assessing the Civil Justice System*, Robert F. Litan, ed. Washington, DC: Brookings.

Lenhardt. R. A. 2004. "Understanding the Mark: Race, Stigma, and Equality in Context." *New York University Law Review* 79:803.

Leonard, Stephen J., and Thomas J. Noel. 1990. *Denver: Mining Camp to Metropolis*. Niwot: University Press of Colorado.

Levit, Nancy. 1998. *The Gender Line: Men, Women, and the Law*. New York: New York University Press.

Levmore, Saul, and Kyle D. Logue. 2003. "Insuring Against Terrorism—and Crime." *Michigan Law Review* 102:268.

Likosky, Michael B. (ed.). 2002. *Transnational Legal Processes*. Cambridge: Cambridge University Press.

Lloyd-Bostock, Sally, and Cheryl Thomas. 2000. "The Continuing Decline of the English Jury," in *World Jury Systems*, Neil Vidmar, ed. New York: Oxford University Press.

Macchiaroli, Jean A. 1989–90. "Medical Malpractice Screening Panels: Proposed Model Legislation to Cure Judicial Ills." *George Washington Law Review* 58:181.

MacCoun, R. J. 1993. "Inside the Black Box: What Empirical Research Tells Us About Decisionmaking by Civil Juries," in *Verdict: Assessing the Civil Justice System,* Robert F. Litan, ed. Washington, DC: Brookings.

MacCoun, Robert J. 1996. "Differential Treatment of Corporate Defendants by Juries: An Examination of the 'Deep-Pockets' Hypothesis." *Law & Society Review* 30:121.

MacKinnon, Catharine A. 1979. *Sexual Harassment of Working Women: A Case of Sex Discrimination.* New Haven, CT, and London: Yale University Press.

MacKinnon, Catharine A. 1989. *Toward a Feminist Theory of the State.* Cambridge, MA: Harvard University Press.

MacKinnon, Catharine A. 2004. "Afterword," in Catharine A. MacKinnon and Reva B. Siegel, eds. *Directions in Sexual Harassment Law.* New Haven, CT, and London: Yale University Press.

MacPherson, William. 1999. *The Stephen Lawrence Inquiry.* London: HMSO.

Madeira, Jody Lynee. 2002. "Law as Reflection of Her/History: Current Institutional Perceptions of, and Possibilities for Protecting Transsexuals' Interest in Legal Determinations of Sex." *University of Pennsylvania Journal of Constitutional Law* 5:128.

Magruder, Calvert. 1936. "Mental and Emotional Disturbance in the Law of Torts." *Harvard Law Review* 44:1047.

Mainichi Daily News. 2003. "Malpractice Victims Demand Vice-Minister's Dismissal." (April 29).

Mainichi Shimbun. 2002. "Hirogaru, Kantei Hanare." (April 16), p. 3.

Mainichi Shimbun. 2003. "Menkyo Torikeshi" (Invalidating Licenses). (June 26).

Malone, Wex. 1956. "Ruminations on Cause-In-Fact." *Stanford Law Review* 9:60.

Mann, Kenneth. 1991. "Punitive Civil Sanctions: The Middleground Between Criminal and Civil Law." *Yale Law Journal* 101:1795.

Manor, James. 1993. *Power, Poverty and Poison: Disaster and Response in an Indian City.* New Delhi: Sage Publications.

Marder, Nancy S. 2006. *The Jury Process.* New York: Foundation Press.

Mather, Lynn. 1998. "Theorizing about Trial Courts: Lawyers, Policymaking, and Tobacco Litigation." *Law and Social Inquiry* 23:897.

McCann, Michael. 1986. *Taking Reform Seriously: Perspectives on Public Interest Liberalism.* Ithaca, NY: Cornell University Press.

McCann, Michael. 1994. *Rights at Work: Pay Equity Reform and the Politics of Legal Mobilization.* Chicago, IL: University of Chicago Press.

McCann, Michael, William Haltom, and Anne Bloom. 2001. "Java Jive: Genealogy of a Juridical Icon." *University of Miami Law Review* 56:113.

McClurg, Andrew J. 2005. "Dead Sorrow: A Story about Loss and a New Theory of Wrongful Death Damages." *Boston University Law Review* 85:1.

McCrystal, Cal. 1993. "The Wrong Side of the Law." *Independent* (November 21).

McKenzie, Ian K., and G. Patrick Gallagher. 1989. *Behind the Uniform: Policing in Britain and America.* New York: St. Martin's.

McNeely, Mary Coates. 1940. "The Genealogy of Liability Insurance Law." *University of Pittsburgh Law Review* 7:169.

McNeely, Mary Coates. 1941. "Illegality as a Factor in Liability Insurance." *Columbia Law Review* 41:26.

Mehta, Yogesh. 2000. *Lok Adalats and Public Interest Litigation.* Ahmedabad: Gujarat State Legal Services Authority.

Mendelsohn, Oliver. 1981. "Pathology of the Indian Legal System." *Modern Asian Studies* 15:823.

Menon, N. R. Madhava. 2000. "Lok Adalat: An Indian Contribution to World Jurisprudence." *Souvenir* 56.

Merry, Sally Engle. 1990. *Getting Justice and Getting Even: Legal Consciousness Among Working Class Americans.* Chicago, IL: University of Chicago Press.

Messick, Richard. 2002. Personal communication with author, January 14.

Metropolitan Police Authority. 2004. *Report of the MPA Scrutiny on MPS Stop and Search Practice.* London: Metropolitan Police Authority.

Milhaupt, Curtis J., and Mark D. West, eds. 2004. *Economic Organizations and Corporate Governance in Japan: The Impact of Formal and Informal Rules.* New York: Oxford University Press.

Mills, Heather. 1995. "Complaints Cost Scotland Yard £1.5M to Settle." *Independent* (September 7).

Mills, Heather. 1996a. "£220,000 Awarded to Police Assault Victim." *Independent* (March 29).

Mills, Heather. 1996b. "Police Chiefs Ignore Claims of Brutality." *Independent* (January 27).

Mills, Heather. 1996c. "Assault Case Settlement Costs £90,000." *Independent* (January 26).

Mills, Heather. 1996d. "Warnings About Neck Holds Failed to Prevent Death." *Independent* (January 26).

Milne, Seumas. 1991. "Police to Pay Pounds 425,000 to 39 Arrested in Miners' Strike." *Guardian* (June 20).

Minow, Martha. 1993. "Surviving Victim Talk." *University of California at Los Angeles Law Review* 40:1411.

Mitra, Sumit. 2000. "Objection Sustained." *India Today* (March 11), at 32.

Moog, Robert. 1997. *Whose Interests are Supreme: Organizational Politics in the Civil Courts in India.* Ann Arbor, MI: Association for Asian Studies.

Mott, Nicole L., Valerie P. Hans, and Lindsay Simpson. 2000. "What's Half a Lung Worth? Civil Jurors' Accounts of their Award Decision Making." *Law and Human Behavior* 24:401.

Mudur, Ganapati. 1998. "Indian doctors call for protection against patients' complaints." *BMJ.* Accessed March 3, 2007, at http://bmj.bmjjournals.com/cgi/content/full/316/7144/1558/a.

Mullin, John. 1994. "Police Damages for Six Wrongly Accused of Possessing Drugs." *Guardian* (July 19).

Muralidhar, S. 2004. The Fact Finding Mission Reports: Legal Aspects. Available online at http://www.bhopalffm.org/Legal%20Aspects.htm.

Murata, Wataru. 2000. "Symposium, Iryō Kago Soshō no Shinri ni tsuite." 1023 *Hanrei Times* (April), p. 18.

Murray, Christopher J. L., et al. 2006, September. "Eight Americas: Investigating Mortality Disparities across Race, Counties, and Race-Counties in the U.S." *PLoSMedicine* 3:260.

Myers, Paul, and Duncan Campbell. 1992. "Woman, 73, Wins 50,000 Pounds Against Met." *Guardian* (March 20).

Nakajima, Kazue et al. 2001. "Medical Malpractice and Legal Resolution Systems in Japan." *Journal of the American Medical Association* 285:1632.

Nakamura, Akiko. 2000. "Zenkoku Yoron Chōsa Shōhō: Isha o Shinrai Rokuwari Jyūni Nenkan de Jiwajiwa Teika." (Detailed Report of the National Public Opinion Survey: Trust in Doctors, 60%, Gradually Declining over 12 Years.) *Asahi Sōken Ripōto* 147:82.

National Law Journal. 1999. "U.K. Tobacco Suits Fail against Hurdle" (March 15), A16.

Nelken, David. 1995. "Understanding/Invoking Legal Culture," in David Nelken (ed.), special issue on "Legal Culture, Diversity and Globalization." *Social and Legal Studies* 4:435.

Nelken, David. (ed.). 1997. *Comparing Legal Cultures*. Aldershot, UK: Dartmouth.

Nelken, David. 1997. "Puzzling out Legal Culture: A Comment on Blankenburg," in *Comparing Legal Cultures*, David Nelken, ed. Aldershot, UK: Dartmouth.

Nelken, David. 2001. "Beyond the Metaphor of Legal Transplants? Consequences of Autopoietic Theory for the study of Cross-Cultural Legal Adaptation," in *Law's New Boundaries: The Consequences of Legal Autopoiesis*, Jiri Priban and David Nelken, eds. Aldershot, UK: Ashgate.

Nelken, David. 2003a. "Comparativists and Transferability," in *Comparative Legal Studies: Traditions and Transition*, Pierre Legrand and Roderick Munday, eds. Cambridge: Cambridge University Press.

Nelken, David. 2003b. "Beyond Compare? Criticising the American Way of Law." *Law and Social Inquiry* 28:181.

Nelken, David. 2004. "Using the Concept of Legal Culture." *Australian Journal of Legal Philosophy* 29:1.

Nelken, David. 2005. "Rethinking Legal Culture," in *Law and Sociology*, Michael Freeman, ed. Oxford, UK: Oxford University Press.

Nelken, David. 2007. "Three Problems in Employing the Concept of Legal Culture," in *Exploring Legal Cultures*, Freek Bussman and David Nelken, eds. Aldershot, UK: Dartmouth.

Nestle, Marion. 2003. *Food Politics: How the Food Industry Influences Nutrition and Health*. Berkeley: University of California Press.

New York Times. 1909. "Negro Not Equal to White: Suffers Less Humiliation in False Arrest, Court Holds" (May 22).

New York Times. 1995. "Mourners of Fire Victims in India Protest Hospital as Inadequate" (December 26), at A9.

New York Times (Editorial). 2006. "Three School Shootings" (October 3).

Nihon Ishikai. 2001. *Nihon Ishikai Ishi Baishō Sekinin Hoken* (The JMA's Medical Responsibility Compensation Insurance). Tokyo: Nihon Ishikai Press.

Nihon Ishikai. 2005. *Ishi News* (June 5), p. 1050. Available online at www.med.or.jp.

Nikkei Shinbun. 2002. "Karute Kantei Nado TV Kaigi De" (April 18).

Nishino, Kiichi. 2000. "Iryō Suijyun to Iryō Kankō" (Medical Standards and Medical Practice), in ta Yukio, ed., *Iryō Kago Soshō Hō* (Medical Malpractice Litigation). Tokyo: Shōrin Shoin.

Noah, Lars. 2001. "Civil Jury Nullification." *Iowa Law Review* 86:1601.

Noel, Thomas J. 1996. *The City and the Saloon, Denver, 1858–1916.* (electronic resource). Niwot: University Press of Colorado.

Nomi, Yoshihisa. 1999. "Medical Liability in Japanese Law." in *Modern Trends in Tort Law: Dutch and Japanese Law Compared,* Ewoud Hondius, ed. Boston, MA: Kluwer Law International.

Oakland Tribune. 1909. "Rights of Negro for Damages" (June 1), p. 6, col. 1.

Olson, Walter K. 1991. *The Litigation Explosion: What Happened When America Unleashed the Lawsuit.* New York: Truman Talley Books.

Painter, Nell Irvin 1992. "Hill, Thomas, and the Use of Racial Stereotype," in *Race-ing Justice, En-gendering Power: Essays on Anita Hill, Clarence Thomas and the Construction of Social Reality,* Toni Morrison, ed. New York: Pantheon Books.

Pandya, Sachin. 2007. "Liability Insurers in America: 1886–1910" (working paper).

Parkes, Debra 2004. "Targeting Workplace Harassment in Quebec: On Exporting a New Legislative Agenda." *Employee Rights and Employment Policy Journal* 8:423.

Pauley, Robin, 1985. "A Fuse Just Waiting to be Lit: Britain's Inner Cities." *Financial Times* (September 12).

Pennington, Nancy, and Reid Hastie. 1992. "Explaining the Evidence: Tests of the Story Model for Juror Decision Making." *Journal of Personality and Social Psychology* 62:189.

Perea, Juan, Richard Delgado, Angela Harris, and Stephanie Wildman. 2000. *Race and Races: Cases and Resources for a Multiracial America.* St. Paul, MN: West Publishing Company.

Pistor, Katherina, and Philip A. Wellons. 1999. *The Role of Law and Legal Institutions in Asian Economic Development, 1960–1995.* New York: Oxford University Press.

Police Complaints Authority. 2004. *National Study on Stop and Search Complaints.* London: Police Complaints Authority.

Polisar, Daniel, and Aaron Wildavsky. 1989. "From Individual to System Blame: A Cultural Analysis of Historical Change in the Law of Torts." *Journal of Policy History* 1:129.

Press Association. 1996. "Yard Chief Warns Against 'Stratospheric' Damages" (May 7).

Prosser, Tony. 1995. "The State, Constitutions and Implementing Economic Policy: Privatisation and Regulation in the UK, France and the USA." *Social and Legal Studies* 4:507.

Prosser, William L. 1939. "Intentional Infliction of Mental Suffering: A New Tort." *Michigan Law Review* 37:888.

Prosser, William L. 1956. "Insult and Outrage." *California Law Review* 44:44.

Pruitt, Lisa 2004. "Her Own Good Name: Two Centuries of Talk About Chastity." *Maryland Law Review* 63:419.

Pryor, Ellen S. 1997. "The Stories We Tell: Intentional Harm and the Quest for Insurance Funding." *Texas Law Review* 75:1721.

Quinn, Beth A. 2000. "The Paradox of Complaining: Law, Humor, and Harassment in the Everyday World." *Law and Social Inquiry* 25:1166.

Rabin, Robert L. 1999. "Enabling Torts." *DePaul Law Review* 49:435.

Rabin, Robert L. 2000. "Reassessing Regulatory Compliance." *Georgetown Law Journal* 88:2049.

Rabin, Robert, and Stephen Sugarman. 2001. *Regulating Tobacco.* New York: Oxford University Press.

Rajiv Gandhi Institute for Contemporary Studies. 1999. "Judicial Delays and its Impact on the Poor" (unpublished manuscript on file with author).

Ramamoorthy, R. 1970. "Difficulties of Tort Litigants in India." *Journal of the Indian Law Institute* 12:313.

Ramanathan, Usha. 2002. "Tort Law in India." *Annual Survey of Indian Law 2001* 615.

Ramaswamy, K. 1997. "Settlement of Disputes Through Lok Adalat Is One of the Effective Alternative Dispute Resolution (ADR) on Statutory Basis," in *Alternative Dispute Resolution: What It Is and How It Works,* P. C. Rao and William Sheffield, eds. Delhi: Universal Law Publications.

Ramseyer, J. Mark. 1988. "Reluctant Litigant Revisited: Rationality and Disputes in Japan." *Journal of Japanese Studies* 12:111.

Ramseyer, J. Mark, & Minoru Nakazato. 1999. *Japanese Law: An Economic Approach.* Chicago, IL: University of Chicago Press.

Rao, Velcheru Narayana. 1990. "Courts and Lawyers in India: Images from Literature and Folklore," in *Boeings and Bullock Carts: Studies in Change and Continuity in Indian Civilization,* Y. K. Malik and D. K. Vajpeyi, eds. Delhi: Chanayka Publications.

Reichman, Nancy, and Sterling, Joyce S. 2004. "Gender Penalties Revisited." Colorado Women's Bar Association. Available online at www.cwba.org.

Reichman, Nancy, and Sterling, Joyce S. 2004. "Sticky Floors, Broken Steps, and Concrete Ceilings in Legal Careers," *Texas Journal of Women and the Law* 14:27.

Reiner, Robert. 1991. *Chief Constables.* Oxford, UK: Oxford University Press.

Reiner, Robert. 1993. "Police Accountability: Principles, Patterns and Practices," in *Accountable Policing: Effectiveness, Empowerment and Equity,* Robert Reiner and Sarah Spencer, eds. London: Institute for Public Policy Research.

Reiner, Robert. 2000. *The Politics of the Police* (3rd edition). Oxford: Oxford University Press.

Republican Study Committee press release (December 2003), "Trial Lawyers Don't Want Religious Jurors." Accessed April 10, 2008, at http://www.house.gov/hensarling/rsc/doc/ATLA%20on%20religious%20jurors.pdf.

Resnik, Judith. 1993. "Finding the Factfinders," in *Verdict: Assessing the Civil Jury System,* Robert E. Litan, ed. Washington, DC: Brookings Institution.

Rice, Robert. 1995. "Business and the Law: When Your Health goes up in Smoke." *Financial Times* (February 7).

Robbennolt, Jennifer K. 2005. "Evaluating Juries by Comparison to Judges: A Benchmark for Judging?" *Florida State University Law Review* 32:469.

Robinson, Paul H., and John Darley. 1995. *Justice, Liability, and Blame: Community Views and the Criminal Law.* Boulder, CO: Westview Press.

Rogers, Kristen Gartman. 1998. "'Mad Plaintiff Disease?' Tobacco Litigation and the British Debate Over Adoption of U.S. Style Tort Litigation Methods." *The Georgia Journal of International and Comparative Law* 27:199.

Rose, Arnold. 1964. *The Negro in America.* Boston, MA: Beacon Press.

Rose, Carol M. 1988. "Crystals and Mud in Property Law." *Stanford Law Review* 40:577.

Rose, David. 1989. "Record Damages Against the Police." *Guardian* (December 6).

Rosen, Lawrence. 2006. *Law as Culture: An Invitation.* Princeton, NJ: Princeton University Press.

Ross, H. Laurence. 1980. *Settled Out of Court: the Social Process of Insurance Claims Adjustments* (2nd edition). Chicago, IL: Aldine Publishing Co.

Rossmiller, David. 2007. "Interpretation and Enforcement of Anti-Concurrent Policy Language in Hurricane Katrina Cases and Beyond." *New Appleman on Insurance: Current Critical Issues in Insurance Law §1,* p. 43.

Saad, Lydia. 2003. "Public Balks at Obesity Lawsuits: Most say food industry should not be held responsible for consumers' weight problems." Available online at http://www.gallup.com/content/?ci=8869.

Saguy, Abigail C., and Kevin W. Riley. 2005. "Weighing Both Sides: Morality, Mortality, and Framing Contests over Obesity." *Journal of Health Politics, Policy and Law* 3:869.

Sakamoto, Noriko et al. 2002. "The Use of Experts in Medical Malpractice Litigation in Japan." *Medical Science Law* 42:200.

Saks, Michael J. 1992. "Do We Really Know Anything about the Behavior of the Tort Litigation System—And Why Not?" *University of Pennsylvania Law Review* 140:1147.

Sanders, Andrew, and Richard Young. 1997. "From Suspect to Trial," in *The Oxford Handbook of Justice* (2nd edition), Mike Maguire, Rod Morgan, and Robert Reiner, eds. Oxford, UK: Clarendon Press.

Sanders, Joseph. 1998. *Bendectin on Trial: A Study of Mass Tort Litigation.* Ann Arbor: University of Michigan Press.

Sasao, Shogo et al. 2006. "Medical Malpractice Litigation in Gastroenterological Practice in Japan: A 22-Yr Review of Civil Court Cases." *American Journal of Gastroenterology* 101:1951.

Sathe, S. P. 2002. *Judicial Activism in India: Transgressing Borders and Enforcing Limits.* New Delhi: Oxford University Press.

Scales, Ann. 2004 "Nooky Nation: On Tort Law and Other Arguments from Nature," in *Directions in Sexual Harassment Law,* Catharine A. MacKinnon and Reva B. Siegel, eds. New Haven, CT, and London: Yale University Press.

Scarman, Lord. 1981. *The Scarman Report: The Brixton Disorders.* London: HMSO.

Schermer, Irvin E., and William J. Schermer. 2004. *Automobile Liability Insurance.* Eagan, MN: Thomson/West.

Scheuerman, William E. 1999. "Globalization and the Fate of Law," in *Recrafting the Rule of Law: The Limits of Legal Order,* David Dyzenhaus, ed. Oxford, UK, and Portland, OR: Hart Publishing.

Schlosser, Eric. 2001. *Fast Food Nation.* New York: Houghton Mifflin Co.

Schuck, Peter H., ed. 1991. *Tort Law and the Public Interest: Competition, Innovation, and Consumer Welfare.* New York: Norton.

Schwartz, David. 2002. "When Is Sex Because of Sex? The Causation Problem in Sexual Harassment Law." *University of Pennsylvania Law Review* 150:1697.

Schwartz, Gary. 1989. "The Character of Early American Tort Law." *UCLA Law Review* 36:641.

Schwartz, Gary T. 1981a. "The Vitality of Negligence and the Ethics of Strict Liability." *Georgia Law Review* 15:963.

Schwartz, Gary T. 1981b. "Tort Law and the Economy in Nineteenth Century America: A Reinterpretation." *Yale Law Journal* 90:1717.

Schwartz, Gary T. 1992. "The Beginning and the Possible End of the Rise of Modern American Tort Law." *Georgia Law Review* 26:601.

Scraton, Philip. 1994. "Denial, Neutralisation and Disqualification: The Royal Commission on Criminal Justice in Context," in *Criminal Justice in Crisis,* Mike McConville and Lee Bridges, eds. Aldershot, UK: Elgar.

Sebok, Anthony J. 2003. "The Fall and Rise of Blame in American Tort Law." *Brooklyn Law Review* 68:1031.

Shakespeare, William. 1604(?). *Measure for Measure.*

Shapo, Marshall S. 2003. *Tort Law and Culture.* Durham, NC: Carolina Academic Press.

Sharfstein, Daniel J. 2003. "The Secret History of Race in the United States." *Yale Law Journal* 112:1473.

Sharkey, Catherine M. 2005. "Revisiting the Noninsurable Costs of Accidents." *Maryland Law Review* 64:409.

Sharkey, Catherine M. 2006. "Dissecting Damages: An Empirical Exploration of Sexual Harassment Awards." *Journal of Empirical Legal Studies* 3:1.

Sharma, Devinder. 2004. "Government's Change: But No Respite from Farmers Suicides." Accessed April 17, 2007, at http://www.mindfully.org/WTO/2004/India-Farmers-Suicides 3jun04.htm.

Shavell, Steven. 1979. "On Moral Hazard and Insurance." *Quarterly Journal of Economics* 93:541.

Shavell, Steven. 1987. *Economic Analysis of Accident Law.* Cambridge, MA: Harvard University Press.

Sherman, Brad. 1997. "Remembering and Forgetting: The Birth of Modern Copyright Law," in *Comparing Legal Cultures,* David Nelken, ed. Aldershot, UK: Dartmouth.

Shriver, Lionel. 2006. "We Need to Talk About Massacres." *The Independent* (October 8).

Simon, Jonathon. 2007. *Governing Through Crime: How the War on Crime Transformed American Democracy and Created a Culture of Fear.* New York: Oxford University Press.

Singer, Richard, and Douglas Husak. 1999. "Of Innocence and Innocents: The Supreme Court and Mens Rea Since Herbert Packer." *Buffalo Criminal Law Review* 2:859.

Sirabionian, Andrei. 2005. "Why Tobacco Litigation has not been Successful in the United Kingdom: A Comparative Analysis of Tobacco Litigation in the United States and the United Kingdom." *Northwestern Journal of International Law and Business* 25:485.

Smith, David J., and Jeremy Gray. 1985. *Police and People in London: The PSI Report.* London: Gower.

Smith, Graham. 1999. "The Legacy of the Stoke Newington Scandal." *International Journal of Police Science and Management* 2:156.

Smith, Graham. 2001. "Police Complaints and Criminal Prosecutions." *Modern Law Review* 65:372.

Smith, Graham. 2005. "A Most Enduring Problem: Police Complaints Reform in England and Wales." *Journal of Social Policy* 35:121.

Smith, Graham, and Martin Walker. 1990. "Letter to the editor." *Independent* (May 14).

Smith, J. Clay, Jr. 1993. *Emancipation: The Making of the Black Lawyer, 1844–1944.* Philadelphia: University of Pennsylvania Press.

Smith, Vicky L., and Christina A. Studebaker. 1996. "What Do You Expect? The Influence of People's Prior Knowledge of Crime Categories on Fact-Finding." *Law and Human Behavior* 20:517.

Smith, Vicky L. 1991. "Prototypes in the Courtroom: Lay Representations of Legal Concepts." *Journal of Personality and Social Psychology* 61:857.

Snyder, Francis. 1999. "Governing Economic Globalisation: Global Legal Pluralism and European Law." *European Law Journal* 5:334.

Solomos, John. 2003. *Race and Racism in Britain* (3rd edition). New York: Palgrave Macmillan.

Sommer, Kristin L., Irwin A. Horowitz, and Martin J. Bourgeois. 2001. "When Juries Fail to Comply with the Law: Biased Evidence Processing in Individual and Group Decision Making." *Personality & Social Psychology Bulletin* 27:309.

Sommers, Samuel R. 2006. "On Racial Diversity and Group Decision Making: Identifying Multiple Effects of Racial Composition on Jury Deliberations." *Journal of Personality and Social Psychology* 90:597.

Spade, Dean. 2003. "Resisting Medicine, Re/Modeling Gender." *Berkeley Women's Law Journal* 18:15.

Spanbauer, Julie M. 1997. "Breast Implants A Beauty Ritual: Woman's Sceptre and Prison." *Yale Journal of Law and Feminism* 92:157.

Stapleton, Jean. 1995. "Tort, Insurance and Ideology." *Modern Law Review* 58:820.

Statistics Bureau, Ministry of Internal Affairs and Communications. Accessed April 14, 2008, at http://www.stat.go.jp/English/data/kokusei/2005/youkei/01.htm.

Steiker, Carol S. 1997. "Punishment and Procedure: Punishment Theory and the Criminal-Civil Procedural Divide." *Georgetown Law Journal* 85:775.

Stengel, James L. 2006. "The Asbestos End-Game." *New York University Annual Survey of American Law* 62:223.

Stern, Seth. 2002. "Fast-food restaurants face legal grilling." *Christian Science Monitor* (August 8). Available online at www.csmonitor.com/2002/0808/p14-usju.html.

Stewart, James. 1985. "Why Suits for Damages Such as Bhopal Claims are Very Rare in India." *Wall Street Journal* (January 23), at 1, col. 1.

Stokes, W. 1887. *The Anglo-Indian Codes* (2 vols.) Oxford, UK: Clarendon Press.

Strathern, Marilyn. 1995. *Shifting Contexts: Transformations in Anthropological Knowledge*. New York: Routledge.

Sunstein, Cass R., Reid Hastie, John W. Payne, David A. Schkade, and W. Kip Viscusi. 2002. *Punitive Damages: How Juries Decide*. Chicago, IL: University of Chicago Press.

Supreme Court of Japan. 2005a. *Iji Kankei Soshō Iinkai Tōshin* (Report of the Medical Malpractice Litigation Commission). Accessed March 14, 2008, at http://www.courts .go.jp/saikosai/about/iinkai/izikankei.

Supreme Court of Japan. 2005b. *Iji Kankei Soshō Iinkai Tōshin* (Report of the Medical Malpractice Litigation Commission). Accessed March 14, 2008, at http://www.courts.go .jp/saikosai/about/iinkai/izikankei/toukci_01.html; accessed April 10, 2008, at http:// www.courts.go.jp/about/siryo/jinsoku/hokoku /02/pdf/351_379.pdf.

Supreme Court of Japan. 2005c. *Iji Kankei Soshō Iinkai Tōshin* (Report of the Medical Malpractice Litigation Commission). Accessed March 14, 2008, at http://www.courts. go.jp/saikosai/about/iinkai/izikankei/toukei_04.html.

Sward, Ellen. 2001. *The Decline of the Civil Jury*. Durham, NC: Carolina Academic Press.

Swidler, Ann. 1986. "Culture in action: symbols and strategies." *American Sociological Review* 51:273.

Syverud, Kent. 1994. "On the Demand for Liability Insurance." *Texas Law Review* 72:1629.

Tamanaha, Brian. 2001. *A General Jurisprudence of Law and Society.* Cambridge: Cambridge University Press.

Tanase, Takao. 1987. "*Saiban no Tokumei-sei* (Anonymity of the Judiciary)." *Jurisuto* 899:47.

Tanase, Takao. 2001. "The Empty Space of the Modern in Japanese Law Discourse," in *Adapting Legal Cultures,* Johannes Feest and David Nelken, eds. Oxford, UK: Hart Publishing.

Tanase, Takao. 2007a. "*Sekinin Kan'nen to Jiyu-shugi* (Attribution of Liability and Liberalism in the United States)." *Jurisuto* 1341:126.

Tanase, Takao. 2007b. *Shimin Shakai to Sekinin* (Civil Society and Responsibility). Tokyo: Yuhikaku Publishing Company.

Taniguchi, Yasuhei. 1997. "The 1996 Code of Civil Procedure of Japan—A Procedure for the Coming Century?" *American Journal of Comparative Law* 45:767.

Taruffo, M. 2003. "Procedural Reform in Italy," in *The Reforms of Civil Procedure in Comparative Perspective,* N. Trocker and V. Varano, eds. (2005). Torino, Italy: Giappichelli.

Taylor, Mike, and John Deane. 1997. "Mixed Reaction to Curb on Police Damages Awards." *Press Association* (February 19).

Teubner, Gunther. 1997. "Global Bukowina: Legal Pluralism in the World Society," in *Global Law without a State,* Gunther Teubner, ed. Aldershot, UK: Dartmouth. 3–38.

Teubner, Gunther. 1998. "Legal Irritants: Good Faith in British Law or How Unifying Law Ends up in New Divergences." *Modern Law Review* 61:11.

Tiersma, Peter 1999. *Legal Language.* Chicago, IL: University of Chicago Press.

Tobacco Industry Litigation Reporter. 1996. "Imperial Tobacco, Gallaher Named in Suit Filed in London." Andrews Publications, Inc. (December 2).

Tokyo Chihō Saibansho Iryō Soshō Taisaku Iinkai. 2003. "Tokyo Chisai Iryō Shūchūbu ni Okeru Iryō Soshō no Shinri no Jijjyō ni Tsuite." 1105 *Hanrei Taimzu* (January 1), p. 34.

Tokyo District Court Practice Dai-ichi Committee. 2000.1018 *Hanrei Times* (March), p. 39.

Tokyo San Bengoshigai Kōtsū Jiko Shori Iinkai. 2002. *Songai Baishō Gakusantei Kijin* (Damage Compensation Computation Standards). Tokyo: Bar Association Press.

Torrant, Julie. 2003. "Let Them Eat Stigma: A Review of Fat Land." *The Red Critique.* Available online at http://redcritique.org/Spring2003/letthemeatstigma.html.

Trautner, Mary Nell. 2006. "Liability v. Likeability: How Lawyers Screen Cases in an Era of Tort Reform." Paper presented at Law & Society Association Annual Meeting, Baltimore, MD.

Travis, Alan. 1997. "Cap on Police Damages." *Guardian* (February 20).

Tribe, Laurence H. 2000. *American Constitutional Law* (3d edition). New York: Foundation Press.

Tsukahara, Mami. 2004. "Hospitals Trying to Overcome Distrust." *Daily Yomiuri* October 11.

Tucker, Henry St. George. 1853. *Memorials of Indian government; being a selection from the papers of Henry St. George Tucker,* John William Kaye (ed.). London: R. Bentley.

U.S. Census Bureau, 1975, 297, Series G, 189–204.

U.S. Census Bureau, *Statistical Abstract of the United States: 2004–2005.*

Upham, Frank. 1987. *Law and Social Change in Postwar Japan.* Cambridge, MA: Harvard University Press.

Varano, Vincenzo, and Allessandra De Luca. 2007. "Access to Justice in Italy." *Global Jurist*: Vol. 7: Iss. 1 (Advances). Art. 6. Available online at http://www.bepress.com/gj/vol7/iss1/art6.

Varley, Nick. 1996. "Victim of Beating by Police Wins £150,000." *Guardian* (June 5).

Victor, Peter. 1996. "Record Payout for Police Victim." *Independent* (April 27).

Vidmar, Neil. 1995. *Medical Malpractice and the American Jury.* Ann Arbor: University of Michigan Press.

Vidmar, Neil. 1999. "Maps, Gaps, Sociolegal Scholarship, and the Tort Reform Debate," in *Social Science, Social Policy, and the Law,* Patricia Ewick, Robert Kagan, and Austin Sarat, eds. New York: Sage Press.

Vidmar, Neil, Felicia Gross, and Mary Rose. 1998. "Jury Awards for Medical Malpractice and Post-Verdict Adjustments of Those Awards." *DePaul Law Review* 48:265.

Vidmar, Neil, and Valerie P. Hans. 2007. *American Juries: The Verdict.* Amherst, NY: Prometheus Books.

Visher, Christie A. 1987. "Juror Decision Making: The Importance of Evidence." *Law and Human Behavior* 11:1.

Volpp, Leti. 1996. "Talking 'Culture': Gender, Race, Nation, and the Politics of Multiculturalism." *Columbia Law Review* 96:1573.

Wada, Yoshitaka, and Shoichi Maeda. 2001. *Iryo Funsō: Medicaru Konfurekuto Manejimento no Teian* (Conflict over Medical Treatment: A Proposal for Medical Conflict Management). Tokyo: Igaku Shoin.

Wagner, Wendy E. 1997. "Choosing Ignorance in the Manufacture of Toxic Products." *Cornell Law Review* 82:773.

Waldron, Jeremy. 1995. "Moments of Carelessness and Massive Loss," in *Philosophical Foundations of Tort Law,* David G. Owen, ed. Oxford, UK: Clarendon Press.

Walker, Clive, and Keir Starmer. 1993. *Justice in Error.* London: Blackstone Press.

Walkowitz, Judith 1998. "Going Public: Shopping, Street Harassment, and Streetwalking in Late Victorian London." *Representations* 62:1.

Wang, Lu-in. 1997. "The Transforming Power of 'Hate': Social Cognition Theory and the Harms of Bias-Related Crimes." *Southern California Law Review* 71:47.

Weil, Elizabeth. 2006. "What if It's (Sort of) a Boy and (Sort of) a Girl?" *New York Times Magazine* (September 24): p. 48.

Weinreb, Ernest J. 1983. "Toward a Moral Theory of Negligence Law." *Law and Philosophy* 2:37.

Welke, Barbara Young. 2001. *Recasting American Liberty: Gender, Race, Law, and the Railroad Revolution, 1865–1920.* Cambridge: Cambridge University Press.

Wenner, David A. 2003. "Juror Bias," in *Litigating Tort Cases,* Roxanne Barton Conlin and Gregory S. Cusimano, eds. Washington, DC: AAJ Press.

Winn, Jane K. 1994. "Relational Practices and the Marginalization of Law: Informal Practices of Small Businesses in Taiwan." *Law and Society Review* 28:193.

Woodward, C. Vann. 1974. *The Strange Career of Jim Crow* (3d edition). New York: Oxford University Press.

World Health Organization. 2002. "Toward Health with Justice: Litigation and public inquiries as tools for tobacco control." Available online at http://www.who.int/tobacco/policy/litigation_report/en.

Wriggins, Jennifer B. 1983. "Rape, Racism, and the Law." *Harvard Women's Law Journal* 6:103.

Wriggins, Jennifer B. 2001. "Domestic Violence Torts." *Southern California Law Review* 75:121.

Wriggins, Jennifer B. 2005a. "Torts, Race, and the Value of Injury, 1900–1949." *Howard Law Journal* 49:99.

Wriggins, Jennifer B. 2005b. "Toward A Feminist Revision of Torts." *American University Journal of Gender, Social Policy & the Law* 13:139.

Wriggins, Jennifer B. 2005c. "The Recognition of Injury: Race, Gender, and Torts" (unpublished paper on file with the author).

Wriggins, Jennifer B. 2005d. Louisiana Cases Database (August 24).

Wriggins, Jennifer B. 2006. *Race, Wrongful Death and Mortality Tables* (work in progress on file with the author).

Yamada, Tetsuya, and Takuitsu Ogawa. 2004. "Tokyo Chihō Irhō Shūchūbu ni Okeru Jiken no Gaisetsu" (An analysis of cases handled by the Tokyo District Court's Consolidation Division). 213 *Minjihō Jyōhō.*

Yamamoto, Noriko. 2000. "Slow Malpractice Suits Under the Knife." *Mainichi Shimbun* (March 20).

Yamana, Manabu, and Hiroshi Ōshima. 2003. "Saikin no Iryō Soshō no Dōkō to Shinri no Jitsujyō" (Current Trends in Medical Malpractice Litigation). *Jiyū to Seigi* (February), pp. 4–21.

Yang, Benson. 2001. "The Breast Implant Controversy: A Prism for Reform." *Risk: Issues in Health and Safety* 12:123.

Yeazell, Stephen C. 2001. "Refinancing Civil Litigation." *DePaul Law Review* 51:183.

Yngvesson, Barbara. 1993. *Virtuous Citizens, Disruptive Subjects: Order and Complaint in a New England Court*. New York: Routledge.

Yoshida, Kenichi et al. 2005. "New Investigative Organization will be Enacted for Potentially Therapeutic Deaths in Japan" (unpublished paper, on file with author).

Yoshino, Kenji 2002. "Covering." *Yale Law Journal* 111:769.

Zedner, Lucia . 1995. "In Pursuit of the Vernacular: Comparing Law and Order Discourse in Britain and Germany," in special issue on "Legal Culture, Diversity and Globalization," David Nelken, ed. *Social and Legal Studies* 4:517.

Zegart, Dan. 2000. *Civil Warriors: The Legal Siege on the Tobacco Industry*. New York: Bantam/Delta.

Zeiler, Kathryn, Bernard S. Black, Charles Silver, David A. Hyman, and William M. Sage. 2007. "Physicians' Insurance Limits and Malpractice Payments: Evidence from Texas Closed Claims, 1990–2003." *Journal of Legal Studies* 36:s9.

Zelizer, Viviana. 1979. *Morals and Markets: The Development of Life Insurance in the United States*. New York: Columbia University Press.

Cases, Statutes, and Agency Reports

Allsop v. Allsop, 23 Vict. 534 (1860).

Allstate Ins. Co. v. Malec, 514 A.2d 832 (N.J. 1986).

Ambassador v. Montes, 388 A.2d 603 (N.J. 1978).

Andrews v. Law Society of British Columbia 1 S.C.R. 143 (1989).

Ard v. Ard, 412 So.2d 1066 (Fla. 1982).

Artiglio v. Superior Court of San Diego County, 22 Cal. App.4th 1388 (1994).

Benzman v. Whitman, 2006 WL 250527 (S.D.N.Y. 2006).

Blackburn v. Louisiana Railway & Navigation Co., 54 So. 865 (La. 1910).

Boeken v. Philip Morris Inc., No. BC 226593 (Superior Court County of Los Angeles, CA, 2001).

Brief of Certain Leading Business Corporations as Amici Curiae in Support of Petitioner, *State Farm Mut. Automobile Insurance Co. v. Campbell,* 538 U.S. 408 (2003) (No. 01-1289).

Buckman v. Plaintiffs' Legal Committee, 531 U.S. 341 (2001).

Bume v. Dr. Roy J. Catanne, No. 184985 (Sup. Ct. Orange County, California. July 21, 1971).

Carter v. Brown & Williamson, No. 95-934-CA CV-B (Fla.Duval Cir.Ct, Dec. 5, 1996) rev'd, 723 So.2d 833 (Fla. 1st Dist. Ct. App. 1998), 778 So. 2d 932 (Fla. 2000).

Castano v. American Tobacco Co., 160 F.R.D. 544 (E.D. La. 1995), rev'd 84 F.3d 734 (5th Cir. 1996).

Cipollone v. Liggett Group, 505 U.S. 504 (1992).

Coates v. Wal-Mart Stores, 976 P.2d 999 (NM 1999).

Colorado & Southern Railway Co. v. McGeorge, 10 P. 747 (Colo. 1909).

Colorado Central v. Martin, 4 P. 1118 (Colo. 1884).

Craig v. Boren, 429 U.S. 190 (1976).

Daubert v. Merrill Dow Pharmaceuticals, 509 U.S. 579 (1993).

Davidson v. Denver Tramway Co., 35 P. 920 (Colo. 1894).

Denver Tramway Co. v. Ann Owens, 36 P. 848 (Colo. 1894).

Denver Tramway Co. v. Jennie Crumbaugh, 48 P. 503 (Colo. 1897).

Denver Tramway Co. v. Nesbit, 45 P. 405 (Colo. 1896).

Denver Tramway v. Wright, 107 P. 1074 (Colo. 1909).

Dickinson v. Scruggs, 242 F. 900 (W.D. Tenn. 1917).

Doe v. Boeing, 846 P.2d 531 (Wash. 1993).

Engle et al. v. Liggett Group, Inc. 945 So.2d 1246 (Fla. 2006),

Engle v R.J. Reynolds Tobacco Co. 2000 WL 33534572 (Fla. Cir. Ct. 2000).

Escola v. Coca-Cola Bottling Co., 150 P.2d 436 (Cal. 1944).

Fisher v. San Pedro Peninsula Hospital, 214 Cal. Rptr. 842 (1989).

Griffin v. Brady, 117 N.Y.S. 1136 (App. Div. 1909) (mem.), *aff'd per curiam*, 118 N.Y.S. 240 (App. Div. 1909), *aff'd.*, 126 N.Y.S. 1130 (App. Div. 1910) (mem.).

Gulf, C. & S.F. Ry. Co. v. Luther, 90 S.W. 44 (Tex. Civ. App.1905).

Harper v. Edgewood Board of Education, 655 F. Supp. 1353 (S.D. Ohio 1987).

Headley et al. v. Denver & R.G.R. Co., 154 P. 731 (Colo. 1915).

Hodgson v. Imperial Tobacco Ltd. and Gallaher, (unreported) Judgment of Justice Wright on pre-trial motion, February, 1999.

Hoffman-LaRoche, Inc. v. Zeltwanger, 144 S.W.3d 438 (Tex. 2004).

In re: A (A Child), 16 Family Law Reporter (Australia) 715 (1993).

In re Breast Implants Litigation, 11 F. Supp.2d 1217 (D. Colo. 1998).

In re Rhone-Poulenc Rorer, Inc., 51 F.3d 1293 (7th Cir. 1995).

In the Matter of the Estate of Marshall G. Gardiner, 42 P.3d 120 (Kan. 2002). *In the Matter of the Estate of Marshall G. Gardiner*, 22 P.3d 1086 (Kan. Ct. App. 2001).

Indian Medical Assn. v. V. P. Shantha, A.I.R. 1996 S.C. 550, [1995] 6 SCC 651.

International Union of Operating Engineers Local No. 68 Welfare Fund v. Merck & Co., 894 A.2d 1136 (N.J. Super. A.D. 2006), appeal pending 902 A. 2d 1232 (N.J. 2006).

Louisiana Civil Code, Sec. 2315 (2005).

Law v. Canada (Minister of Employment and Immigration), 1 S.C.R. 497 (1999).

Lindsey v. Dow Corning Corp., No. CV 92-P-10000-S, No. Civ. A. 94-P-11558-S, 1994 WL 578353 (N. D. Ala. Sept. 1, 1994).

Littleton v. Prange, 9 S.W.3d 223 (Tex. Ct. App. 1999), cert. denied 531 U.S. 872 (2000).

Lucerno-Nelson v. Washington Metropolitan Area Transit Authority, 1 F. Supp.2d 1 (D.D.C. 1998).

Markman v. Westview Instruments Inc., 517 U.S. 370 (1996).

McTear v. Imperial Tobacco Ltd., 2005 2 S.C.1 [2005] CSOH 69 OH.

Michael M. v. Superior Court of Sonoma County, 450 U.S. 464 (1981).

Nguyen v. INS, 533 U.S. 43 (2001).

Nucci v. Colorado and Southern Railway Co., 169 P. 273 (Colo. 1917).

Oxendine v. Merrell Dow Pharmaceuticals, Inc., 506 A.2d 1100 (D.C. Ct. App. 1986).

Patterson v. Risher, 221 S.W. 468 (Ark. 1920).

Philbin v. Denver City Tramway, 85 P. 630 (Colo. 1906).

Philip Morris USA v. Williams, 549 U.S 346 (2007).

Prince v. Ridge, 66 N.Y.S. 454 (1900).

R v. Chief Constable ex parte Wiley, 1 AC 274, House of Lords (1995).

Reed v. Maley, 74 S.W. 1079 (Ky. 1903).

The Saginaw and the Hamilton, 139 F. 906 (S.D.N.Y. 1905), aff'd 146 F. 724 (2d. Cir. 1906), aff'd sub nom Old Dominion S.S. v. Gilmore, 207 U.S. 398 (1907).

Sentencia SU-337/99 (Colombia 1999).

Sentencia T-477 (Colombia 1995).

Sentencia T-551/99 (Colombia 1999).

Sindell v. Abbott Laboratories, 607 P.2d 924 (Cal. 1980).

State Farm Mut. Auto Ins. Co. v. Campbell, 538 U.S. 408 (2003).

State Farm Mut. Auto Ins. Co. v. Wertz, 540 N.W.2d 636 (S.D. 1995).

Symes v. Her Majesty the Queen, 4 S.C.R. 695 (1993).

Tamimim v. Howard Johnson Co., 807 F.2d 1550 (11th Cir. 1987).

Taylor v. Vicksburg, Shreveport & Pac. R.R., 91 So. 732 (La. 1922).

Thompson and Hsu v. Commissioner of Police of the Metropolis, 2 All England Reports 762 (1997).

Town of Castle Rock v. Gonzales, 545 U.S. 748 (2005).

Union Carbide Corporation v. Union of India (1991) 4 SCC 584.

Union Carbide Corporation v. Union of India (2004) 7 SCALE 259.

U.S. v. Philip Morris et al., 449 F. Supp.2d 1 (D.D.C. 2006).

Walker v. Richie, O.J. No. 1600 (On. C.) (2005).

Washington v. Davis, 426 U.S. 229 (1976).

Williams v. Philip Morris et al., 48 P.3d 824 (Ore. Ct. App. 2002); *Philip Morris et al. v. Williams,* 540 U.S. 801 (2003); *Williams v. Philip Morris et al.,* 127 P.3d 1165 (Ore. 2006); *Philip Morris et al. v. Williams,* 549 U.S. 346 (2007); and *Williams v. Philip Morris et al.,* 176 P.3d 1255 (Ore. 2008).

Young v. Broussard, 189 So. 477 (La. Ct. App. 1939).

Index

Abbott, Carl, 289
Abel, Richard L., 208
Abraham, Kenneth, 67, 69
Abrams, Kathryn, 133
Acharyya, Bijay Kisor, 47, 48
Action on Smoking and Health (ASH), 105, 204
Adjin-Tettey, Elizabeth, 284
African Americans: compensation for whites vs., 14, 159–72, 270, 318n6; lynching of, 318n3; as plaintiffs, 157, 159–72, 318n3; unequal treatment by judges, 157, 161–67, 170–71, 172. *See also* racial discrimination
age discrimination, 42
Agent Orange litigation, 283
Agyemang, Tracy, 285
Albertson, Stephanie, 87
Albright, Audra A., 200, 202, 205
Allen, Charlotte, 151
Allen, Ronald J., 82, 86
Allsop v. Allsop, 123
Allstate, 314n14
Allstate Ins. Co. v. Malec, 314n12
Ambassador Insurance v. Montes, 74, 313nn6,9,11
American Association of Pediatrics Policy 2000, 141, 152
American Law Institute: Products Liability Restatement, 7; Second Restatement of Torts, 84, 122, 124; Third Restatement of Torts, 282

American Obesity Association (AOA), 99–100
Amsterdam, Anthony: *Minding the Law,* 94
Andrews v. Law Society of British Columbia, 284
Ard v. Ard, 3131
Arizona civil jury trials, 93
arson, 75
Artiglio v. Superior Court of San Diego County, 153
Asahi Shimbun, 222, 223, 225
asbestos litigation: in Japan, 16, 233–34, 235–48; Johns-Manville case, 283; lawyers' fees in, 195–96, 206, 233; mesothelioma and cancer caused by asbestos, 233, 234–35, 243–44, 325nn2,4; in United States, 246, 283, 326n14, 333–34
Associated Press, 114
ATLA's Litigating Tort Cases, 266
Austin, Regina, 131, 134, 318n5
Australia: medical malpractice cases in, 153–54
automobiles, 68; automobile insurance, 69, 73. *See also* road accidents

Bacon, Sir Francis, 286
Baker, Tom, 4, 11–12
Balen, Paul, 200
Balsara, S. D., 49
Bangladesh: sexual identity in, 143
Banzhaf, John F., III, 104–6, 316n2

Barber, Caesar, 104, 112–13
Barr, Robert, 184, 203
Bartlett, Katharine T., 147
Barton, Peter, 273
Bates, Clive, 203
battery, 159
Batts, Deborah A., 328n2
Bearak, Barry, 53
Becker, Gary S., 67
Beisner, E. Calvin, 266
Bell, John, 23
Ben-Asher, Noa, 139, 141, 142
Benda-Beckmann, Keebet von, 10–11, 88, 193
Bendectin litigation, 261–62, 264–65, 268
Bennetto, Jason, 184, 185
Benzman v. Whitman, 328n2
Berdella, Robert A., 76–77
Berger, Margaret A., 86, 273; "Eliminating General Causation," 282–84
Bergstrom, Randolph E., 263–64, 265, 288
Bernstein, Anita, 131
Berridge, Virginia, 193
Bharti, Harish, 316n2
Bhatt, Raju, 181, 184–85
Bhopal disaster, 55–58
Biklen, Molly, 273
Bjorkman, Neil, 51
Black, Bernard S., 66
Blackburn v. Louisiana Railway & Naviga- tion Co., 170
Blackless, Melanie, 140
Blankenburg, Erhard, 23, 33, 34
Blasi, Gary, 157
Bloom, Anne, 13–14, 276; Regulating Middlesex, 131
Blorkman, Neil, 312
Boeken v. Philip Morris Inc., 197, 206, 208
Bogart, W. A., 281
Boot, Max, 4
Bora, Pranab, 56
Bornstein, Brian H., 85
Bourgeois, Martin J., 95
Bowling, Ben, 179
Bragge, Lily, 153
Braman, Don, 83
breast implants, 150–53, 273
Brickley, Kathleen F., 67

Brief of Certain Leading Business Corpo- rations as Amici Curiae in Support of Petitioner, 83
Briffa, Tony, 153–54
British Broadcasting Corp.: Secret Policeman, 191
Bronaugh, Richard, 273
Brown, Arthur, 179
Brown, Colin, 183
Brownell, Kelly D., 99
Bruinsma, Freek, 23, 34
Bruner, Jerome: Minding the Law, 94
Bryant, Kobe, 275
Buckman v. Plaintiffs' Legal Committee, 281
Buddhism: compassion and forgiveness in, 255, 256–57, 260; karma in, 251, 252, 254–57, 258, 259–60, 262, 263, 264, 267, 270, 277, 288, 327n6
Bume v. Dr. Roy J. Catanne, 150
Burns, John F., 56
Bush, George W., 196, 281
Butler, Judith: Bodies That Matter, 144–46, 152
Byers, William, 290

Cadden, Joan, 143
Cady, Troy L., 281
Cain, Maureen, 25
Caldwell, Paulette A., 133
California, 122, 147; Escola v. Coca-Cola Bottling Co., 277; Sindell v. Abbott Laboratories, 272; tobacco litigation in, 197, 206, 208
Campbell, Duncan, 181, 182, 183, 184, 185, 186
Canada, 9; equal treatment and human dignity in, 132–33; equal treatment and intent to discriminate in, 284; Supreme Court, 284; vs. United States, 132–33, 281, 284–85; universal health care in, 281
cancer and asbestos, 233, 234–35, 243–44, 325nn2,4
Carbado, Devon, 133
Care, Alan, 206
Carroll, Stephen J., 233
Carter v. Brown & Williamson, 197
Case, Mary Ann, 133

Castano v. American Tobacco Co., 196, 208
causation: vs. association/correlation, 272;
    and Bendectin litigation, 261–62,
    264–65, 268; causal chains, 245–46;
    and Christianity, 265–67, 268; cultural
    values and norms regarding, 16–17,
    251–52, 253–68, 269, 288, 304, 327n3;
    epidemiological evidence for, 272–73,
    282; and gender discrimination, 17,
    269–86; and judges, 272–74; and karma/
    misdeeds of injured person, 251, 252,
    254–57, 258, 259–60, 262, 263, 264, 267,
    270, 277, 288, 327n6; and malevolent
    ghosts, 255–56, 257, 258, 259–60, 263, 270,
    277; Malone on, 16, 253–54, 255, 259,
    260–61, 262, 267, 268, 327n3; as mono-
    causal, 17, 270–71; proximate cause, 7,
    80; relationship to habits of inference,
    271–72, 273–74; relationship to litigation
    rates, 252, 258–59, 260, 267, 268, 327n4;
    relationship to responsibility, 21, 251,
    252–57, 262, 265, 269, 271, 272–73; in
    tort law, 251–54, 255, 258–68, 269–86
Central Law Journal, 163
Chadbourn, James H., 318n3
Chakravarty, Sayantan, 60
Chamallas, Martha, 13, 146, 148, 150, 278,
    280–81, 284, 318nn1,5
Chase, Oscar, 8
Cheffins, Brian R., 66
Chiarloni, Sergio, 50
Chicago Jury Project, 92
Chikuho Jinpai case, 325n5
chinoform, 237, 243
Chodesh, Hiram, 52, 53
Christianity and causation, 265–67, 268
Cipollone v. Liggett Group, 194–95
civil law jurisdictions, 318n7, 321n10,
    327n7; vs. common law jurisdictions,
    30–31, 34–35, 168, 215; doctrinal
    commentary in, 30–31
civil rights law and tort law, 13, 119–36,
    284–85; intentional infliction torts,
    119, 120, 121–22, 130–36; variations
    among states, 121–22
class differentiation: and criminal law
    system, 40–41; and fast food, 114,
    317n11; and intentional infliction torts,

131; and tort law systems, 9, 11, 41, 42,
    114, 131; in United States, 131
Clayton, Richard, 178, 179, 180, 319n1
Clermont, Kevin M., 82, 321n10
Clifford, James, 32
Clinton, Bill, 196
Cloatre, Emilie, 50
Coates v. Wal-Mart Stores, 122
Coca Cola: vending machines in Seattle,
    104
Colapinto, John: *As Nature Made Him*,
    137–38
Colbert, Douglas L., 158
Cole, Anthony, 211
Coleman, Brady, 131
Collins, Cindy, 153
Colombia: Constitutional Court, 138–39,
    154; medical malpractice cases in, 153;
    sex change operations in, 138–39;
    surgery on intersexed infants in,
    153, 154
colonialism, 10, 24
Colorado Central v. Martin, 297–98
Colorado Court of Appeals, 294, 302
*Colorado & Southern Railway Co. v.
    McGeorge*, 301–2
Colorado state legislature: Employer
    Liability Acts, 298
Colorado Supreme Court, 17, 292, 293–94,
    295–303; *Colorado Central v. Martin*,
    297–98; *Colorado & Southern Railway
    Co. v. McGeorge*, 301–2; *Davidson v.
    Denver Tramway Co.*, 305–6; *Denver
    Tramway Co. v. Jennie Crumbaugh*, 298;
    Denver Tramway Co. v. Nesbit, 292;
    Denver Tramway Co. v. Wright, 300;
    and fellow-servant rule, 297–98, 302,
    304; *Nucci v. Colorado and Southern
    Railway Co.*, 299–90; *Philbin v. Denver
    City Tramway*, 300–301
common law jurisdictions, 8, 23, 47, 77–78,
    82; vs. civil law jurisdictions, 30–31,
    34–35, 168, 215; and constabulary
    independence, 178; sovereign
    immunity in, 242
communication networks, 24
community: as changing, 41–43; as foun-
    dation of tort law, 39–40, 43–44;

community: *(continued)*
heterogeneity of communities, 41–43; imagined communities, 25; juries as representatives of, 10–11, 40–44; and news media, 41, 42; shared cultural values and norms in, 10–11, 39–44; shared experience in, 41, 42–43; shared knowledge in, 41, 42–43; as unit of legal culture, 10–11, 39–44

comparative cross-cultural studies, 2, 5, 8–10, 21–26; and globalization, 23–24, 25, 26; and justice, 38; social science approach vs. interpretive approach, 33–35; units of study, 10, 22, 23–25, 26–29, 32, 39–40, 311n.2

comparative historical studies, 2, 9

compensation, 3, 7, 8; for African Americans vs. whites, 14, 159–72, 270, 318n6; appropriateness of, 12, 80, 88, 91, 159–72, 227–32; in Berdella case, 76–77; equality in, 235, 248; fault vs. no fault, 59; as full, 235; for industrial accidents, 55–58; in Italy, 311n6; in Japan, 215, 217, 233–48, 324n36, 325nn3,4, 326n12; in sexual harassment cases, 120–21; in Thailand, 257–58, 260, 267; in tobacco legislation, 192, 196, 197–98; in United Kingdom, 175–76, 181–82, 193, 324n36; in United States, 14, 76–77, 85, 86, 87, 88, 92, 93, 159–72, 160–64, 170, 190–91, 194–95, 216, 217, 231, 233, 235, 242, 246, 247, 262, 264, 266, 268, 270, 287, 288–89, 293, 294, 314n15, 318nn3,6, 324n36

conditional fees, 201–2, 206, 209, 210

Condon, Sir Paul, 185, 187

Coniff, Ruth, 151

Conley, John M., 6

consumer fraud law, 285

continental law systems, 23, 26, 34–35, 36

contingency fees, 35, 54, 55, 200, 247; vs. conditional fees, 201–2, 206, 209; in Japan, 35, 216, 326n10; in United States, 8, 31, 159–60, 168, 169, 205–6, 207, 231

Conway-Jones, Danielle, 273

Cook, Douglas H., 265–66

Coombe, Rosemary J., 25

copyright law, 24–25

corporate producers and vendors of fast food, 97, 98–99, 100–106; Burger King, 99, 104; Culver's, 99; Hardee's, 99; KFC, 104; McDonald's, 88, 100, 104, 114; news media coverage of, 110, 111, 112; public attitudes toward, 108–9; responsibilities of, 107, 108–9, 316nn6,7; Wendy's, 104. *See also* fast food litigation

corporate products, mass-produced, 12, 17

corporatism, legal, 245–46

Costanzo, Mark, 89

Cotterell, Roger: on community, 39–40, 43, 312n1; on legal culture, 32, 37, 39–40, 43

Cover, Robert M., 146

Craig v. Boren, 146

Crawford, William E., 168

Crenshaw, Kimberle, 133

criminal justice systems: and attitudes toward justice, 89–90; empirical research regarding, 3–4; in India, 11, 48, 55, 59, 61, 65; juries in, 40–41; and jury nullification, 84; prison rates, 8, 22, 26; and race, 14; vs. tort law systems, 3–4, 11–12, 14, 30, 40–41, 48, 55, 61, 65, 66–79, 88, 92, 94, 314n15, 320n7, 322n15

Crisis, The, 160

Critser, Greg, 317n11

cultural values and norms, 3, 5–8, 9–10, 12; adversarialism, 3, 15, 16, 26, 30, 62; antidiscrimination, 121; regarding body and mind, 13; regarding causation, 16–17, 251–52, 253–68, 269, 288, 304, 327n3; collective action, 31; corporate responsibility, 254, 263, 265; demand for "total justice," 33, 36, 193, 247; equality, 14, 16, 132–33, 135, 157, 235, 244, 248; female honor, 122–23, 124–25, 128–29, 132, 135, 148–49, 158; government responsibility, 242–44, 247–48; group loyalty, 31; in guilt cultures vs. shame cultures, 22; human dignity, 132–33; individualism, 3, 12, 16, 17, 26, 28, 29, 31, 265, 288, 297, 304; informalism, 61–63; regarding injury, 3, 7, 8, 12, 13, 15, 21, 80, 122–23, 124–25, 128–29, 132, 135, 148–49, 157, 158,

159–72, 318n3; institutional responsibility, 190–91; interpersonal obligations, 263–64, 265; invented traditions, 25; and judges, 2, 3, 6, 7, 12, 13, 27, 28, 39–40, 43, 44, 81, 85, 92–94, 157, 193, 204, 253, 296–97, 304–6; and juries, 2, 6, 7, 12, 40–44, 80–96, 151, 152–53, 155, 175–77, 194, 252–53, 266, 268, 327n3; and lawyers, 2, 6, 12, 176–77, 192, 193, 194, 205–10; male sexual initiative, 123–27, 128–29, 132, 136, 149; mediation, 61–63; and news media, 41, 42, 107–9, 112–13, 114–15, 176, 177–78, 189, 265; personal responsibility, 12, 17, 37–38, 97, 98–101, 102–3, 105, 107–9, 112–13, 176, 178, 189, 190, 193, 195, 197, 199, 203, 204, 209, 254, 258, 260, 263, 265–67, 271, 288, 297, 304; regarding personhood, 13; preservation of social harmony, 211; regarding insiders vs. outsiders, 304–5; relationship to tort law systems, 5–8, 13, 16–17, 22, 39–40, 43–44, 120, 122–23, 124–25, 128–29, 132, 132–33, 135–36, 138–40, 156–72, 189–91, 268, 287–306; reliance upon others, 247–48; reluctance to litigate, 33; rights consciousness, 3, 7, 29, 34, 50, 61–62, 325n7; regarding risk, 3, 7, 8, 14, 21, 254, 263, 287, 293, 299, 303, 304, 306; regarding role of law, 192, 197, 210; regarding sexual identity, 138–40, 141–55; as shared by communities, 10–11, 39–44; white supremacy, 14, 127–28, 129–30, 135, 156–72. *See also* gender discrimination; racial discrimination

Dailey, Anne, 313n10
Daily Yomiuri, 213
Daniels, Stephen, 4, 5, 208
Darley, John, 88
Daubert v. Merrell Dow Pharmaceuticals, 86, 261–62, 272
Davidson v. Denver Tramway Co., 305–6
Davies, Patricia Wynn, 187
Davis, Stephen, 203, 204, 205
Day, Martyn, 200–201, 202–3, 207
Daynard, Richard A., 195, 203, 204, 207, 208

Debroy, Bibek, 52, 53
defamation cases, 48
delay of litigation, 31, 35; in India, 29, 47, 51, 52–55, 57–58, 61, 65; in Italy, 50–51; in Japan, 211, 213, 219–21, 227
De Luca, Allessandra, 50
democracy, 242, 244
Denmark and European Union law, 22
Denver City Tramway Co., 290, 292, 298
Denver District Court, 293, 298, 299, 301, 305
Denver Horse Railroad Co., 290
Denver Tramway Co. v. Ann Owens, 302
Denver Tramway Co. v. Jennie Crumbaugh, 298
Denver Tramway Co. v. Nesbit, 292
Denver Tramway Co. v. Wright, 300
Desai, D. A., 53
DES litigation, 272, 279
Dethloff, Henry C., 169
Dezalay, Yves, 24
Dhavan, Rajeev, 61
Diamond, Shari Seidman, 87, 90, 92, 93
Dickinson v. Scruggs, 125–27, 128
diethylstilbestrol (DES) litigation, 272, 279
dignitary harms, 119, 120, 127, 131, 136, 150; to female honor, 122–23, 124–25, 128–29, 132–33, 135, 148–49, 158
Dingwall, Robert, 50
Dixon, Bill, 187
Dixon, David, 179
Dobbs, Dan B., 67, 164, 168, 252
Doe v. Boeing, 147
domestic violence, 66, 74, 77, 78, 275, 313n10, 314n13
Dorsett, Lyle W., 289
driving under the influence (DUI), 70, 313n.10
due process, 41
Dugro, Philip, 161–64
duty, 7, 16, 17, 288, 303; of care, 21, 65, 80, 215, 293, 298, 299–302, 321n9
Dworkin, Andrea: on pharmaceuticals for women, 278–79
Dyer, Clare, 182, 188

economics and law, 26, 28, 34–35
Economy Fire and Casualty Co., 76–77

Edwards, Pamela K., 71

Ehrenreich, Rose, 131

Eidsmore, Daniel C., 71, 76

Eisenberg, Theodore, 92

Eligman, David, 273

Ellman, Ira Mark, 313n10

Ellsworth, Phoebe, 83

empiricism, 271–77; empirical research on tort law system, 3–5, 7–8, 12, 29–30, 211n.3; and feminism, 274–77

enforcement of law, 22

Engel, David, 8, 16–17, 36, 38, 88, 91, 269, 270, 277, 312n9; research on Sander County, 288, 304–5

Engle v. Liggett Group, Inc., 197

Engle v. R.J. Reynolds Tobacco Co., 197

Enron, 67

environmental harms, 228

Epp, Charles R., 14–15, 29, 37–38, 206

Epstein, Richard A., 252

equal treatment under law, 14, 16, 157, 160–61, 163–64, 172

Ericson, Richard, 77

Escola v. Coca-Cola Bottling Co., 277

Espinoza, Leslie, 318n2

ethnicity and tort law systems, 9, 11, 88

Eugenides, Jeffrey: *Middlesex,* 137, 139, 141

European Committee for the Prevention of Torture, 188

European Union, 2, 22, 26, 30

Evans, John, 290

Evening Standard (UK), 182

Ewald, Francois, 77

Ewick, Patricia, 80

execution of judgments, 54

Executive Risk Indemnity, 315nn16,17

exemplary damage awards. *See* punitive damage awards

expert witnesses: in France and Germany, 322n18; in Japan, 212, 220, 221–23, 322nn18,19,21,22; and judges, 86, 204, 221, 222, 223–24, 261–62, 272–74, 322n18; in medical malpractice litigation, 212, 220, 221–23, 227, 231, 322nn18,19,21

Farley, Erin, 87

Farrell, Sean, 203

fast food litigation, 97–101, 190; Barber lawsuit, 104, 112–13; and health care costs, 104–5; and health experts, 99–100, 101; and liberal public interest litigators, 100, 101–6, 109, 114; McDonald's coffee spill case, 88, 176, 276–77; McDonald's french fries case, 100, 104, 114, 315n1, 316n2; news media coverage of, 12–13, 15, 97, 101, 103, 106–15, 176, 276, 277, 316n3; vs. tobacco litigation, 97, 100, 101–6, 114

Federal Trade Commission (FTC), 100

Feigenson, Neal: *Legal Blame,* 89, 90, 264

Feinberg, Kenneth R., 164, 318n5

Feld, Andrew, 320n1

Feldman, Eric A., 15–16, 23, 29, 34, 35, 36, 177, 211, 218, 226, 311n7

fellow servant rule, 297–98, 302, 304

Felstiner, William L. F., 157

feminism, 9, 120, 130–31, 134–35, 143; and empiricism, 274–77

Field, Richard H., 82, 95

Field, Stewart, 30

Finkel, Norman J.: *Commonsense Justice,* 89–90

Finland: prison rates in, 26

Finley, Lucinda M., 5, 273, 278, 281

Fiore, Michael C., 196

Fisher v. San Pedro Peninsula Hospital, 122

Fisk, Catherine L., 131

Flood, John, 208

Florida: tobacco litigation in, 196, 197

Food and Drug Administration (FDA), 100, 102, 113, 151, 152; and pharmaceutical products, 279, 281–82, 284

Ford, Richard, 184, 186, 187

France: expert witnesses in, 322n18; legal culture in, 34, 318n7; vs. United States, 34

Francey, Neil, 203

Franke, Katherine, 121

Friedman, Jonathan, 5, 26, 34, 204

Friedman, L., 204, 207, 208

Friedman, Lawrence M., 294, 318n7; on American racism, 158; on demand for total justice, 33, 36, 193; on Denver's railroads and tramways, 291; on legal

culture, 32–33, 36, 37–38, 193; on subsidies through tort system, 287, 303–4
Fukuda Takahisa, 224
Fuller, L. L., 273
Fye, Cameron, 203–4, 208

Galanter, Marc, 4, 5, 11, 28, 29–30, 85, 86, 106, 157
Gallagher, G. Patrick, 178
Gandhi, Indira: assassination of, 63
Garapon, Antoine, 25
Gardner, David, 54
Garland, David, 26
Garth, Bryant, 24
Geertz, Clifford, 34
gender discrimination: and attitudes toward causation, 17, 269–86; and empiricism, 274–77; and Genesis, 277–78; and intentional infliction torts, 119–36; and intersexuals, 137, 139, 140–46, 153–54; among Native Americans, 143; and pharmaceuticals, 17, 278–86; and poverty, 280–81; and sex change operations, 137–39, 141–42; and tort law systems, 9, 11, 13–14, 17, 27, 42, 88, 119–36, 138–40, 148–55, 269–86, 327n1; and transsexuals, 138–39, 140, 142–43, 147–48, 149–50, 153; in United States, 119–36, 137–38, 139–55, 207, 269–86
Gergen, Mark, 136
Gerlin, Andrea, 276
Germany: expert witnesses in, 322n18; vs. Holland, 25, 33; legal culture in, 25, 31, 33; litigation rate in, 22, 33; Nazi Germany, 25; pedestrian crossings in, 23; Weimar Republic, 25
Gertner, Nancy, 82
Gessner, Volkmar, 23
Gilles, Stephen, 72, 74
Ginsberg, Tom, 227, 320n6
Givelber, Daniel, 121
Gladwell, Malcolm, 151
Gledhill, Alan, 49
Glenn, Brian, 165, 166, 318n5
globalization, 9, 10, 15, 23–24, 25, 26, 35
God's providence, 265–66

Golanski, Alani, 283
Goodstein, Phil, 289, 290
Gray, Jeremy, 178
Gray, Steven, 99, 114
Great Depression, 50
Green, Leon, 86–87
Greene, Edie, 85
Greenhouse, Carol J., 7, 262, 265
Griffin v. Brady, 161–64, 167
Griffith, Sean S., 66
Gross, Ariela J., 318n2
Gross, Felicia, 4
Guardian, 182, 183, 184, 186
Gulf, C. & S.F. Ry. Co. v. Luther, 127–28, 158
Gunn, Alan, 162
Guthrie, Chris, 94

Hadfield, Gillian K., 312n4
Halarnkar, Samar, 60
Haley, John, 211
Hall, Stuart, 177–78
Haltom, William, 4, 6, 7, 12–13, 27, 81, 88, 91, 176, 177, 189, 199, 208, 265, 266, 276, 277
Hamilton, V. Lee, 33
Hampton, Jean, 74
Haney Lopez, Ian F., 318n2
Hannaford, Paula L., 92, 93
Hans, Valerie P., 4, 12, 38, 113, 155, 194
Harding, Andrew, 24
Harper v. Edgewood Board of Education, 147
Harris, Angela P., 318n2
Harris, Cheryl J., 318n2
Harrison, John, 180
Hart, H. L. A., 67, 71
Hastie, Reid, 87, 88
hate crimes, 285
Hayden, Lisa A., 280
Hayden, Robert M., 4
Hayes, Brian, 186
Headley et al. v. Denver & Rio Grande Railroad Company, 291–92
health care costs, 104–5, 193, 195–96, 225, 238, 281
health experts: and fast food litigation, 99–100, 101; and tobacco litigation, 195, 199

health insurance, 281
HealthSouth, 67
Hebert, L. Camille, 131
Hegde, Sasheej, 53
Heimer, Carol, 69
Heller, Janice, 276
Henderson, James A., 96
Hensler, Deborah R., 326n16
Hermer, Laura, 140
Heuer, Larry, 92
Heyderbrand, Wolf, 26
Higginbotham, Patrick, 85–86
Hill, Anita, 275
HIV-infection in Japan, 243
Hodgson v. Imperial Tobacco Ltd. and Gallaher, 199, 200–203, 204, 205, 206, 209–10
Hoeland, Armin, 23
Hoetker, Glenn, 227, 320n6
Hoffman, Beatrix, 166
Hoffman, David, 83
Hoffman, Frederick L.: *Race Traits and Tendencies of the American Negro,* 166–67
Hoffman-LaRoche, Inc. v. Zeltwanger, 121
Holland: German occupation, 25; vs. Germany, 25, 33; legal culture in, 25, 33, 34; litigation rate in, 22, 33; prison rates in, 26
Holmes, Oliver Wendell: on judges, 92
homeowners' insurance, 71
Horgen, Katharine Battle, 99
Horowitz, Irwin A., 95
Horowitz, Morton, 287
Howard, Philip K., 4
Howells, Geraint, 201, 205
Hsu, Kenneth, 186
Huber, Peter, 4
human dignity, 132–33, 135
Hume, David: on causation, 271–72
Hunter, Sir William, 48
Huntley, Jill E., 89
Husack, Douglas, 67

Ilminen, Gary R., 278
imitation of other systems, 24
immigration, 24, 42, 177

income differentiation and tort law systems, 88
Independent (UK), 183, 184, 185, 186
India: Bhopal disaster, 55–58; Civil Justice Committee, 47, 48; Civil Procedure Code, 53; compensation in, 54, 55–58, 59, 60–61, 63–64, 65; compliance with caregiving duties torts, 11; Constitution, 312n3; Consumer Protection Act, 59; Consumer Tribunals, 59–60, 63, 65; courts in, 11, 48, 52–53, 54, 57, 58, 59, 60, 62, 65; criminal justice system in, 11, 48, 55, 59, 61, 65; delay of litigation in, 29, 47, 51, 52–55, 57–58, 61, 65; downed electrical line cases in, 51; ex gratia payments in, 55, 56–57, 59, 63–64, 65; fees for court use in, 48, 54, 59; fees for lawyers in, 54; Fourth Law Commission, 47; government bodies as litigants in, 54, 60–61; High Courts, 52, 54, 57, 60–61, 64, 65, 312n1; Indian Court Fees Act of 1870, 48; industrial accidents in, 51, 55–58; informalism in, 59, 61–63; vs. Italy, 29–30, 50–51; vs. Japan, 52; judges in, 52–53, 54, 56, 62, 63; lawyers in, 50, 52, 53, 55–56, 60, 63; Legal Services Authorities Act, 62; litigation rates/litigiousness in, 11, 28, 36, 48–55, 64–65; Lok Adalats, 59, 61–63; medical malpractice cases in, 51, 59–60, 65; money damage suits in, 49–50, 54–55; Motor Accident Claims Tribunals (MACTs), 59, 62, 63, 65; Motor Vehicles Act, 59; negligence torts. vs. intentional torts in, 48–49, 51, 64–65; news media in, 52–53; Penal Code, 48; personal dignity torts in, 11, 65; rent and title suits in, 49; Republic of India vs. British India, 49–50, 312n2; road accident cases in, 54, 59, 62; sexual identity in, 143; vs. South Korea, 52; Supreme Court, 52, 57, 58, 59, 61, 312n1; tort law practice in, 9, 11, 47–65; tort reform by bypass in, 58–63; tribunals in, 52, 54, 55, 58, 59–60, 63, 312n3; vs. United Kingdom, 47; vs. United States, 11, 28–29, 52, 56,

57, 64–65; Uphaar Cinema fire, 60–61; Uttar Pradesh, 54, 312n2; writ petition procedure in, 52, 58, 59, 60–61, 65

Indian Law Institute: *All-India Reporter*, 48, 51, 312n1; *Annual Survey of Indian Law*, 49

Indian Medical Assn v. V. P. Shantha, 59

individualized claim resolution, 156–57, 159–60, 161, 163, 167, 168, 172

industrial accidents, 51; Bhopal disaster, 55–58

industrialization, 68

inequality, 13, 15, 38, 127; for African American plaintiffs, 156–57, 158, 159, 160–67, 170–71, 172, 270. *See also* gender discrimination; racial discrimination

informed consent, 283

injury: cultural values and norms regarding, 3, 7, 8, 12, 13, 15, 21, 80, 122–23, 124–25, 128–29, 132, 135, 148–49, 157, 158, 159–72, 318n3; location of accident, 17; relationship of parties involved, 17; types of, 17, 31. *See also* causation; dignitary harms; fast food litigation; gender discrimination; medical malpractice litigation; racial discrimination; road accidents; tobacco litigation; workers' compensation; wrongful death cases

In re: A (A Child), 16 Family Law Reporter, 153–54

In re: Breast Implants Litigation, 273

In re: Rhone-Poulenc Rorer, Inc., 325n8

insanity defense, 90

insurance industry, 8, 28; fire insurers, 68; in India, 59; insurance adjuster, 68, 76; insurance regulators, 79; insurance vs. gambling, 11–12, 166; in Italy, 37; liability insurance, 11–12, 66–79, 313nn1,4,8; life insurers, 68; mortality tables, 164–67, 172

intentional torts: intentional infliction torts after civil rights, 119, 120, 121–22, 130–36; intentional infliction torts before civil rights, 122–30, 135; vs.

negligence torts, 27, 48–49, 51, 64–65, 77–78, 85

interdisciplinary research, 1–2, 3

intermediate scrutiny standard, 146–47

International Union of Operating Engineers Local No. 68 Welfare Fund v. Merck & Co., 285

Internet, 37, 41, 224

Intersex Society of America, 145

In the Matter of the Estate of Marshall G. Gardiner, 147–48

Irish Republican Army (IRA), 178, 185

Italy: accident brokers in, 31; Berlusconi, 311n6; compensation in, 311n6; delay of litigation in, 50–51; and European Union law, 22; vs. India, 29–30, 50–51; insurance industry in, 37; job security in, 31; judges in, 311n5; lawyers in, 31, 51; litigation rates in, 50–51; pedestrian crossings in, 23; political conditions in, 29; road accidents in, 31, 36–37, 311nn6,8; Sicily, 36–37; tort law in, 9, 10, 29–31, 36, 50; vs. United States, 31; workplace injuries and deaths in, 30

Iwata, Futoshi, 217, 218, 225, 320n7, 322n15

Jacoby, Russell, 271

Jagannadha Rao, M., 52, 53

Jain, M. P., 47; *Outlines of Indian Legal History*, 49

Jain, Sarah S. Lochlann, 265

Japan: adversarial legalism in, 15, 16; Adverse Drug Reaction Fund (ADRF), 323n28; asbestos litigation, in Japan, 16, 233–34, 235–48; attitudes toward elites in, 224–25, 230; automobile accidents in, 227–28; Bar Association, 216; vs. Canada, 324n36; Civil Code (Article 709), 215; Code of Civil Procedure, 221, 231, 322n22; contingency fees in, 35, 216, 326n10; courts in, 214, 222, 223, 224, 237–38, 239–40, 241, 244, 245, 249, 320nn3,4, 321n10, 322n30, 324n32, 325nn5,9; Criminal Code (Article 171), 222; damage awards in, 211, 227; delay of litigation in, 211, 213,

Japan: *(continued)*
219–21, 227; determination of damages
in, 217; expert witnesses in, 212, 220,
221–23, 322nn18,19,21,22; extrajudicial
approaches to personal harms in, 211,
213, 227–30; filing fees in, 211, 216, 217,
218, 227, 322n13; Freedom of Information Act, 231; government policies
in, 35, 213, 227–31, 234–36, 239, 241,
242–45; Higaisha Renrakukai, 320n5;
vs. India, 52; Inoculation Act of 1948/
Vaccination Compensation system,
324n28, 326n12; Japan Board of Medical Societies, 323n27; Japan Council
for Quality Health Care, 323n27;
Japan Medical Association (JMA), 229,
321n10, 323n27, 324nn29–31; judges
in, 239–40, 241, 245, 323n25, 324n32,
325n9; Justice System Reform Council,
221, 222; Kanazawa District Court,
323n28; labor unions in, 234, 235;
Law for the Compensation of Pollution
Related Health Injury, 228; lawyers'
fees in, 35, 216, 240, 326n10; lawyers
in, 35, 211, 212, 213, 216, 218, 231, 239,
240–42, 245, 247, 320n2, 322nn12,16,
326n10; legal transplants in, 24, 30, 37;
litigation rates in, 15, 28, 29, 33, 36, 52,
64, 211, 212–15, 218–19, 220, 224–27,
229–30, 320n6; Medical Act (Article 21),
214; Medical Ethics Council, 323n27;
medical malpractice courts in, 212,
213, 220, 223–24, 231; medical malpractice litigation in, 15, 29, 31, 211–32;
Medical Practitioners Law, 321n10,
323n27; Ministry of Health, Labor and
Welfare, 228, 237–38, 243, 245, 321n10,
323nn27,28; Ministry of Labor, 236;
Ministry of Trade and Industry, 325n5;
modernization of, 24, 241, 244–45,
326n13; National SMON Conference,
238; news media in, 225, 226, 247–48;
Osaka District Court, 240; Personal
Information Protection Law, 321n10;
preservation of social harmony in, 211;
Red Book, 217–18; rights consciousness
in, 34, 325n7, 328; road accidents in,
217–18, 227–28; SMON litigation in,

237–39, 240, 241, 242–43, 244, 245,
323n28, 326n10; Supreme Court, 214,
239, 249, 320nn3,4, 325nn5,9; Tokyo
District Court, 222, 223, 224, 237–38,
240, 244, 322n20; tort reform in, 212,
213, 219–24, 229–31; Traffic Accident
Dispute Resolution Centers, 228; vs.
United Kingdom, 324n36; vs. United
States, 9, 14, 28, 29, 31, 35, 216, 217–18,
226, 231–32, 239, 241, 242–45, 246–47,
321n8, 324nn29,30,35,36, 325n8,
326n11; workers' compensation in, 16,
233–37, 246–47; and WWII, 241

Jettinghoff, Alex, 25
job security, 31
Johns-Manville asbestos case, 283
Johnson, David, 23
Johnson, Vincent, 162
Jones, Robert R., 169
Jones, Trina, 318n2
Jost, John T., 157
Judd, David, 175
judges: in appellate courts, 3, 7, 158, 162,
164, 165–70, 196, 197, 209, 261–62, 264,
296; appointment of, 8, 22; attitudes toward justice among, 94; and causation,
272–74; control of, 8, 22; and cultural
values and norms, 2, 3, 6, 7, 12, 13, 27,
28, 39–40, 43, 44, 81, 85, 92–94, 157, 193,
204, 253, 296–97, 304–6; discretion of,
7; dismissal of cases by, 2; and expert
witnesses, 86, 204, 221, 222, 223–24,
261–62, 272–74, 322n18; in India, 52–53,
54, 56, 62, 63; instructions to juries, 7,
85; in Italy, 311n5; in Japan, 239–40,
241, 245, 323n25, 324n32, 325n9; and
law-fact distinction, 82–83, 86, 253,
261–62, 268, 296–97; and litigation
explosion debate, 3; relations with
juries, 7, 27, 85, 253, 268; role in punitive damages awards, 40, 276; rulings on
evidence admissibility, 82, 86; rulings
on motions to dismiss, 82; and settlement of lawsuits, 85–86; unequal treatment of African Americans by, 157,
161–67, 170–71, 172; in United Kingdom,
15, 40, 193, 203, 204; in United States,
82–83, 85–86, 92–94, 96, 157, 158,

170–71, 172, 261–67, 264, 328n2. *See also* Colorado Supreme Court; United States Supreme Court

juries: attitudes toward breast implants, 151, 152–53; attitudes toward corporate litigants, 91, 93; attitudes toward justice in, 81, 83, 89–92, 94, 95, 96; attitudes toward personal responsibility, 90, 91–92, 95; attitudes toward plaintiffs vs. defendants, 91; and common law, 8; as community representatives, 10–11, 40–44, 83–85, 94, 96; and complexity exceptions, 82; composition of, 81, 83–84; constitutional guarantees regarding, 81–82; and cultural values and norms, 2, 6, 7, 12, 40–44, 80–96, 151, 152–53, 155, 175–77, 194, 252–53, 266, 268, 327n3; damages awarded by, 4–5, 14, 76–77, 85, 86, 87, 88, 92, 93, 155, 160–64, 170, 181–83, 185–87, 189, 190–91, 194–95, 197–98, 206–7, 217–18, 247, 262, 294; fact-finding by, 82–83, 86, 88–89, 252–53, 261–62, 268; instructions by judges, 85; and insurance, 90; vs. judges regarding verdicts, 92–94; and litigation explosion debate, 4; nullification by civil juries, 81, 94–95; racial diversity on, 83–84; and reasonable person standard, 2, 80, 84–85, 91; relations with judges, 7, 27, 85, 253, 268; role in punitive damages awards, 40, 42, 44, 82–83; Schuck on, 80, 81, 84; selection of, 266; story model of juror decision making, 87–89, 94; and strict products liability, 7; in United Kingdom, 175–76, 180, 181–83, 185–87, 189–91, 194, 319n1; in United States, 15, 40, 76–77, 80–96, 160–64, 170, 176, 194, 197–98, 217, 231, 239, 262, 268, 294, 324n32

justice: attitudes of juries toward, 81, 83, 89–92, 94, 95, 96; commonsense vs. legal, 89–92; corrective justice, 272, 273; distributive justice, 95, 272, 273

Kagan, Robert, 26, 30, 200
Kahan, Dan, 83
Kalven, Harry, Jr., 92, 93

Kamir, Orit, 129
Kansas, 147–48
Kansas City Star, 163
Kaplan, Benjamin, 82
Karlen, Josh, 202
Karsten, Peter, 159
Kassebaum, Gene, 62
Kaufman, Marc, 281
Kaur, Naunidhi, 60
Kawabata, Yoshiharu, 226
Kawashima, Takeyoshi, 211
Keeton, W. Page, 163, 252
Keleman, R. Dan, 231, 324n35
Kelsey, Tim, 184
Kennedy, Randall: on lynching, 318n3
Kentucky, 125
Keren-Paz, Tsachi, 273
Kerr, Norbert, 84
Kersh, Rogan, 98
Kessler, David A., 152
Kessler, Gladys, 196
Keyes, Charles F., 327n6
Khan, Sadiq, 186
Kim, Joyce, 273
Kirby, Terry, 182
Kirkland, Anna, 100
Klausner, Michael, 66
Kodama, Yashushi, 226
Koizumi, Junichiro, 230
Kōmi, Masakatsu, 229
Kramer, Geoffrey P., 84
Krishnan, Jayanth, 52, 62
Kritzer, Herbert M., 200, 281
Kubota Corp., 234, 243
Kulkarni, Niketa, 49
Kuper, Adam, 32
Kuroyanagi, Tatsuo, 225
Kurtz, Michelle, 150

labor law, 30
Ladinsky, Jack, 36
Laquer, Thomas, 137, 143, 144, 145
Latin America, 22
Lawrence, Stephen, 188
Law v. Canada (Minister of Employment and Immigration), 133
lawyers: attitudes toward, 97, 106–7, 110, 111, 112, 114, 226, 316n7; choices of, 28;

lawyers: *(continued)*
conditional fees, 201–2, 206, 209; contingency fees, 8, 31, 35, 54, 55, 74, 159–60, 168, 169, 199, 200, 201–2, 205–6, 207, 209, 216, 231, 247, 326n10; and cultural values and norms, 2, 6, 12, 176–77, 192, 193, 194, 205–10; government prosecutors, 160; in India, 50, 52, 53, 55–56, 60, 63; interviews with, 5, 7; in Italy, 31, 51; in Japan, 35, 211, 212, 213, 216, 218, 231, 239, 240–42, 245, 247, 320n2, 322nn12,16, 326n10; jury selection, 266; and liability insurance, 66, 67; and litigation explosion debate, 3, 4; number of, 8, 22, 212, 218, 219, 231; payment in advance, 35; relations with news media, 208, 209; specialization of, 23, 30, 35, 55; and tobacco tort litigation, 101–2, 192; in United Kingdom, 15, 177–78, 180–81, 184–85, 186, 187–88, 192, 193, 194, 199–210; in United States, 15, 35, 57, 97, 101–2, 104–7, 114, 177, 192, 193, 194–99, 200, 201–3, 205–10, 241, 246, 264, 326n11; as white, 157, 160; women as, 219

Lead Discovery, Ltd., 278

Leflar, Robert B., 217, 218, 225, 320n7, 322n15

legal culture, 15, 21–37, 80–81; changes in, 25, 32, 33, 36, 96, 208–9, 251–52; community as unit of, 10–11, 39–44; definition of, 22–23, 32, 156; empirical study of, 97; internal vs. external, 32–33, 37; interpretive approach to, 33–35, 38; and legal transplants/transfers, 24–26, 30; and liability, 38; role of mass media in, 114–15; social science approach to, 33–35; and technology, 32, 37; units of, 10, 22, 23–25, 26–29, 32, 39–44. *See also* cultural values and norms; judges; juries; litigation rates; news media

Legal Realism, 274

legal transplants/transfers, 24–26, 30

Lempert, Richard O., 4, 82

Lenhardt, R. A., 121

Leonard, Stephen J., 290

Levit, Nancy, 142, 146, 147

Levmore, Saul, 77

liability, 3, 21; criminal vs. tort, 11–12, 66–79, 314n15; determination of, 12, 17, 22, 28, 38, 80, 86, 155, 160, 235–39, 242–44, 291–306; as fault-based, 27; individual vs. corporate, 91, 247; and inequality/discrimination, 38; joint and several liability, 4, 77; product liability, 7, 13, 17, 27, 51, 69, 74, 95, 149, 150–53, 200, 206, 207, 277, 278–86; as risk-based, 27; strict products liability, 7, 95, 153; vicarious liability, 180. *See also* fast food litigation; intentional torts; negligence; tobacco litigation

liability insurance: for automobiles, 314nn13,15; and consequentialist reasoning, 69, 70; criminal defense costs covered by, 67, 69–70, 71–72, 75–79, 315nn16–18; and economic incentives, 69, 72, 79; exclusionary provisions in, 68–69, 70–72, 73–77, 78, 313n11, 314nn13,14; and intentional harm, 70, 71, 73–78; and lawyers, 66, 67, 76–77; and legal culture, 66; McNeely on, 68–69, 70, 73, 75; medical liability insurance, 79, 229, 315n17, 324nn30,31; and moral hazard, 69, 70, 72–75, 79; professional liability insurance, 67, 71, 79, 315n16; as protection for defendants, 67, 69, 75–76, 78; and punitive damages, 71; relationship to morality, 69, 70–71, 72–75, 76–77, 78; relationship to tort-crime boundary, 11–12, 66–79, 314n15; social insurance approach to, 69, 74; and subrogation, 73–74, 313n8, 314nn11,13; as victim compensation fund, 69

libel cases, 51

Liebeck, Stella. *See* McDonald's coffee spill case

lifestyle drugs, 280

Likosky, Michael B., 24

Lindsey v. Dow Corning Corp., 151

litigants: African Americans as plaintiffs, 157, 159–72, 318n3; corporations as, 91, 93; and litigation explosion debate, 3, 4; public attitudes toward, 106–15

litigation rates: in India, 11, 28, 48–55, 64–65; in Italy, 50–51; in Japan, 15, 28,

29, 33, 36, 52, 64, 211, 212–15, 218–19, 220, 224–27, 229–30, 320n6; relationship to attitudes regarding causation, 252, 258–59, 260, 267, 268, 327n4; in South Korea, 52; in Thailand, 252, 258–59, 260, 267, 268, 327n4; and tort reform debate, 3–5, 8, 27, 52, 87, 209, 246; in United Kingdom, 29, 50, 180–81, 189; in United States, 29, 50, 85–86, 252, 263–64, 321n8

Littleton, Christie, 149–50
Littleton v. Prange, 149–50
Lloyd-Bostock, Sally, 82
Locke, John, 143
Logue, Kyle D., 77
Louisiana, 14; appellate courts in, 167–70; Civil Code, 167–70, 319nn7,8; Supreme Court of, 170; wrongful death and survival civil code provision in, 167–70
Luban, David, 5
Lucerno-Nelson v. Washington Metropolitan Area Transit Authority, 134
lynching of African Americans, 318n3

Macchiaroli, Jean A., 324n29
MacCoun, Robert J., 4, 84, 91
MacKinnon, Catharine, 134, 135; on rules, 273; *Sexual Harassment of Working Women,* 130–31; *Toward a Feminist Theory of the State,* 132, 273
Maeda, Shoichi, 216
Magruder, William: on intentional infliction torts, 122, 123–24, 125
Maine, Sir Henry, 47
Mainichi Daily News, 226
malicious prosecution cases, 48, 51
Malone, Wex: "Ruminations on Cause-In-Fact," 16, 253–54, 255, 259, 260–61, 262, 267, 268, 327n3
Mann, Kenneth, 67
Manor, James, 313n5
Marcus, George, 32
Markman v. Westview Instruments, Inc., 82
Martin, Joanne, 4, 5
Mather, Lynn, 15, 21, 29, 102, 104, 113, 176, 177, 188, 195, 198
Matsuda, Mari, 276

McCann, Michael, 4, 5, 6, 8, 12–13, 27, 81, 88, 91, 176, 177, 189, 199, 208, 265, 266, 276, 277
McCarthy, Michael, 289
McClurg, Andrew J., 164
McCool, Geraldine, 200
McCrystal, Cal, 182, 183, 184
McDonald's coffee spill case, 88, 176, 276–77
McDonald's french fries case, 100, 104, 114, 315n1, 316n2
McKenzie, Ian K., 178
McNeely, Mary Coates, 68–69, 70, 73, 75, 313n2, 314nn11,15
McPherson, Sir William, 188
McTear v. Imperial Tobacco Ltd., 199, 203–5, 206, 207, 208, 210
medical malpractice litigation, 13, 27; in Colombia, 153; expert witnesses in, 212, 220, 221–23, 227, 231, 322nn18,19,21; involving impaired newborns, 216; in India, 51, 59–60; and informed consent, 283; in Japan, 15, 29, 31, 211–32, 320n4, 321nn8–11, 322nn13,15,16, 323n27, 324nn35,36; and malpractice insurance, 229; news media coverage of, 226, 227; and public trust in doctors, 224–25; screening panels for, 4; under tort law vs. contract law, 321n9; in United Kingdom, 36; in United States, 138, 149–50, 153, 154, 216, 217, 218, 226, 231, 321n8
Mehta, Yogesh, 62
Mendelsohn, Oliver, 50
Menon, N. R. Madhava, 62
Merry, Sally Engle, 6, 146
mesothelioma and asbestos, 233, 234–35, 243–44, 325nn2,4
Messick, Richard, 54
Mexico City: explosion of natural gas storage facility in, 57
Michael M. v. Superior Court of Sonoma County, 146–47
Milhaupt, Curtis J., 320n2
Miller, Russell, 180
Mills, Heather, 185, 186
Milne, Seumas, 181
Minnesota: tobacco litigation in, 196

Minow, Martha, 276
Mississippi: tobacco litigation in, 195–96
Mitra, Sumit, 53
Mizer, Judith H., 82
molestation, 66, 71, 77
Moog, Robert, 50, 53, 62
Moore, Mike, 195–96
moral hazard, 69, 70, 72–75, 313n8
Morone, James, 98
Mott, Nicole L., 85
Mudur, Ganapati, 59
Mullin, Chris, 185–86, 188
Mullin, John, 184
Munsterman, G. Thomas, 92
Muralidhar, S., 58, 59
Murata, Wataru, 221
Murray, Christopher J. L., 318n5
Myers, Paul, 183

Nakajima, Kazue, 324n31
Nakamura, Akiko, 323n26
Nakazato, Minoru, 321nn9,11
National Association for the Advance-
    ment of Colored People (NAACP), 160
National Rifle Association: liability
    insurance for members, 79, 315n18
National Thermal Power Corp., 64
negligence, 172, 296–97; comparative
    negligence regime, 94–95, 270–71;
    contributory negligence regime, 94–95;
    determination of, 10, 85, 88–89, 94–95,
    256–59, 260, 262–63, 291–306; doctrine
    of negligence per se, 67; in Japanese
    tort law, 235–36; negligence torts vs.
    intentional torts, 27, 48–49, 51, 64–65,
    77–78, 85. See also medical malpractice
    litigation
Nelken, David, 5, 8, 10, 50, 156, 311n.1
Nestle, Marion, 99, 104
New Jersey Supreme Court: *Ambassador
    Insurance v. Montes*, 74, 313nn6,9,11
news media: coverage of fast food litiga-
    tion, 12–13, 15, 97, 101, 103, 106–15, 176,
    276, 277, 316n3; coverage of medical
    malpractice litigation, 226, 227; cover-
    age of public interest tort litigation,
    12–13, 15, 97, 101, 103, 106–15, 176,
    195, 196, 198–99, 208, 276, 277, 316n3;

coverage of tobacco litigation, 195, 196,
    198–99, 208; and cultural norms and
    values, 41, 42, 107–9, 112–13, 114–15,
    176, 177–78, 189, 265; in India, 52–53;
    in Japan, 225, 226, 247–48; relations
    with lawyers, 208, 209; role in com-
    munity formation, 41, 42; in United
    Kingdom, 15, 35, 176, 177–78, 182, 184,
    185, 186–87, 189, 191, 208, 316n4; in
    United States, 12–13, 15, 35, 97, 176,
    189, 208, 209, 226, 265, 316nn3,4; and
    use of tort law, 27, 52–53
New Statesman, 204
New York City, 263–64, 265, 288
New York State, 125
New York Times, 161–62, 271
Nguyen v. INS, 147
Nihon Ishikai, 323n27, 324n31
Nikkei Shimbun, 222
Nishino, Kiichi, 215
Noah, Lars, 94
Noel, Thomas J., 289, 290, 291
Nomi, Yoshihisa, 321n11
*Nucci v. Colorado and Southern Railway
    Co.,* 299–90

Oakland Tribune, 163
O'Barr, William M., 6
obligation. *See* duty
Occidentalism, 25
Ogawa, Takuitsu, 223
Olson, Walter K., 4
Oregon: tobacco litigation in, 197–98, 206
Orientalism, 25
Orucu, Elsin, 24
Ōshima, Hiroshi, 224, 322n23
*Oxendine v. Merrell Dow Pharmaceuticals,
    Inc.,* 328n9

Painter, Nell Irvin, 127
Pakistan: sexual identity in, 143
Pandya, Sachin, 68
Pardo, Michael S., 82, 86
Parker, Kathleen, 113
Parkes, Debra, 131
Parlodel, 278
Patterson, Edwin, 313n2
Patterson v. Risher, 159

Pauley, Robin, 181
Pennington, Nancy, 87, 88
Penrod, Steven D., 92
Perdue, William R., Jr., 273
Perea, Juan, 318n2
pharmaceuticals: and FDA, 279, 281–82, 284; and women, 17, 278–86. *See also* Bendectin litigation; DES litigation
Philbin v. Denver City Tramway, 300–301
Philip Morris et al. v. Williams (2003), 197–98
Philip Morris et al. v. Williams (2007), 83, 198
Phillips, Coretta, 179
Pistor, Katherina, 50
police abuse, 15, 35–36, 37, 175–91
Polisar, Daniel, 287–88
politics, 29, 34–35, 38
Pollock, Sir Frederick, 47
postadjudication processing, 5
pretrial discovery, 8
Prince v. Ridge, 125
principle of equal justice, 16
principle of equal treatment, 14
private enforcement, 157
Prosser, Tony, 32
Prosser, William: "Insult and Outrage," 124–25, 126–27; on intentional infliction torts, 122, 123, 124–25, 126–27
proximate cause, 7, 80
Pruitt, Lisa, 122
Pryor, Ellen S., 71, 74, 78
public health systems, 35, 225
public interest tort litigation: attitudes in United States toward, 97; and health care costs, 104–5; news media coverage of, 12–13, 15, 97, 101, 103, 106–15, 176, 195, 196, 198–99, 208, 276, 277, 316n3. *See also* fast food litigation; tobacco litigation
punitive damage awards, 4, 5, 10, 31, 105, 187, 190, 247; appropriateness of, 197–98, 206–7, 209; caps on, 281; vs. criminal fines, 71; and liability insurance, 71, 313n7; role of judges in, 40, 276; role of juries in, 40, 42, 44, 82–83, 197; in tobacco litigation, 197–98, 206–7; in United Kingdom, 175–76,

181–82, 206–7; in United States, 197, 206, 209, 217, 231, 262, 276, 285

Quinn, Beth A., 134–35

Rabin, Robert L., 67, 74, 193, 322n23; on enabling torts, 77
Rachlinski, Jeffrey J., 94
racial discrimination, 318n2, 319n9; against African American plaintiffs, 156–57, 158, 159, 160–67, 170–71, 172, 270; compensation for African Americans vs. whites, 14, 159–72, 270, 318n6; and criminal law system, 40–41, 83–84; Jim Crow laws, 127, 158; in juries, 83–84, 318n4; lynching, 318n3; scientific racism, 165, 166–67; and tort law systems, 9, 11, 13, 14, 27, 41, 42, 83–84, 88, 114, 119, 120, 122, 125–28, 129–30, 133, 135–36, 146, 270, 275–76; in United Kingdom, 15, 27, 35–36, 175–91; in United States, 14, 125–28, 129–30, 133, 154–55, 156–72, 179, 207, 270; white privilege, 14, 127–28, 129–30, 133
Racketeer Influenced and Corrupt Organizations (RICO) Act, 196
railroads: blame for accidents involving, 291–306; in India, 51, 63; litigation involving, 17, 35, 36, 51, 91, 160, 172, 288–306; as subsidized by tort system, 287, 296–97, 303–4; vs. tramways, 288–306
Rajiv Gandhi Institute, 53
Ramamoorthy, R., 48, 51
Ramanathan, Usha, 60
Ramaswamy, K., 62
Ramseyer, J. Mark, 321nn9,11, 322n14
Rao, Velcheru Narayana, 53
rape, 74, 75, 77, 78, 125–27, 276–77
reasonable force, 84
reasonable person standard, 12; and judges, 2; and juries, 2, 80, 84–85, 91
Reed v. Maley, 125
Reichman, Nancy, 17, 28, 35, 91, 265, 274
Reimer, David, 137–38, 139, 142–43, 145, 153
Reiner, Robert, 177, 178, 179, 180

religion, 9, 88. *See also* Buddhism; Christianity and causation
Republican Study Committee, "Trial
  Lawyers Don't Want Religious Jurors,"
  266
Resnik, Judith, 86
responsibility: corporate responsibility as
  cultural value, 254, 263, 265; personal
  responsibility as cultural value, 12, 17,
  37–38, 97, 98–101, 102–3, 105, 107–9,
  112–13, 176, 178, 189, 190, 193, 195, 197,
  199, 203, 204, 209, 254, 258, 260, 263,
  265–67, 271, 288, 297, 304; personal
  responsibility in United States, 12,
  17, 97, 98–101, 102–3, 105, 106, 107–9,
  112–13, 176, 263, 265–67, 271, 316n6.
  See also negligence
Rice, Robert, 194
Richardson, Frank K., 272
right-to-die cases, 90
Riley, Kevin W., 98
risk: assumption of, 7, 197; cultural values
  and norms regarding, 3, 7, 8, 14, 21, 254,
  263, 267, 287, 293, 299, 303, 304, 306;
  and informed consent, 283; in pharmaceuticals use, 17, 278–86; relative risk,
  262; risk-based liability, 27; the risk
  society, 27
Roach, Colin, 181
road accidents: and DUI, 70, 74; in India,
  54, 59, 62; in Italy, 31, 36–37, 311nn6,8;
  in Japan, 217–18, 227–28; and jury
  trials, 87; and liability insurance, 70, 73;
  in Thailand, 256–57, 258–59, 327n8
Robbennolt, Jennifer K., 92
Robinson, Paul H., 88
Rogers, Kristen Gartman, 202, 206, 207
Rose, Arnold, 169
Rose, Carol M.: on property law, 96
Rose, David, 175, 182
Rose, Mary, 4
Rosen, Lawrence, 6
Ross, H. Laurence, 28, 78, 80, 88
Rossmiller, David, 68
rule of law, 26, 160–61, 324n34
Russell, Thomas, 287, 294
R v. Chief Constable ex parte Wiley,
  184–85

Saad, Lydia, 113
Saguy, Abigail C., 98
Sakamoto, Noriko, 221
Saks, Michael J., 4, 5, 157
Sanders, Andrew, 180
Sanders, Joseph, 33, 261–62
Sasao, Shogo, 231, 324n35
Sathe, S. P., 61
Scales, Ann, 17, 38, 131, 253, 265,
  273, 293
Scarman, Lord, 179, 188
Schermer, Irvin E., 313n10, 315n15
Schermer, William J., 313n10, 315n15
Scheuerman, William E., 26
Schlosser, Eric, 98
Schuck, Peter H.: on juries, 80, 81, 84; *Tort
  Law and the Public Interest*, 80
Schwartz, David, 131, 133
Schwartz, Gary T., 69, 287
Scraton, Philip, 180
Scruggs, Cora, 125–27, 128
Sebok, Anthony J., 69
Secret Policman, The, 191
Seirei Hamamatsu General Hospital, 225
self-defense cases, 90
Sentencia SU-337/99, 154
Sentencia T-477/95, 138, 154
Sentencia T-551/99, 154
September 11th attacks, 328n2
sexual harassment cases, 89, 91, 119,
  120–22, 129, 130–36
sexuality, 120, 122–23; discrimination
  based on sexual orientation, 133; male
  sexual solicitations, 123–27, 128–29,
  132, 136, 149; sexual identity, 13–14,
  137–55
Shapo, Marshall S., 3, 27
Sharfstein, Daniel J., 318n2
Sharkey, Catherine M., 71, 120–21, 313n7
Sharma, Devinder, 63
Shavell, Steven, 72
Sherman, Brad, 25
Shriver, Lionel, 271
Sibbitt, Eric C., 231, 324n35
Silbey, Susan S., 80
silicone breast implant litigation, 150–53,
  273
Simon, Jonathon, 67

Sindell v. Abbott Laboratories, 272
Singer, Richard, 67
Sirabionian, Andrei, 205, 210
Smith, David J., 178
Smith, Graham, 179, 180, 181, 182, 183–84, 187, 188
Smith, J. Clay, Jr., 158
Smith, Lord Nimmo, 204
Smith, Vicky L., 89
SMON litigation in Japan, 237–39, 240, 241, 242–43, 244, 245, 323n28, 326n10
Snyder, Francis, 24
social differentiation and tort law, 9–10
social equality, 119, 122, 130, 132–33, 135, 162
Solomos, John, 177
Sommer, Kristin L., 95
Sommers, Samuel R., 83–84
South Africa, 24
South Korea: vs. India, 52; litigation rates in, 52
sovereign immunity, 236, 242
Spade, Dean, 142
Spanbauer, Julie M., 151
Stapleton, Jean, 66, 68, 69, 74
Starmer, Keir, 178
State Farm, 314n14
State Farm Mut. Auto. Inc. Co. v. Campbell, 82–83, 198
State Farm Mut. Auto. Inc. Co. v. Wertz, 313n5
Steiker, Carol S., 67
Stengel, James L., 326n16
Stephen, Sir James, 47–48
Sterling, Joyce S., 17, 28, 35, 91, 265, 274
Stern, Seth, 104, 106
steroids, 328n1
Stetz, Michael, 112
Stewart, James, 57
stigmatization, 13
Stokes, W., 47
Strathern, Marilyn, 25
strict scrutiny standard, 146
Studebaker, Christina A., 89
subacute myelo optico neuropathy. *See* SMON litigation in Japan
Sugarman, Stephen, 193, 313n10
Sunstein, Cass R., 264–65

Suzuki Toshihiro, 224
Sward, Ellen, 82
Sweet, Robert, 315n1
Swidler, Ann, 6
Symes v. Her Majesty the Queen, 284
Syverud, Kent, 68

Tamanaha, Brian, 23
Tamimim v. Howard Johnson Co., 147
Tanase, Takao, 16, 29, 35, 36, 97, 177
Taniguchi, Yasuhei, 321n10
Tanzania: attitudes toward causation in, 269
Taruffo, M., 51
Taylor, Lord, 183
Taylor, Rupert, 175
Taylor v. Vicksburg, Shreveport & Pac. R.R., 158
technology, 32, 37, 49
Teubner, Gunther, 24
Texas, 127–28, 149–50; tobacco litigation in, 196
textbook writers, 27
Thailand, 9, 327n7; attitudes toward ghosts in, 255–56, 257, 258, 259–60, 263, 270, 277; attitudes toward karma in, 251, 252, 254–57, 258, 259–60, 262, 263, 264, 267, 270, 277, 288, 327n6; Chiangmai Provincial Court, 258–59, 327nn4,8; litigation rates in, 252, 258–59, 260, 267, 268, 327n4; road accidents in, 256–57, 258–59, 327n8; vs. United States, 16, 36, 251–68
thalidomide, 323n28
The Saginaw and the Hamilton, 165–67, 318n6
"third cultures," 24
Thomas, Cheryl, 82
Thompson and Hsu v. Commissioner of Police, 187, 189
Tiersma, Peter, 85
Time Out, 184
tobacco litigation, 21, 192–210; class/multiparty actions, 195, 196–97, 199, 200–204, 206, 207, 209, 210; damage awards in, 192, 196, 197–98; vs. fast food litigation, 97, 100, 101–6, 114; government litigation, 195–96, 205–6, 208;

tobacco litigation *(continued)*
  individual lawsuits, 195, 197–98,
  199, 200, 203–5; Master Settlement
  Agreement with states, 192, 196, 198;
  new media coverage of, 195, 196, 198–99,
  208; and tobacco industry deception,
  194, 195, 196, 197, 198, 202–3, 209; in
  United Kingdom, 15, 35–36, 192–94,
  199–210; in United States, 15, 192–99,
  202–3, 205–10
Tobacco Products Liability Project
  (TPLP), 195
Tocqueville, Alexis de, 195
Tokio Marine, 324n30
Tomlinson, Hugh, 178, 179, 180, 319n1
Torrant, Julie, 114
tort reform debate, 3–5, 8, 27, 52, 87, 209,
  246
Town of Castle Rock v. Gonzales, 275
toxic tort litigation, 272–74
trade, international, 24
trade unions, 31
tramways: blame for accidents involving,
  291–306; litigation involving, 17, 35, 91,
  288–306; vs. railroads, 288–306
transsexuals, 13–14, 138–39, 140, 142–43,
  147–48, 149–50, 153
Trautner, Mary Nell, 206
Travis, Alan, 187
Traynor, Roger, 277
trespasser/licensee relationships, 299–300
Tribe, Laurence H., 146
Tsukahara, Mami, 225
Tucker, Henry St. George, 48
Turkey: legal culture in, 24
Twerski, Aaron, 283

Union Carbide Corp.: Bhopal disaster,
  55–58; and Dow Chemical, 58
*Union Carbide Corporation v. Union of
  India* (1991), 58
*Union Carbide Corporation v. Union of
  India* (2004), 58
United Kingdom: admiralty courts, 82;
  Association of Personal Injury Lawyers,
  207; attitudes toward lawsuits seeking
  recovery for injuries in, 15; Brixton
  riots, 179; civil juries in, 82; compensation in, 175–76, 181–82, 193, 324n36;
  conditional fee agreements (CFAs) in,
  201–2, 206; court fees in, 50; Court of
  Appeal, 187, 189; Crown Prosecution
  Service (CPS), 179, 183, 184, 185, 188;
  and European Union law, 22; Freedom
  of Information Act, 188; Hackney Community Defence Association, 181,
  182–84, 188; health care system in,
  193; Her Majesty's Inspectorate of
  the Constabulary (HMIC), 179, 187;
  immigration to, 177; vs. India, 47;
  judges in, 15, 40, 193, 203, 204; Labour
  Party, 188, 202; lawyers in, 15, 177–78,
  180–81, 184–85, 186, 187–88, 192,
  193, 194, 199–210; Legal Aid Board,
  200–201, 203, 206; legal aid in, 181, 189,
  200–201, 203, 205, 206, 209; libel law
  in, 176, 184; litigation rates in, 29, 50,
  180–81, 189; "loser pays" rule in, 181,
  189, 202, 203, 205; medical malpractice
  cases in, 36; National Union of Miners
  (NUM), 181; news media in, 15, 35, 176,
  177–78, 182, 184, 185, 186–87, 189, 191,
  208, 316n4; Operation Jackpot, 182,
  183–84; pedestrian crossings in, 23;
  police abuse and racial discrimination
  in, 15, 35–36, 37, 175–91; Police and
  Criminal Evidence (PACE) Act, 179;
  Police Complaints Authority, 179, 183,
  186; Police Lawyers Group (PALG),
  181; Race Relations (Amendment) Act,
  188; sex scandals and corruption in,
  22; statute of limitations in, 35; Stoke
  Newington police station, 181–84;
  tobacco litigation in, 15, 35–36, 192–94,
  199–210; top-down managerial
  approaches to accountability in,
  14–15; vs. United States, 14–15, 22,
  26, 29, 30, 31, 35, 39–40, 82, 176–77,
  179, 180, 189, 190, 192–210, 316n4;
  vicarious liability in, 180
United States: adversarial legalism in, 26,
  29; American Association for Justice/
  Association of Trial Lawyers of America, 207; American Bar Association,
  326n11; asbestos litigation in, 246, 283,
  326n14, 333–34; attitudes toward civil

plaintiffs in, 106–7, 108, 109, 110, 111, 112–13, 114, 156–57, 158, 159, 160–67, 170–71, 172, 270; attitudes toward lawsuits seeking recovery for injuries in, 15, 326n14; attitudes toward personal injury lawyers in, 97, 106–7; vs. Australia, 153–54; vs. Canada, 132–33, 281, 284–85; vs. Colombia, 138–40, 153, 154; community in, 39–44; compensation in, 14, 76–77, 85, 86, 87, 88, 92, 93, 159–72, 160–64, 170, 190–91, 194–95, 216, 217, 231, 233, 235, 242, 246, 247, 262, 264, 266, 268, 270, 287, 288–89, 293, 294, 314n15, 318nn3,6, 324n36; Congress, 82, 195; contingency fees in, 8, 31, 159–60, 168, 169, 205–6, 207, 231; death penalty in, 26; Department of Justice, 196; Environmental Protection Agency (EPA), 328n2; vs. France, 34; government regulation/responsibility in, 100, 101, 102, 105, 106, 107, 108, 109, 113, 114, 246; vs. India, 11, 28–29, 52, 56, 57, 64–65; vs. Italy, 31; vs. Japan, 9, 14, 28, 29, 31, 35, 216, 217–18, 226, 231–32, 239, 241, 242–45, 246–47, 321n8, 324nn29,30,35,36, 325n8, 326n11; judges in, 82–83, 85–86, 92–94, 96, 157, 158, 170–71, 172, 261–67, 264, 328n2; juries in, 15, 40, 76–77, 80–96, 160–64, 170, 176, 194, 197–98, 217, 231, 239, 262, 268, 294, 324n32; lawyers in, 15, 35, 57, 97, 101–2, 104–7, 114, 177, 192, 193, 194–99, 200, 201–3, 205–10, 241, 246, 264, 326n11; litigation rates in, 29, 50, 85–86, 252, 263–64, 321n8; medical malpractice litigation in, 29, 138, 149–50, 153, 154, 216, 217, 218, 226, 231, 321n8; news media in, 12–13, 15, 35, 97, 176, 189, 208, 209, 226, 265, 316nn3,4; personal responsibility in, 12, 17, 97, 98–101, 102–3, 105, 106, 107–9, 112–13, 176, 263, 265–67, 271, 316n6; police and African Americans in, 179; populist approaches to accountability in, 14–15; sex scandals and corruption in, 22; sovereign immunity in, 242; vs. Thailand, 16, 36, 251–68; tobacco litigation in, 15, 192–99, 202–3, 205–10;

vs. United Kingdom, 14–15, 22, 26, 29, 30, 31, 35, 39–40, 82, 176–77, 179, 180, 189, 190, 192–210, 316n4; workers' compensation in, 233–34, 315n15. *See also* Food and Drug Administration (FDA); United States Constitution; United States Supreme Court

United States Constitution, 121, 194; Equal Protection, 284, 285; Seventh Amendment, 81–82

United States Supreme Court: *Buckman v. Plaintiffs' Legal Committee,* 281; *Cipollone v. Liggett Group,* 194–95; *Craig v. Boren,* 146; *Daubert v. Merrill Dow Pharmaceuticals,* 86, 261–62, 272; decisions regarding juries, 82, 83; *Harper v. Edgewood Board of Education,* 147; *Michael M. v. Superior Court of Sonoma County,* 146–47; *Nguyen v. INS,* 147; *Philip Morris et al. v. Williams (2003),* 197–98; *Philip Morris et al. v. Williams (2007),* 83, 198; *State Farm Mutual Automobile Inc. Co. v. Campbell,* 82–83, 198; *Tamimim v. Howard Johnson Co.,* 147; *The Saginaw and the Hamilton,* 165–67, 318n6; *Town of Castle Rock v. Gonzales,* 275; *Washington v. Davis,* 284

United States Surgeon General, 113

United States Third Circuit Court of Appeals, 82

University of Denver College of Law, 275

Uphaar Cinema fire, 60–61

Upham, Frank, 211

U.S. v. Philip Morris et al., 196

Van Voris, Bob, 202

Varano, Vincenzo, 50

Varga, Carba, 23

Varley, Nick, 186

Viagra litigation, 280

Victor, Peter, 186

Vidmar, Neil, 4, 83, 87, 90, 92, 281

Virginia Law Register, 163

Volpp, Leti, 276

Wada, Yoshitaka, 216

Wagner, Wendy E., 273, 282, 284

Waldron, Jeremy, 68
Walker, Clive, 178
Walker, Martin, 182
Walker v. Richie, 284
Walkowitz, Judith, 128
Wang, Lu-in, 121
Washington State Supreme Court:
    Doe v. Boeing, 147
Washington v. Davis, 284
Weil, Elizabeth, 145
Weinreb, Ernest J., 272
Weinstein, Jack, 283
Welke, Barbara Young, 128, 158, 159, 160
Wellons, Philip A., 50
Wenner, David A., 266
West, Mark D., 320n2
Whitman, Christine Todd, 328n2
Wildavsky, Aaron, 287–88
Williams v. Philip Morris et al. (Ore. 2006),
    198
Williams v. Philip Morris et al. (Ore. 2008),
    198
*Williams v. Philip Morris et al. (Ore. Ct.
    App. 2002)*, 197–98, 206
Winn, Jane K., 34
Winning the Race, 187
Wistrich, Andrew J., 94
women: and breast implants, 150–53, 273;
    feminism, 9, 120, 130–31, 134–35, 143,
    274–77; as lawyers, 219; and pharma-
    ceuticals, 17, 278–86. *See also* gender
    discrimination
Woodbury, Roger W., 290
Woodward, C. Vann, 158
Woolf, Lord, 187
workers' compensation, 69, 74; asbestos
    causation, 234–35; equal vs. full com-
pensation, 235; in Japan, 16, 233–37,
    246–47; relationship to litigation,
    236–37, 247; in United States, 233–34,
    315n15
workplace discrimination, 13, 119, 120–22,
    130–36
WorldCom, 67
World Health Organization, and tobacco
    control, 199
Wriggins, Jennifer, 14, 67, 74, 120, 127–28,
    154, 158, 159, 160, 165, 168, 169, 170,
    171, 270, 313n8, 314n13
Wright, Michael, 203
wrongful death cases, 14, 76–77, 149–50,
    158, 185, 258–59, 313n11; involving
    African Americans, 164–72, 318n3; and
    estimates of life expectancy, 164–67,
    318n5

Yamada, Tetsuya, 223
Yamamoto, Noriko, 322n22
Yamana, Manabu, 224
Yang, Benson, 152
Yeazell, Stephen C., 68
Yngvesson, Barbara, 6, 7
Yomiuri Shimbun, 225
Yoshida, Kenichi, 214
Yoshino, Kenji, 133
Young, Richard, 180
Young v. Broussard, 171

Zedner, Lucia, 34
Zegart, Dan, 102
Zeiler, Kathryn, 66
Zeisel, Hans, 92, 93
Zelizer, Viviana, 68, 166

THE CULTURAL LIVES OF LAW

Austin Sarat, Editor

The Cultural Lives of Law series brings insights and approaches from cultural studies to law and tries to secure for law a place in cultural analysis. Books in the series focus on the production, interpretation, consumption, and circulation of legal meanings. They take up the challenges posed as boundaries collapse between, as well as within cultures, and as the circulation of legal meanings becomes more fluid. They also attend to the ways law's power in cultural production is renewed and resisted.

Lex Populi: The Jurisprudence of Popular Culture
William P. MacNeil
2007

The Cultural Lives of Capital Punishment: Comparative Perspectives
Edited by Austin Sarat and Christian Boulanger
2005